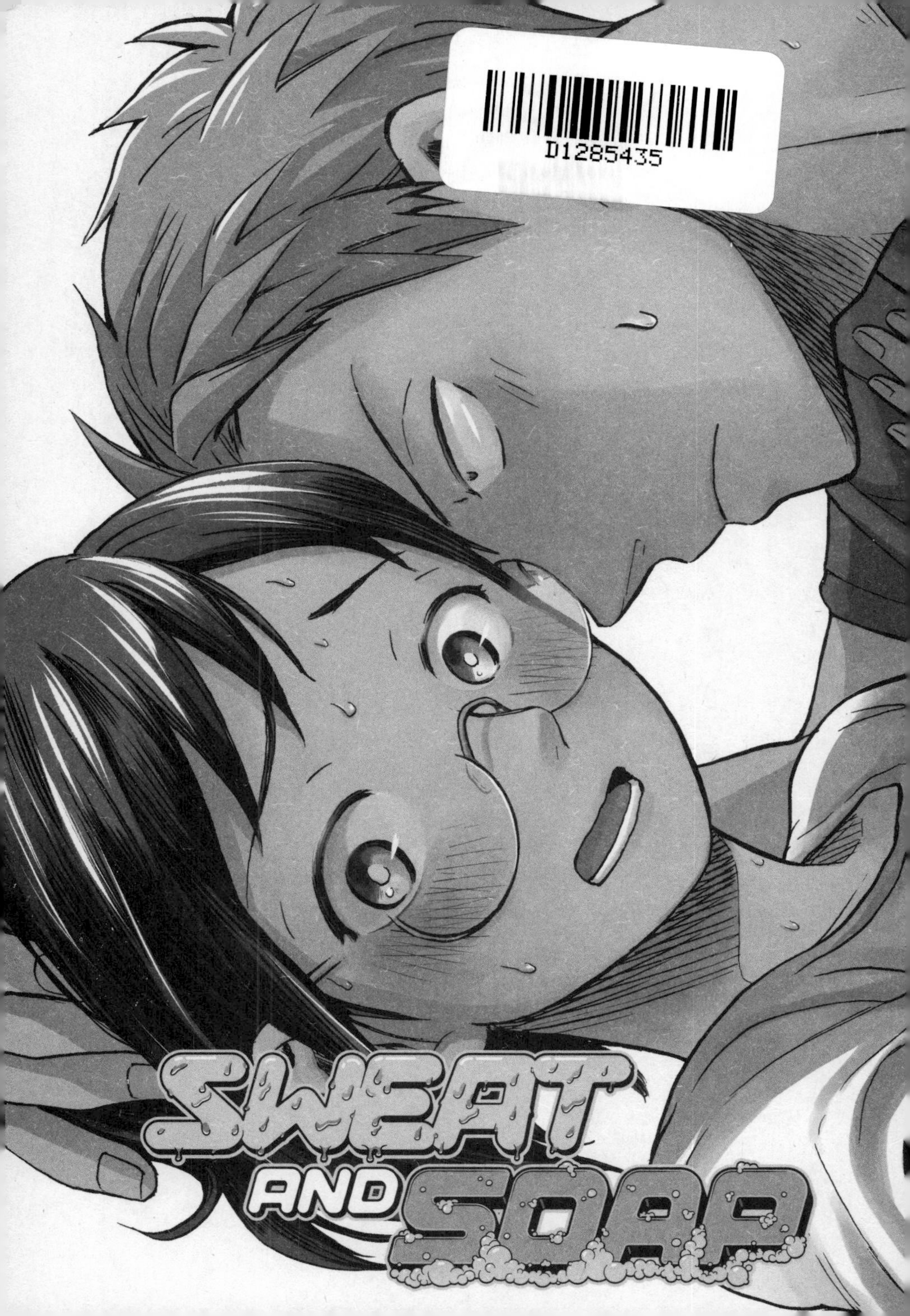
SWEAT
AND
SOAP

C O N T E N T S

chapter **9** Not to Anyone 003

chapter **10** Little by Little 025

chapter **11** Natori's Secret 041

chapter **12** Young Natori 061

chapter **13** I Have You Now 083

chapter **14** Family 107

chapter **15** I'll Be the Judge 129

chapter **16** First Impressions 149

chapter **17** What I Want 167

Bonus Mini-Chapter **13.5** I Just Want to Hold You 191

Exclusive Character Profiles! 200

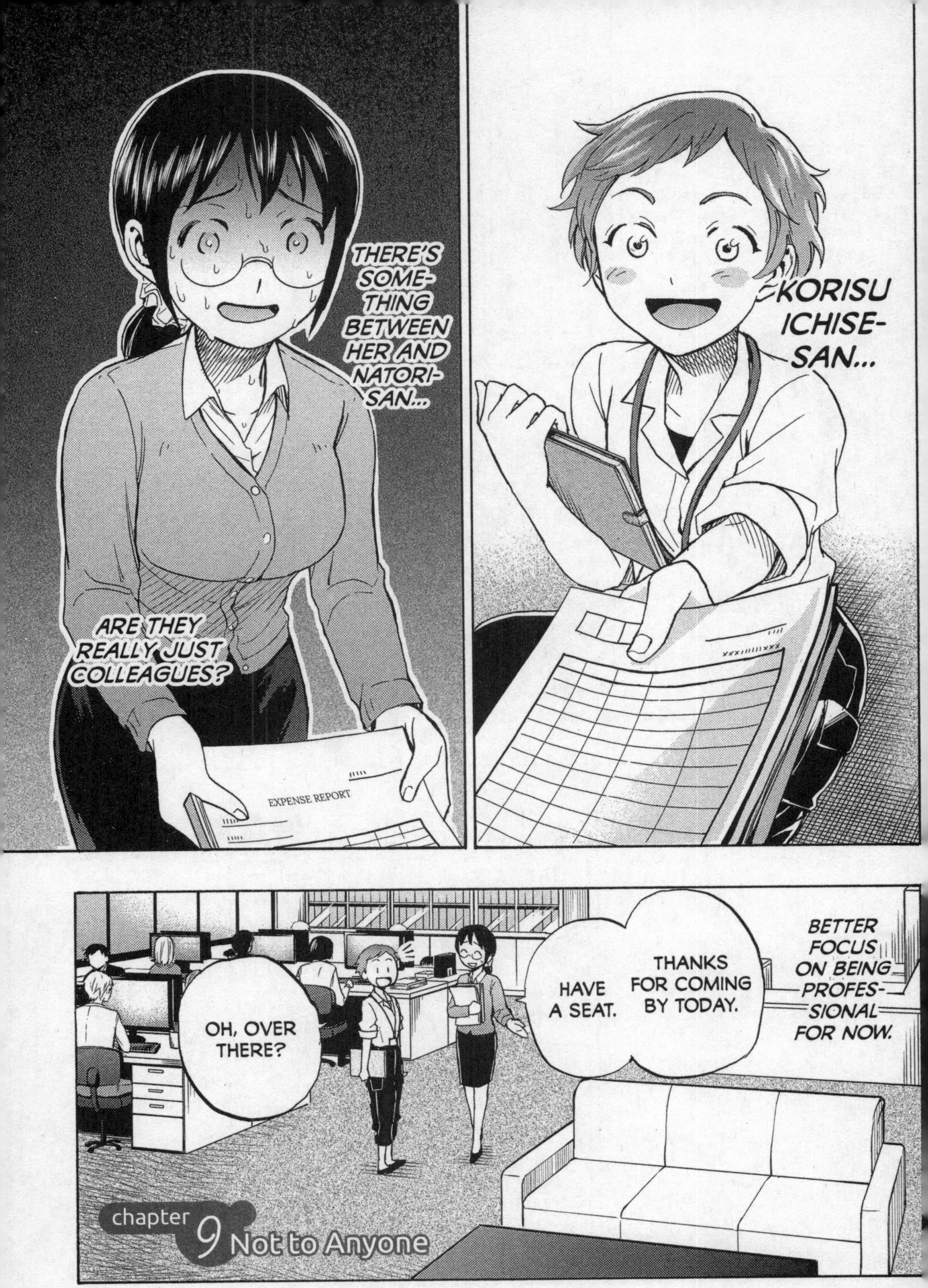
KORISU ICHISE-SAN...
THERE'S SOMETHING BETWEEN HER AND NATORI-SAN...
ARE THEY REALLY JUST COLLEAGUES?
EXPENSE REPORT
BETTER FOCUS ON BEING PROFESSIONAL FOR NOW.
THANKS FOR COMING BY TODAY.
HAVE A SEAT.
OH, OVER THERE?
chapter 9 Not to Anyone

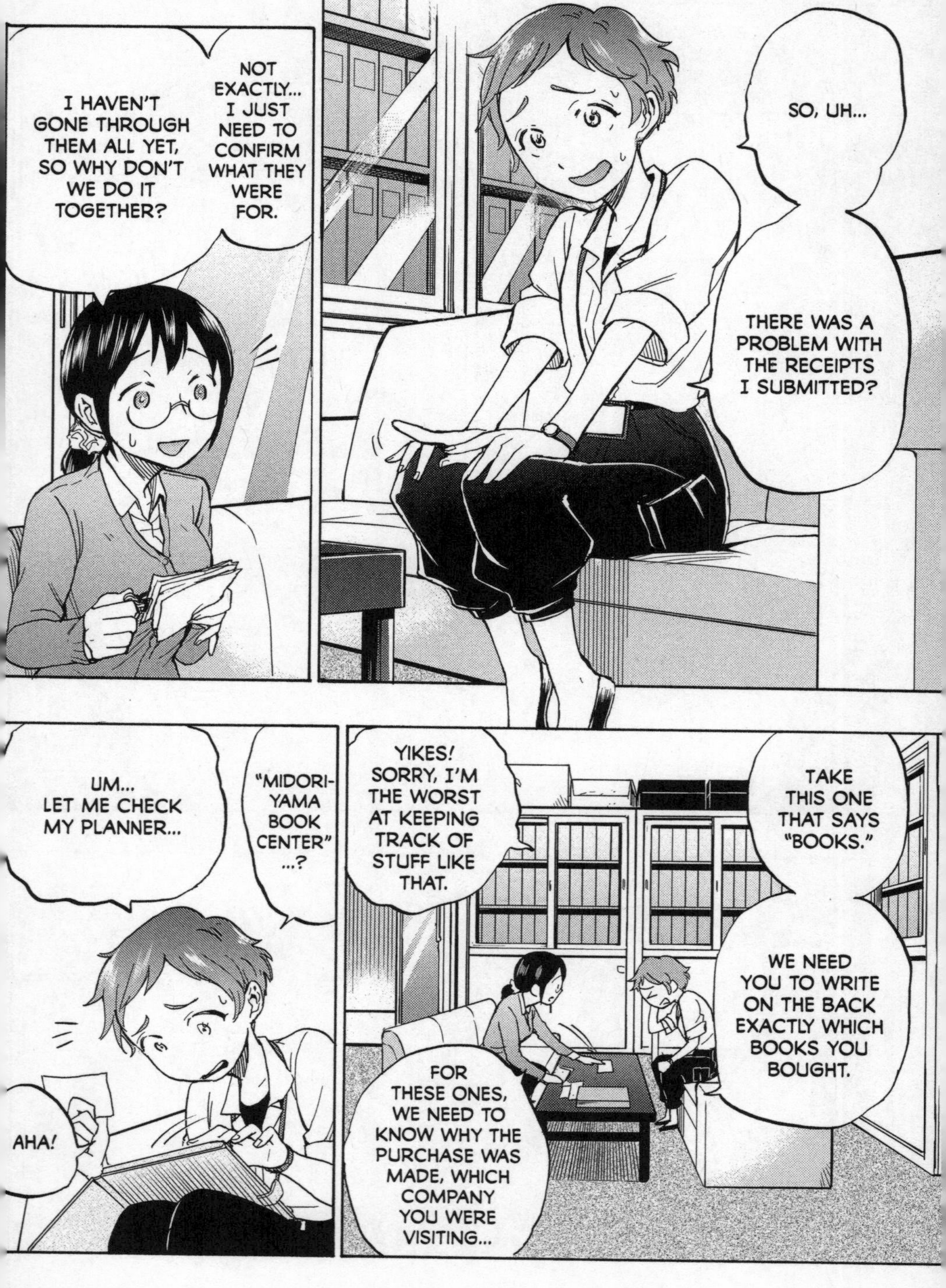
SO, UH...
THERE WAS A PROBLEM WITH THE RECEIPTS I SUBMITTED?
NOT EXACTLY... I JUST NEED TO CONFIRM WHAT THEY WERE FOR.
I HAVEN'T GONE THROUGH THEM ALL YET, SO WHY DON'T WE DO IT TOGETHER?
TAKE THIS ONE THAT SAYS "BOOKS."
WE NEED YOU TO WRITE ON THE BACK EXACTLY WHICH BOOKS YOU BOUGHT.
YIKES! SORRY, I'M THE WORST AT KEEPING TRACK OF STUFF LIKE THAT.
FOR THESE ONES, WE NEED TO KNOW WHY THE PURCHASE WAS MADE, WHICH COMPANY YOU WERE VISITING...
"MIDORI-YAMA BOOK CENTER" ...?
UM... LET ME CHECK MY PLANNER...
AHA!

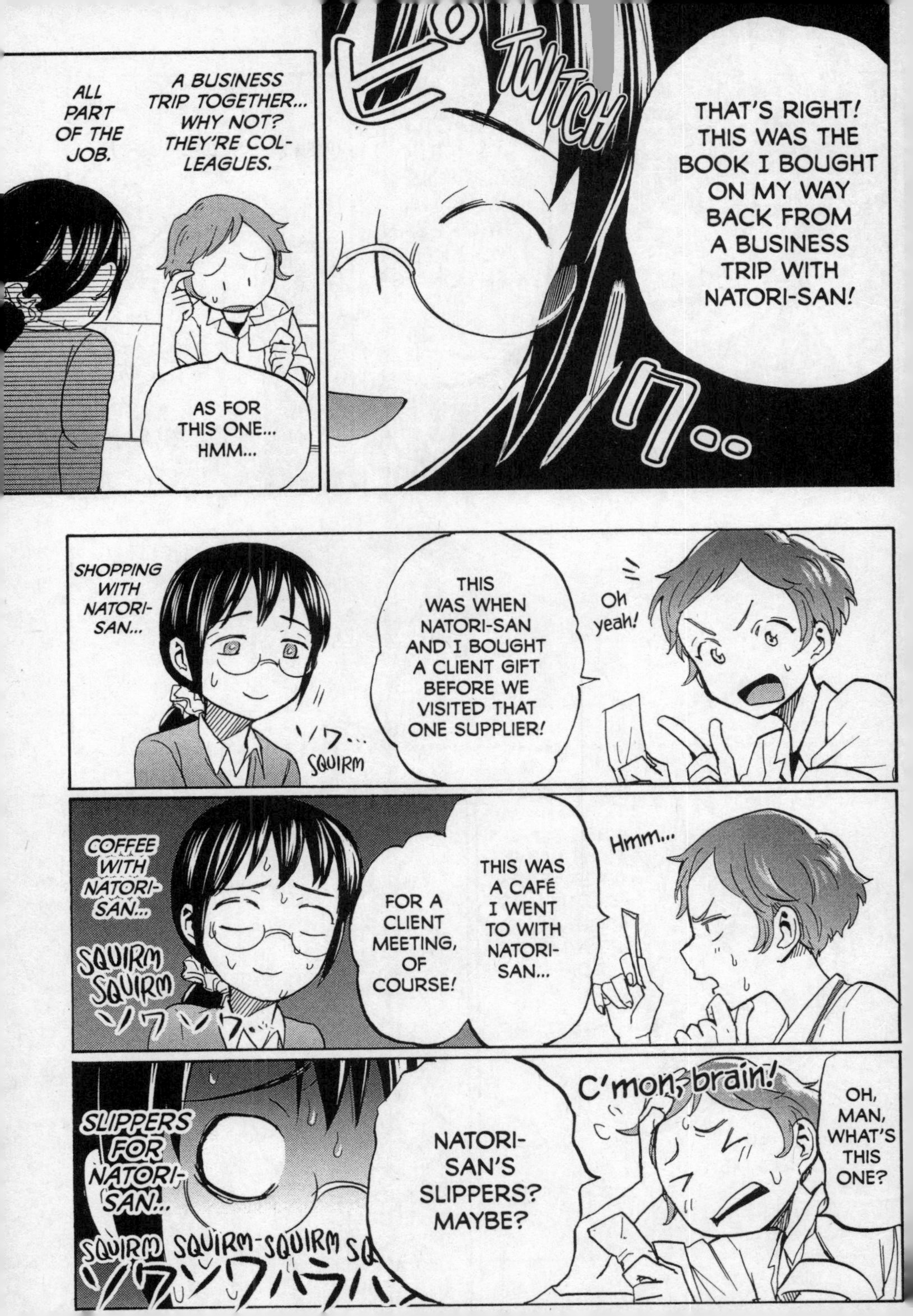
TWITCH
THAT'S RIGHT! THIS WAS THE BOOK I BOUGHT ON MY WAY BACK FROM A BUSINESS TRIP WITH NATORI-SAN!
A BUSINESS TRIP TOGETHER... WHY NOT? THEY'RE COL-LEAGUES.
ALL PART OF THE JOB.
AS FOR THIS ONE... HMM...
Oh yeah!
THIS WAS WHEN NATORI-SAN AND I BOUGHT A CLIENT GIFT BEFORE WE VISITED THAT ONE SUPPLIER!
SQUIRM
SHOPPING WITH NATORI-SAN...
Hmm...
THIS WAS A CAFÉ I WENT TO WITH NATORI-SAN...
FOR A CLIENT MEETING, OF COURSE!
COFFEE WITH NATORI-SAN...
SQUIRM SQUIRM
OH, MAN, WHAT'S THIS ONE?
C'mon, brain!
NATORI-SAN'S SLIPPERS? MAYBE?
SLIPPERS FOR NATORI-SAN...
SQUIRM SQUIRM-SQUIRM SQ

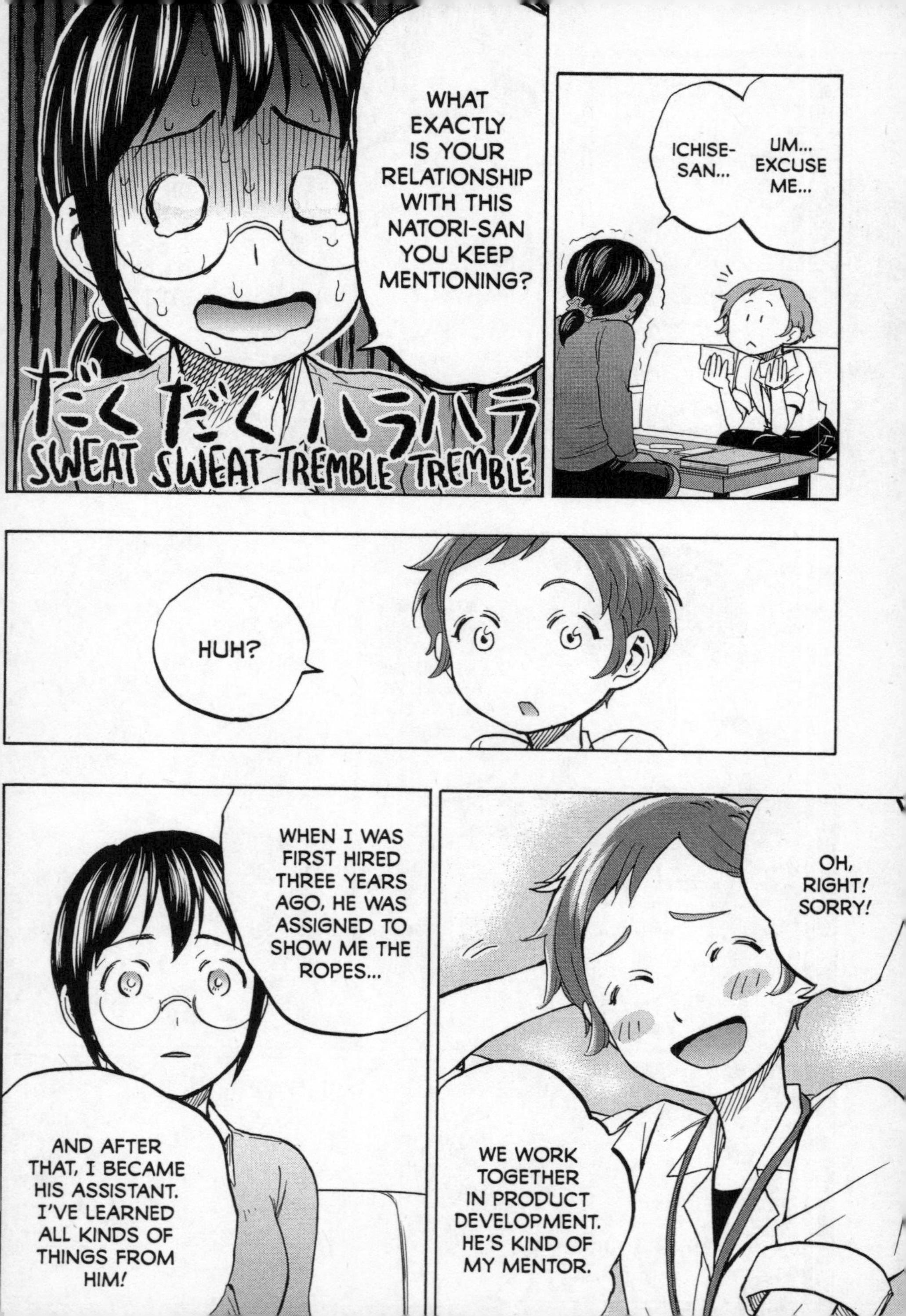
UM... EXCUSE ME...
ICHISE-SAN...
WHAT EXACTLY IS YOUR RELATIONSHIP WITH THIS NATORI-SAN YOU KEEP MENTIONING?
だくだくハラハラ
SWEAT SWEAT TREMBLE TREMBLE
HUH?
OH, RIGHT! SORRY!
WE WORK TOGETHER IN PRODUCT DEVELOPMENT. HE'S KIND OF MY MENTOR.
WHEN I WAS FIRST HIRED THREE YEARS AGO, HE WAS ASSIGNED TO SHOW ME THE ROPES...
AND AFTER THAT, I BECAME HIS ASSISTANT. I'VE LEARNED ALL KINDS OF THINGS FROM HIM!

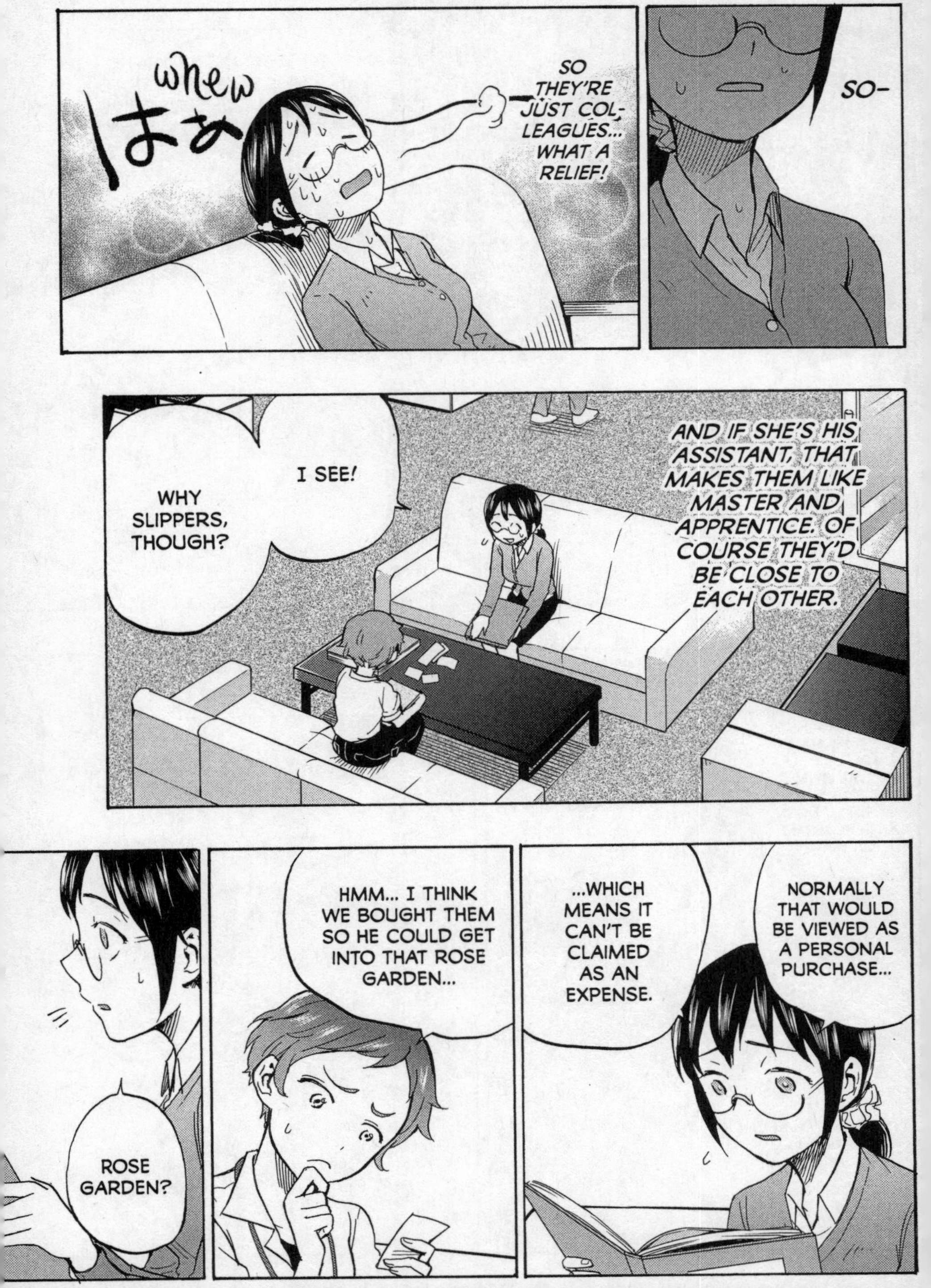
SO-
SO THEY'RE JUST COLLEAGUES... WHAT A RELIEF!
はぁ
whew
AND IF SHE'S HIS ASSISTANT, THAT MAKES THEM LIKE MASTER AND APPRENTICE. OF COURSE THEY'D BE CLOSE TO EACH OTHER.
I SEE!
WHY SLIPPERS, THOUGH?
NORMALLY THAT WOULD BE VIEWED AS A PERSONAL PURCHASE...
...WHICH MEANS IT CAN'T BE CLAIMED AS AN EXPENSE.
HMM... I THINK WE BOUGHT THEM SO HE COULD GET INTO THAT ROSE GARDEN...
ROSE GARDEN?

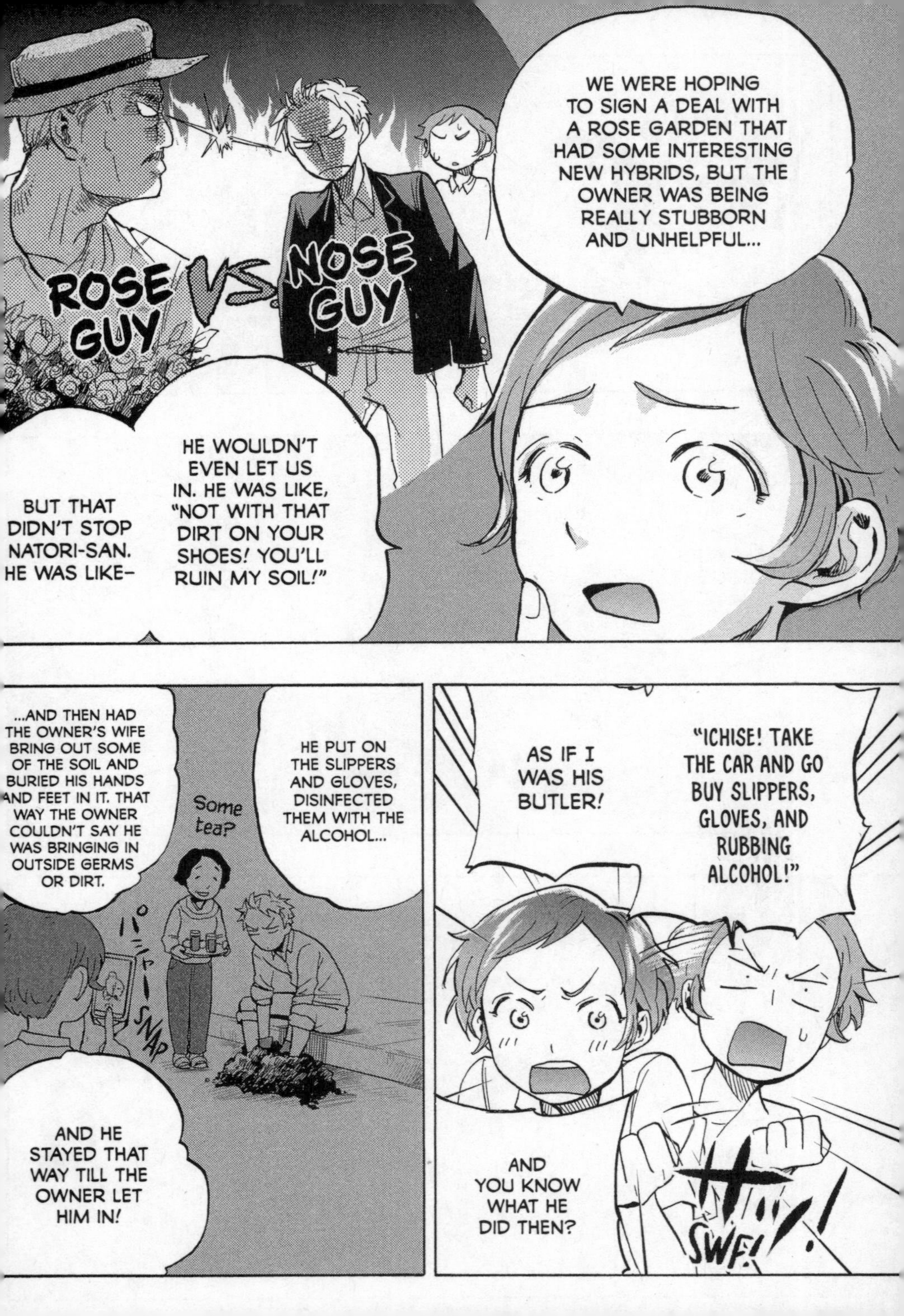
WE WERE HOPING TO SIGN A DEAL WITH A ROSE GARDEN THAT HAD SOME INTERESTING NEW HYBRIDS, BUT THE OWNER WAS BEING REALLY STUBBORN AND UNHELPFUL...
ROSE GUY VS. NOSE GUY
HE WOULDN'T EVEN LET US IN. HE WAS LIKE, "NOT WITH THAT DIRT ON YOUR SHOES! YOU'LL RUIN MY SOIL!"
BUT THAT DIDN'T STOP NATORI-SAN. HE WAS LIKE–
"ICHISE! TAKE THE CAR AND GO BUY SLIPPERS, GLOVES, AND RUBBING ALCOHOL!"
AS IF I WAS HIS BUTLER!
AND YOU KNOW WHAT HE DID THEN?
SWF!
HE PUT ON THE SLIPPERS AND GLOVES, DISINFECTED THEM WITH THE ALCOHOL...
...AND THEN HAD THE OWNER'S WIFE BRING OUT SOME OF THE SOIL AND BURIED HIS HANDS AND FEET IN IT. THAT WAY THE OWNER COULDN'T SAY HE WAS BRINGING IN OUTSIDE GERMS OR DIRT.
Some tea?
SNAP
AND HE STAYED THAT WAY TILL THE OWNER LET HIM IN!

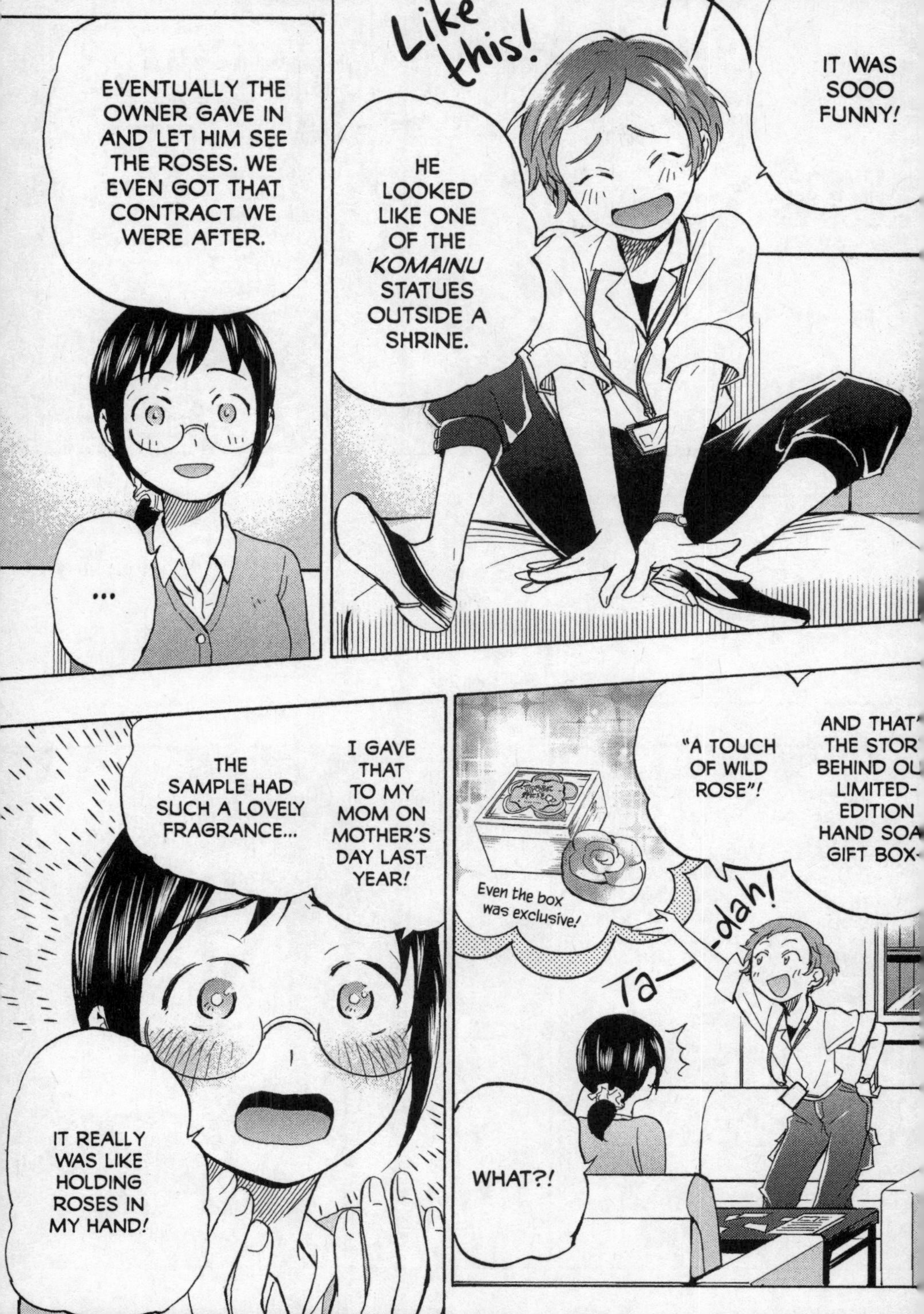
IT WAS SOOO FUNNY!
Like this!
HE LOOKED LIKE ONE OF THE *KOMAINU* STATUES OUTSIDE A SHRINE.
EVENTUALLY THE OWNER GAVE IN AND LET HIM SEE THE ROSES. WE EVEN GOT THAT CONTRACT WE WERE AFTER.
...
AND THAT' THE STOR' BEHIND OU LIMITED-EDITION HAND SOA GIFT BOX-
"A TOUCH OF WILD ROSE"!
Ta—dah!
Even the box was exclusive!
WHAT?!
I GAVE THAT TO MY MOM ON MOTHER'S DAY LAST YEAR!
THE SAMPLE HAD SUCH A LOVELY FRAGRANCE...
IT REALLY WAS LIKE HOLDING ROSES IN MY HAND!

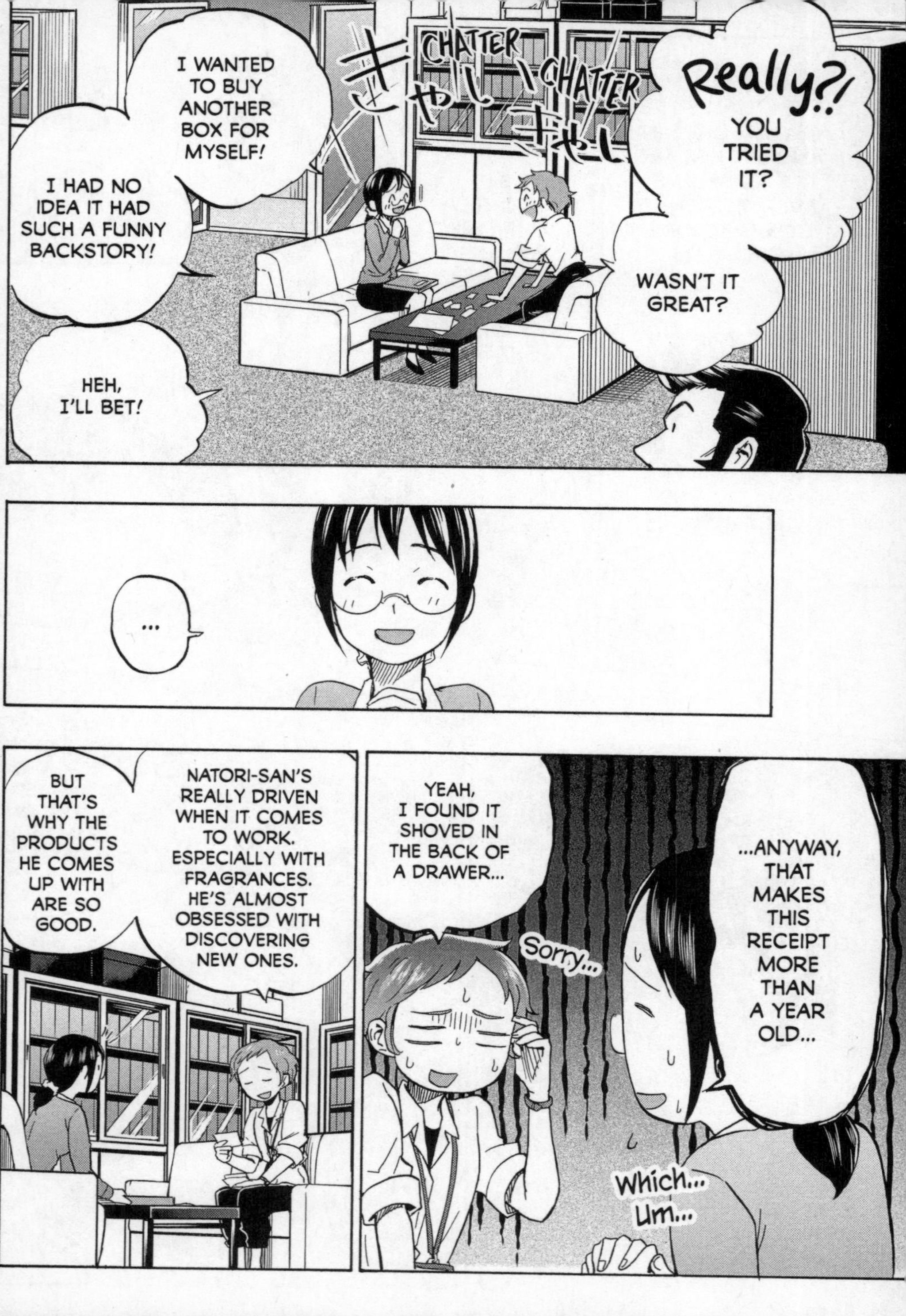
Really?!
YOU TRIED IT?
CHATTER CHATTER
WASN'T IT GREAT?
I WANTED TO BUY ANOTHER BOX FOR MYSELF!
I HAD NO IDEA IT HAD SUCH A FUNNY BACKSTORY!
HEH, I'LL BET!
...
...ANYWAY, THAT MAKES THIS RECEIPT MORE THAN A YEAR OLD...
YEAH, I FOUND IT SHOVED IN THE BACK OF A DRAWER...
Sorry...
Which... Um...
NATORI-SAN'S REALLY DRIVEN WHEN IT COMES TO WORK. ESPECIALLY WITH FRAGRANCES. HE'S ALMOST OBSESSED WITH DISCOVERING NEW ONES.
BUT THAT'S WHY THE PRODUCTS HE COMES UP WITH ARE SO GOOD.

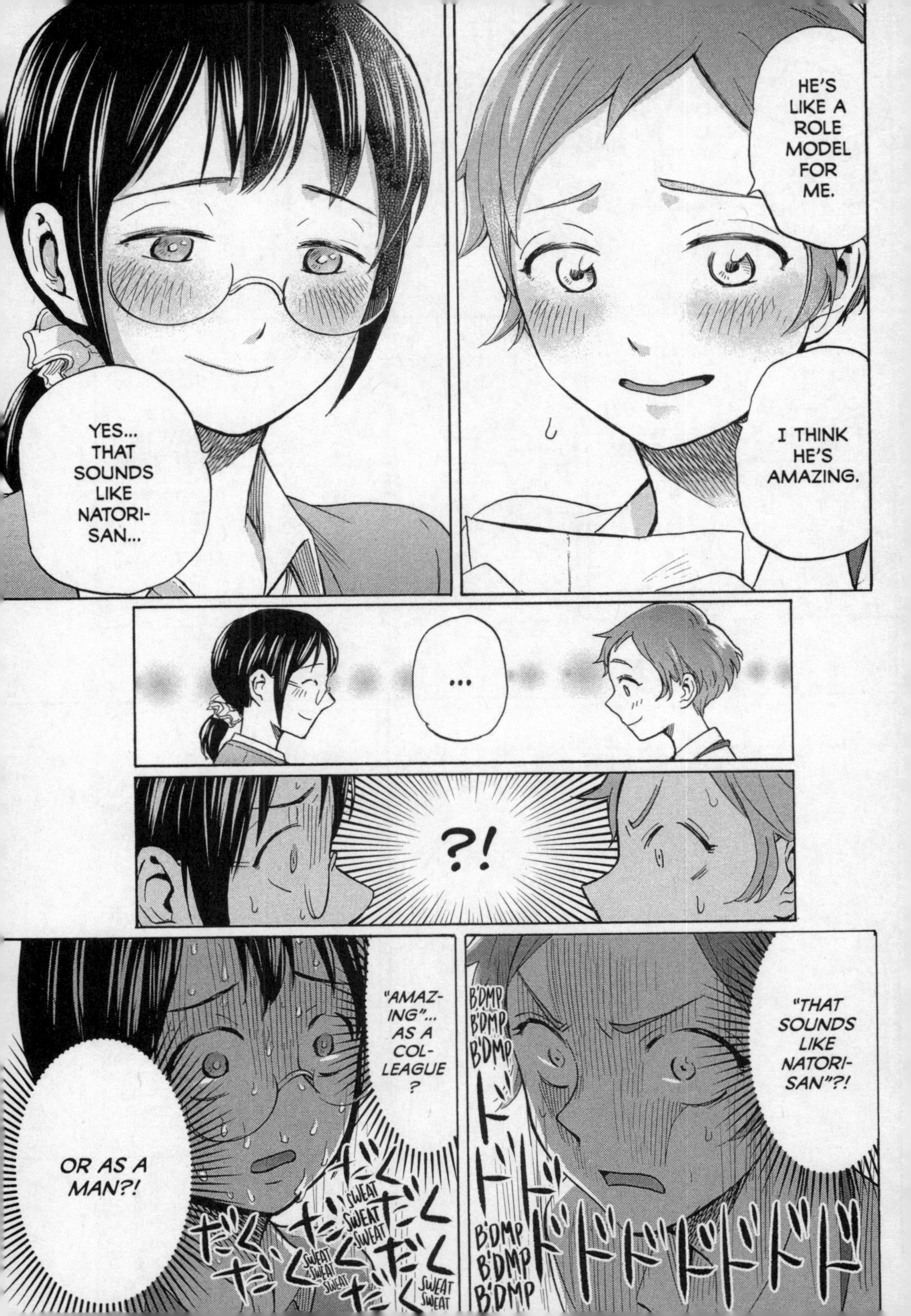
HE'S LIKE A ROLE MODEL FOR ME.
I THINK HE'S AMAZING.
YES... THAT SOUNDS LIKE NATORI-SAN...
...
?!
"THAT SOUNDS LIKE NATORI-SAN"?!
B'DMP B'DMP B'DMP
ドドドドドドドドド
B'DMP B'DMP B'DMP
"AMAZ-ING"... AS A COL-LEAGUE?
OR AS A MAN?!
だくだくだくだくだく
SWEAT SWEAT SWEAT
SWEAT SWEAT
SWEAT SWEAT

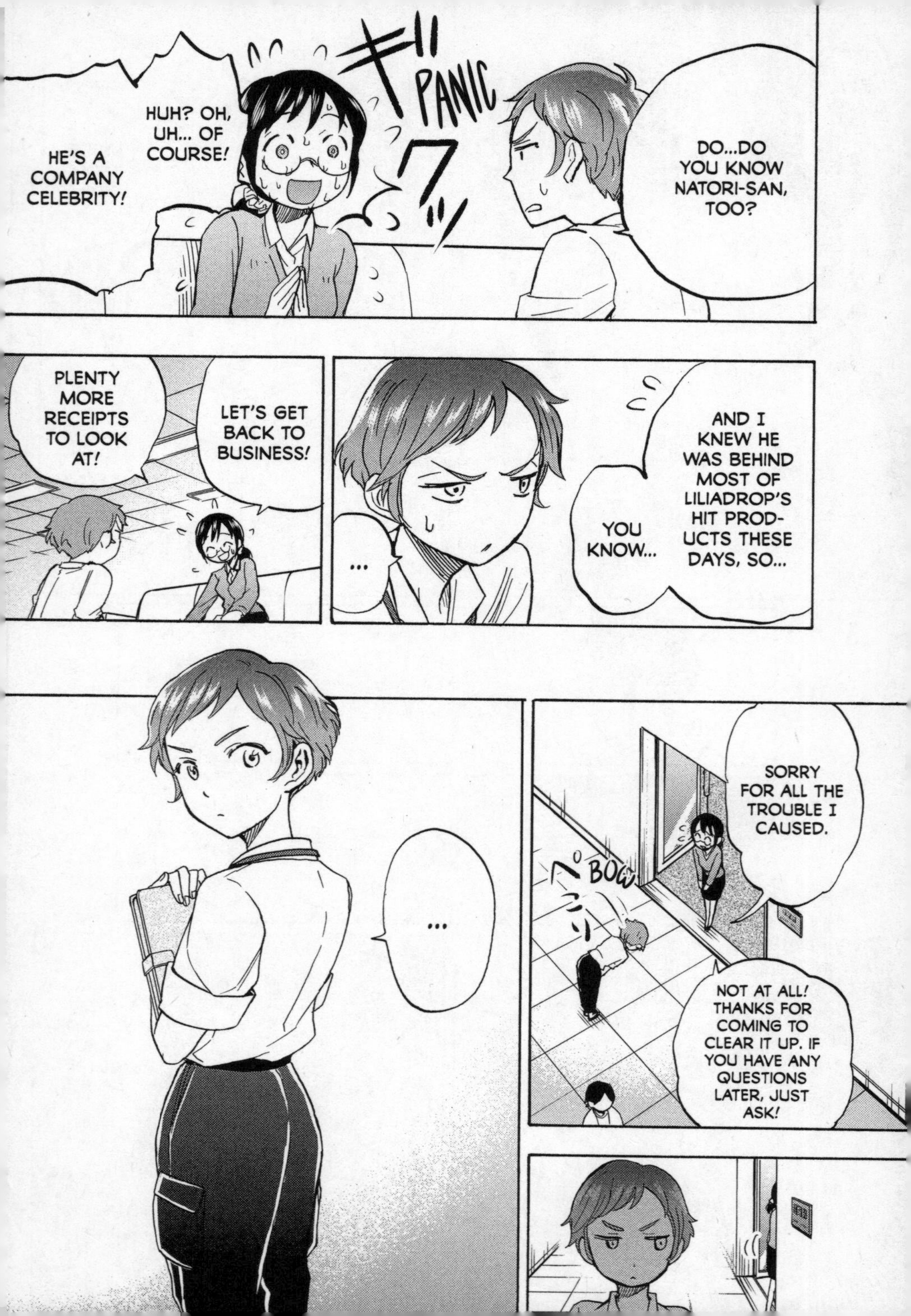
DO...DO YOU KNOW NATORI-SAN, TOO?
PANIC
HUH? OH, UH... OF COURSE!
HE'S A COMPANY CELEBRITY!
AND I KNEW HE WAS BEHIND MOST OF LILIADROP'S HIT PROD-UCTS THESE DAYS, SO...
YOU KNOW...
...
LET'S GET BACK TO BUSINESS!
PLENTY MORE RECEIPTS TO LOOK AT!
SORRY FOR ALL THE TROUBLE I CAUSED.
BOW
NOT AT ALL! THANKS FOR COMING TO CLEAR IT UP. IF YOU HAVE ANY QUESTIONS LATER, JUST ASK!
...

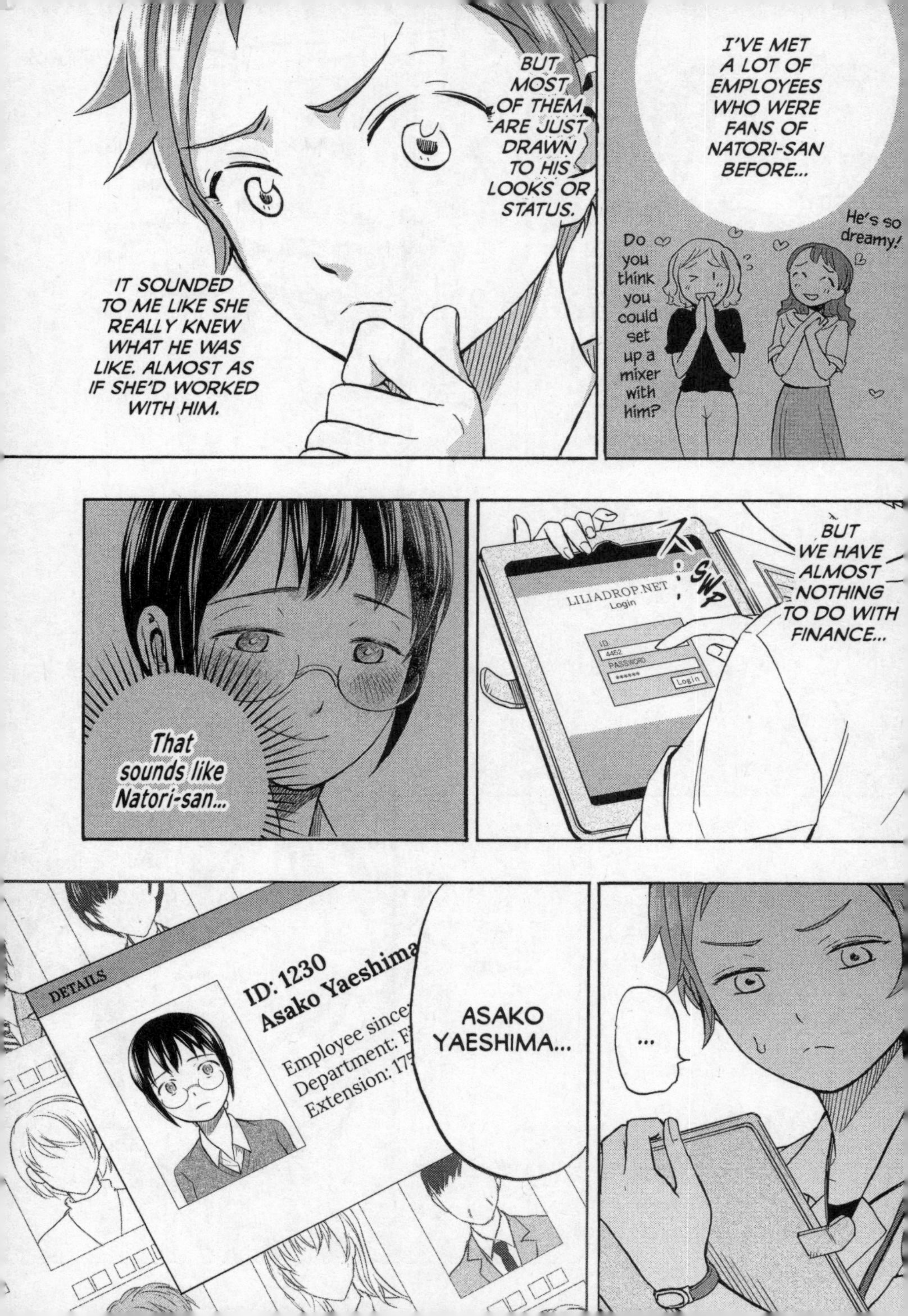
I'VE MET A LOT OF EMPLOYEES WHO WERE FANS OF NATORI-SAN BEFORE...
He's so dreamy!
Do you think you could set up a mixer with him?
BUT MOST OF THEM ARE JUST DRAWN TO HIS LOOKS OR STATUS.
IT SOUNDED TO ME LIKE SHE REALLY KNEW WHAT HE WAS LIKE. ALMOST AS IF SHE'D WORKED WITH HIM.
BUT WE HAVE ALMOST NOTHING TO DO WITH FINANCE...
SWP
LILIADROP.NET
Login
ID
4452
PASSWORD
******
Login
That sounds like Natori-san...
...
ASAKO YAESHIMA...
DETAILS
ID: 1230
Asako Yaeshima
Employee since
Department:
Extension:

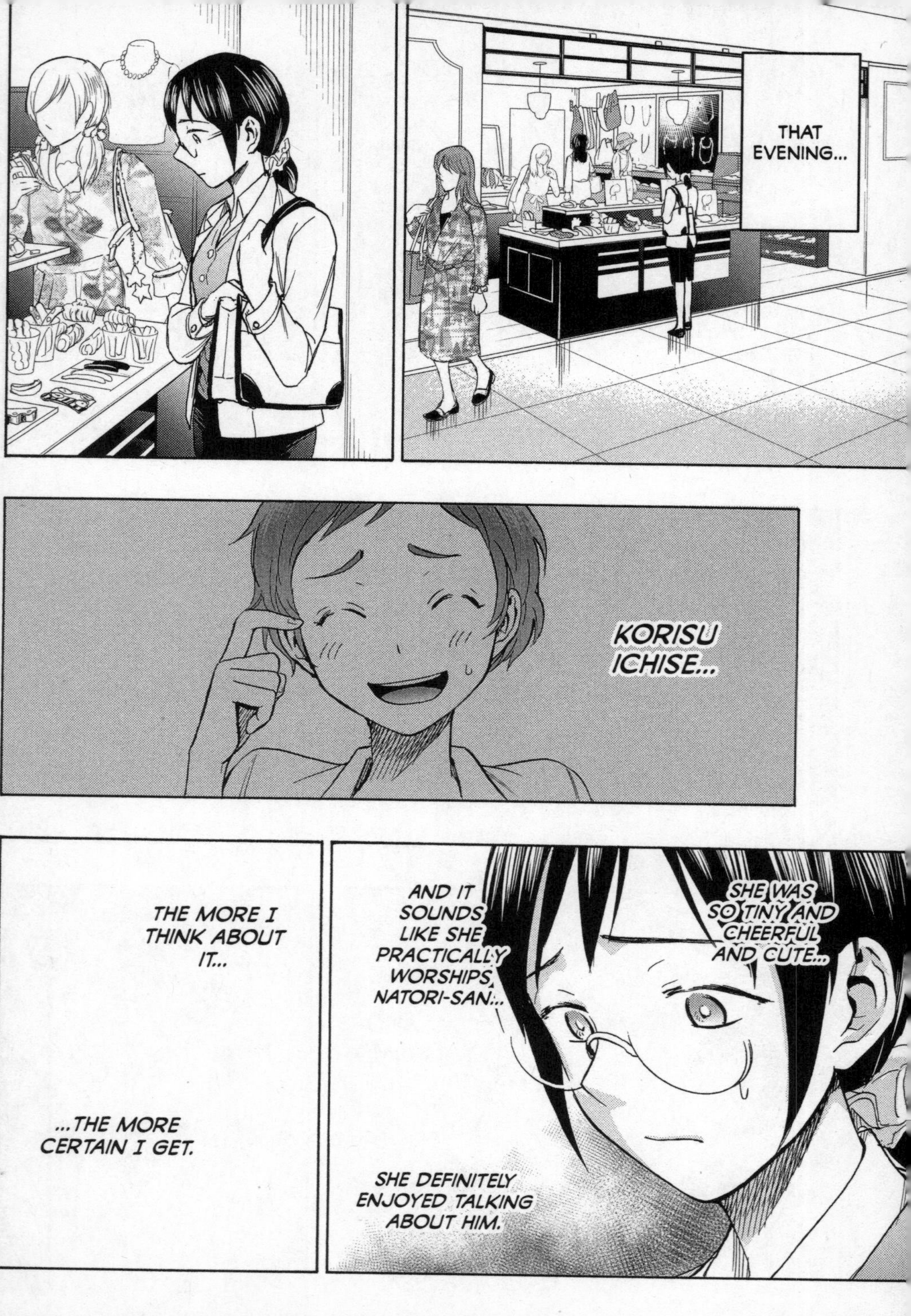
THAT EVENING...
KORISU ICHISE...
SHE WAS SO TINY AND CHEERFUL AND CUTE...
AND IT SOUNDS LIKE SHE PRACTICALLY WORSHIPS NATORI-SAN...
SHE DEFINITELY ENJOYED TALKING ABOUT HIM.
THE MORE I THINK ABOUT IT...
...THE MORE CERTAIN I GET.

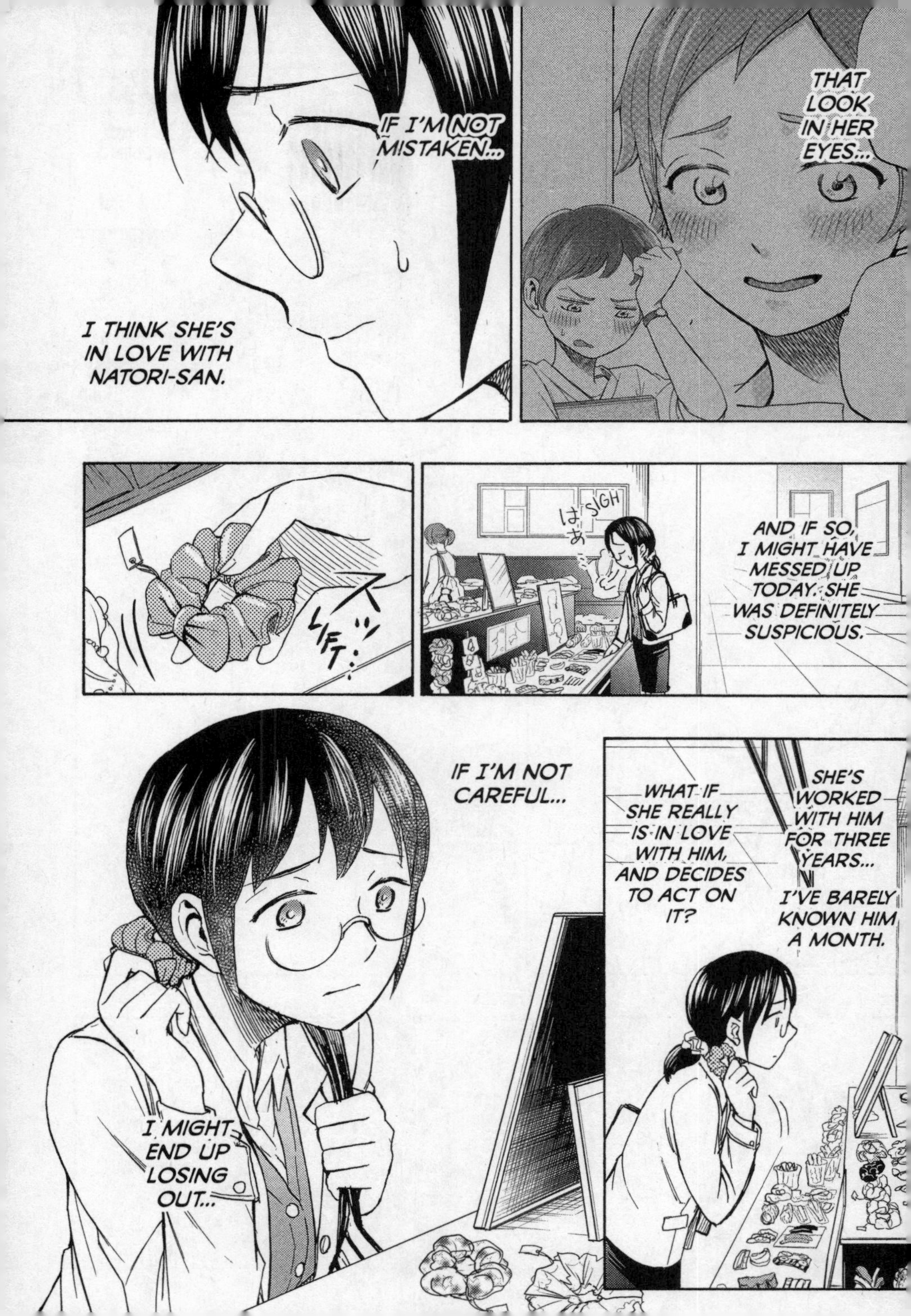
THAT LOOK IN HER EYES...
IF I'M NOT MISTAKEN...
I THINK SHE'S IN LOVE WITH NATORI-SAN.
AND IF SO, I MIGHT HAVE MESSED UP TODAY. SHE WAS DEFINITELY SUSPICIOUS.
はぁ
SIGH
LIFT...
SHE'S WORKED WITH HIM FOR THREE YEARS...
I'VE BARELY KNOWN HIM A MONTH.
WHAT IF SHE REALLY IS IN LOVE WITH HIM, AND DECIDES TO ACT ON IT?
IF I'M NOT CAREFUL...
I MIGHT END UP LOSING OUT...

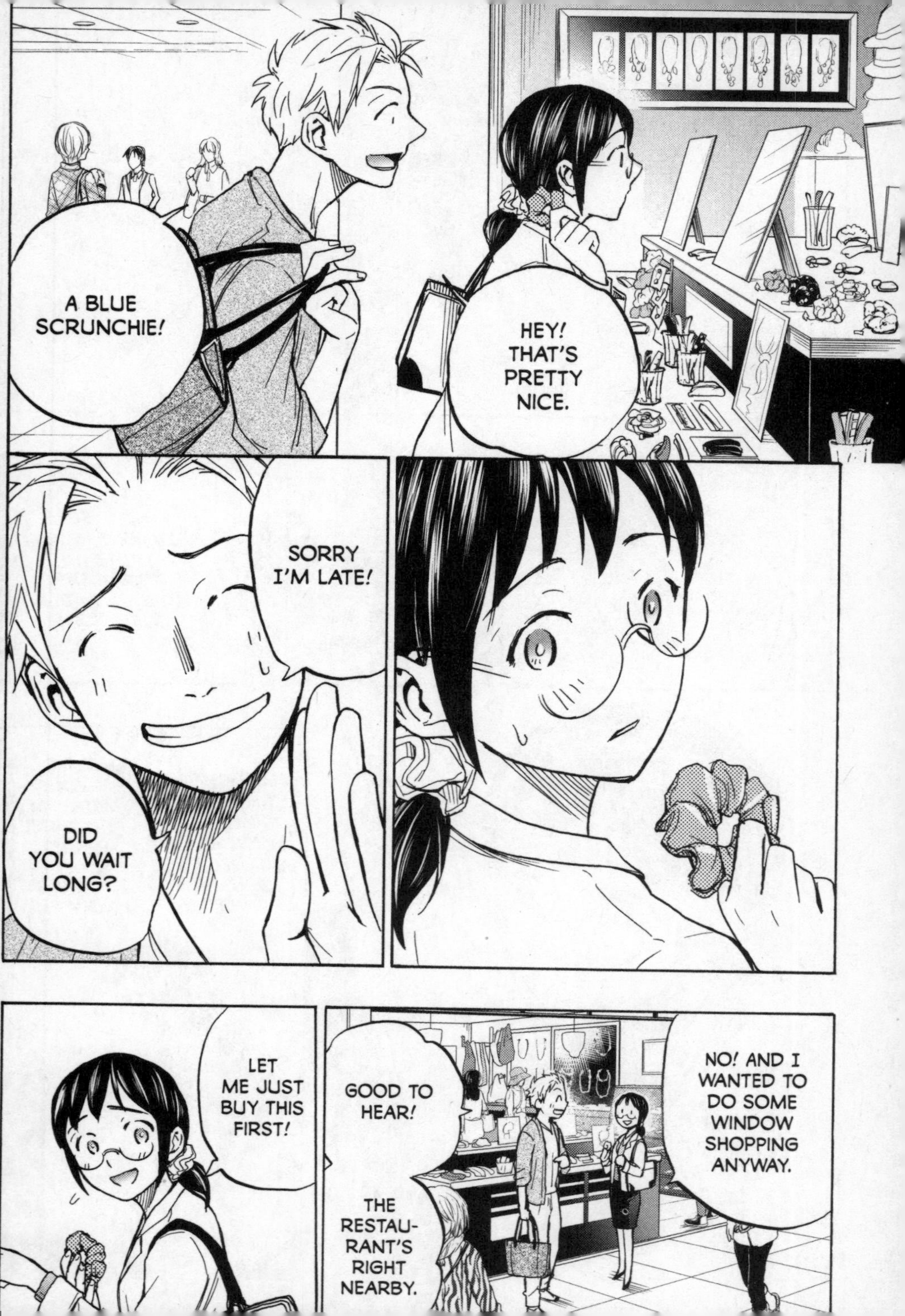
HEY! THAT'S PRETTY NICE.
A BLUE SCRUNCHIE!
SORRY I'M LATE!
DID YOU WAIT LONG?
NO! AND I WANTED TO DO SOME WINDOW SHOPPING ANYWAY.
GOOD TO HEAR!
THE RESTAU-RANT'S RIGHT NEARBY.
LET ME JUST BUY THIS FIRST!

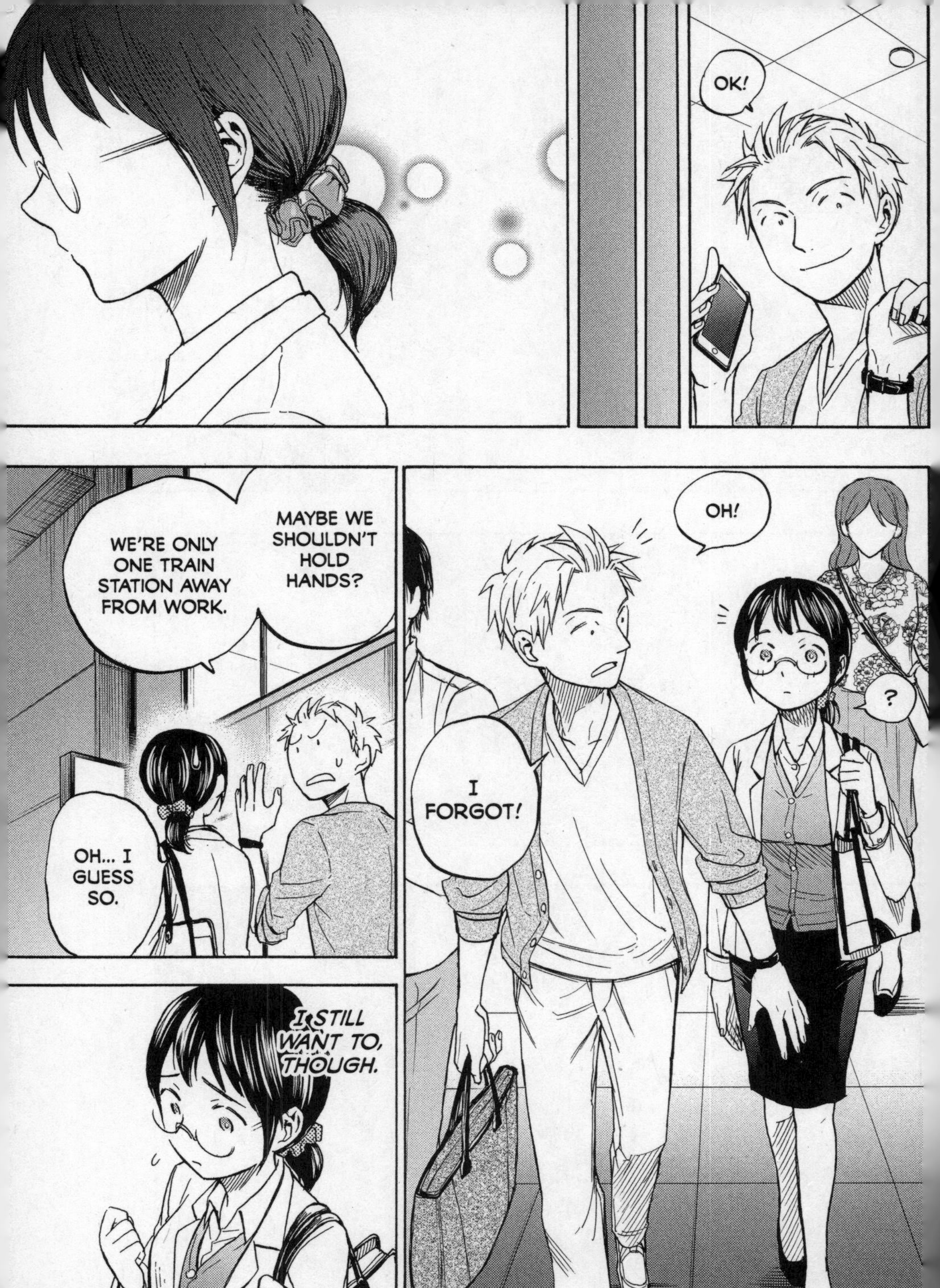
OK!
OH!
?
I FORGOT!
MAYBE WE SHOULDN'T HOLD HANDS?
WE'RE ONLY ONE TRAIN STATION AWAY FROM WORK.
OH... I GUESS SO.
I STILL WANT TO, THOUGH.

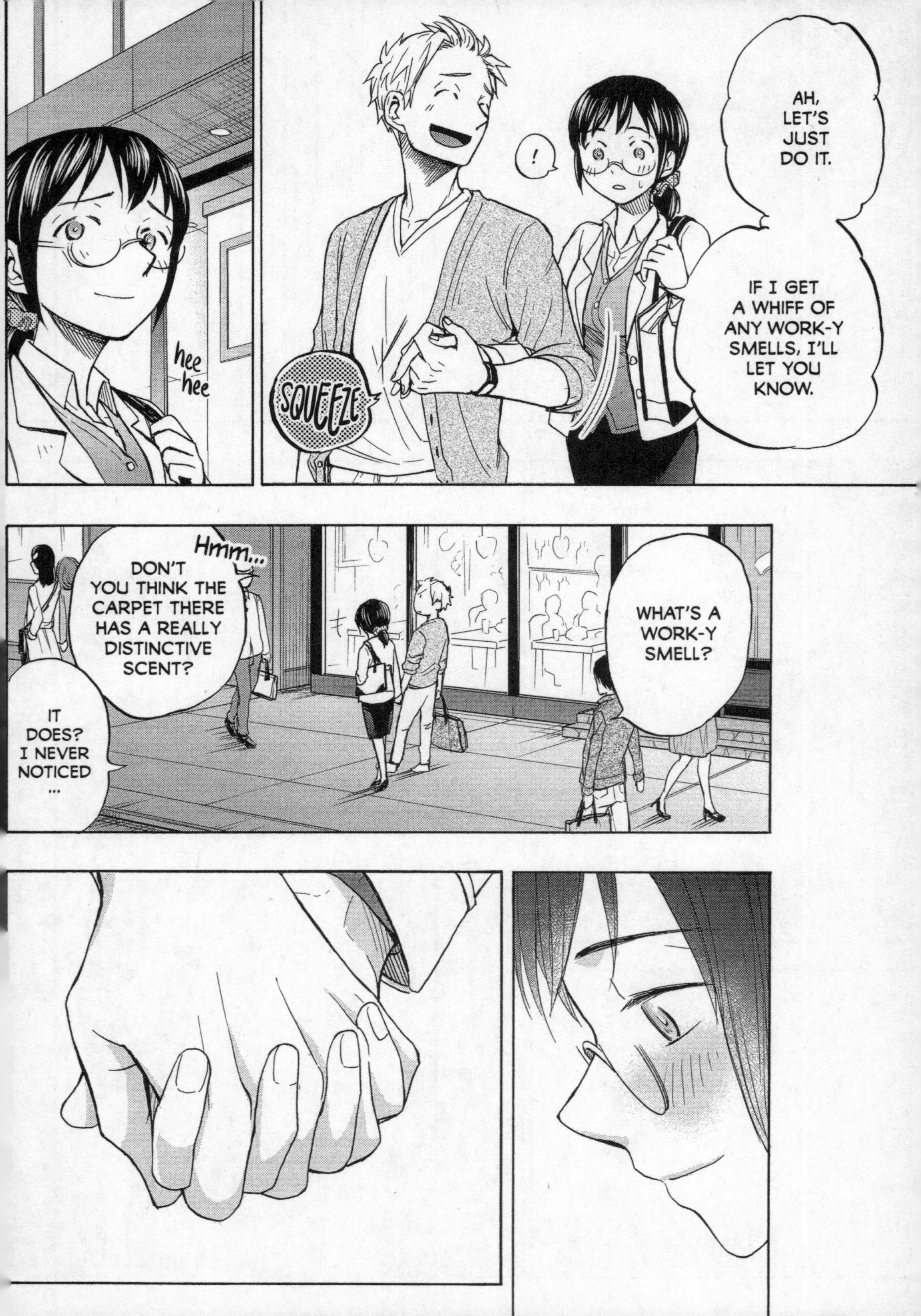
AH, LET'S JUST DO IT.
IF I GET A WHIFF OF ANY WORK-Y SMELLS, I'LL LET YOU KNOW.
!
SQUEEZE
hee hee
WHAT'S A WORK-Y SMELL?
Hmm...
DON'T YOU THINK THE CARPET THERE HAS A REALLY DISTINCTIVE SCENT?
IT DOES? I NEVER NOTICED ...

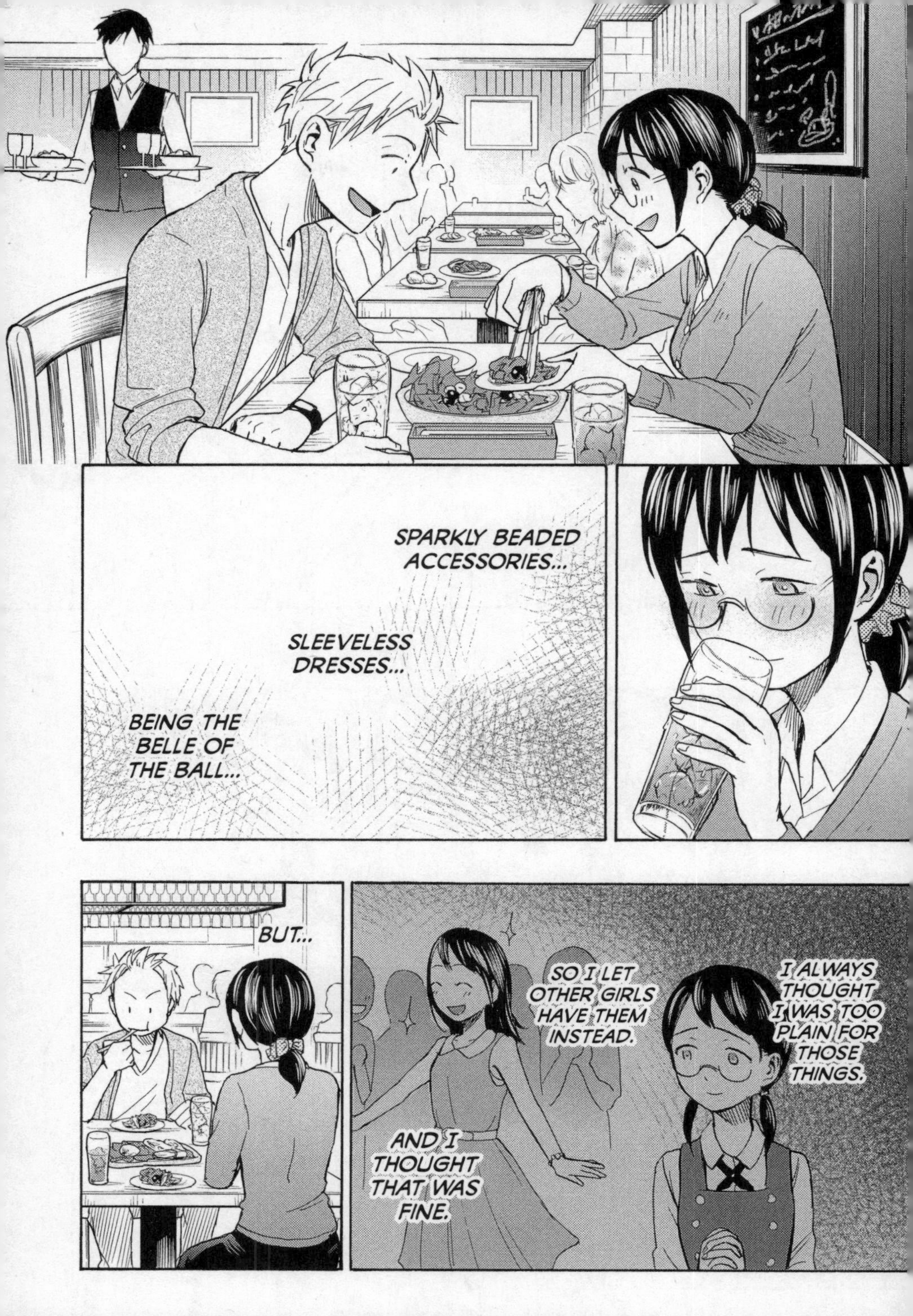
SPARKLY BEADED ACCESSORIES...
SLEEVELESS DRESSES...
BEING THE BELLE OF THE BALL...
I ALWAYS THOUGHT I WAS TOO PLAIN FOR THOSE THINGS.
SO I LET OTHER GIRLS HAVE THEM INSTEAD.
AND I THOUGHT THAT WAS FINE.
BUT...

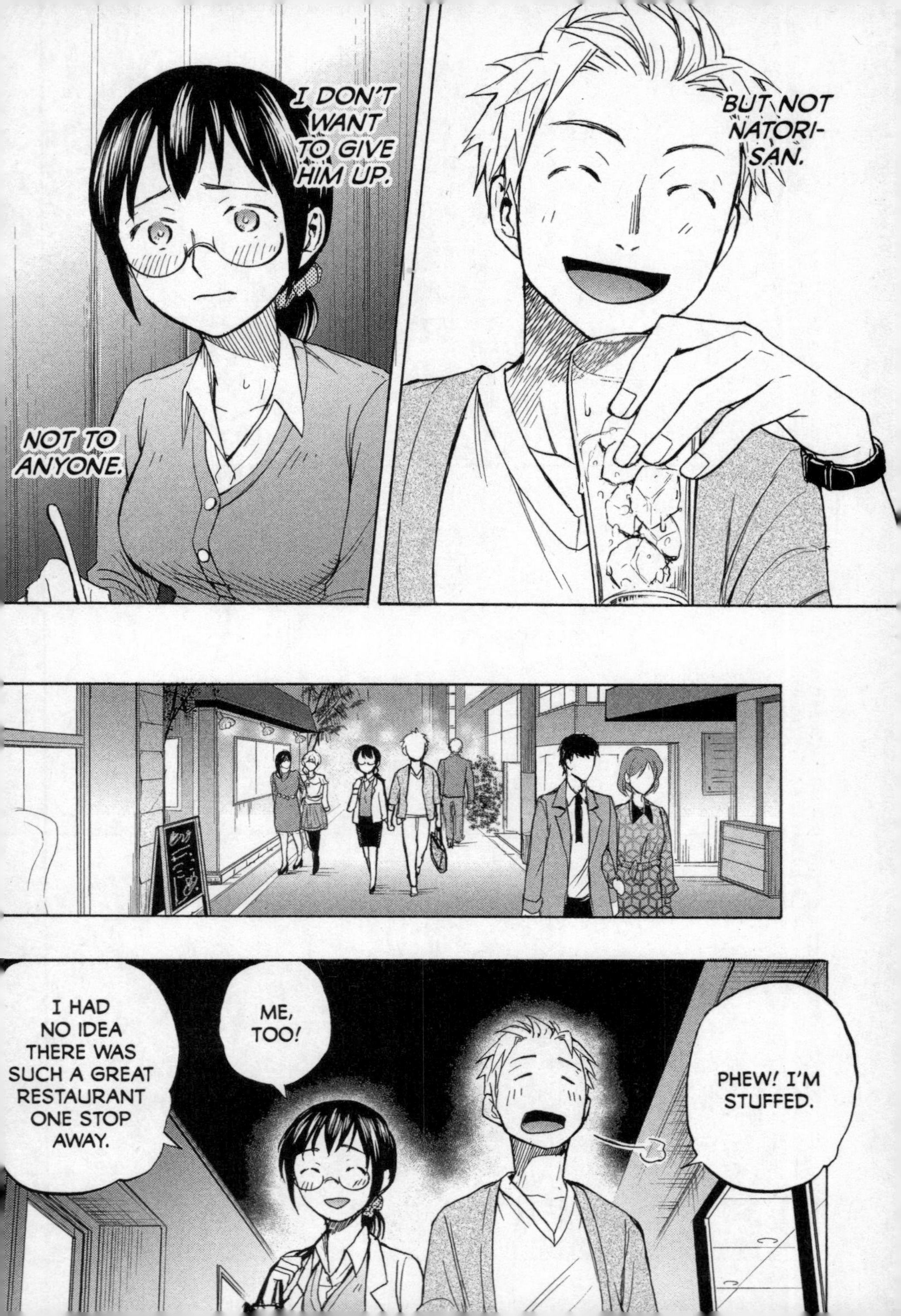
BUT NOT NATORI-SAN.
I DON'T WANT TO GIVE HIM UP.
NOT TO ANYONE.
PHEW! I'M STUFFED.
ME, TOO!
I HAD NO IDEA THERE WAS SUCH A GREAT RESTAURANT ONE STOP AWAY.

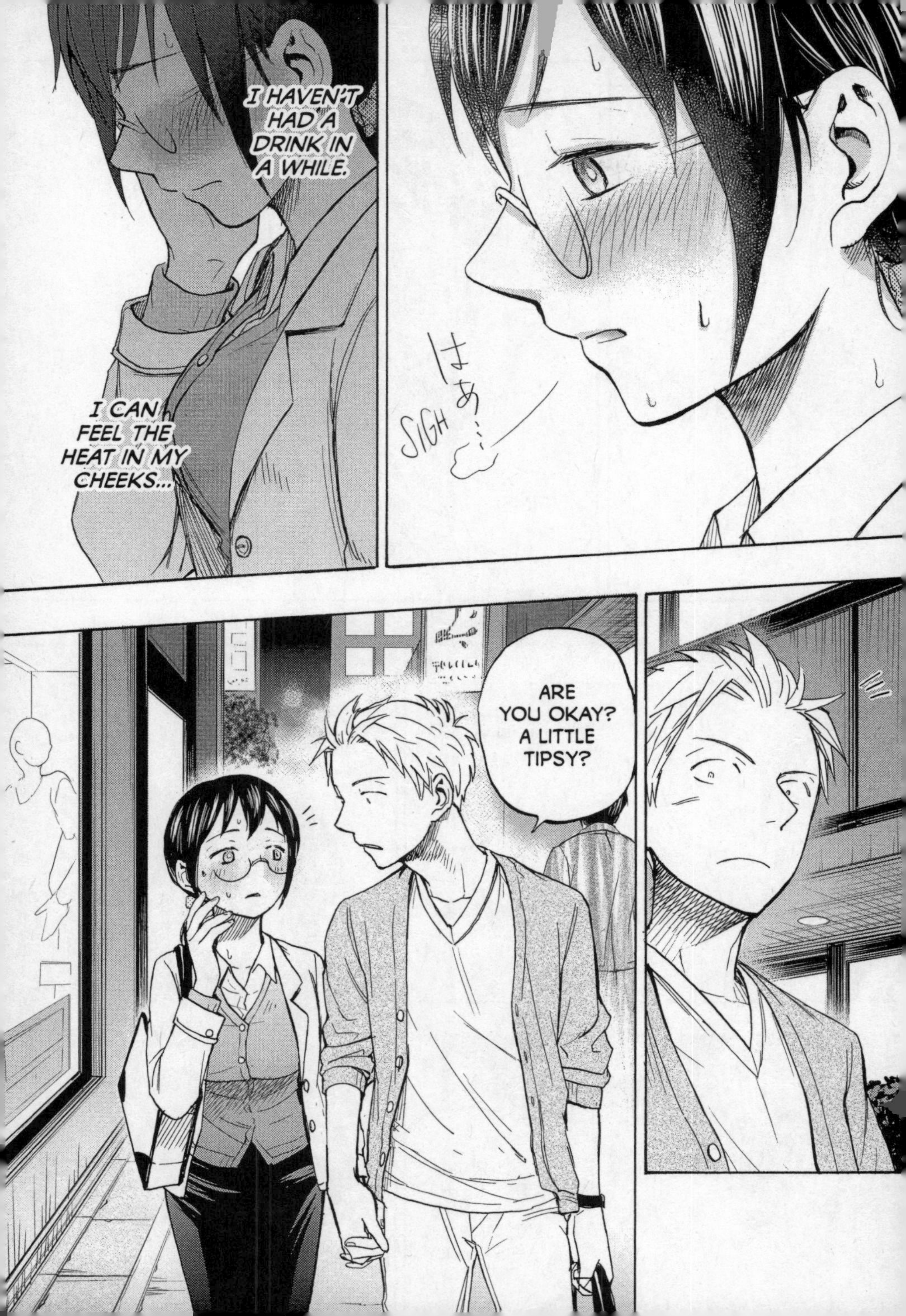
はぁ…
SIGH
I HAVEN'T HAD A DRINK IN A WHILE.
I CAN FEEL THE HEAT IN MY CHEEKS...
ARE YOU OKAY? A LITTLE TIPSY?

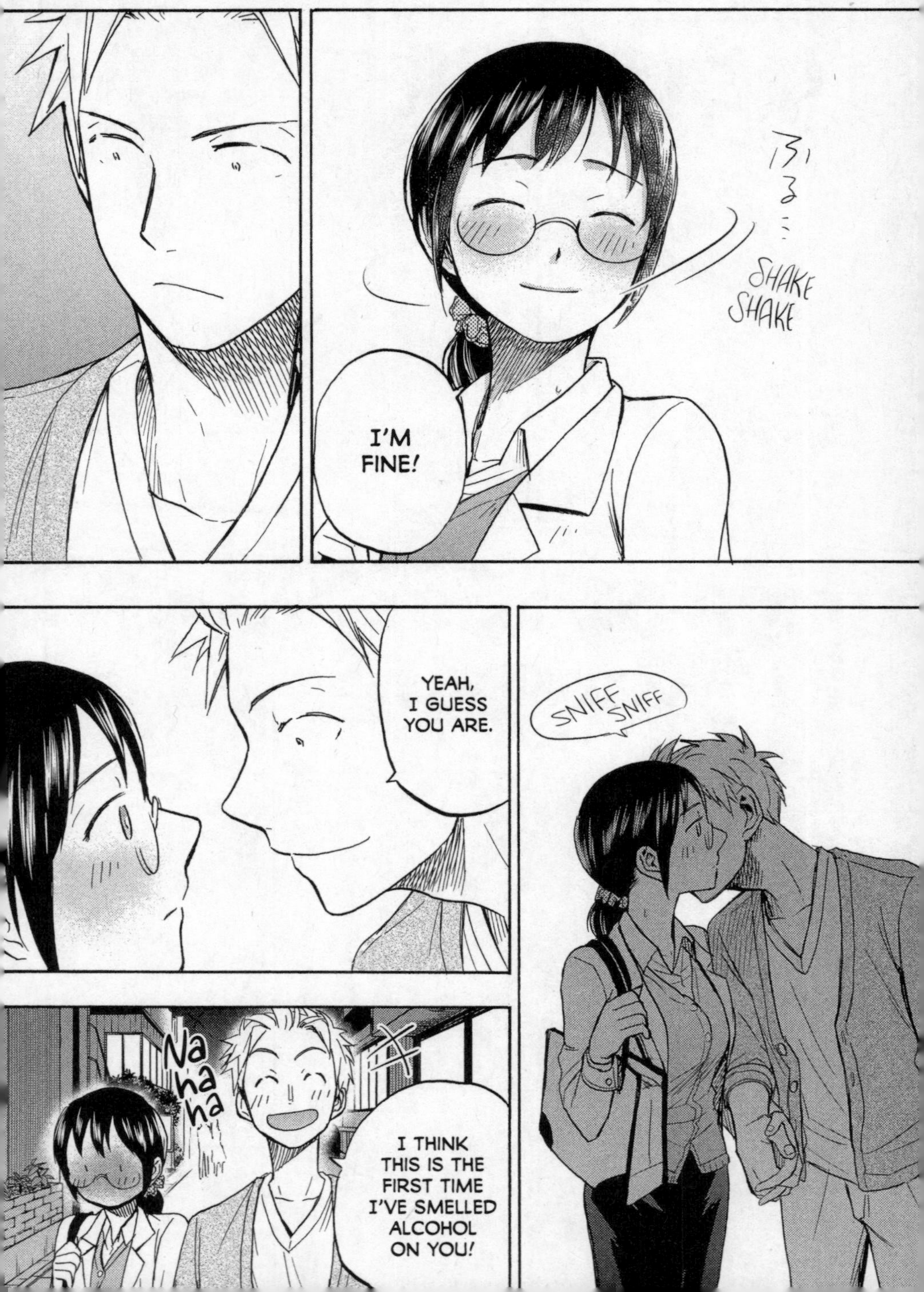
ふる
SHAKE SHAKE
I'M FINE!
SNIFF SNIFF
YEAH, I GUESS YOU ARE.
Na ha ha ha
I THINK THIS IS THE FIRST TIME I'VE SMELLED ALCOHOL ON YOU!

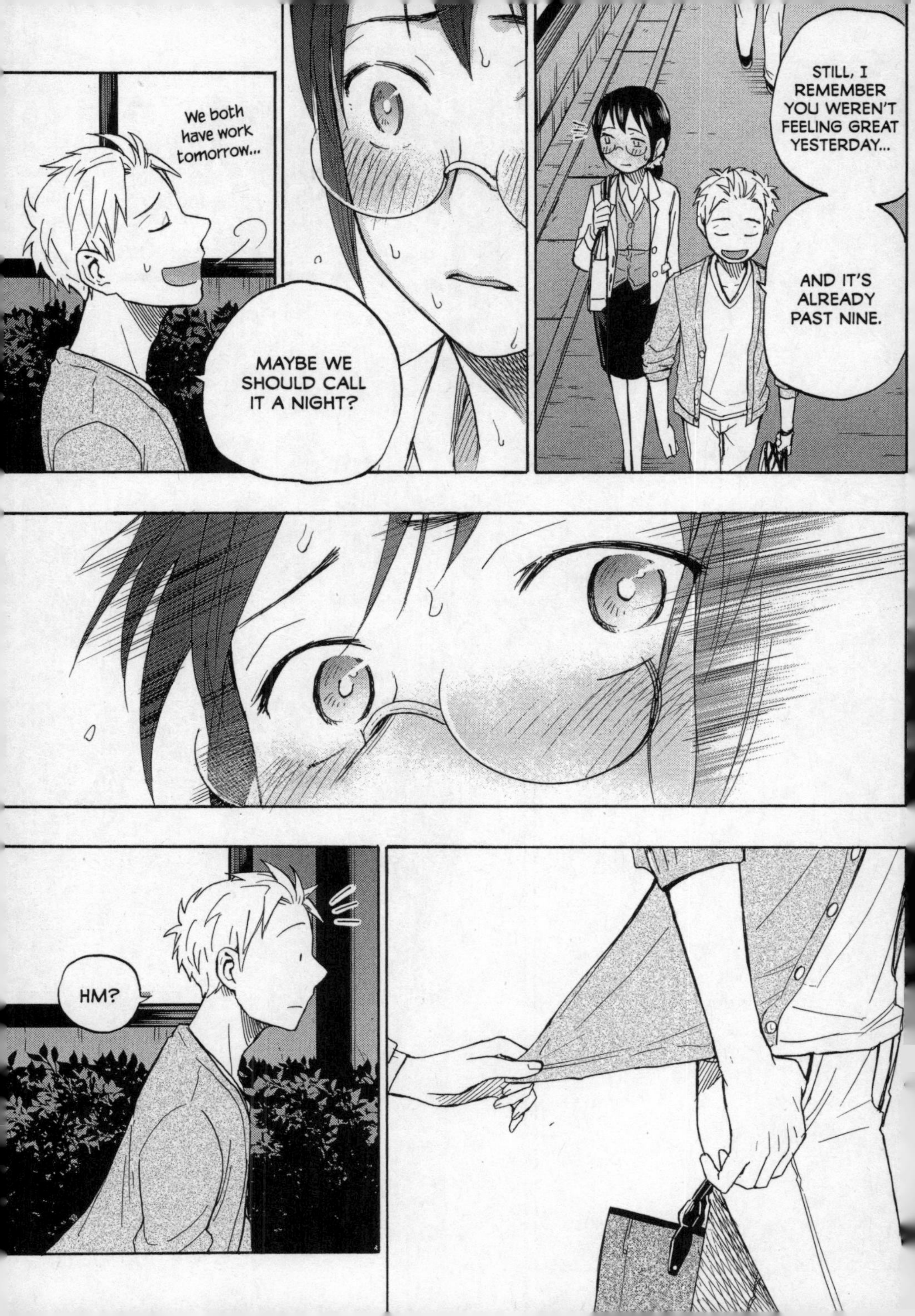
STILL, I REMEMBER YOU WEREN'T FEELING GREAT YESTERDAY...
AND IT'S ALREADY PAST NINE.
We both have work tomorrow...
MAYBE WE SHOULD CALL IT A NIGHT?
HM?

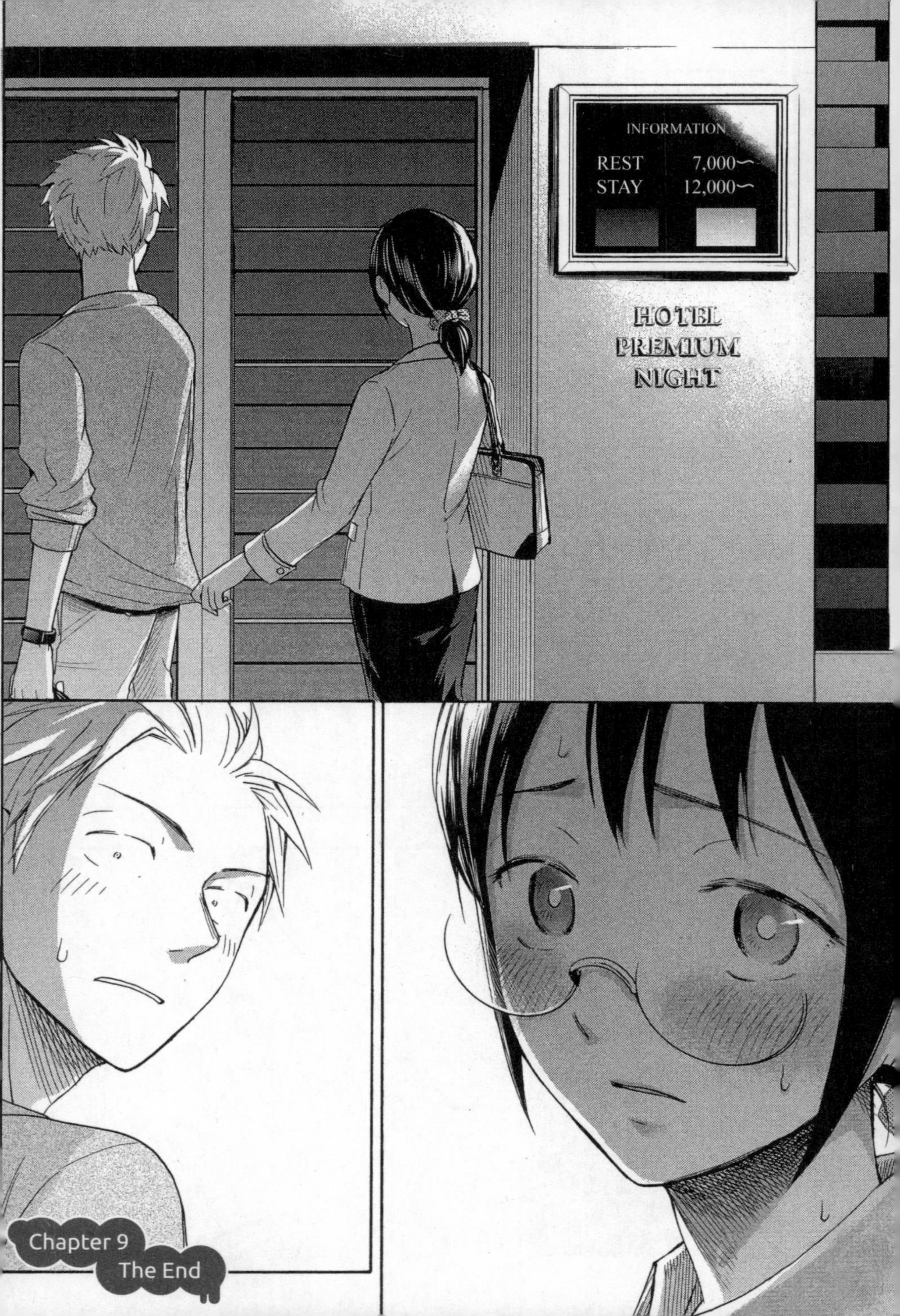
INFORMATION
REST 7,000～
STAY 12,000～
HOTEL
PREMIUM
NIGHT
Chapter 9
The End

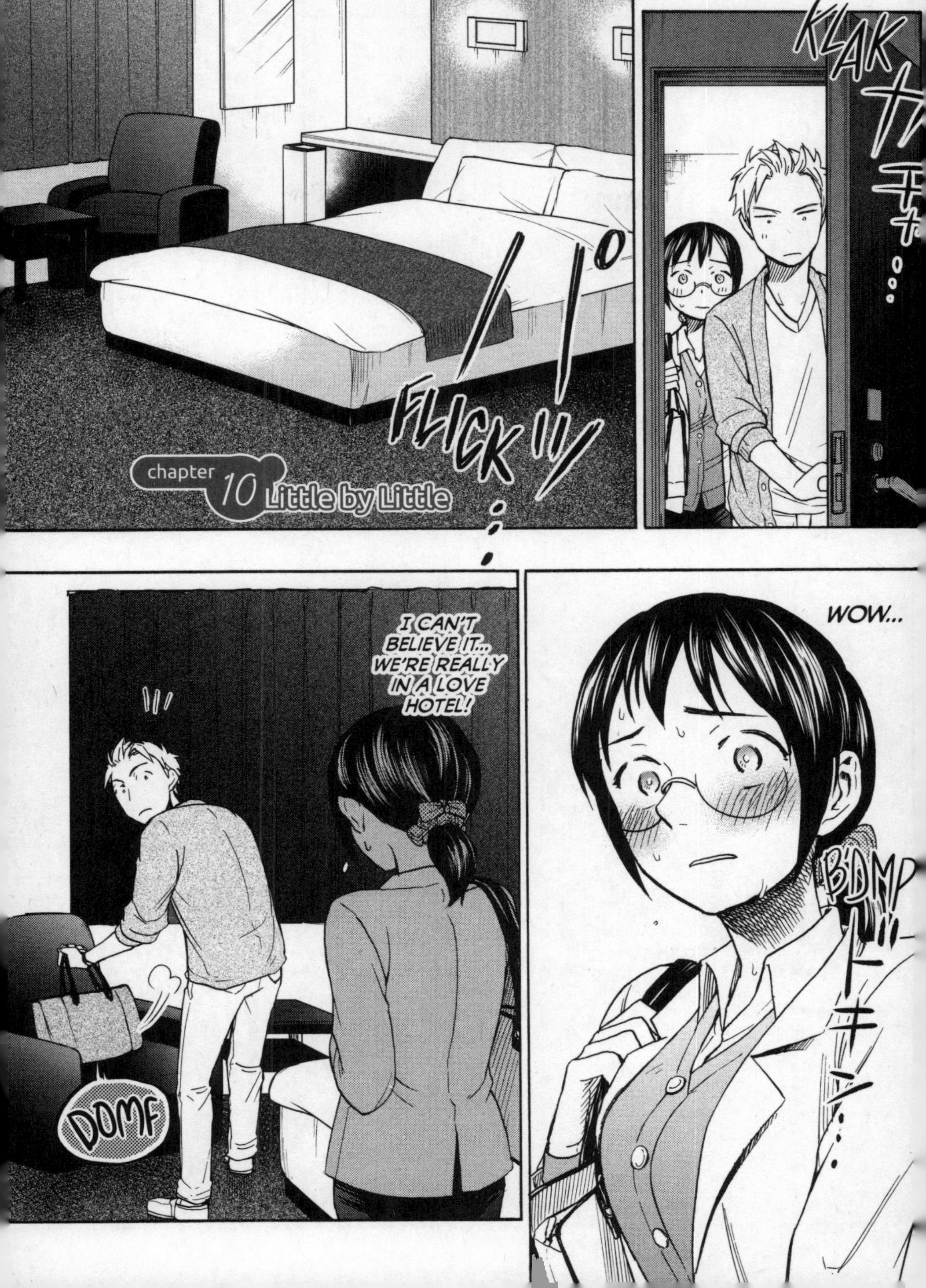
KLAK
FLICK
chapter 10 Little by Little
WOW...
BDMP
I CAN'T BELIEVE IT... WE'RE REALLY IN A LOVE HOTEL!
DOMF

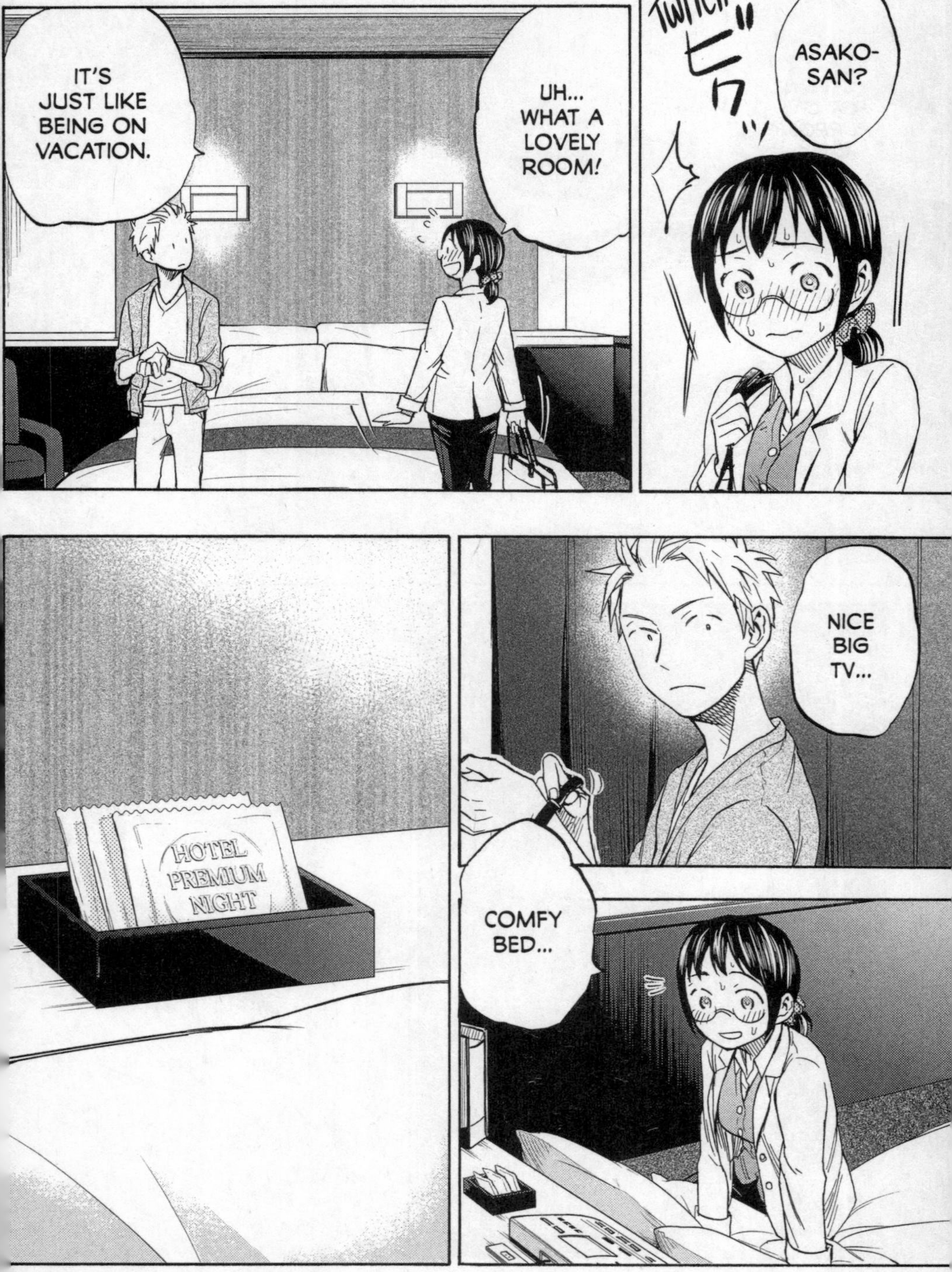
TWITCH
ビクッ
ASAKO-SAN?
UH... WHAT A LOVELY ROOM!
IT'S JUST LIKE BEING ON VACATION.
NICE BIG TV...
COMFY BED...
HOTEL PREMIUM NIGHT

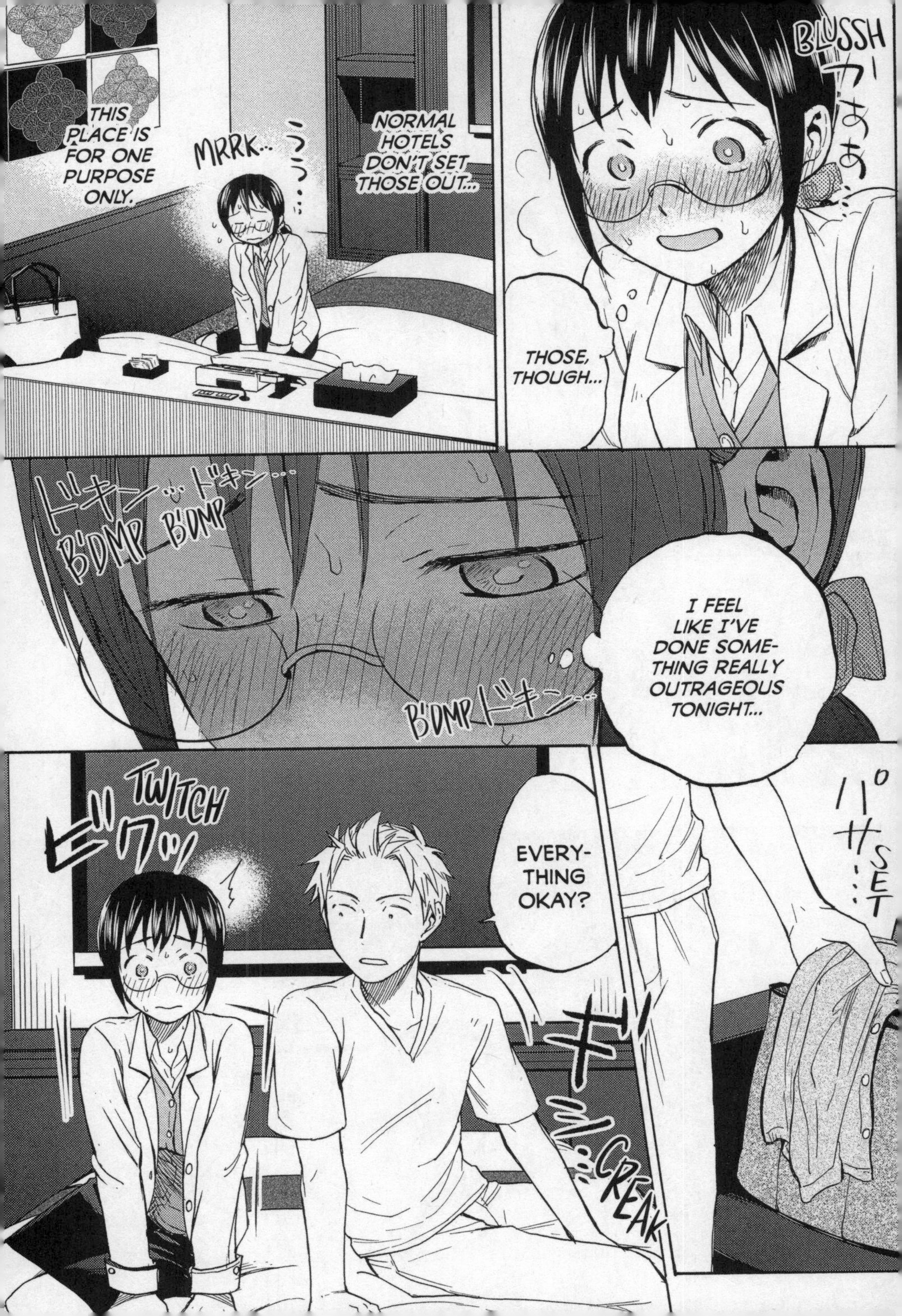
BLUSSH
かぁぁ…
THOSE, THOUGH...
NORMAL HOTELS DON'T SET THOSE OUT...
MRRK...
うう…
THIS PLACE IS FOR ONE PURPOSE ONLY.
ドキン…ドキン…
B'DMP B'DMP
I FEEL LIKE I'VE DONE SOME-THING REALLY OUTRAGEOUS TONIGHT...
B'DMP
ドキン…
パサ…
SET
EVERY-THING OKAY?
ギシ…
CREAK
TWITCH
ビクッ

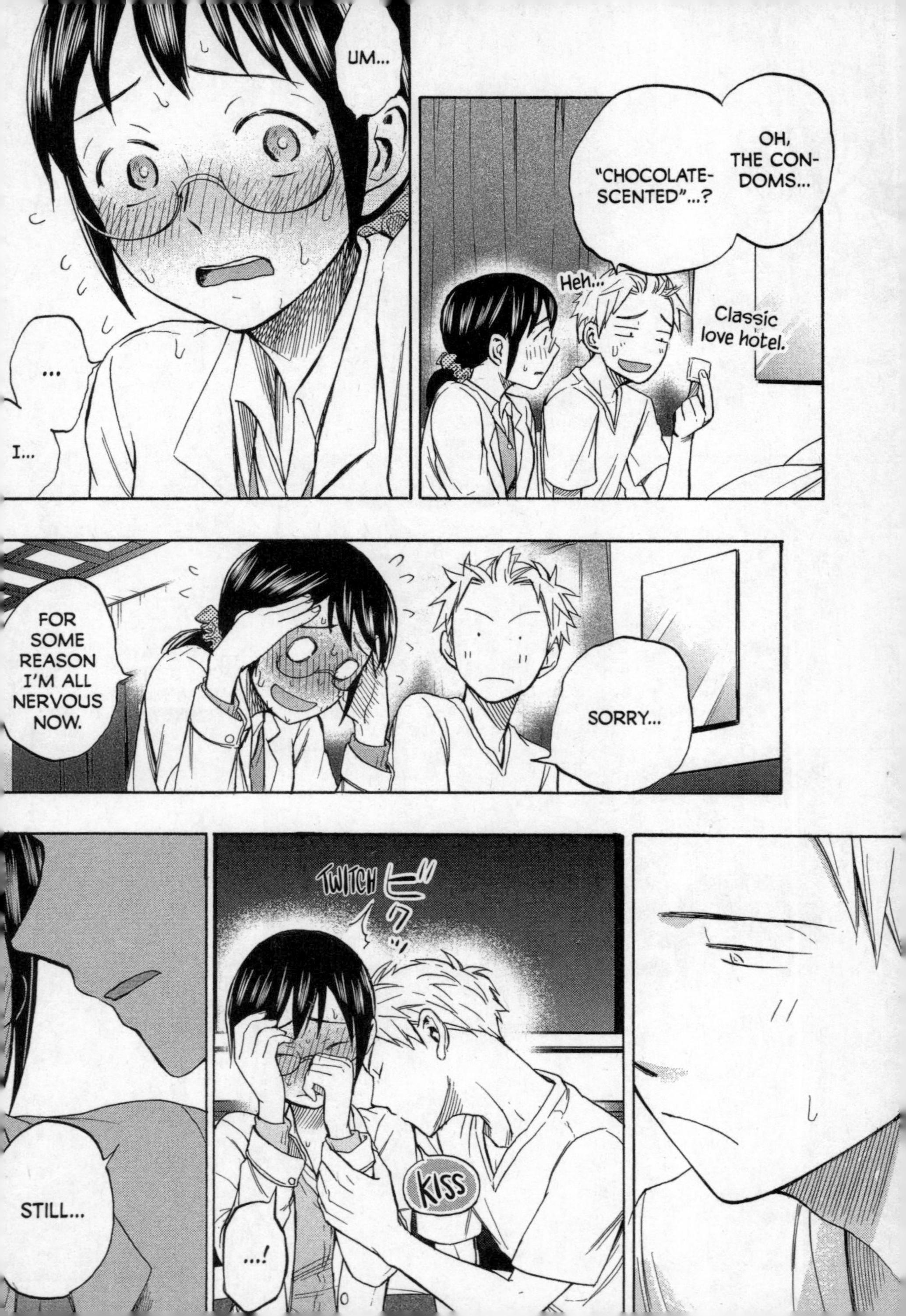
OH, THE CON-DOMS...
"CHOCOLATE-SCENTED"...?
Heh...
Classic love hotel.
UM...
...
I...
FOR SOME REASON I'M ALL NERVOUS NOW.
SORRY...
TWITCH
ビクッ
KISS
...!
STILL...

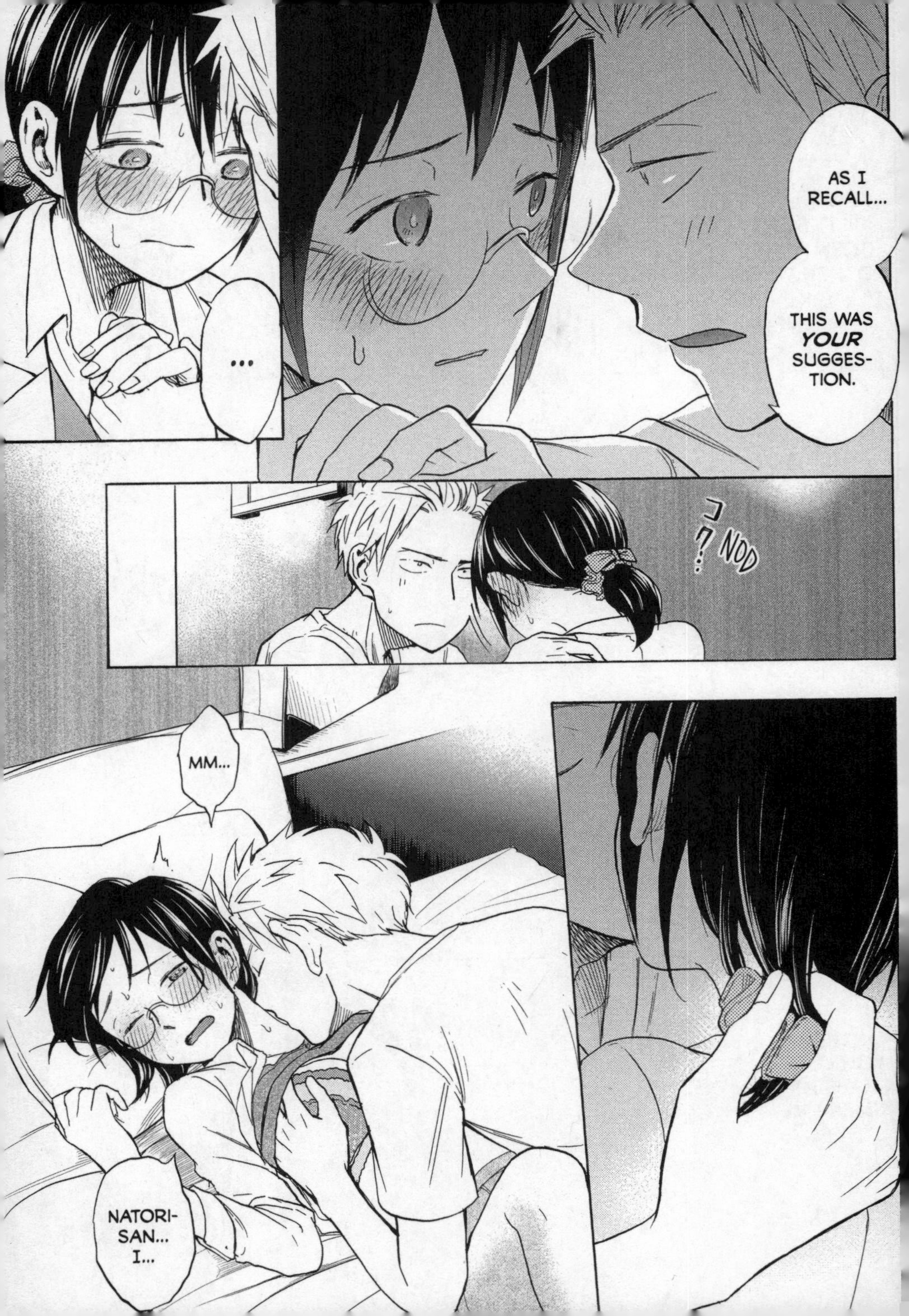
AS I RECALL...
THIS WAS *YOUR* SUGGESTION.
...
コク NOD
MM...
NATORI-SAN... I...

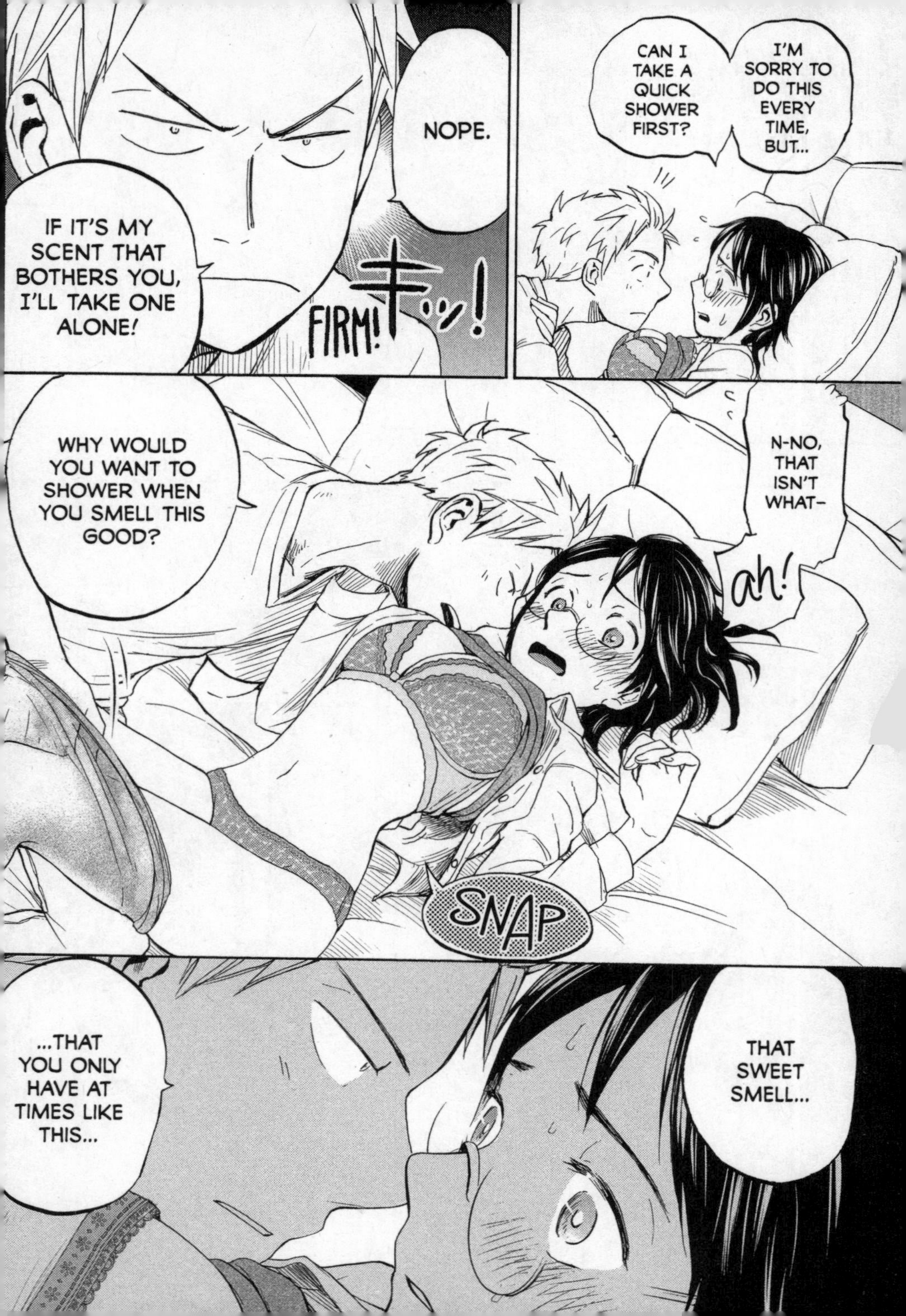
I'M SORRY TO DO THIS EVERY TIME, BUT...
CAN I TAKE A QUICK SHOWER FIRST?
NOPE.
IF IT'S MY SCENT THAT BOTHERS YOU, I'LL TAKE ONE ALONE!
キッ!
FIRM!
N-NO, THAT ISN'T WHAT–
ah!
WHY WOULD YOU WANT TO SHOWER WHEN YOU SMELL THIS GOOD?
SNAP
THAT SWEET SMELL...
...THAT YOU ONLY HAVE AT TIMES LIKE THIS...

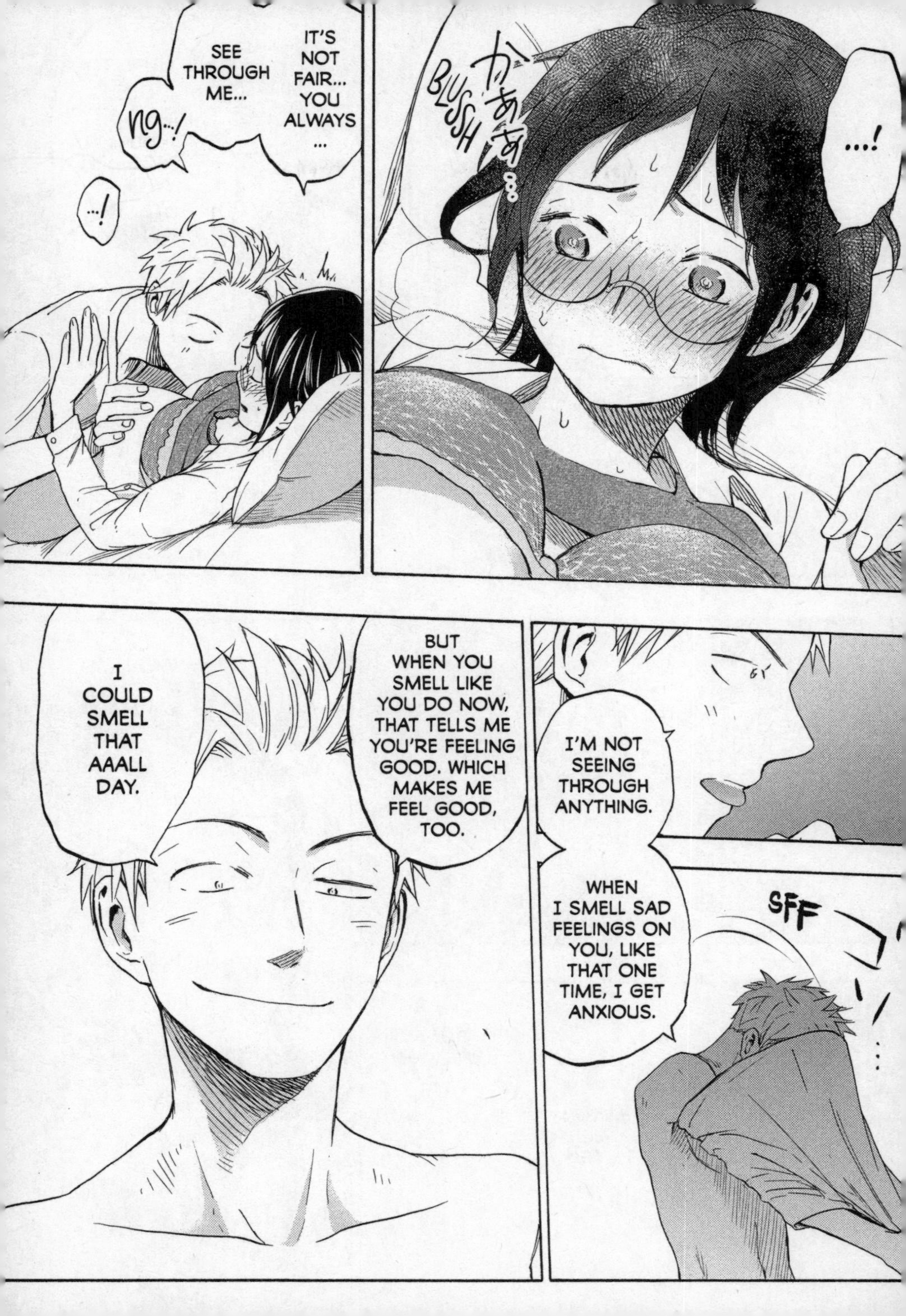
...!
BLUSSH
IT'S NOT FAIR... YOU ALWAYS ...
SEE THROUGH ME...
ng...!
...!
I'M NOT SEEING THROUGH ANYTHING.
WHEN I SMELL SAD FEELINGS ON YOU, LIKE THAT ONE TIME, I GET ANXIOUS.
SFF
BUT WHEN YOU SMELL LIKE YOU DO NOW, THAT TELLS ME YOU'RE FEELING GOOD. WHICH MAKES ME FEEL GOOD, TOO.
I COULD SMELL THAT AAALL DAY.

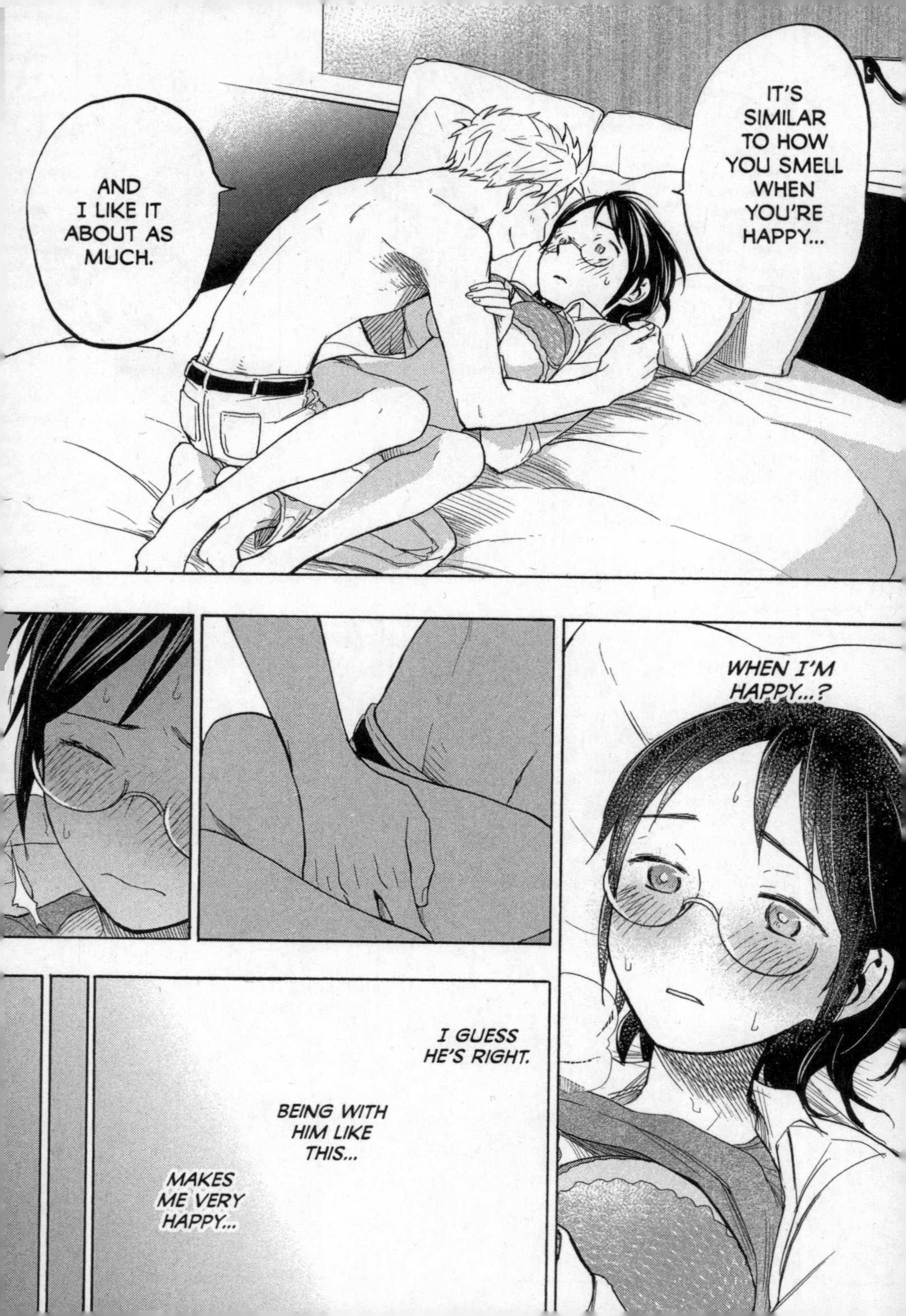
IT'S SIMILAR TO HOW YOU SMELL WHEN YOU'RE HAPPY...
AND I LIKE IT ABOUT AS MUCH.
WHEN I'M HAPPY...?
I GUESS HE'S RIGHT.
BEING WITH HIM LIKE THIS...
MAKES ME VERY HAPPY...

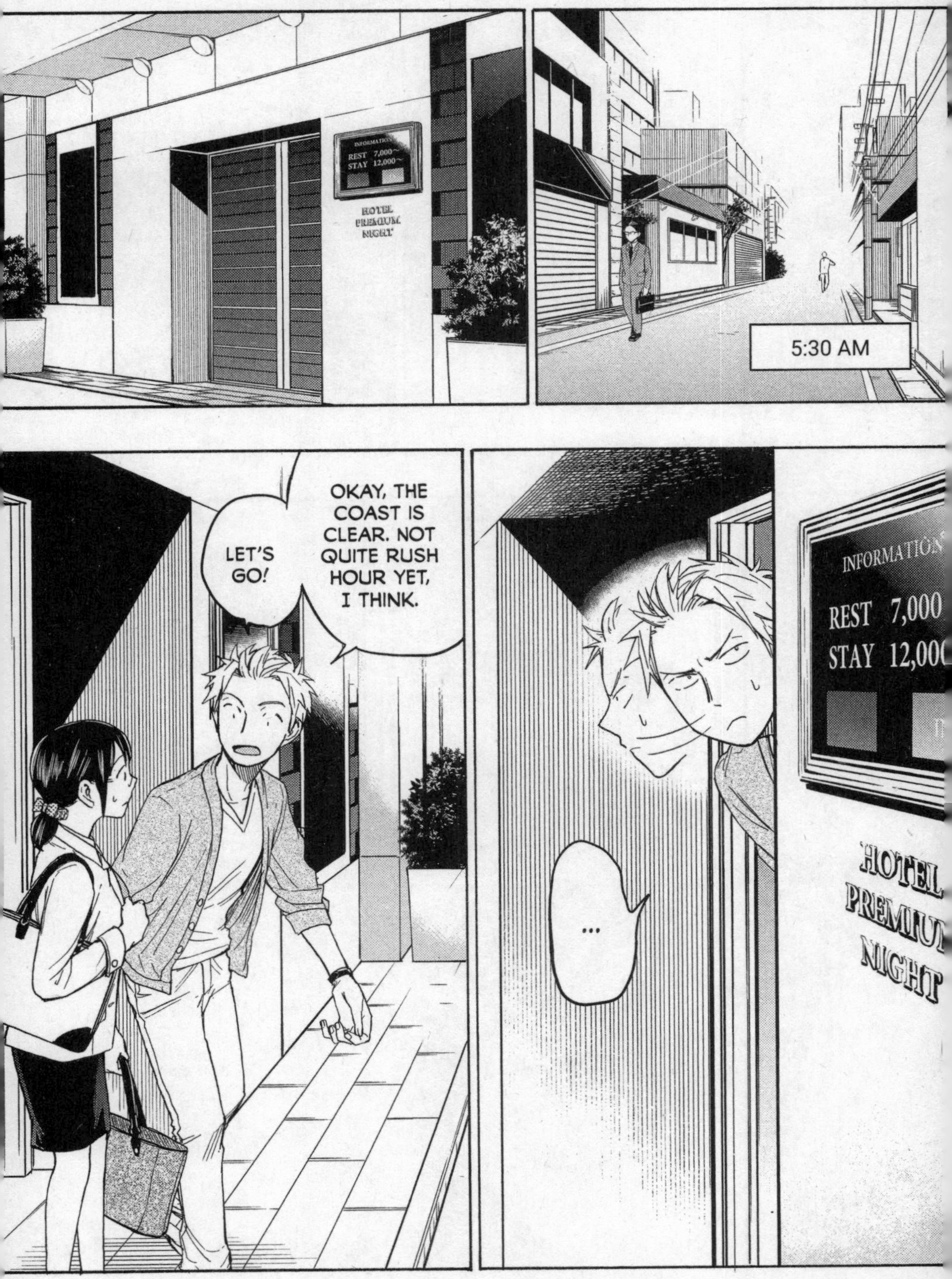
5:30 AM
INFORMATION
REST 7,000~
STAY 12,000~
HOTEL
PREMIUM
NIGHT
INFORMATION
REST 7,000
STAY 12,00
HOTEL
PREMIU
NIGHT
...
OKAY, THE COAST IS CLEAR. NOT QUITE RUSH HOUR YET, I THINK.
LET'S GO!

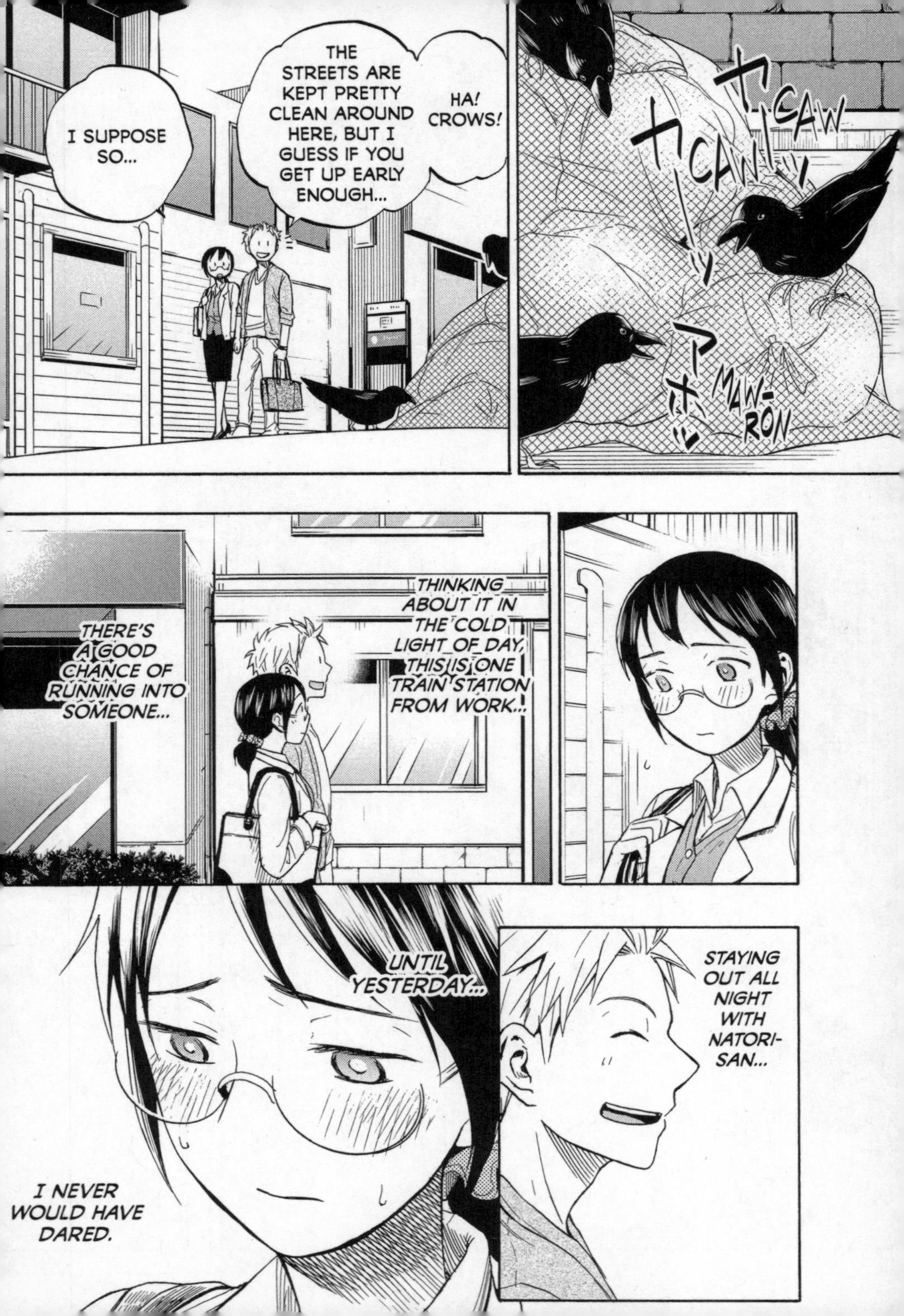
CAW
CAW
MAW-RON
HA! CROWS!
THE STREETS ARE KEPT PRETTY CLEAN AROUND HERE, BUT I GUESS IF YOU GET UP EARLY ENOUGH...
I SUPPOSE SO...
THINKING ABOUT IT IN THE COLD LIGHT OF DAY, THIS IS ONE TRAIN STATION FROM WORK...
THERE'S A GOOD CHANCE OF RUNNING INTO SOMEONE...
STAYING OUT ALL NIGHT WITH NATORI-SAN...
UNTIL YESTERDAY...
I NEVER WOULD HAVE DARED.

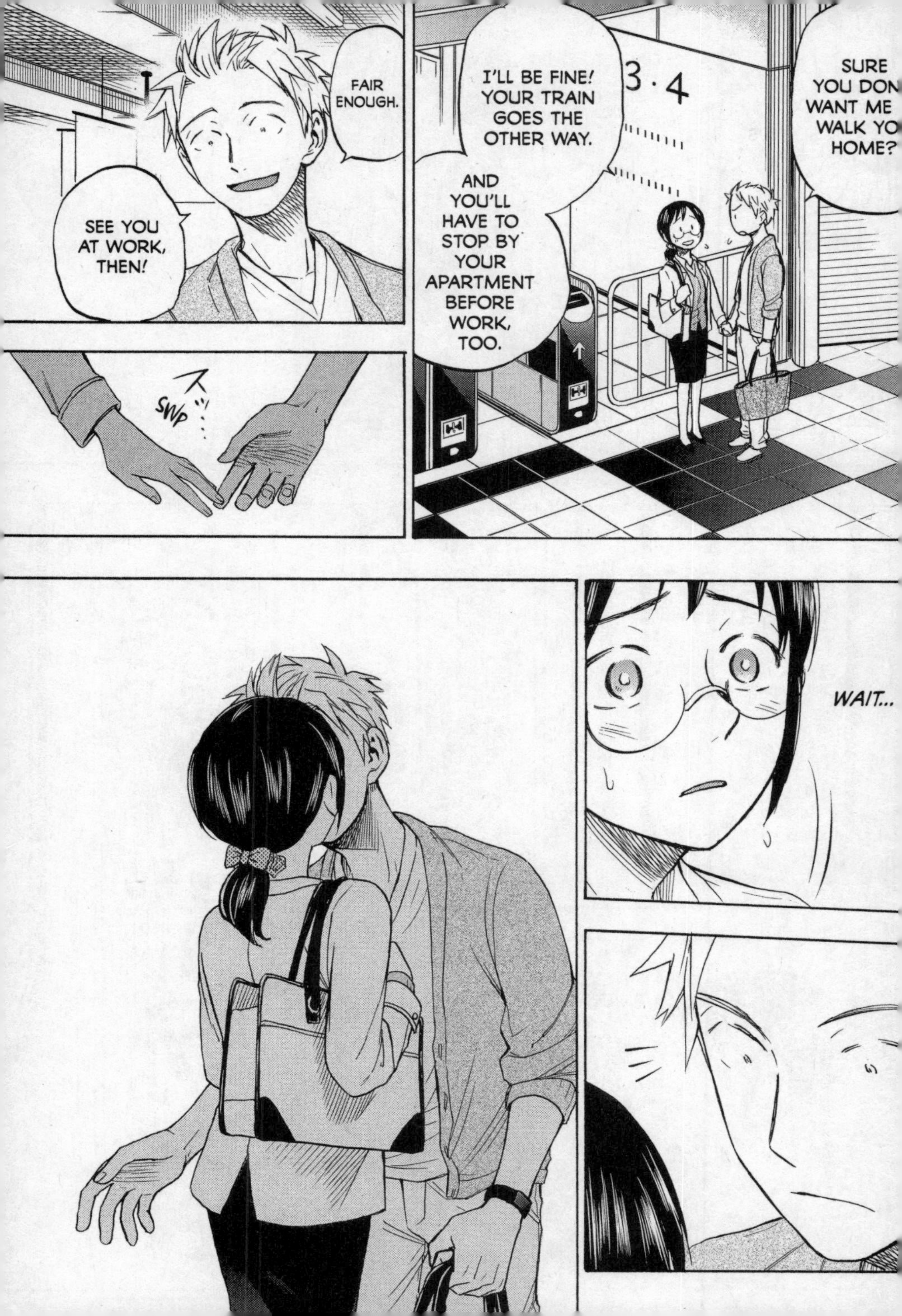
SURE YOU DON WANT ME WALK YO HOME?
I'LL BE FINE! YOUR TRAIN GOES THE OTHER WAY.
AND YOU'LL HAVE TO STOP BY YOUR APARTMENT BEFORE WORK, TOO.
FAIR ENOUGH.
SEE YOU AT WORK, THEN!
スッ
SWP
WAIT...

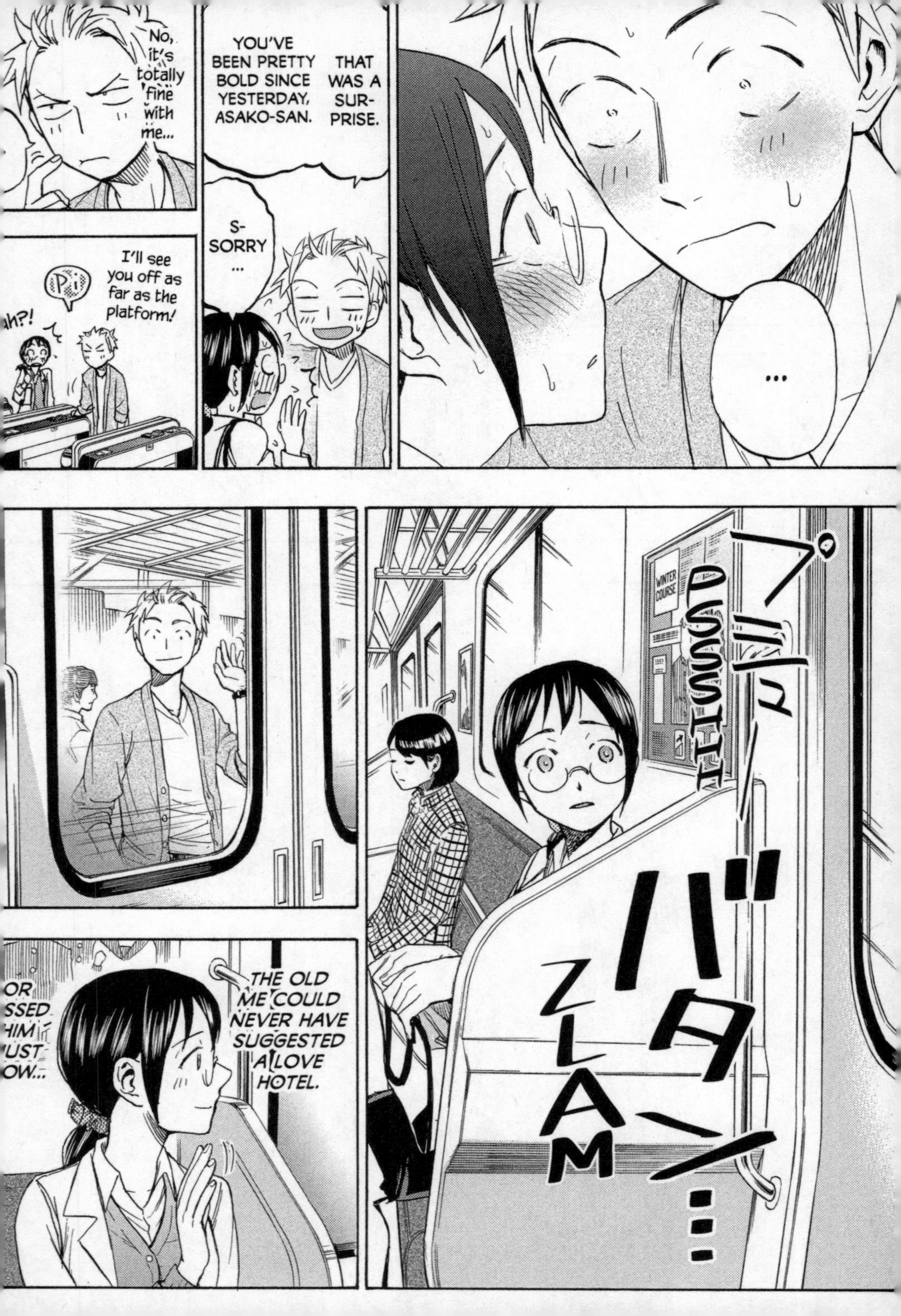
...
YOU'VE BEEN PRETTY BOLD SINCE YESTERDAY, ASAKO-SAN.
THAT WAS A SURPRISE.
S-SORRY ...
No, it's totally fine with me...
Pi
I'll see you off as far as the platform!
PSSSHH
WINTER COURSE
SLAM
THE OLD ME COULD NEVER HAVE SUGGESTED A LOVE HOTEL.

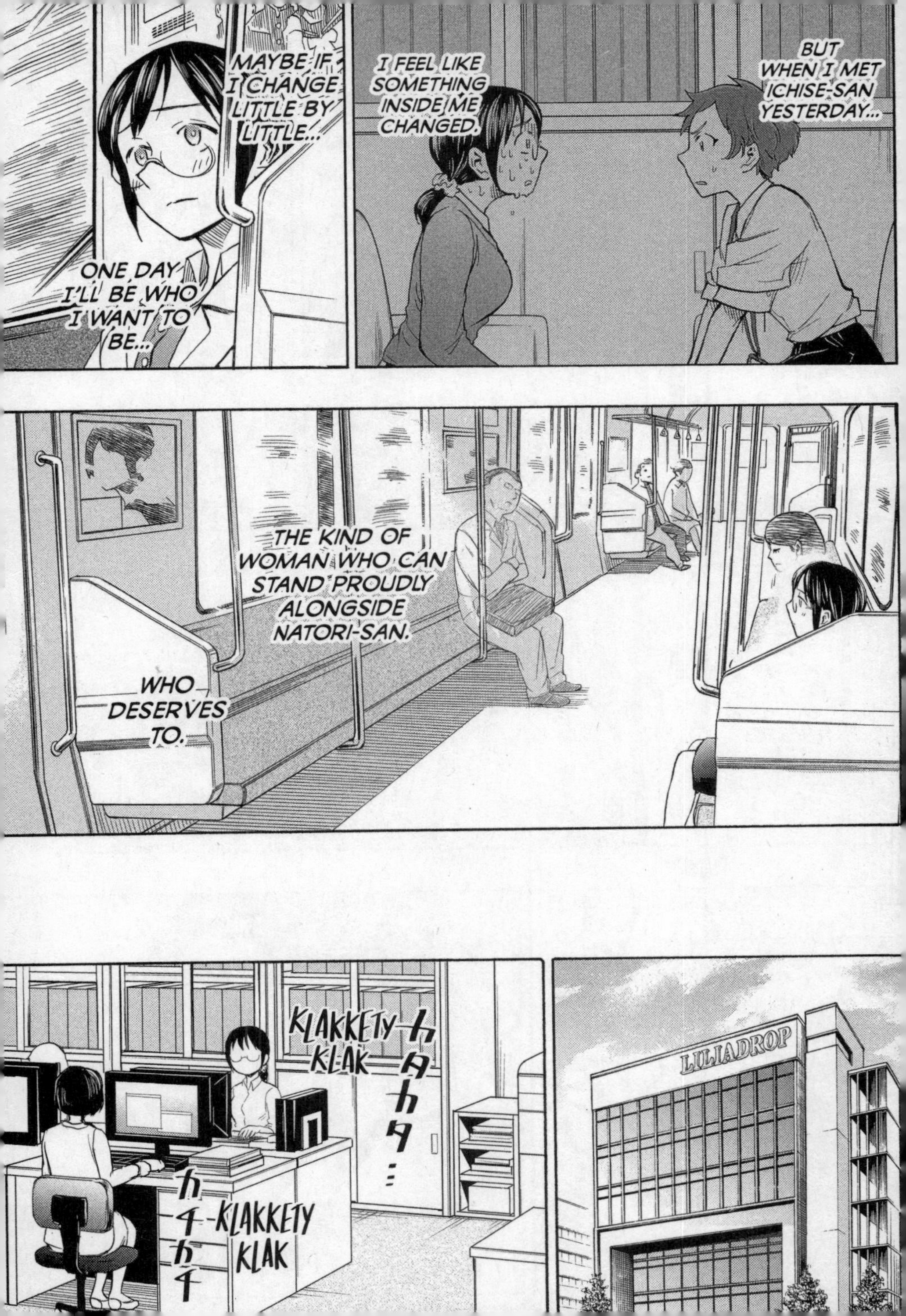
BUT WHEN I MET ICHISE-SAN YESTERDAY...
I FEEL LIKE SOMETHING INSIDE ME CHANGED.
MAYBE IF I CHANGE LITTLE BY LITTLE...
ONE DAY I'LL BE WHO I WANT TO BE...
THE KIND OF WOMAN WHO CAN STAND PROUDLY ALONGSIDE NATORI-SAN.
WHO DESERVES TO.
LULIADROP
KLAKKETY-KLAK
カタカタ…
カチカチ
-KLAKKETY KLAK

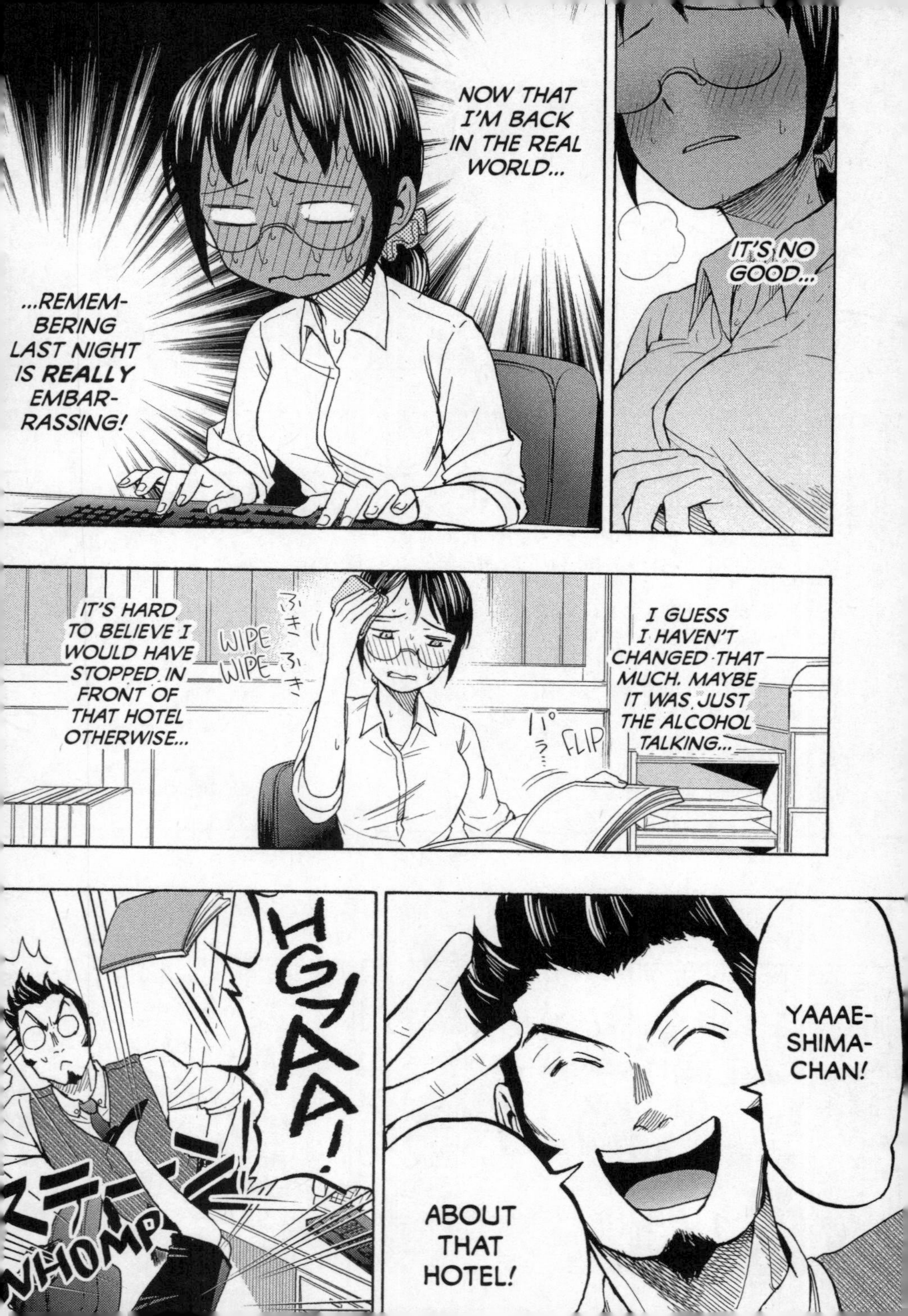
IT'S NO GOOD...
NOW THAT I'M BACK IN THE REAL WORLD...
...REMEMBERING LAST NIGHT IS **REALLY** EMBARRASSING!
I GUESS I HAVEN'T CHANGED THAT MUCH. MAYBE IT WAS JUST THE ALCOHOL TALKING...
パラ
FLIP
ふき ふき
WIPE WIPE
IT'S HARD TO BELIEVE I WOULD HAVE STOPPED IN FRONT OF THAT HOTEL OTHERWISE...
YAAAE-SHIMA-CHAN!
ABOUT THAT HOTEL!
HGYAA!
WHOMP

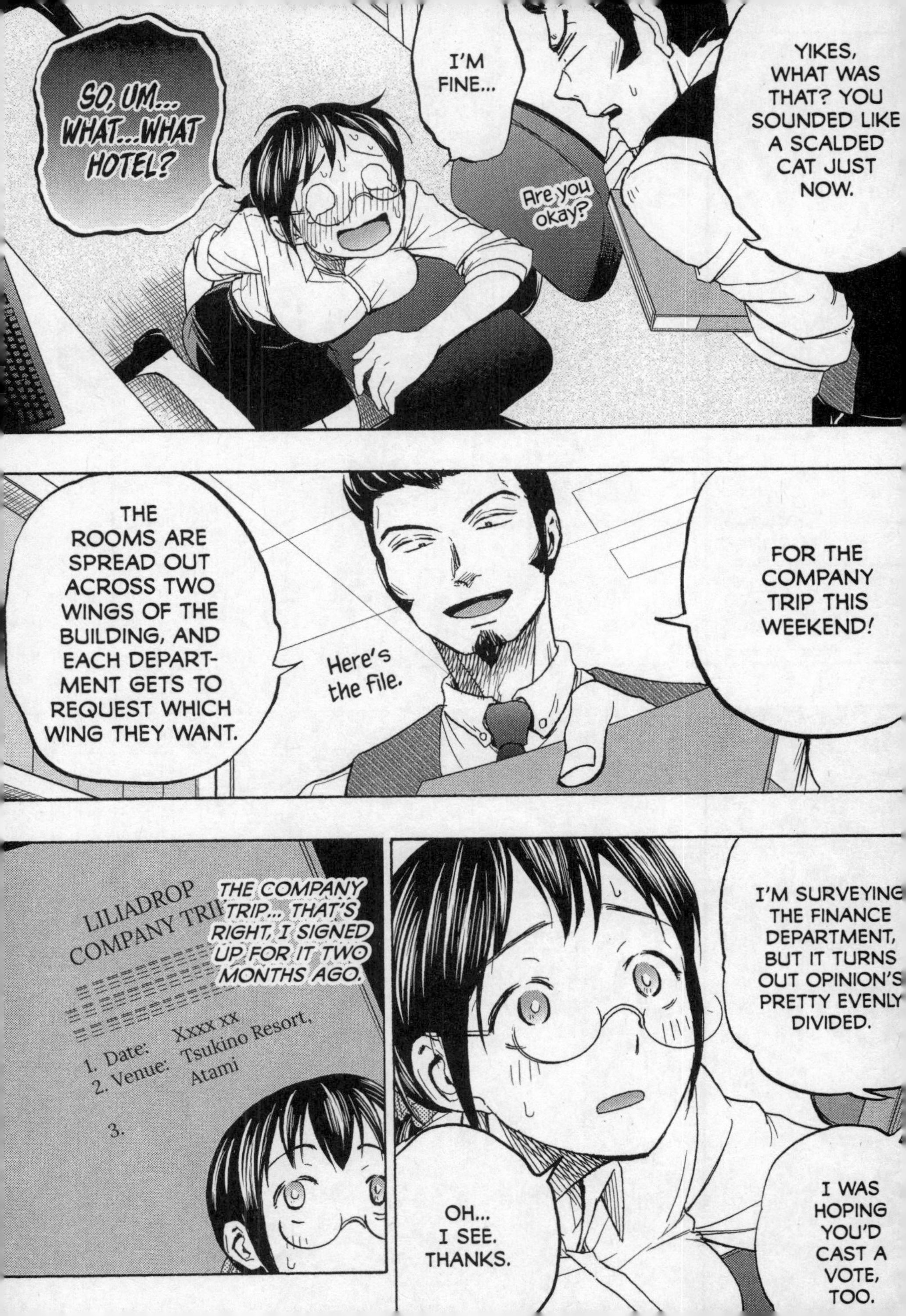
YIKES, WHAT WAS THAT? YOU SOUNDED LIKE A SCALDED CAT JUST NOW.
Are you okay?
I'M FINE...
SO, UM... WHAT...WHAT HOTEL?
FOR THE COMPANY TRIP THIS WEEKEND!
Here's the file.
THE ROOMS ARE SPREAD OUT ACROSS TWO WINGS OF THE BUILDING, AND EACH DEPARTMENT GETS TO REQUEST WHICH WING THEY WANT.
I'M SURVEYING THE FINANCE DEPARTMENT, BUT IT TURNS OUT OPINION'S PRETTY EVENLY DIVIDED.
I WAS HOPING YOU'D CAST A VOTE, TOO.
OH... I SEE. THANKS.
THE COMPANY TRIP... THAT'S RIGHT, I SIGNED UP FOR IT TWO MONTHS AGO.
LILIADROP
COMPANY TRI
1. Date: Xxxx xx
2. Venue: Tsukino Resort, Atami
3.

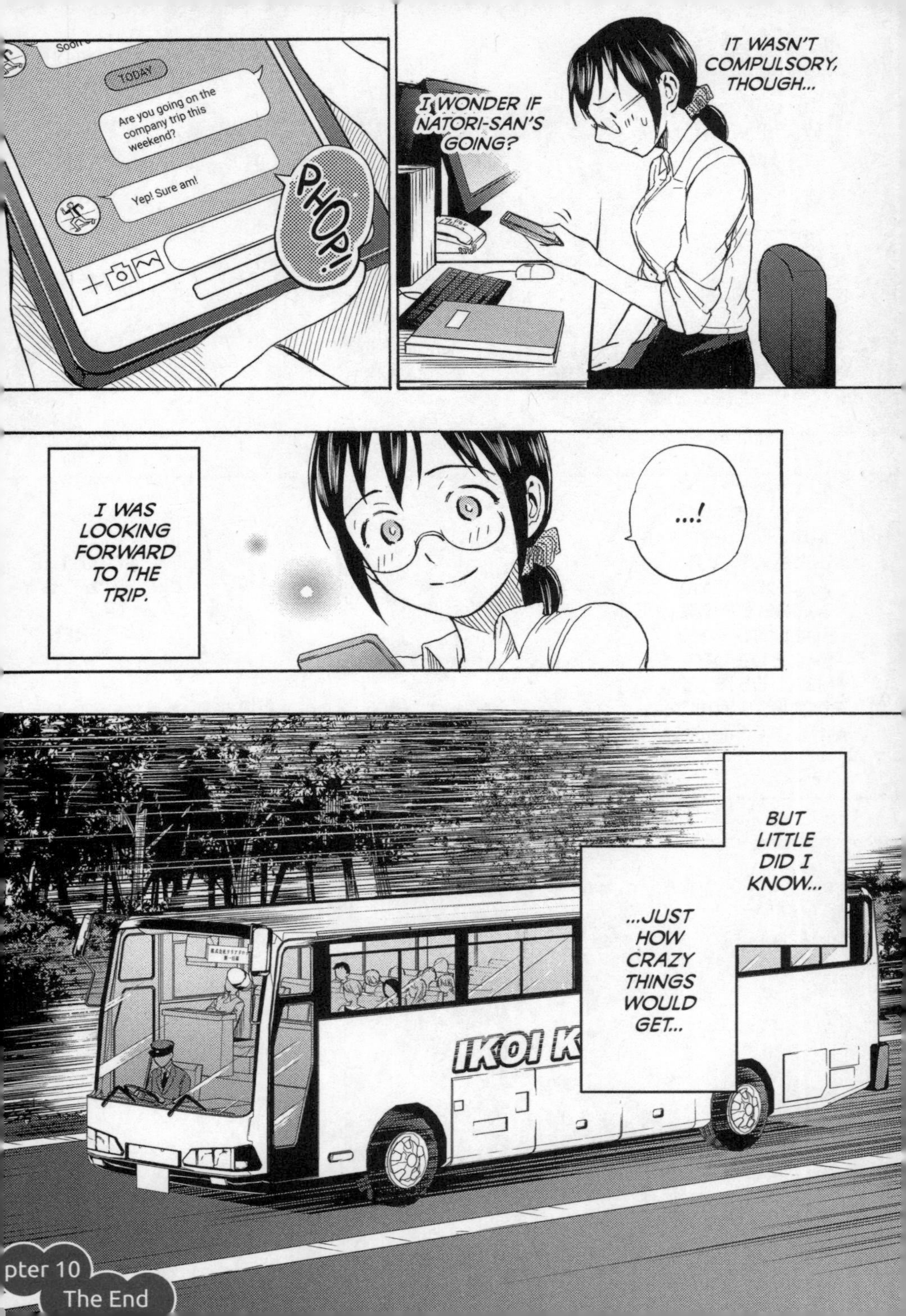
IT WASN'T COMPULSORY, THOUGH...
I WONDER IF NATORI-SAN'S GOING?
TODAY
Are you going on the company trip this weekend?
Yep! Sure am!
PHOP!
...!
I WAS LOOKING FORWARD TO THE TRIP.
BUT LITTLE DID I KNOW...
...JUST HOW CRAZY THINGS WOULD GET...
IKOI K
pter 10
The End

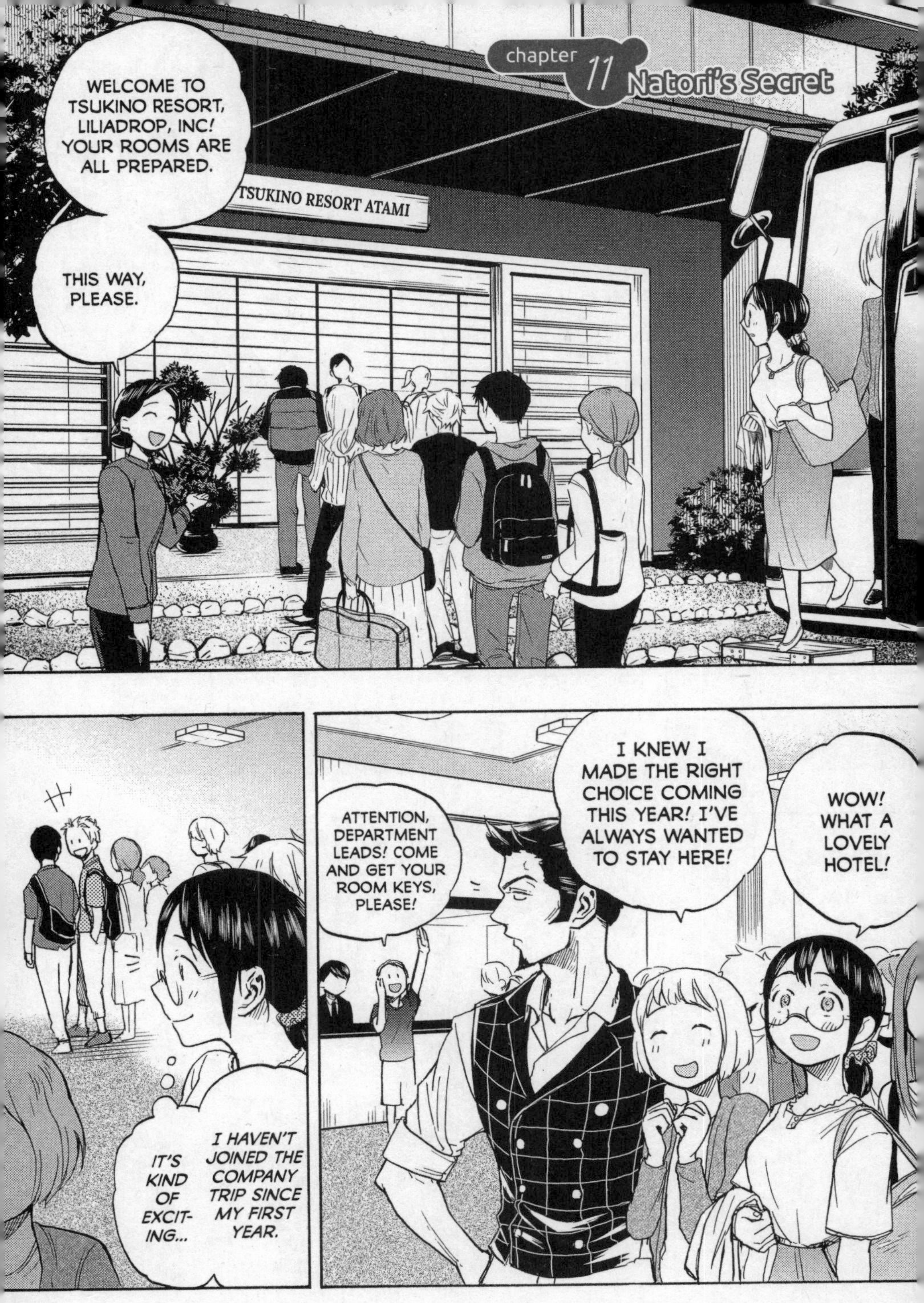
chapter 11 Natori's Secret
WELCOME TO TSUKINO RESORT, LILIADROP, INC! YOUR ROOMS ARE ALL PREPARED.
TSUKINO RESORT ATAMI
THIS WAY, PLEASE.
WOW! WHAT A LOVELY HOTEL!
I KNEW I MADE THE RIGHT CHOICE COMING THIS YEAR! I'VE ALWAYS WANTED TO STAY HERE!
ATTENTION, DEPARTMENT LEADS! COME AND GET YOUR ROOM KEYS, PLEASE!
I HAVEN'T JOINED THE COMPANY TRIP SINCE MY FIRST YEAR.
IT'S KIND OF EXCITING...

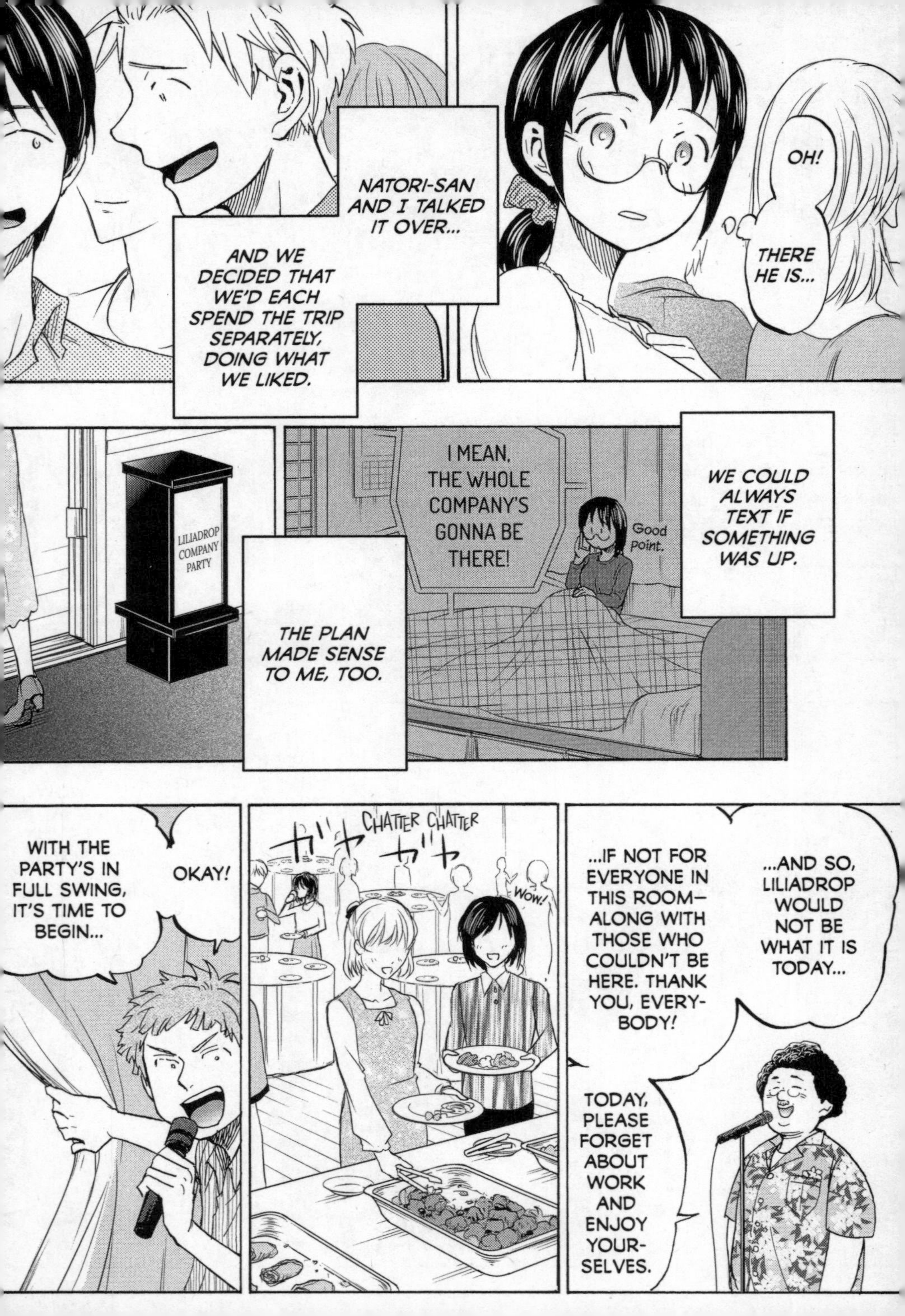
OH!
THERE HE IS...
NATORI-SAN AND I TALKED IT OVER...
AND WE DECIDED THAT WE'D EACH SPEND THE TRIP SEPARATELY, DOING WHAT WE LIKED.
WE COULD ALWAYS TEXT IF SOMETHING WAS UP.
I MEAN, THE WHOLE COMPANY'S GONNA BE THERE!
Good point.
THE PLAN MADE SENSE TO ME, TOO.
LILIADROP COMPANY PARTY
...AND SO, LILIADROP WOULD NOT BE WHAT IT IS TODAY...
...IF NOT FOR EVERYONE IN THIS ROOM—ALONG WITH THOSE WHO COULDN'T BE HERE. THANK YOU, EVERY-BODY!
TODAY, PLEASE FORGET ABOUT WORK AND ENJOY YOUR-SELVES.
CHATTER CHATTER
ガヤガヤ
WOW!
OKAY!
WITH THE PARTY'S IN FULL SWING, IT'S TIME TO BEGIN...

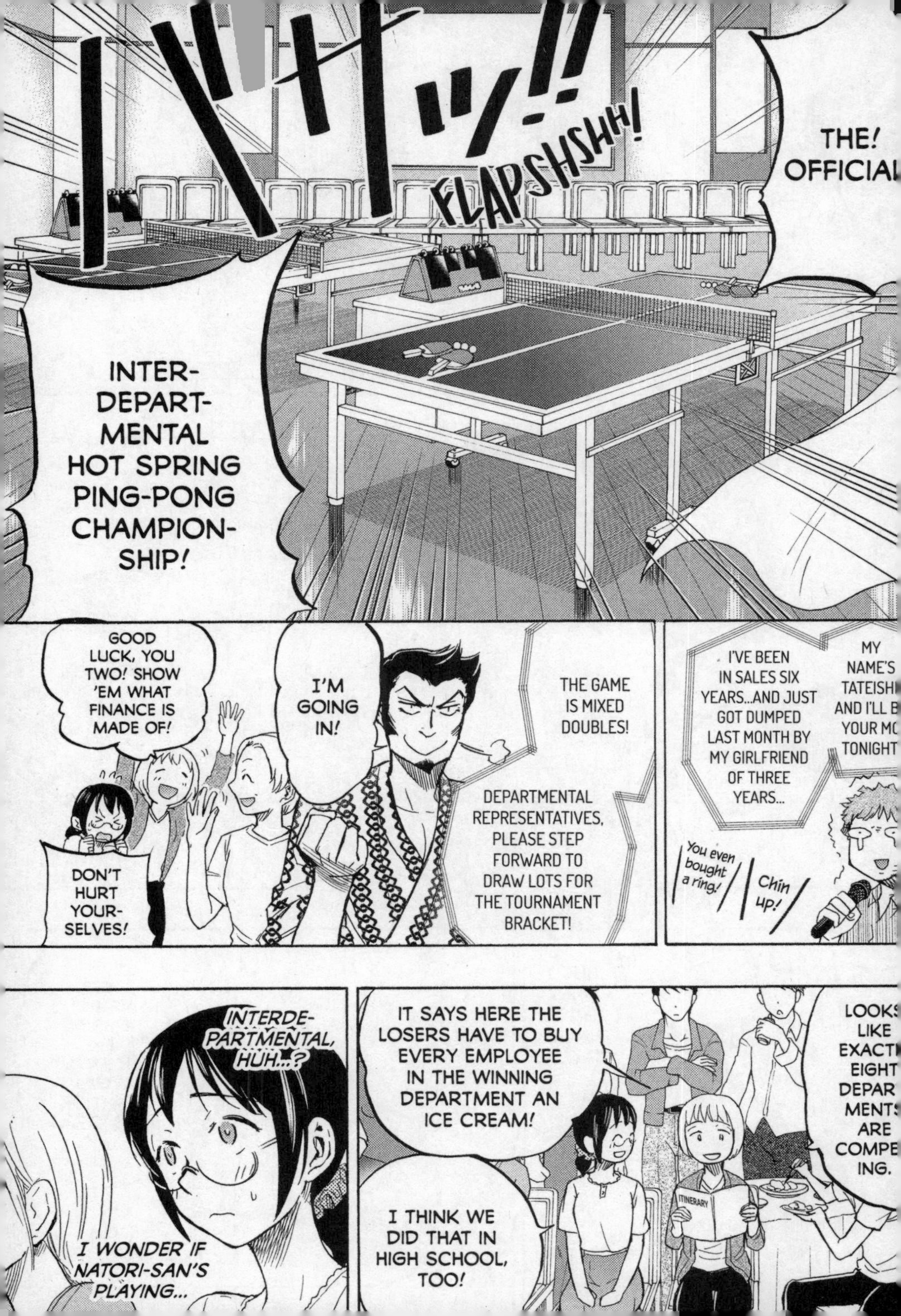
FLAPSHSHH!
THE! OFFICIAL
INTER-DEPARTMENTAL HOT SPRING PING-PONG CHAMPIONSHIP!
MY NAME'S TATEISH AND I'LL B YOUR MC TONIGHT
I'VE BEEN IN SALES SIX YEARS...AND JUST GOT DUMPED LAST MONTH BY MY GIRLFRIEND OF THREE YEARS...
You even bought a ring!
Chin up!
THE GAME IS MIXED DOUBLES!
DEPARTMENTAL REPRESENTATIVES, PLEASE STEP FORWARD TO DRAW LOTS FOR THE TOURNAMENT BRACKET!
I'M GOING IN!
GOOD LUCK, YOU TWO! SHOW 'EM WHAT FINANCE IS MADE OF!
DON'T HURT YOURSELVES!
LOOKS LIKE EXACT EIGHT DEPAR MENTS ARE COMPE ING.
IT SAYS HERE THE LOSERS HAVE TO BUY EVERY EMPLOYEE IN THE WINNING DEPARTMENT AN ICE CREAM!
ITINERARY
I THINK WE DID THAT IN HIGH SCHOOL, TOO!
INTERDEPARTMENTAL, HUH...?
I WONDER IF NATORI-SAN'S PLAYING...

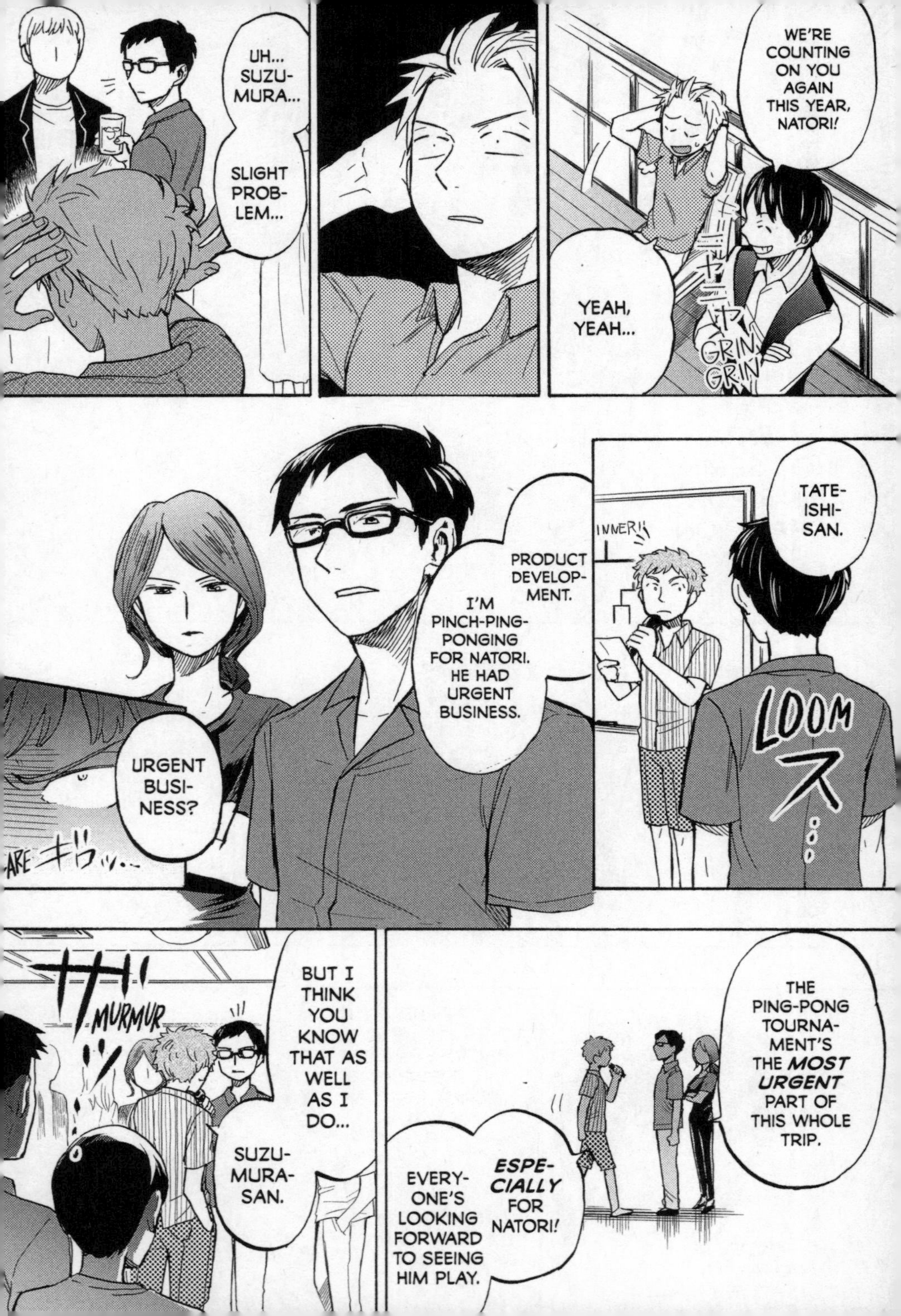
WE'RE COUNTING ON YOU AGAIN THIS YEAR, NATORI!
YEAH, YEAH...
ニヤニヤ GRIN GRIN
UH... SUZU-MURA...
SLIGHT PROB-LEM...
TATE-ISHI-SAN.
INNER!!
ス... LOOM
PRODUCT DEVELOP-MENT.
I'M PINCH-PING-PONGING FOR NATORI. HE HAD URGENT BUSINESS.
URGENT BUSI-NESS?
ARE ギロッ...
THE PING-PONG TOURNA-MENT'S THE ***MOST URGENT*** PART OF THIS WHOLE TRIP.
ESPE-CIALLY FOR NATORI!
EVERY-ONE'S LOOKING FORWARD TO SEEING HIM PLAY.
BUT I THINK YOU KNOW THAT AS WELL AS I DO...
SUZU-MURA-SAN.
ザワ MURMUR

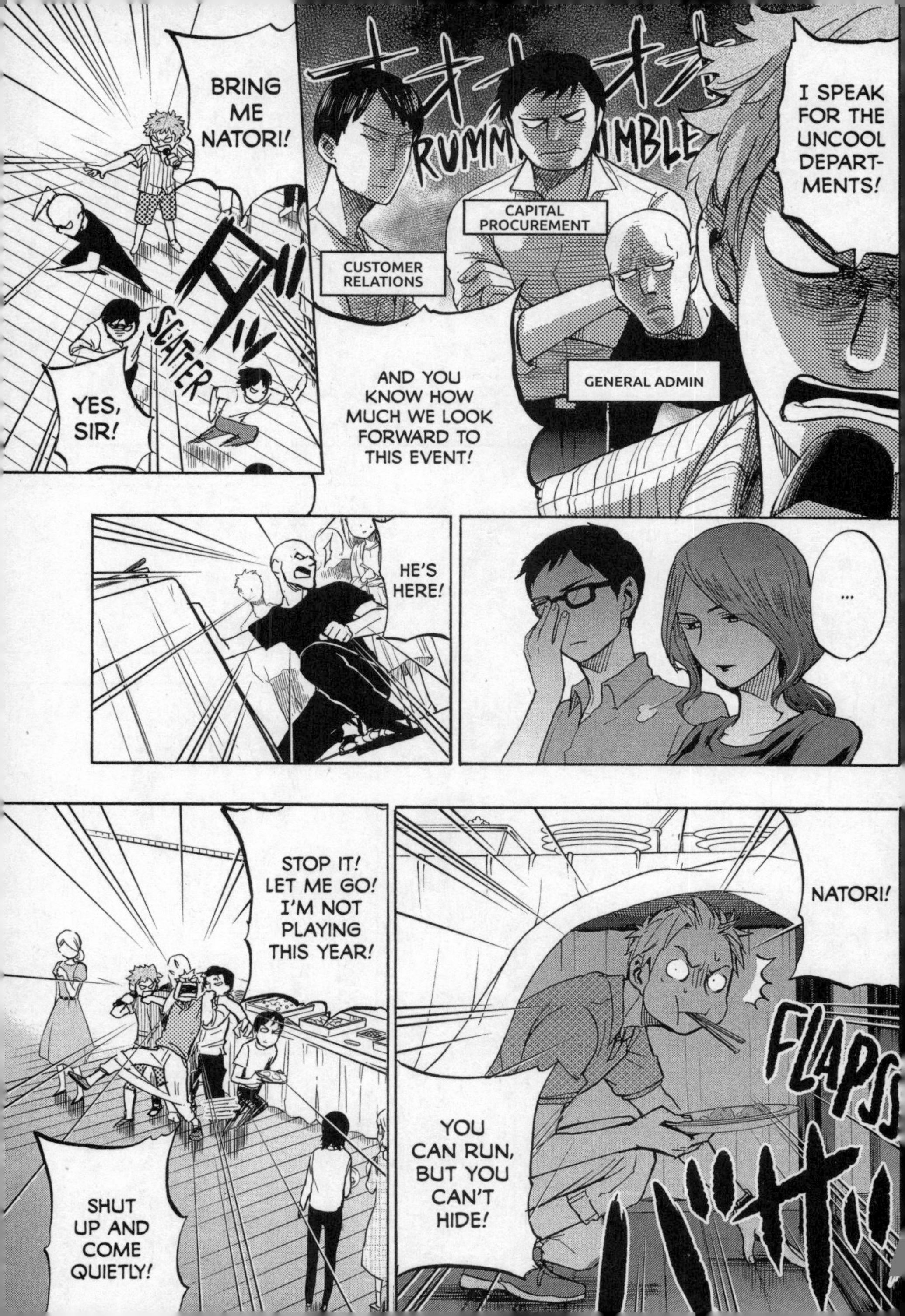
I SPEAK FOR THE UNCOOL DEPART-MENTS!
CAPITAL PROCUREMENT
CUSTOMER RELATIONS
GENERAL ADMIN
AND YOU KNOW HOW MUCH WE LOOK FORWARD TO THIS EVENT!
BRING ME NATORI!
SCATTER
YES, SIR!
...
HE'S HERE!
NATORI!
FLAPS
YOU CAN RUN, BUT YOU CAN'T HIDE!
STOP IT! LET ME GO! I'M NOT PLAYING THIS YEAR!
SHUT UP AND COME QUIETLY!

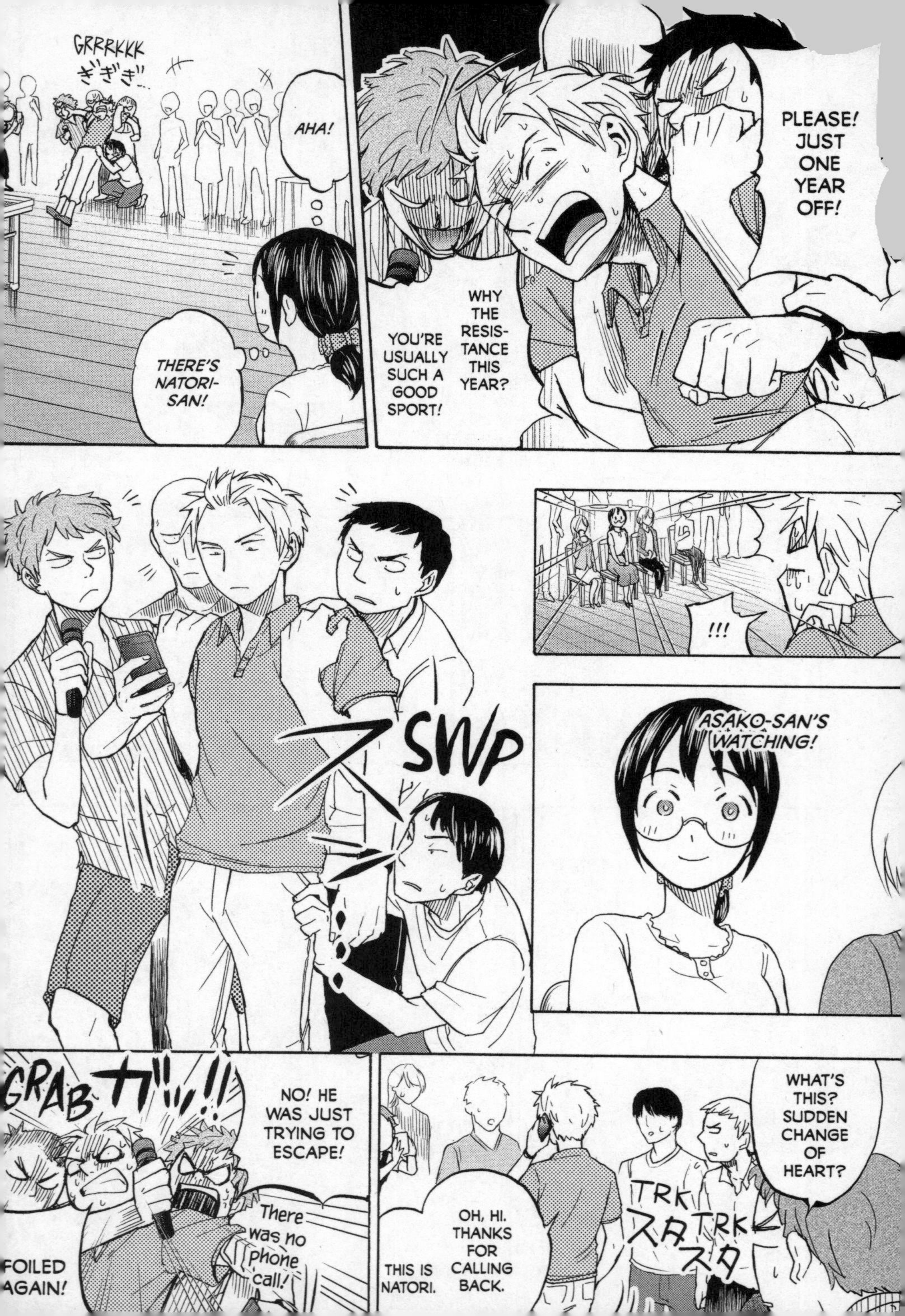
PLEASE! JUST ONE YEAR OFF!
WHY THE RESISTANCE THIS YEAR?
YOU'RE USUALLY SUCH A GOOD SPORT!
GRRRKKK ぎぎぎ...
AHA!
THERE'S NATORI-SAN!
!!!
ASAKO-SAN'S WATCHING!
SWP
WHAT'S THIS? SUDDEN CHANGE OF HEART?
TRK スタ TRK スタ
OH, HI. THANKS FOR CALLING BACK.
THIS IS NATORI.
GRAB ガッ!!
NO! HE WAS JUST TRYING TO ESCAPE!
There was no phone call!
FOILED AGAIN!

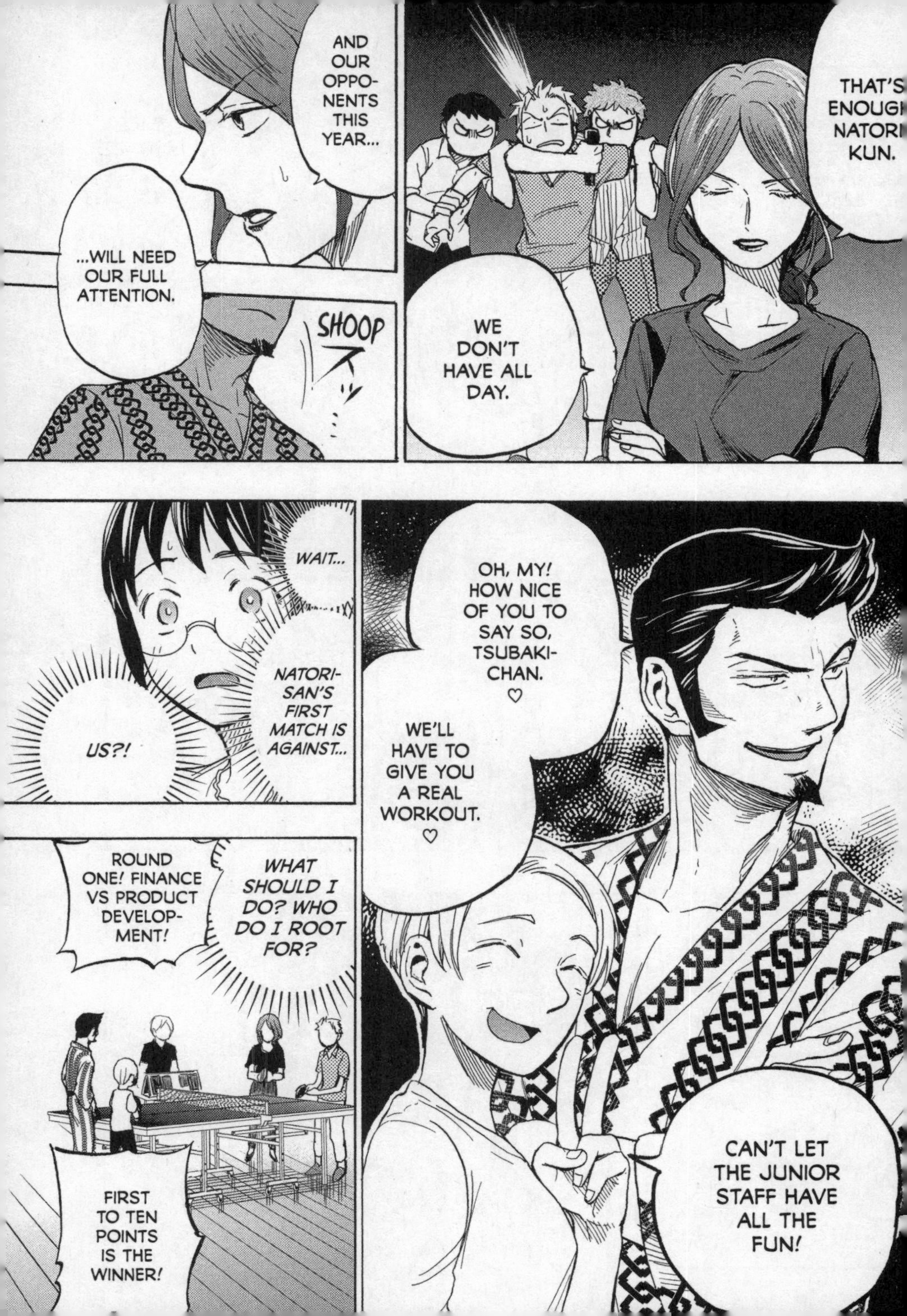
THAT'S ENOUG NATORI KUN.
WE DON'T HAVE ALL DAY.
AND OUR OPPO-NENTS THIS YEAR...
...WILL NEED OUR FULL ATTENTION.
SHOOP
OH, MY! HOW NICE OF YOU TO SAY SO, TSUBAKI-CHAN. ♡
WE'LL HAVE TO GIVE YOU A REAL WORKOUT. ♡
CAN'T LET THE JUNIOR STAFF HAVE ALL THE FUN!
WAIT...
NATORI-SAN'S FIRST MATCH IS AGAINST...
US?!
WHAT SHOULD I DO? WHO DO I ROOT FOR?
ROUND ONE! FINANCE VS PRODUCT DEVELOP-MENT!
FIRST TO TEN POINTS IS THE WINNER!

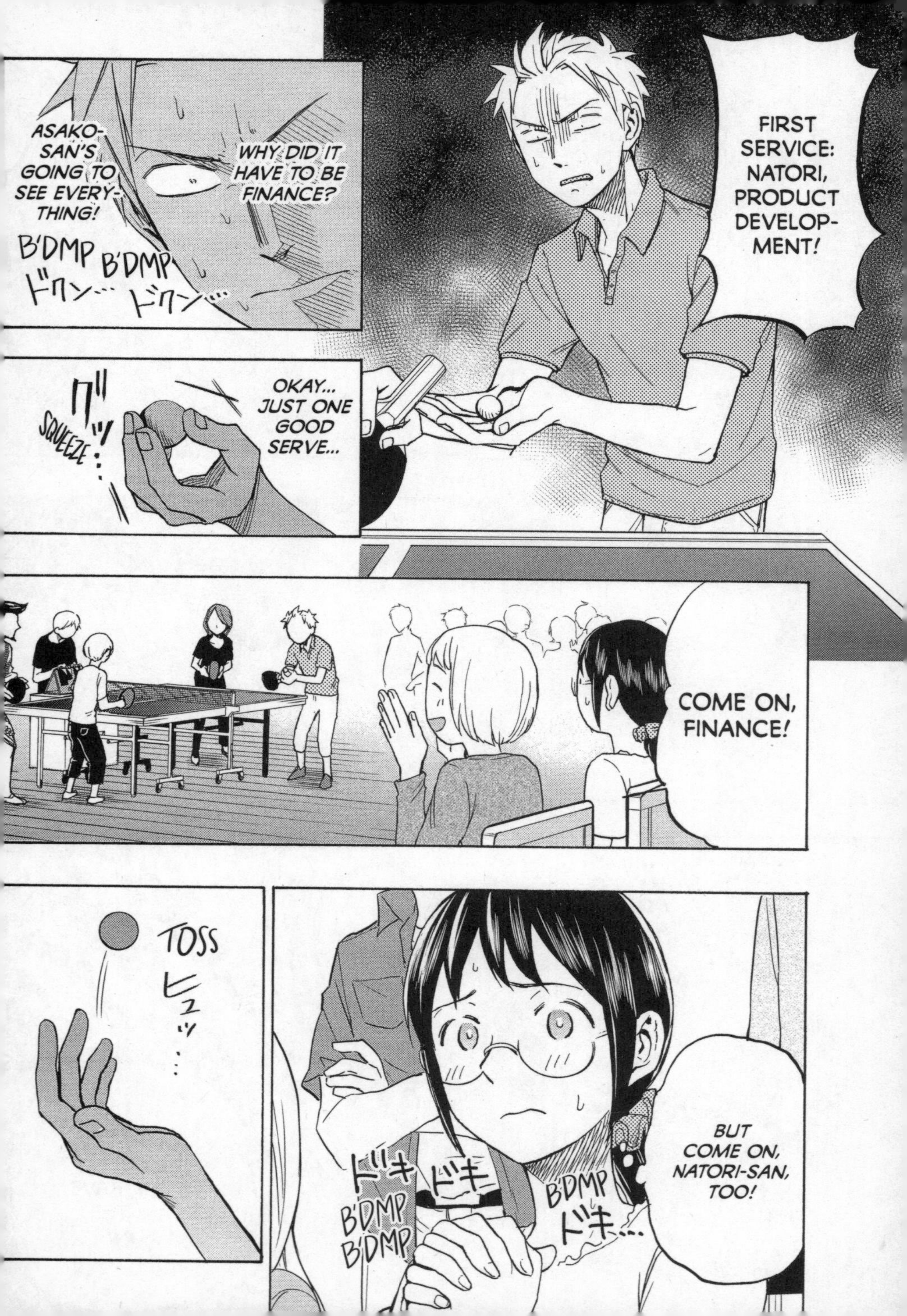
FIRST SERVICE: NATORI, PRODUCT DEVELOPMENT!
WHY DID IT HAVE TO BE FINANCE?
ASAKO-SAN'S GOING TO SEE EVERYTHING!
B'DMP B'DMP
ドクン… ドクン…
OKAY... JUST ONE GOOD SERVE...
グッ
SQUEEZE
COME ON, FINANCE!
BUT COME ON, NATORI-SAN, TOO!
B'DMP
ドキ…
ドキ ドキ
B'DMP B'DMP
TOSS
ヒュッ

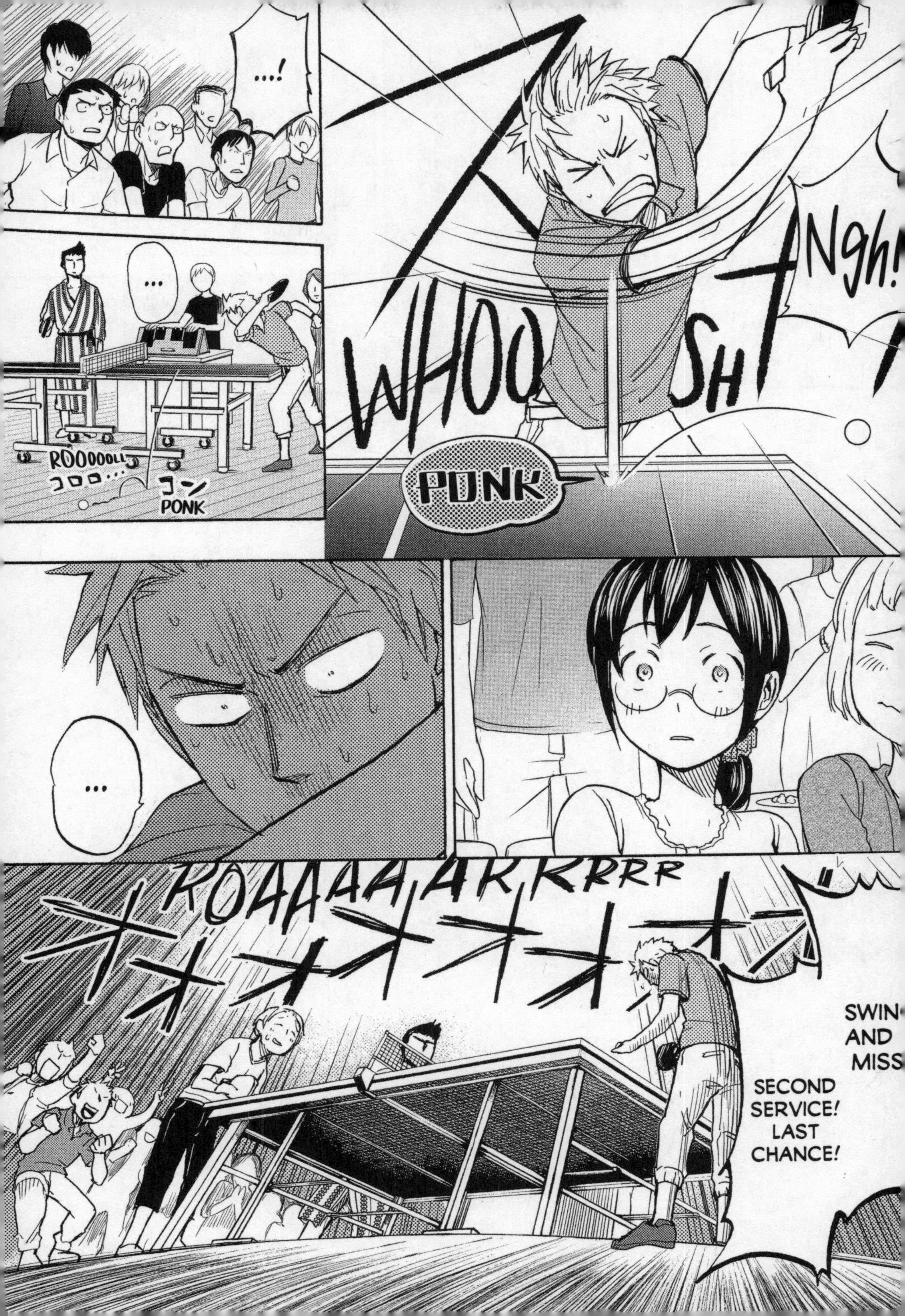
WHOOSH
Angh!
PONK
...!
...
ROOOOOLL
コロロ...
コン
PONK
...
ROAAAAARRRRR
オオオオオオ
SWIN
AND
MISS
SECOND SERVICE! LAST CHANCE!

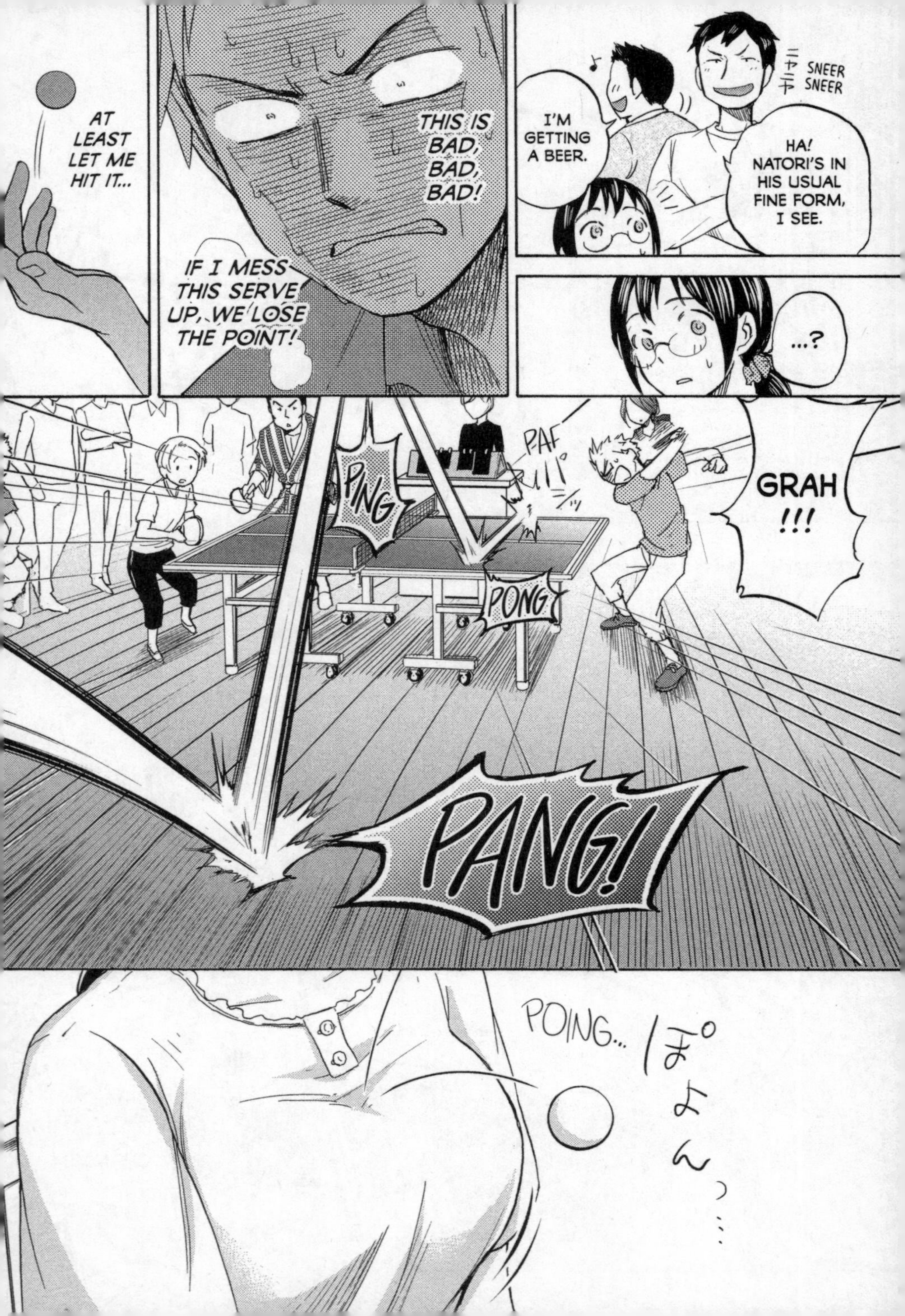
ニヤニヤ
SNEER SNEER
HA! NATORI'S IN HIS USUAL FINE FORM, I SEE.
I'M GETTING A BEER.
...?
THIS IS BAD, BAD, BAD!
IF I MESS THIS SERVE UP, WE LOSE THE POINT!
AT LEAST LET ME HIT IT...
GRAH!!!
PAF
PING
PONG
PANG!
POING...
ぽよんっ...

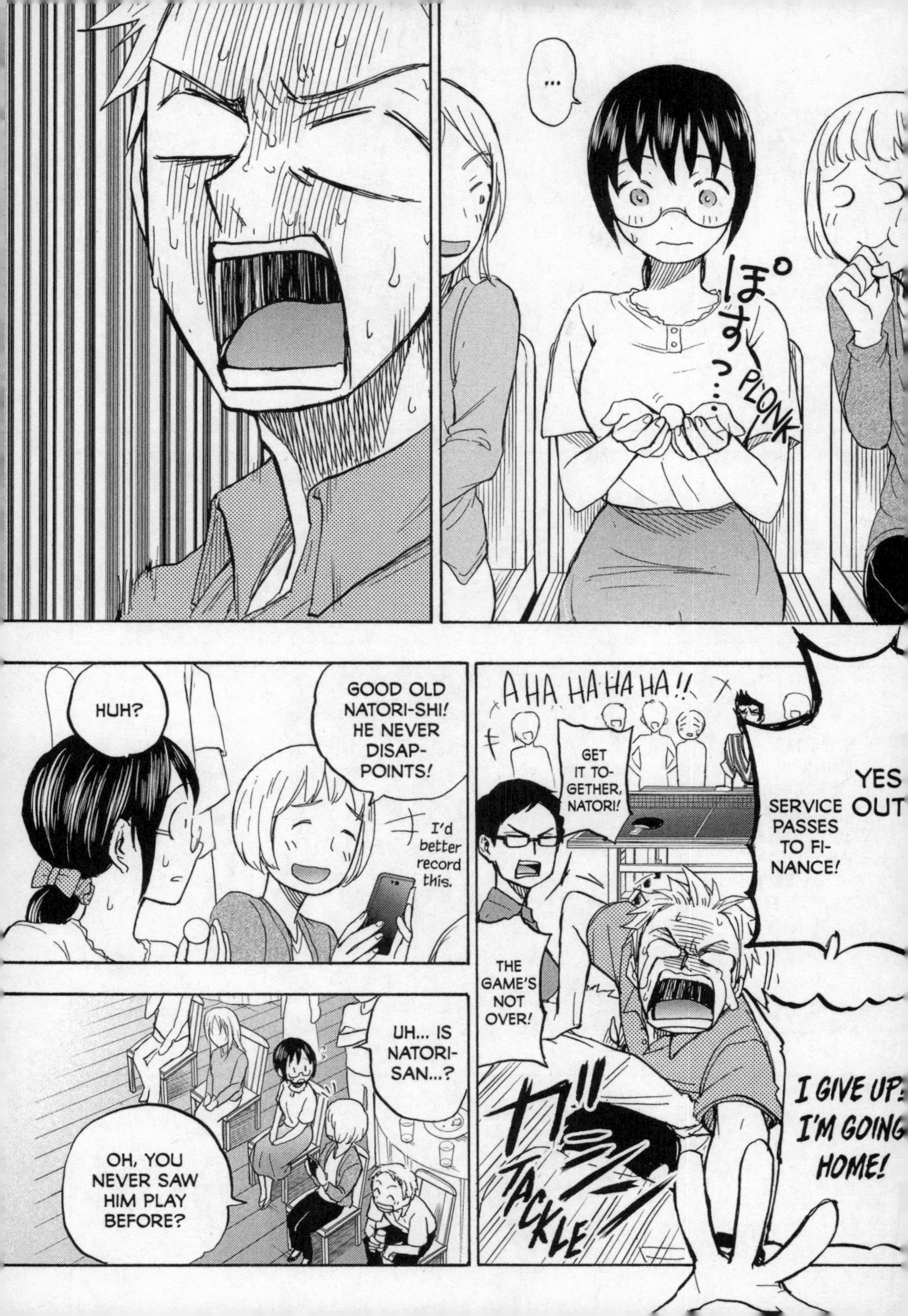
...
ぽすっ…
PLONK
YES OUT
SERVICE PASSES TO FI-NANCE!
I GIVE UP! I'M GOING HOME!
AHA HA HA HA HA!!
GET IT TO-GETHER, NATORI!
THE GAME'S NOT OVER!
カッ
TACKLE
GOOD OLD NATORI-SHI! HE NEVER DISAP-POINTS!
HUH?
I'd better record this.
UH... IS NATORI-SAN...?
OH, YOU NEVER SAW HIM PLAY BEFORE?

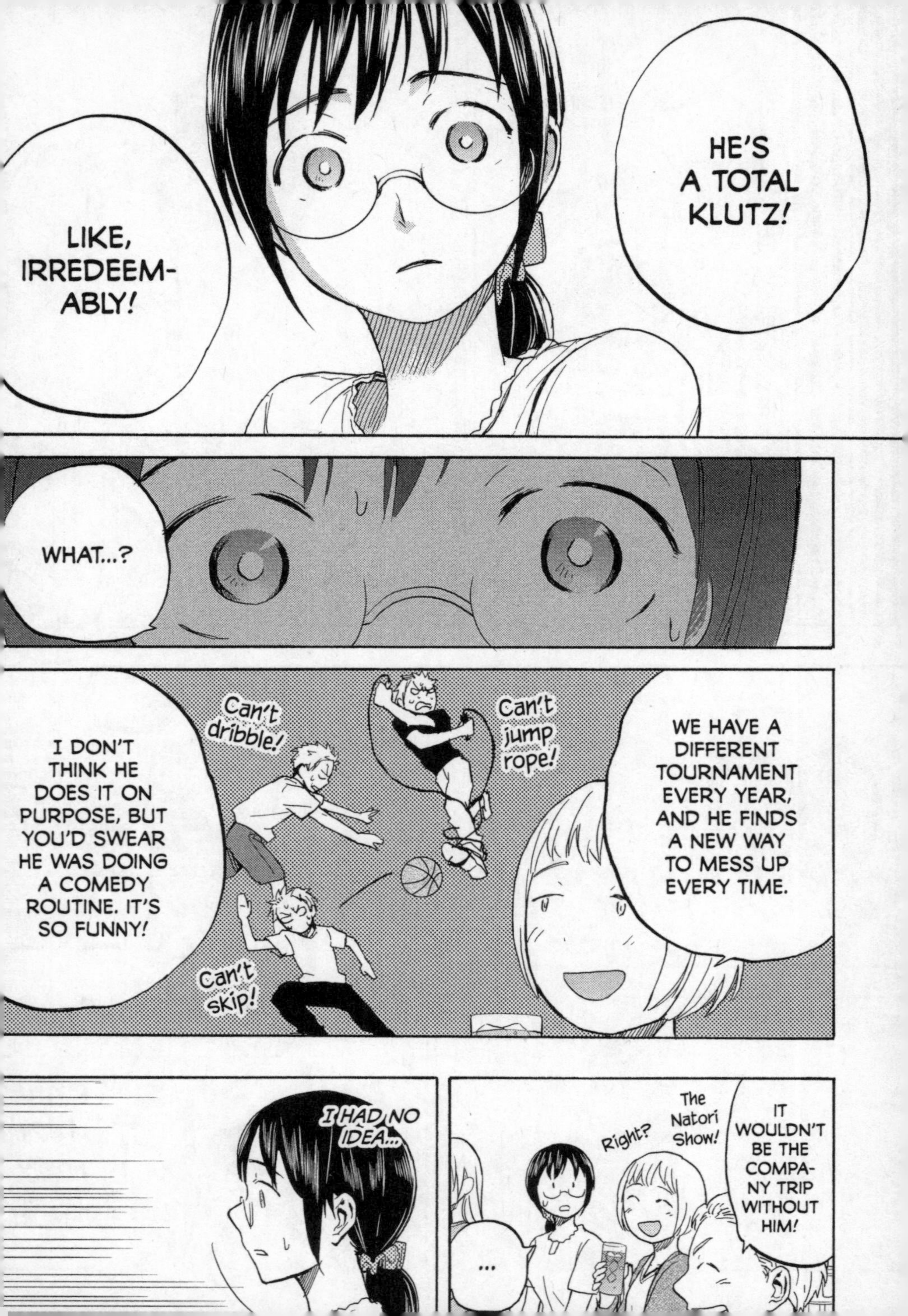
HE'S A TOTAL KLUTZ!
LIKE, IRREDEEMABLY!
WHAT...?
WE HAVE A DIFFERENT TOURNAMENT EVERY YEAR, AND HE FINDS A NEW WAY TO MESS UP EVERY TIME.
Can't jump rope!
Can't dribble!
Can't skip!
I DON'T THINK HE DOES IT ON PURPOSE, BUT YOU'D SWEAR HE WAS DOING A COMEDY ROUTINE. IT'S SO FUNNY!
IT WOULDN'T BE THE COMPANY TRIP WITHOUT HIM!
The Natori Show!
Right?
...
I HAD NO IDEA...

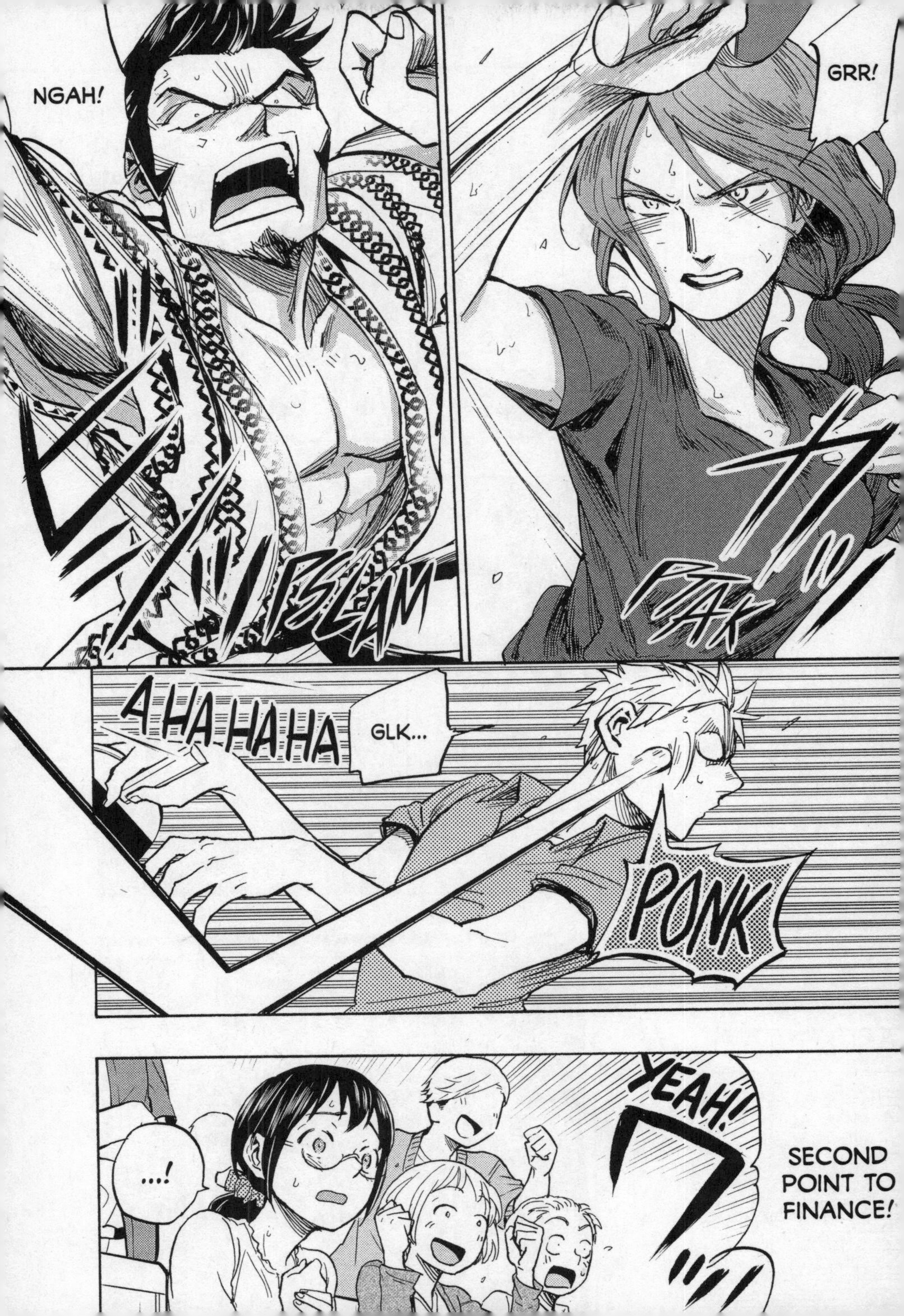
GRR!
PTAK
NGAH!
BSLAM
GLK...
AHAHAHA
PONK
SECOND POINT TO FINANCE!
YEAH!
...!

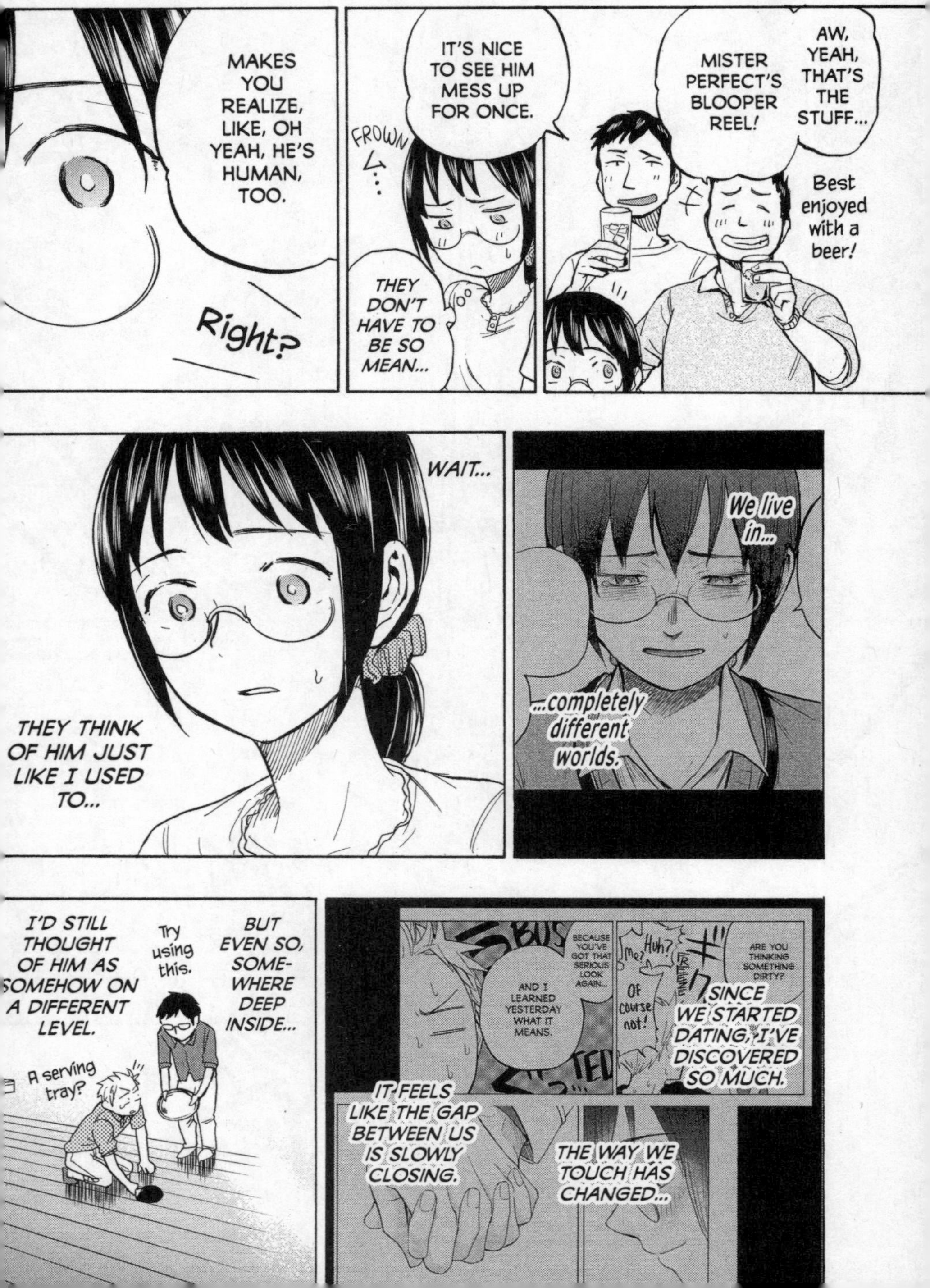
AW, YEAH, THAT'S THE STUFF...
MISTER PERFECT'S BLOOPER REEL!
Best enjoyed with a beer!
IT'S NICE TO SEE HIM MESS UP FOR ONCE.
FROWN
THEY DON'T HAVE TO BE SO MEAN...
MAKES YOU REALIZE, LIKE, OH YEAH, HE'S HUMAN, TOO.
Right?
We live in...
...completely different worlds.
WAIT...
THEY THINK OF HIM JUST LIKE I USED TO...
SINCE WE STARTED DATING, I'VE DISCOVERED SO MUCH.
ARE YOU THINKING SOMETHING DIRTY?
Huh? Me?
Of course not!
BECAUSE YOU'VE GOT THAT SERIOUS LOOK AGAIN...
AND I LEARNED YESTERDAY WHAT IT MEANS.
THE WAY WE TOUCH HAS CHANGED...
IT FEELS LIKE THE GAP BETWEEN US IS SLOWLY CLOSING.
BUT EVEN SO, SOMEWHERE DEEP INSIDE...
I'D STILL THOUGHT OF HIM AS SOMEHOW ON A DIFFERENT LEVEL.
Try using this.
A serving tray?

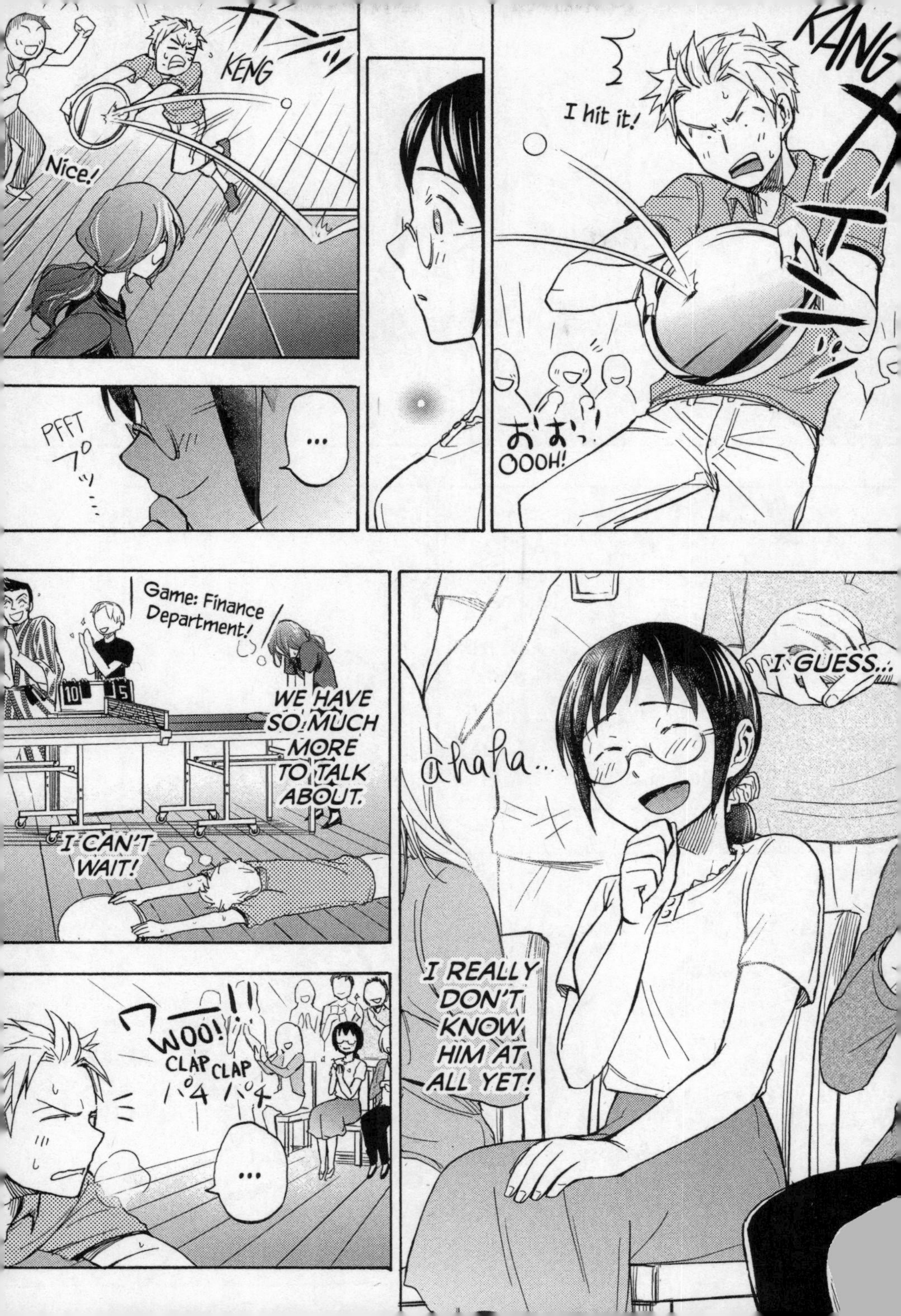
KANG
I hit it!
おおっ!
OOOH!
KENG
Nice!
PFFT
プッ
...
I GUESS...
ahaha...
I REALLY DON'T KNOW HIM AT ALL YET!
Game: Finance Department!
WE HAVE SO MUCH MORE TO TALK ABOUT.
I CAN'T WAIT!
WOO!
CLAP CLAP
パチパチ
...

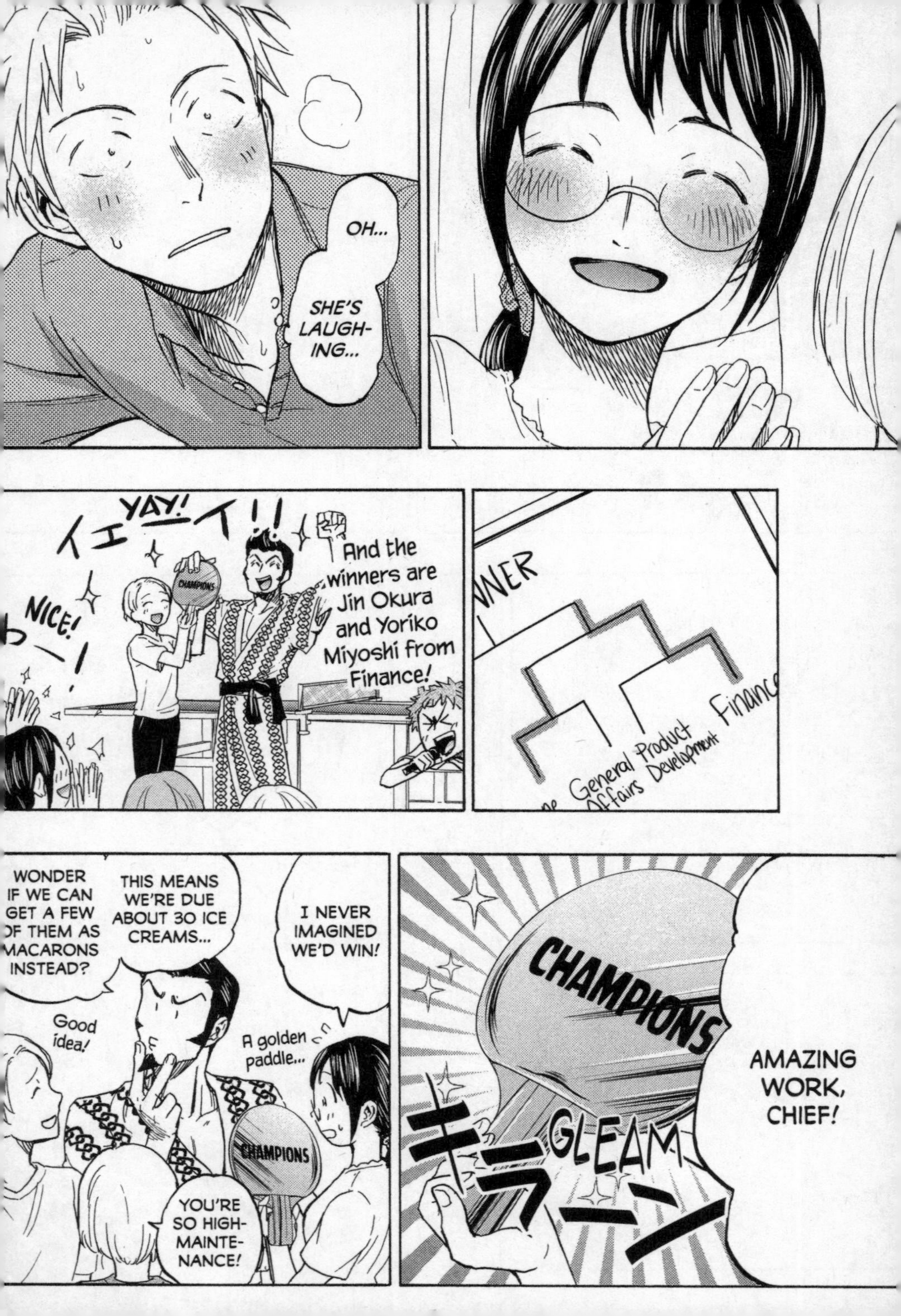
OH...
SHE'S LAUGHING...
NNER
General Product
Affairs Development
Finance
And the winners are Jin Okura and Yoriko Miyoshi from Finance!
YAY!
イエーイ!!
CHAMPIONS
NICE!
CHAMPIONS
AMAZING WORK, CHIEF!
GLEAM
キラーン
I NEVER IMAGINED WE'D WIN!
THIS MEANS WE'RE DUE ABOUT 30 ICE CREAMS...
WONDER IF WE CAN GET A FEW OF THEM AS MACARONS INSTEAD?
Good idea!
A golden paddle...
CHAMPIONS
YOU'RE SO HIGH-MAINTENANCE!

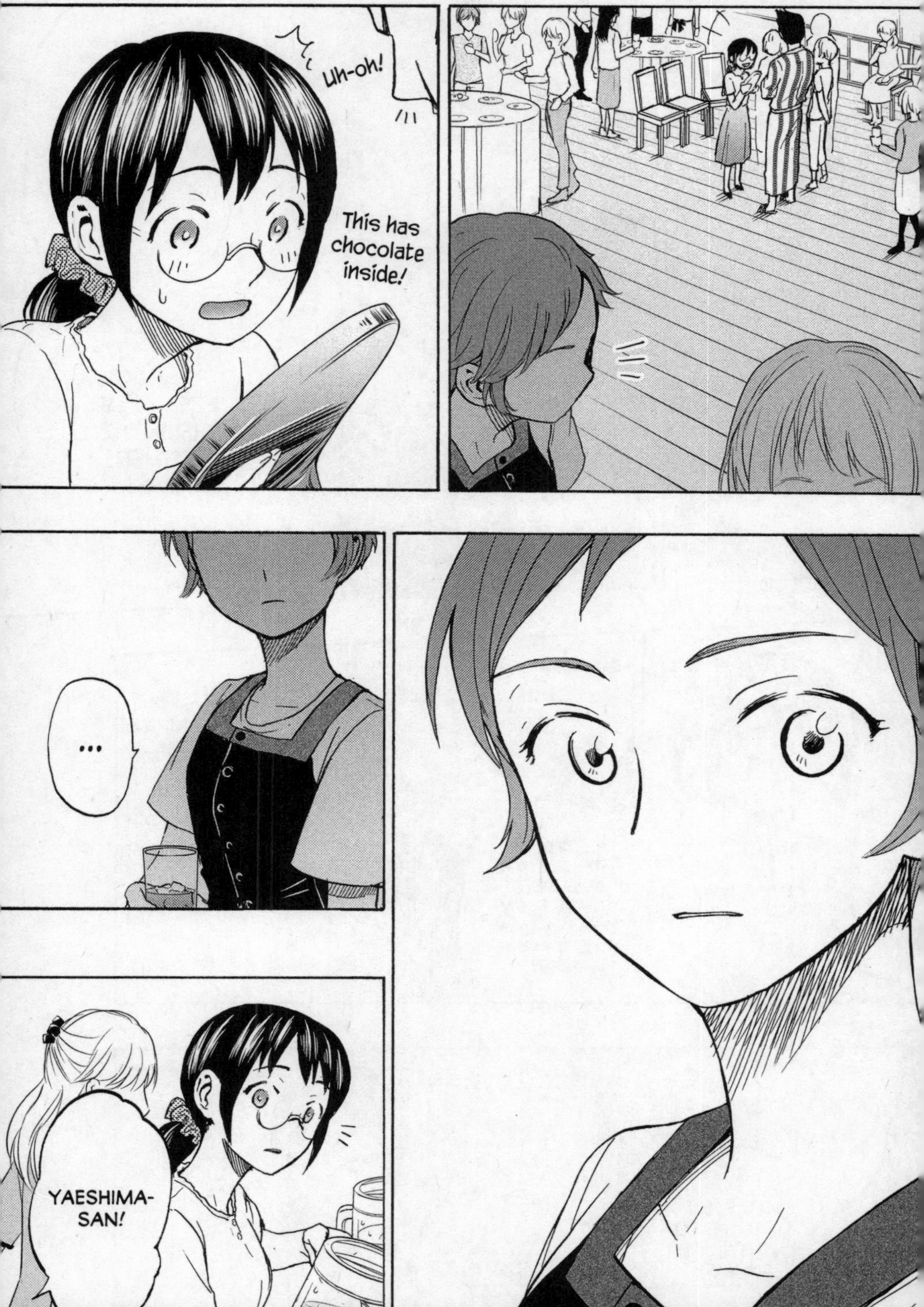

Uh-oh!
This has chocolate inside!
...
YAESHIMA-SAN!

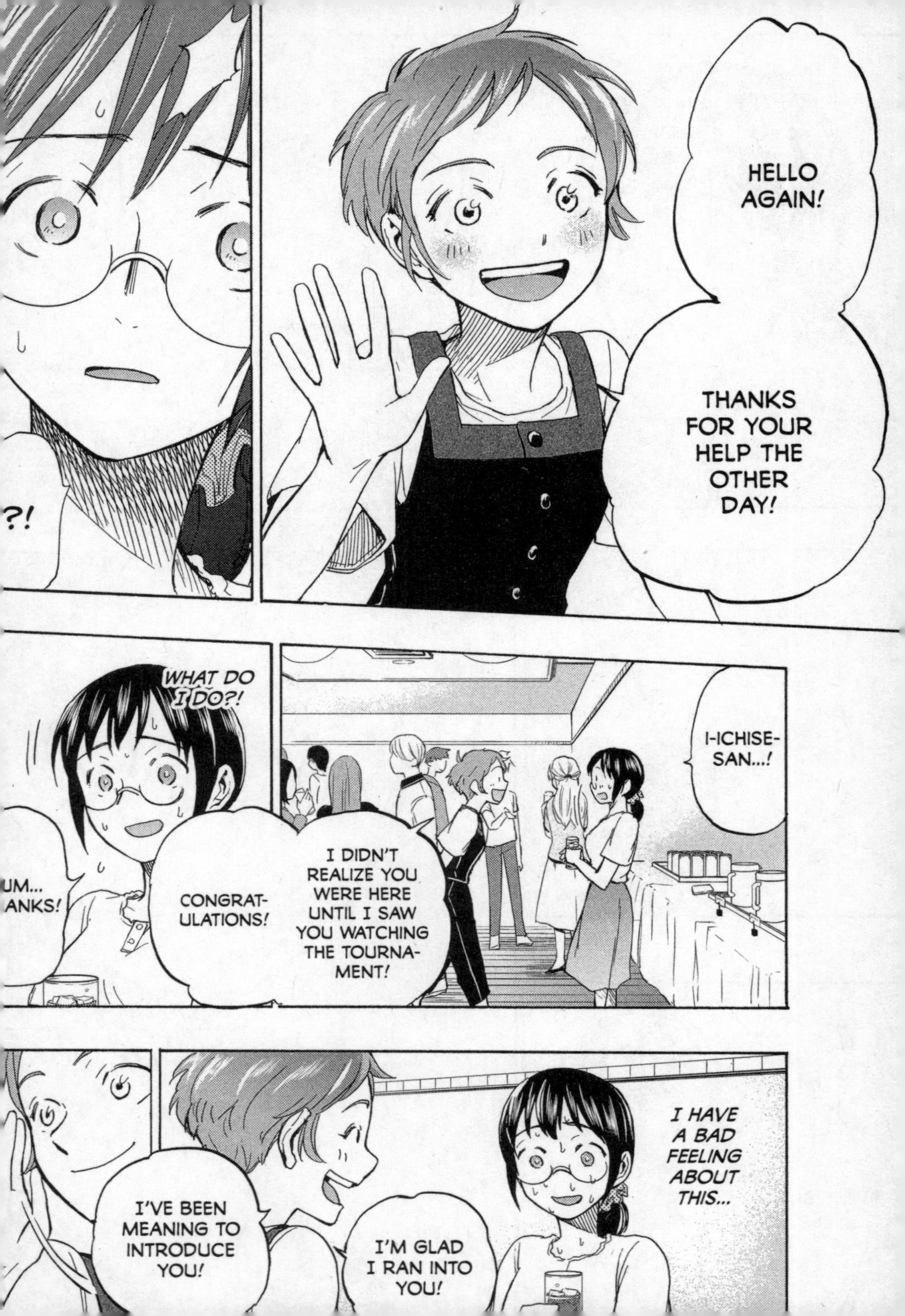
HELLO AGAIN!
THANKS FOR YOUR HELP THE OTHER DAY!
?!
I-ICHISE-SAN...!
WHAT DO I DO?!
I DIDN'T REALIZE YOU WERE HERE UNTIL I SAW YOU WATCHING THE TOURNAMENT!
CONGRATULATIONS!
UM... ANKS!
I HAVE A BAD FEELING ABOUT THIS...
I'M GLAD I RAN INTO YOU!
I'VE BEEN MEANING TO INTRODUCE YOU!

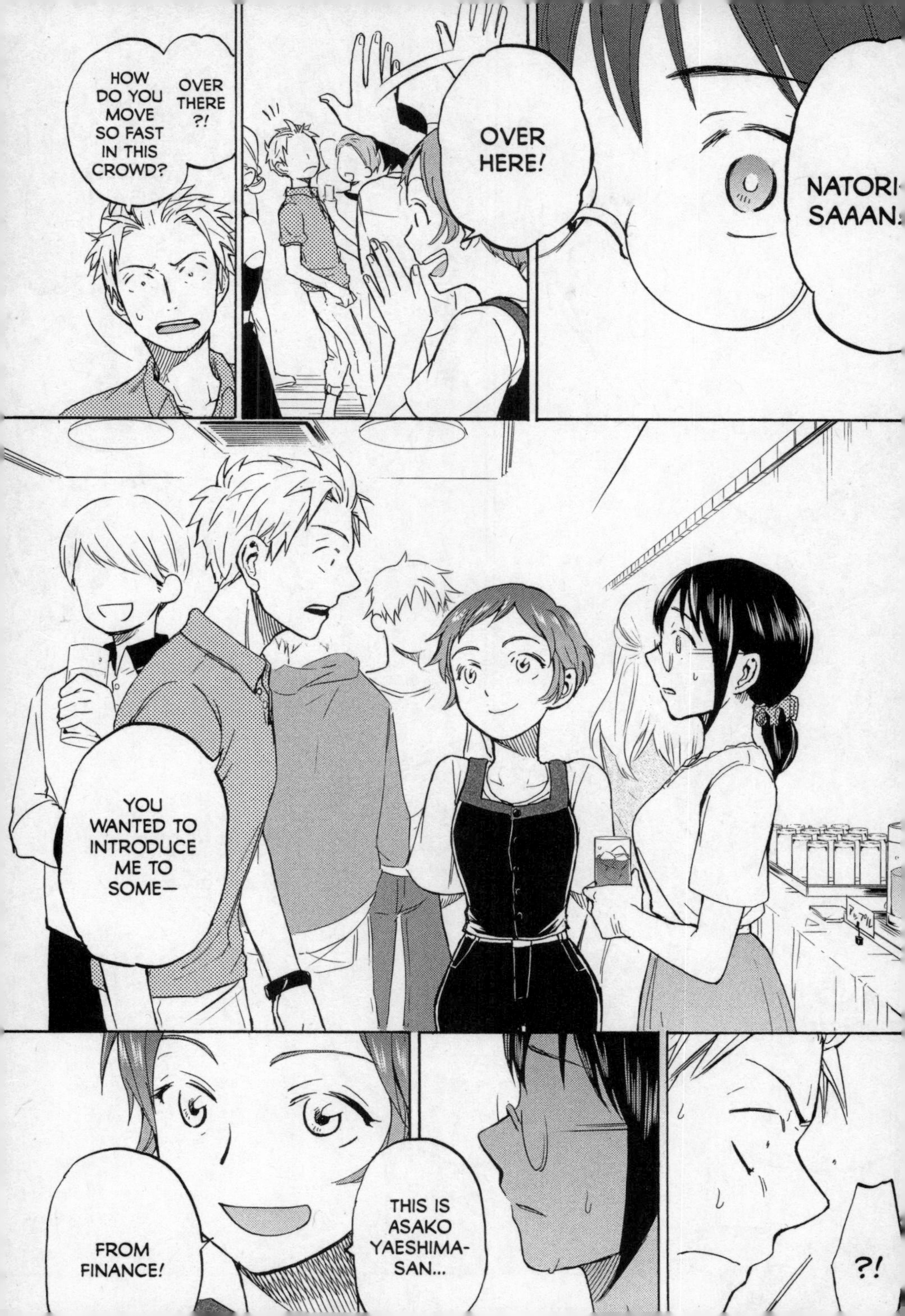
NATORI-SAAAN!
OVER HERE!
OVER THERE?!
HOW DO YOU MOVE SO FAST IN THIS CROWD?
YOU WANTED TO INTRODUCE ME TO SOME—
?!
THIS IS ASAKO YAESHIMA-SAN...
FROM FINANCE!

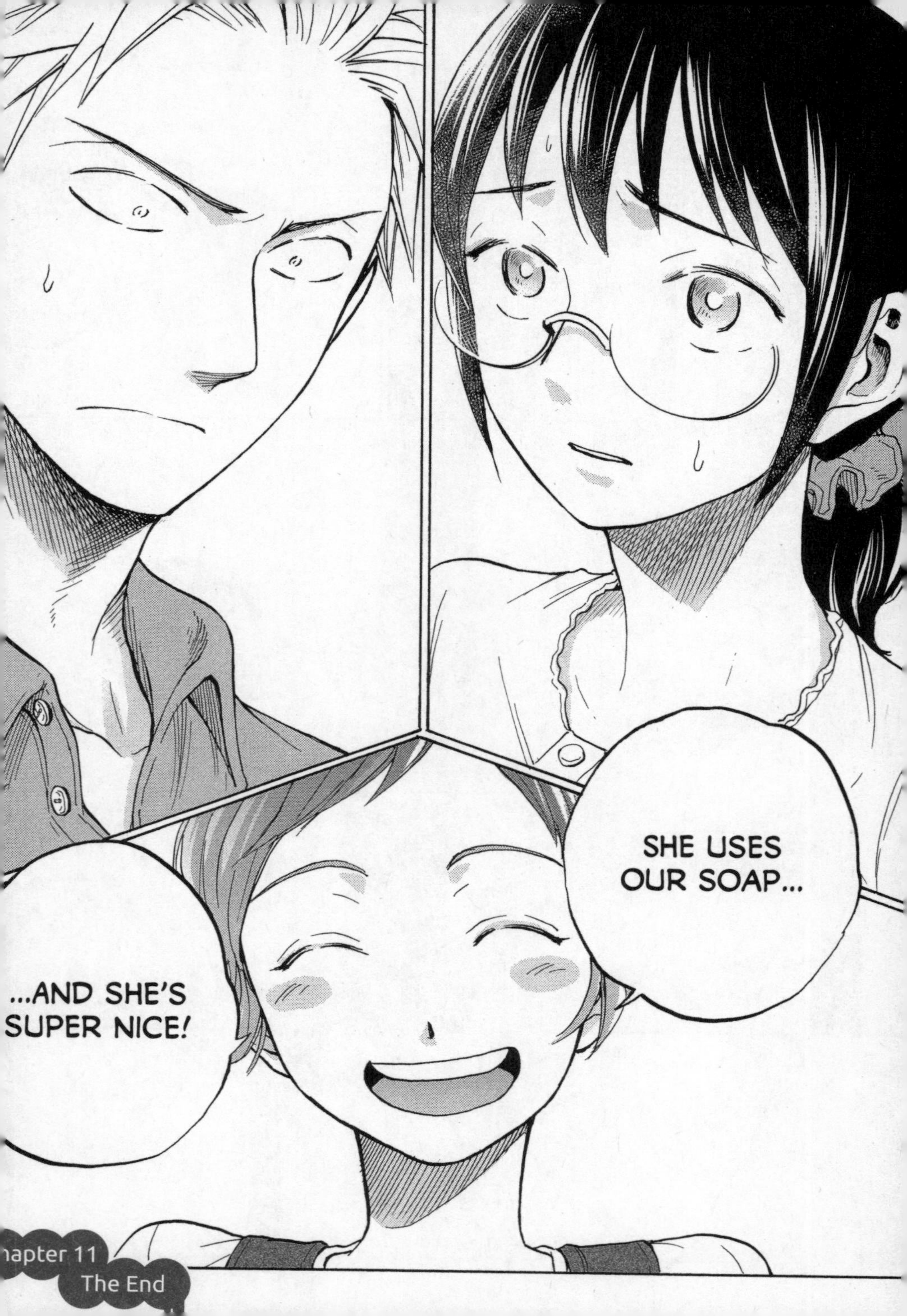
SHE USES OUR SOAP...
...AND SHE'S SUPER NICE!
hapter 11
The End

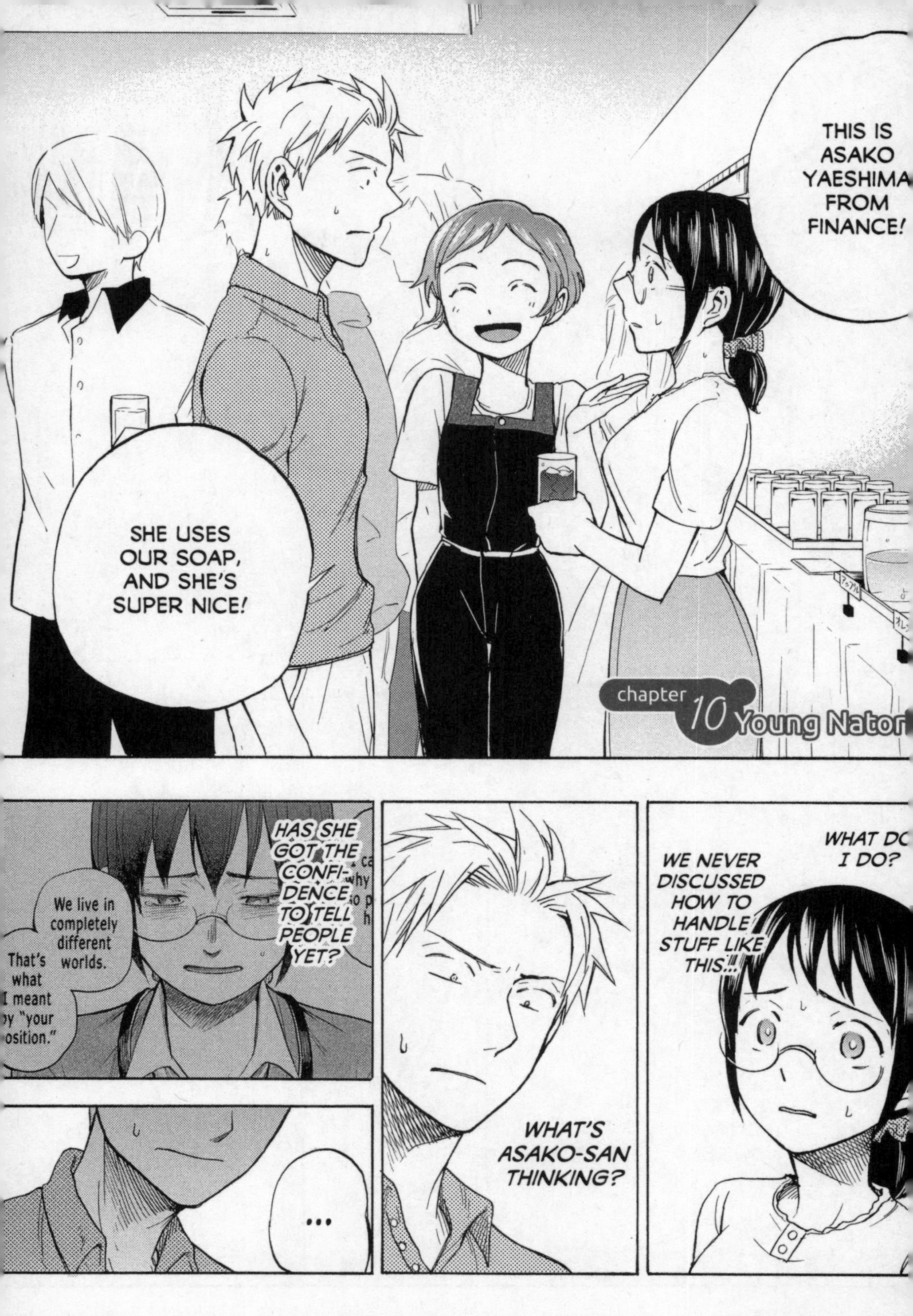
THIS IS ASAKO YAESHIMA FROM FINANCE!
SHE USES OUR SOAP, AND SHE'S SUPER NICE!
chapter 10 Young Natori
WHAT DO I DO?
WE NEVER DISCUSSED HOW TO HANDLE STUFF LIKE THIS...
WHAT'S ASAKO-SAN THINKING?
HAS SHE GOT THE CONFI-DENCE TO TELL PEOPLE YET?
We live in completely different worlds. That's what I meant by "your position."
...

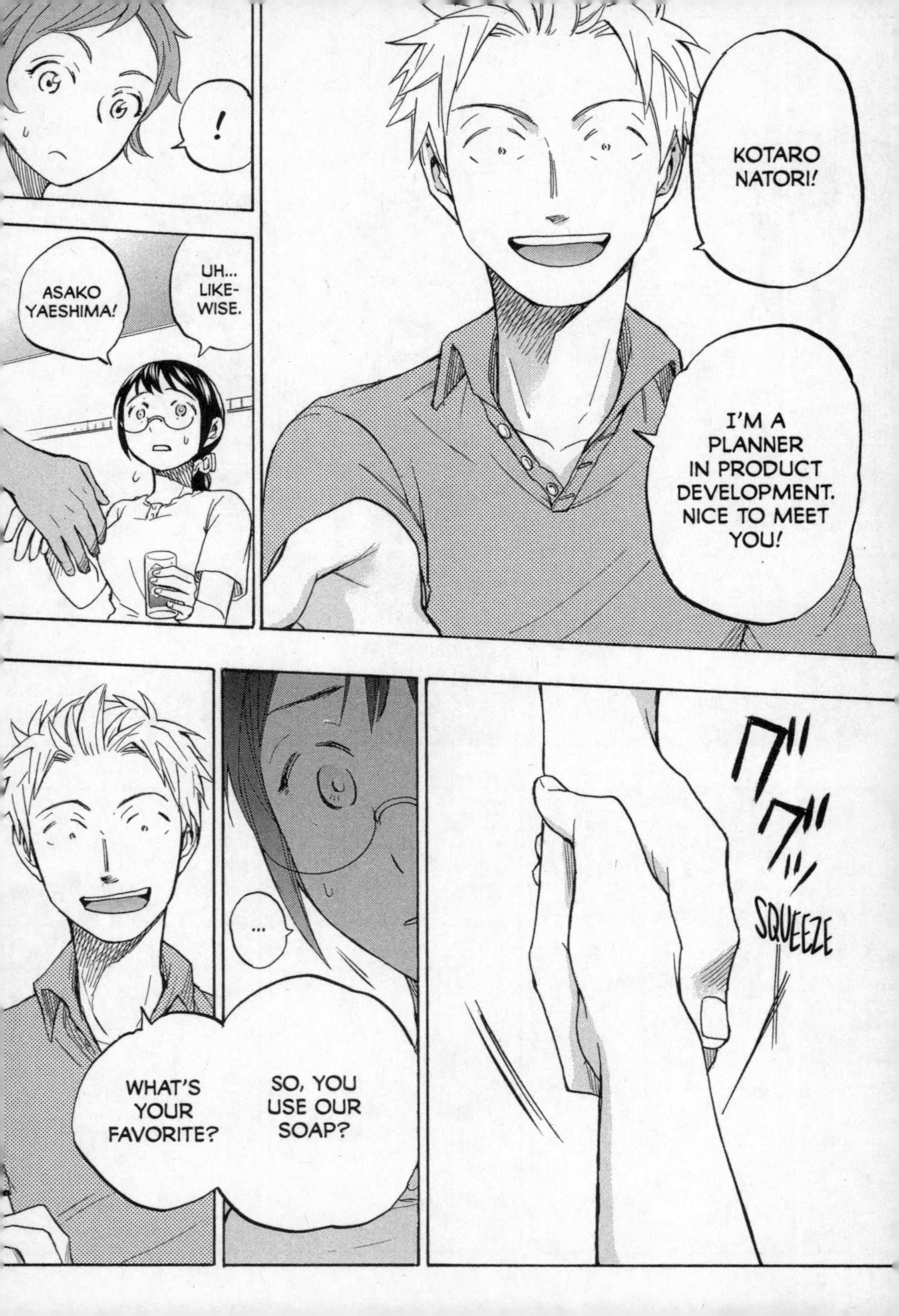

KOTARO NATORI!
I'M A PLANNER IN PRODUCT DEVELOPMENT. NICE TO MEET YOU!
!
UH... LIKE-WISE.
ASAKO YAESHIMA!
SQUEEZE
...
SO, YOU USE OUR SOAP?
WHAT'S YOUR FAVORITE?

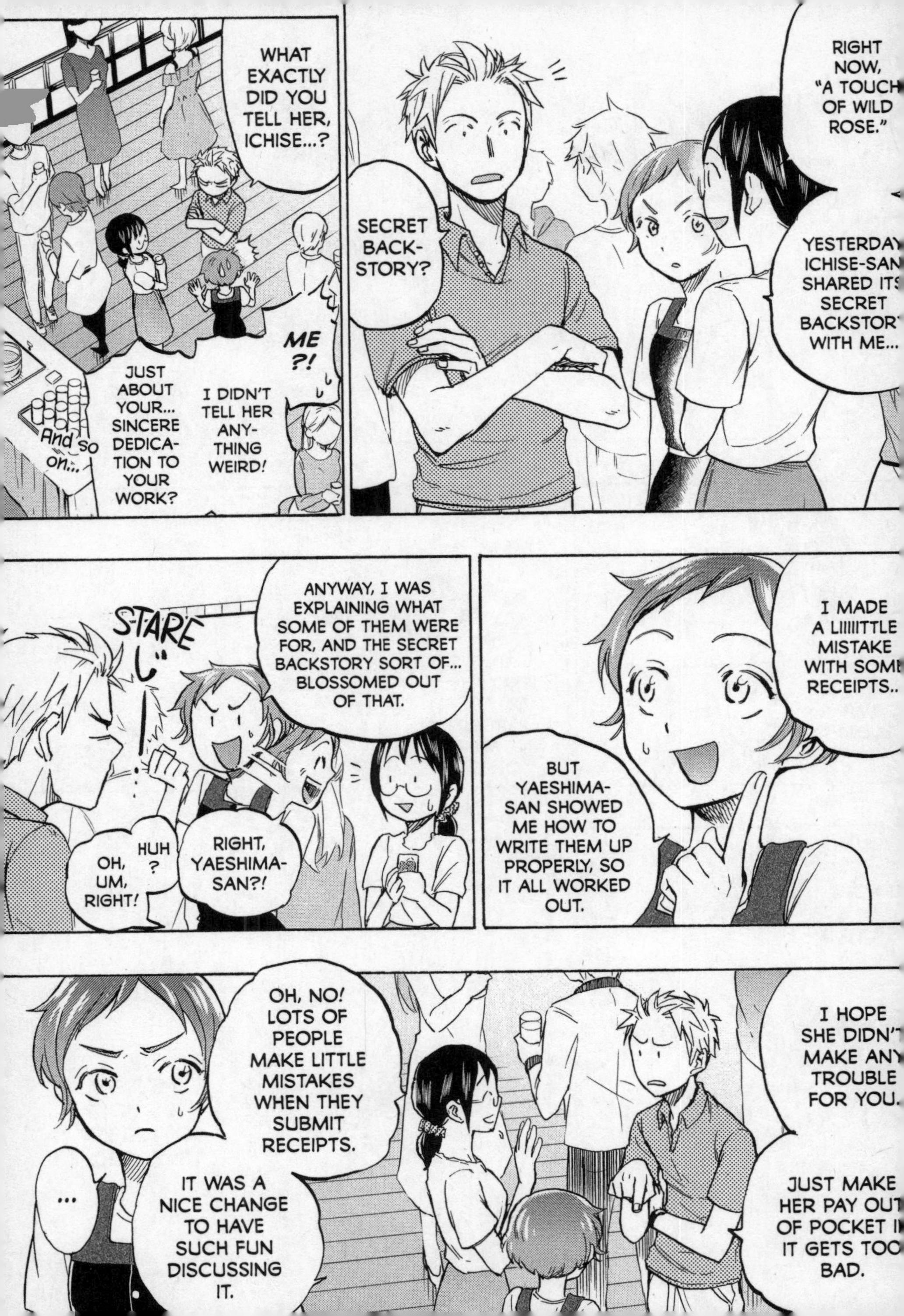
RIGHT NOW, "A TOUCH OF WILD ROSE."
YESTERDAY ICHISE-SAN SHARED ITS SECRET BACKSTORY WITH ME...
SECRET BACK-STORY?
WHAT EXACTLY DID YOU TELL HER, ICHISE...?
ME?!
I DIDN'T TELL HER ANY-THING WEIRD!
JUST ABOUT YOUR... SINCERE DEDICA-TION TO YOUR WORK?
And so on...
I MADE A LIIIITTLE MISTAKE WITH SOME RECEIPTS..
BUT YAESHIMA-SAN SHOWED ME HOW TO WRITE THEM UP PROPERLY, SO IT ALL WORKED OUT.
ANYWAY, I WAS EXPLAINING WHAT SOME OF THEM WERE FOR, AND THE SECRET BACKSTORY SORT OF... BLOSSOMED OUT OF THAT.
STARE
RIGHT, YAESHIMA-SAN?!
HUH?
OH, UM, RIGHT!
I HOPE SHE DIDN'T MAKE ANY TROUBLE FOR YOU.
JUST MAKE HER PAY OUT OF POCKET IF IT GETS TOO BAD.
OH, NO! LOTS OF PEOPLE MAKE LITTLE MISTAKES WHEN THEY SUBMIT RECEIPTS.
IT WAS A NICE CHANGE TO HAVE SUCH FUN DISCUSSING IT.
...

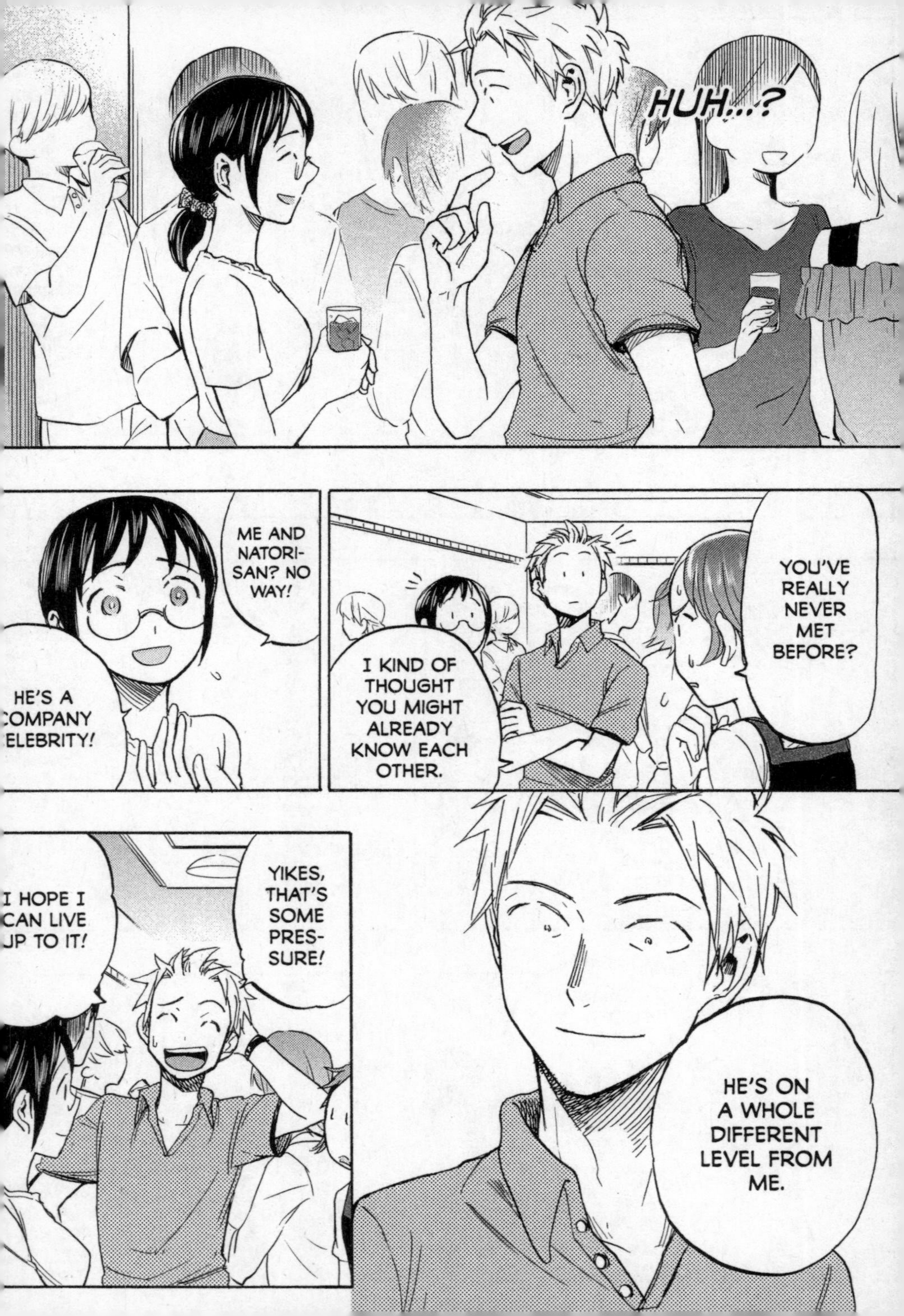
HUH...?
YOU'VE REALLY NEVER MET BEFORE?
I KIND OF THOUGHT YOU MIGHT ALREADY KNOW EACH OTHER.
ME AND NATORI-SAN? NO WAY!
HE'S A COMPANY CELEBRITY!
HE'S ON A WHOLE DIFFERENT LEVEL FROM ME.
YIKES, THAT'S SOME PRES-SURE!
I HOPE I CAN LIVE UP TO IT!

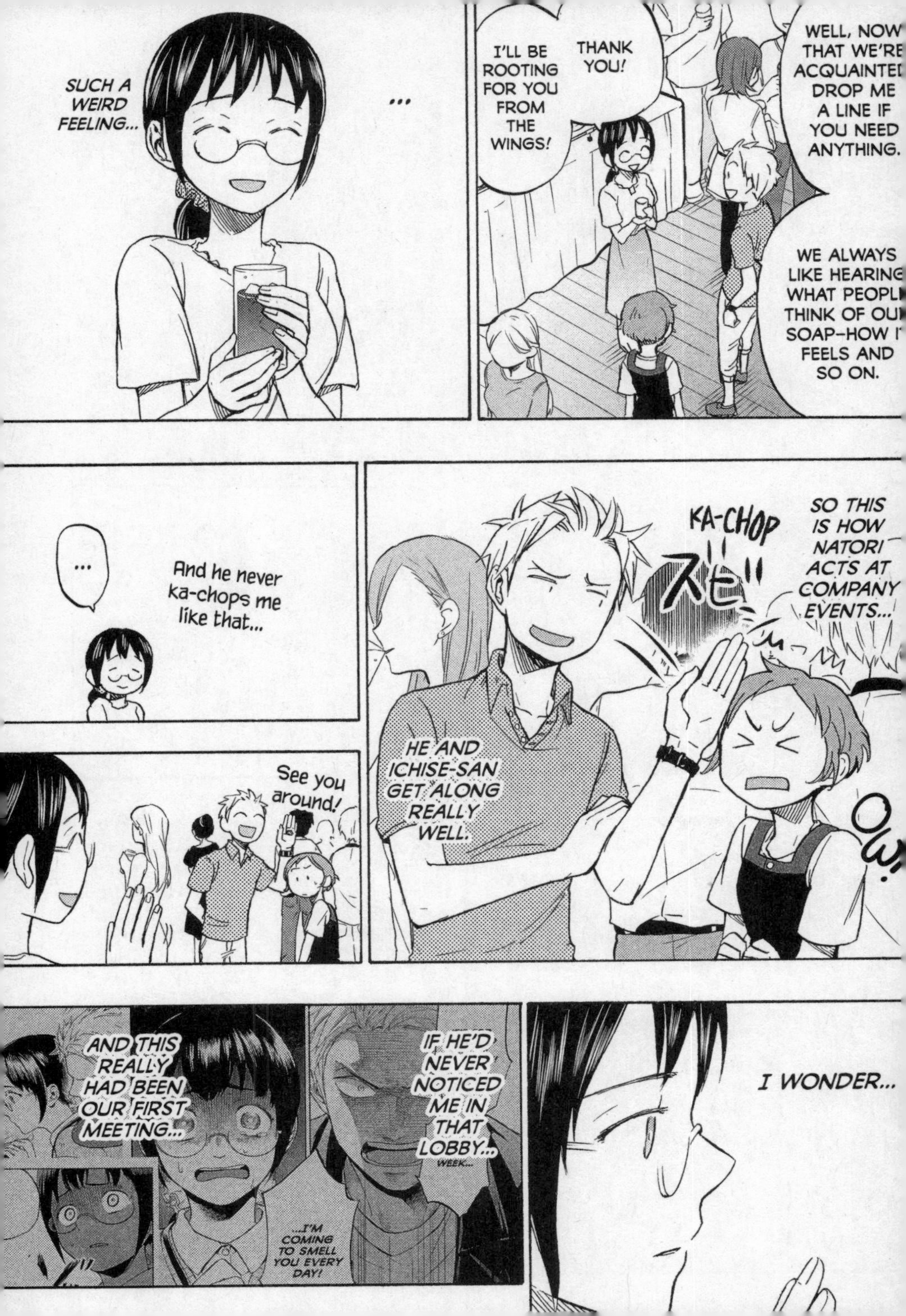
WELL, NOW THAT WE'RE ACQUAINTED DROP ME A LINE IF YOU NEED ANYTHING.
WE ALWAYS LIKE HEARING WHAT PEOPLE THINK OF OUR SOAP—HOW IT FEELS AND SO ON.
THANK YOU!
I'LL BE ROOTING FOR YOU FROM THE WINGS!
...
SUCH A WEIRD FEELING...
SO THIS IS HOW NATORI ACTS AT COMPANY EVENTS...
KA-CHOP
OW!
HE AND ICHISE-SAN GET ALONG REALLY WELL.
...
And he never ka-chops me like that...
See you around!
I WONDER...
IF HE'D NEVER NOTICED ME IN THAT LOBBY...
WEEK...
...I'M COMING TO SMELL YOU EVERY DAY!
AND THIS REALLY HAD BEEN OUR FIRST MEETING...

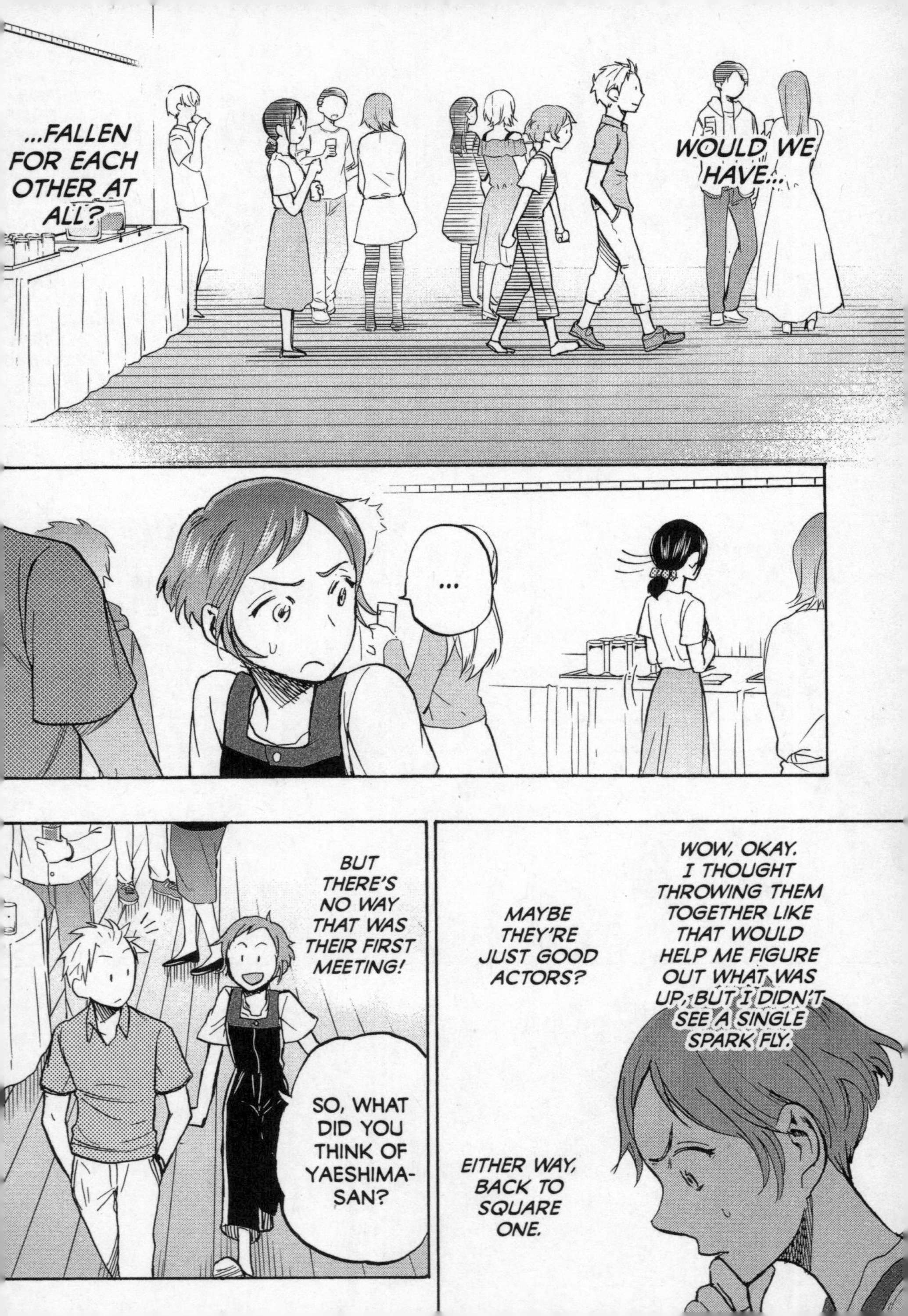
WOULD WE HAVE...
...FALLEN FOR EACH OTHER AT ALL?
...
WOW, OKAY. I THOUGHT THROWING THEM TOGETHER LIKE THAT WOULD HELP ME FIGURE OUT WHAT WAS UP, BUT I DIDN'T SEE A SINGLE SPARK FLY.
MAYBE THEY'RE JUST GOOD ACTORS?
EITHER WAY, BACK TO SQUARE ONE.
BUT THERE'S NO WAY THAT WAS THEIR FIRST MEETING!
SO, WHAT DID YOU THINK OF YAESHIMA-SAN?

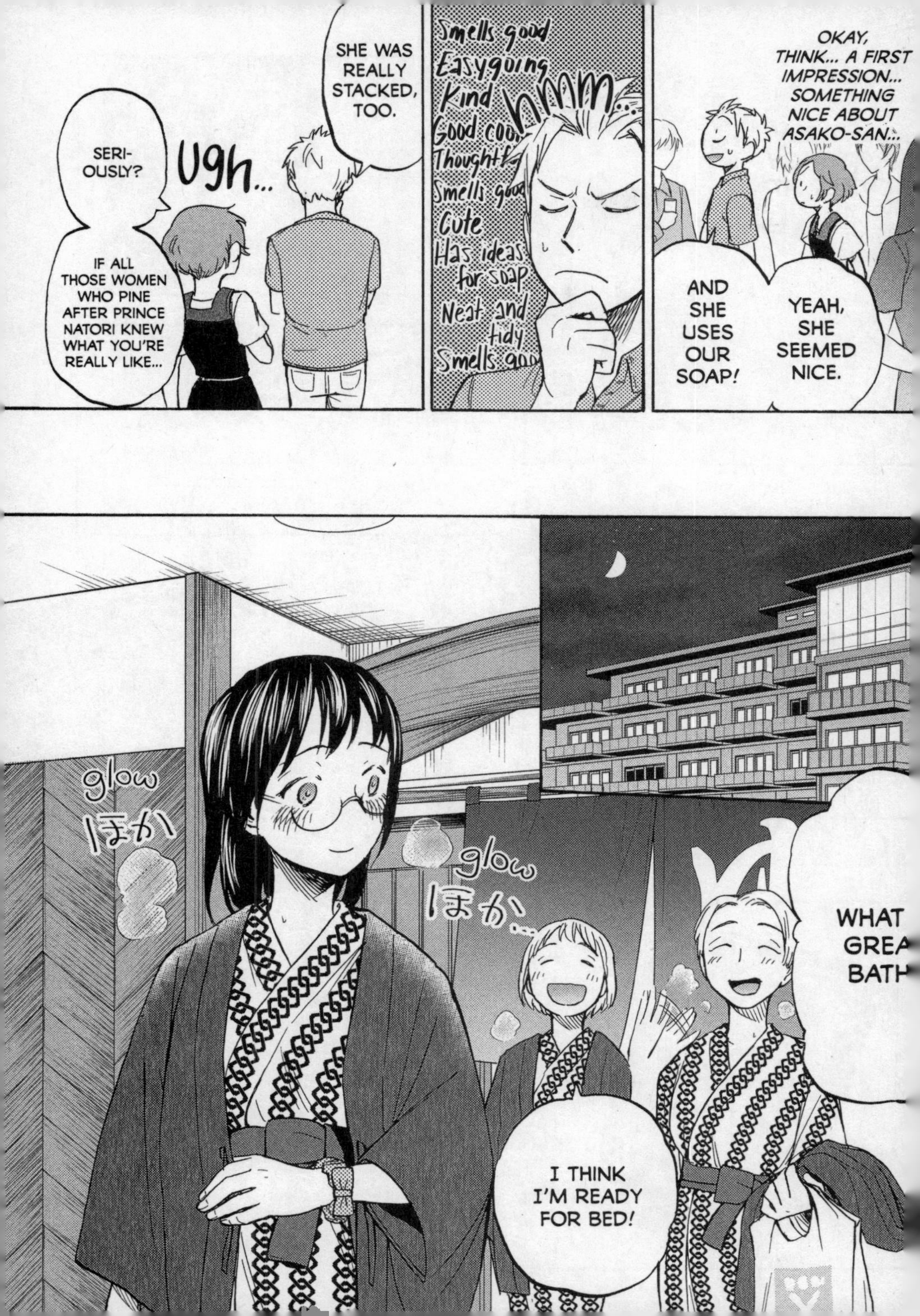
OKAY, THINK... A FIRST IMPRESSION... SOMETHING NICE ABOUT ASAKO-SAN...
YEAH, SHE SEEMED NICE.
AND SHE USES OUR SOAP!
hmm
Smells good
Easygoing
Kind
Good coo
Thoughtf
Smells goo
Cute
Has ideas for soap
Neat and tidy
Smells goo
SHE WAS REALLY STACKED, TOO.
Ugh...
SERI-OUSLY?
IF ALL THOSE WOMEN WHO PINE AFTER PRINCE NATORI KNEW WHAT YOU'RE REALLY LIKE...
WHAT GREA BATH
I THINK I'M READY FOR BED!
glow
ほか...
glow
ほか

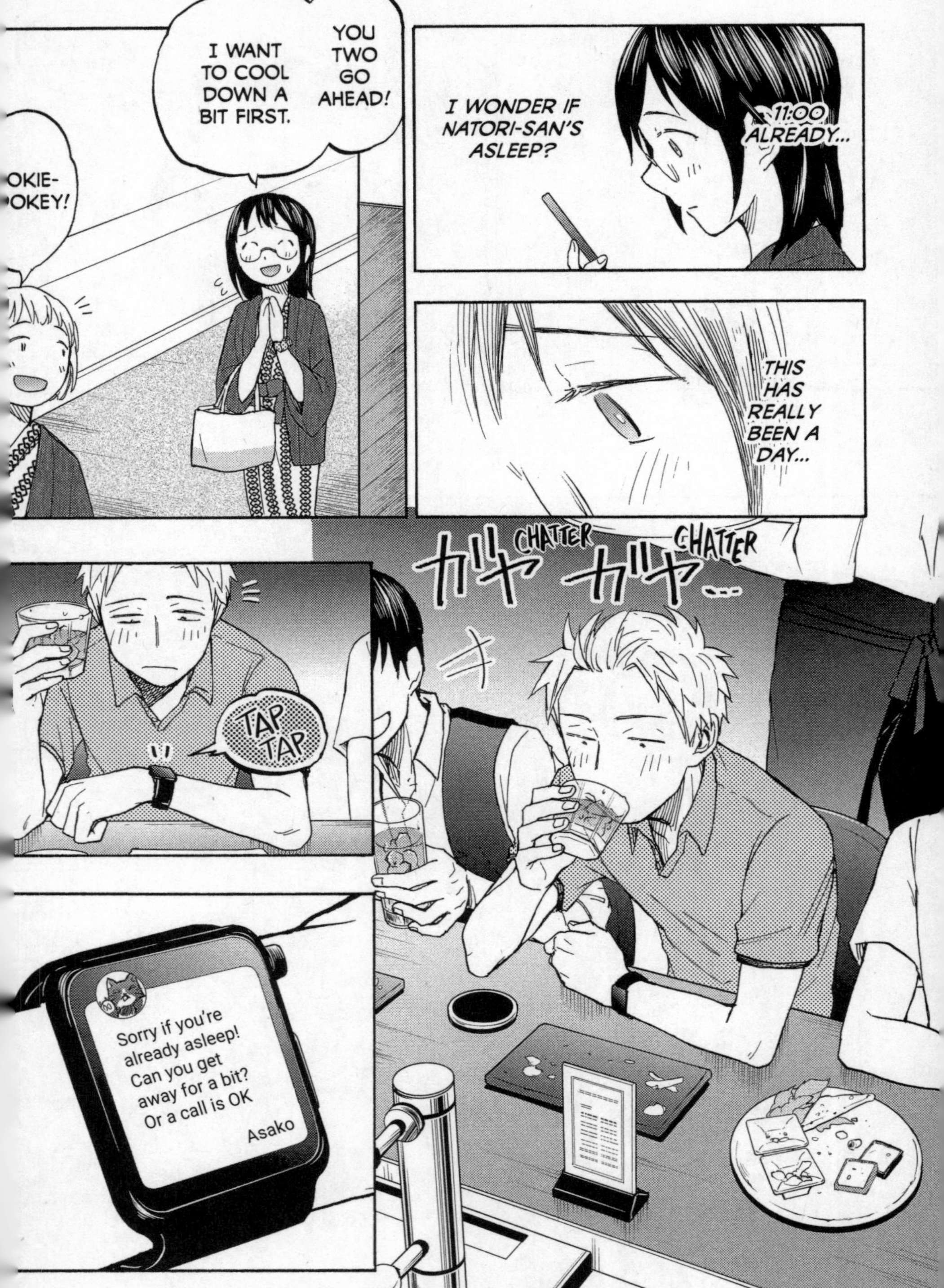
11:00 ALREADY...
I WONDER IF NATORI-SAN'S ASLEEP?
THIS HAS REALLY BEEN A DAY...
YOU TWO GO AHEAD!
I WANT TO COOL DOWN A BIT FIRST.
OKIE-
OKEY!
ガヤ CHATTER
ガヤ... CHATTER
TAP TAP
Sorry if you're already asleep! Can you get away for a bit? Or a call is OK
Asako

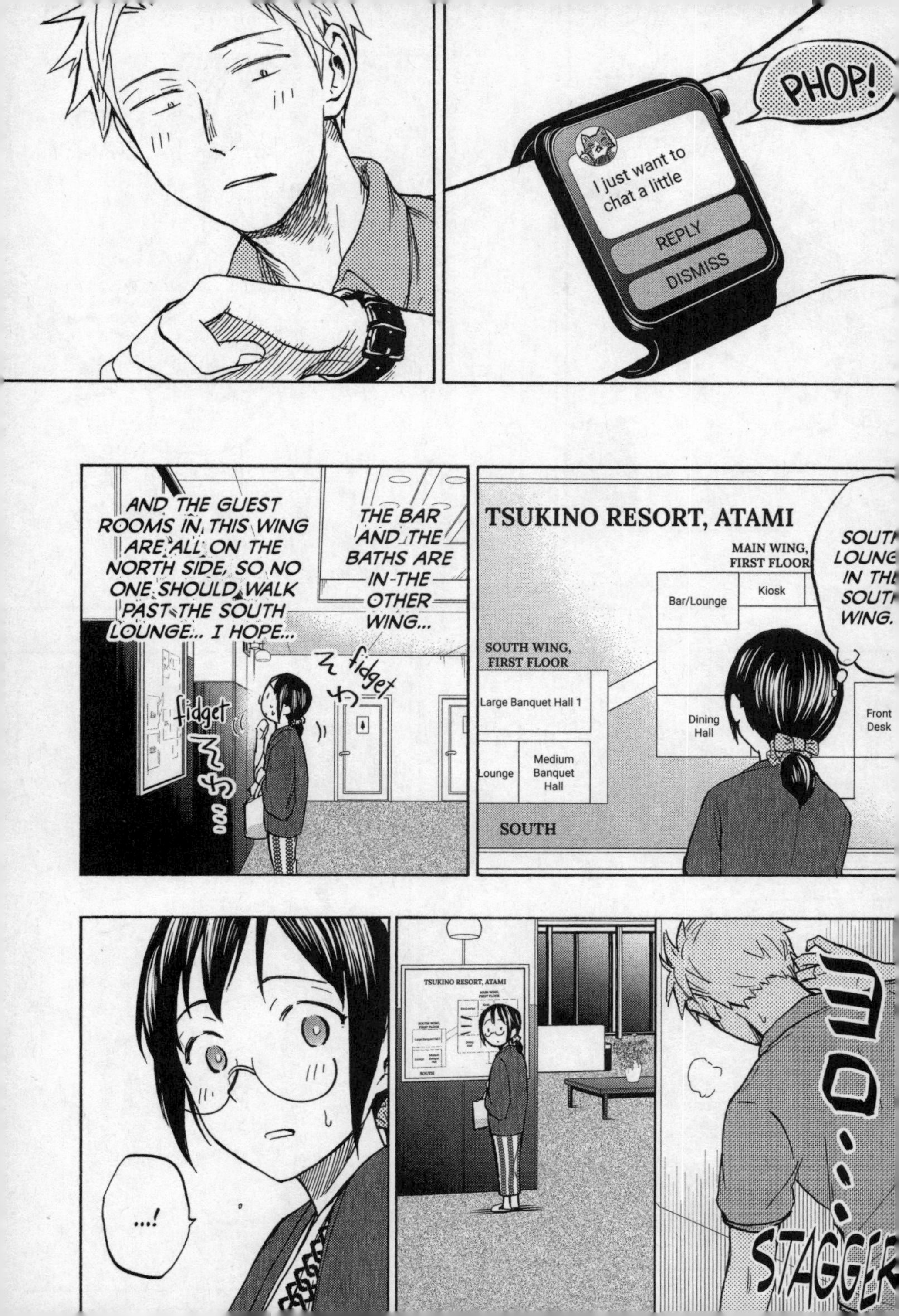
PHOP!
I just want to chat a little
REPLY
DISMISS
TSUKINO RESORT, ATAMI
MAIN WING, FIRST FLOOR
Bar/Lounge
Kiosk
SOUTH WING, FIRST FLOOR
Large Banquet Hall 1
Dining Hall
Front Desk
Lounge
Medium Banquet Hall
SOUTH
AND THE GUEST ROOMS IN THIS WING ARE ALL ON THE NORTH SIDE, SO NO ONE SHOULD WALK PAST THE SOUTH LOUNGE... I HOPE...
THE BAR AND THE BATHS ARE IN THE OTHER WING...
fidget
fidget
STAGGER
...!

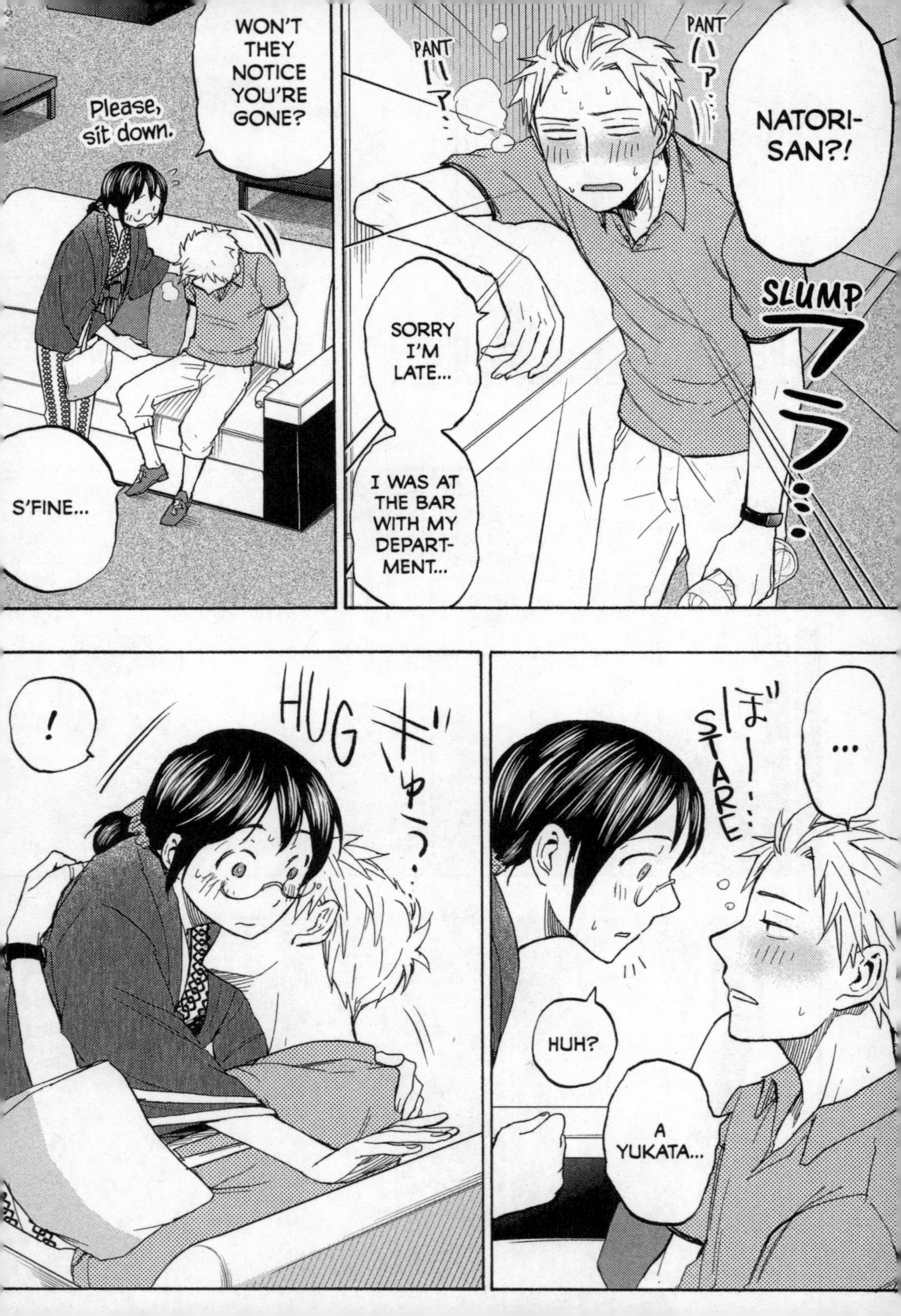
NATORI-SAN?!
PANT ハア…
PANT ハア…
SLUMP フラ…
SORRY I'M LATE...
I WAS AT THE BAR WITH MY DEPARTMENT...
WON'T THEY NOTICE YOU'RE GONE?
Please, sit down.
S'FINE...
...
STARE ぼー…
HUH?
A YUKATA...
!
HUG ぎゅう…

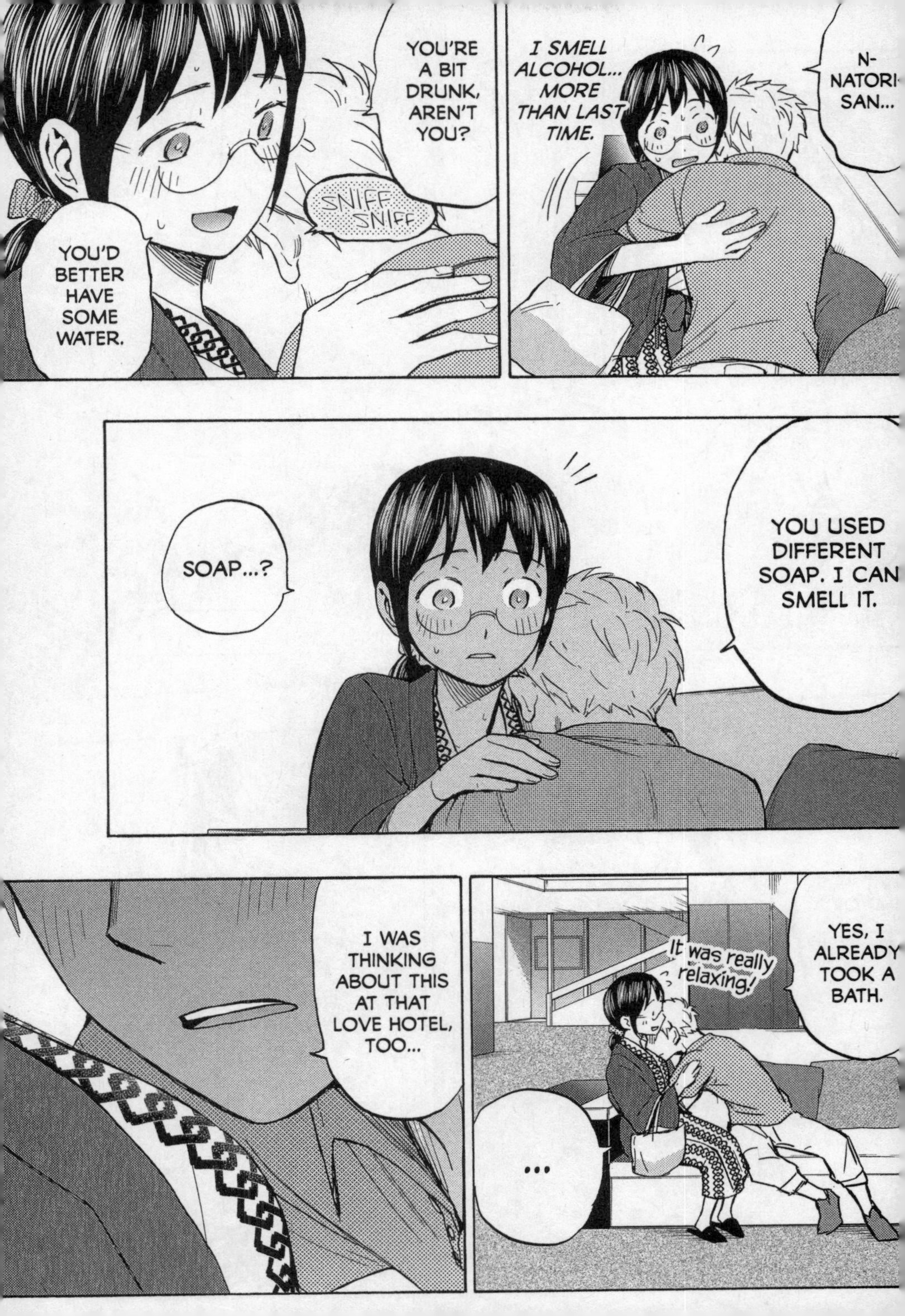
N-NATORI-SAN...
I SMELL ALCOHOL... MORE THAN LAST TIME.
YOU'RE A BIT DRUNK, AREN'T YOU?
SNIFF SNIFF
YOU'D BETTER HAVE SOME WATER.
YOU USED DIFFERENT SOAP. I CAN SMELL IT.
SOAP...?
YES, I ALREADY TOOK A BATH.
It was really relaxing!
...
I WAS THINKING ABOUT THIS AT THAT LOVE HOTEL, TOO...

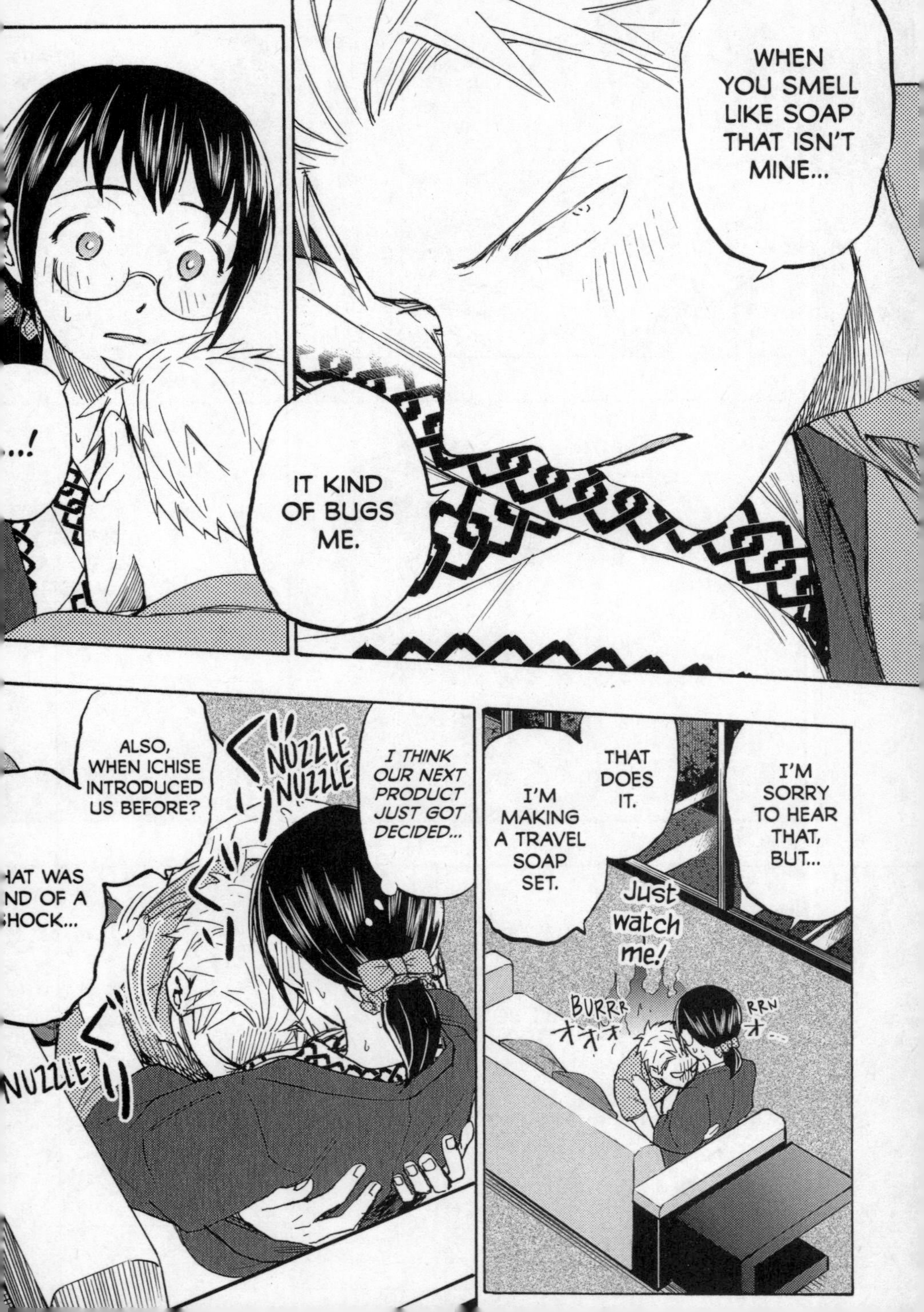
WHEN YOU SMELL LIKE SOAP THAT ISN'T MINE...
IT KIND OF BUGS ME.
...!
I'M SORRY TO HEAR THAT, BUT...
THAT DOES IT.
I'M MAKING A TRAVEL SOAP SET.
Just watch me!
BURRR
RRN
I THINK OUR NEXT PRODUCT JUST GOT DECIDED...
NUZZLE NUZZLE
ALSO, WHEN ICHISE INTRODUCED US BEFORE?
HAT WAS ND OF A HOCK...
NUZZLE

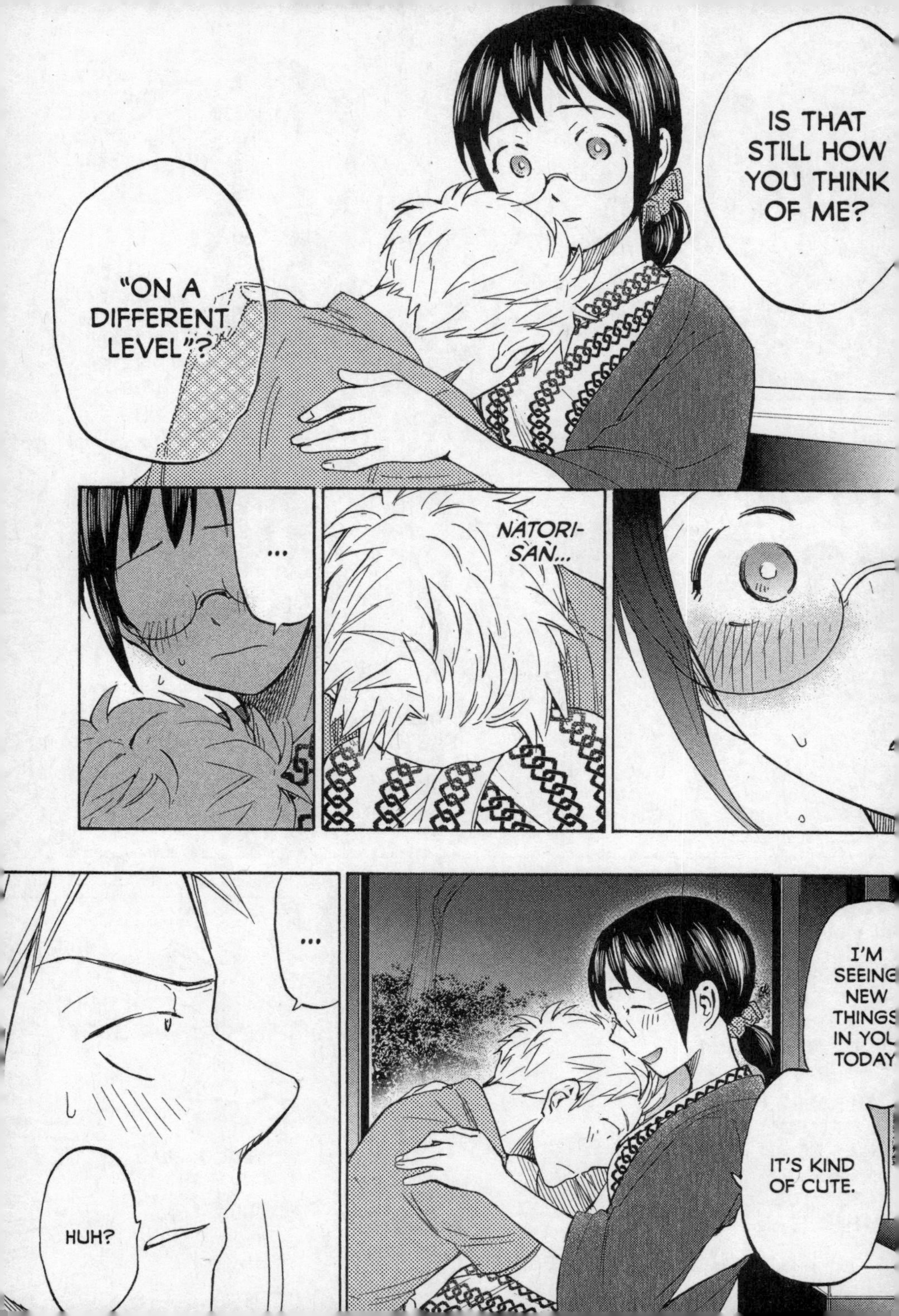
IS THAT STILL HOW YOU THINK OF ME?
"ON A DIFFERENT LEVEL"?
NATORI-SAN...
...
I'M SEEING NEW THINGS IN YOU TODAY
IT'S KIND OF CUTE.
...
HUH?

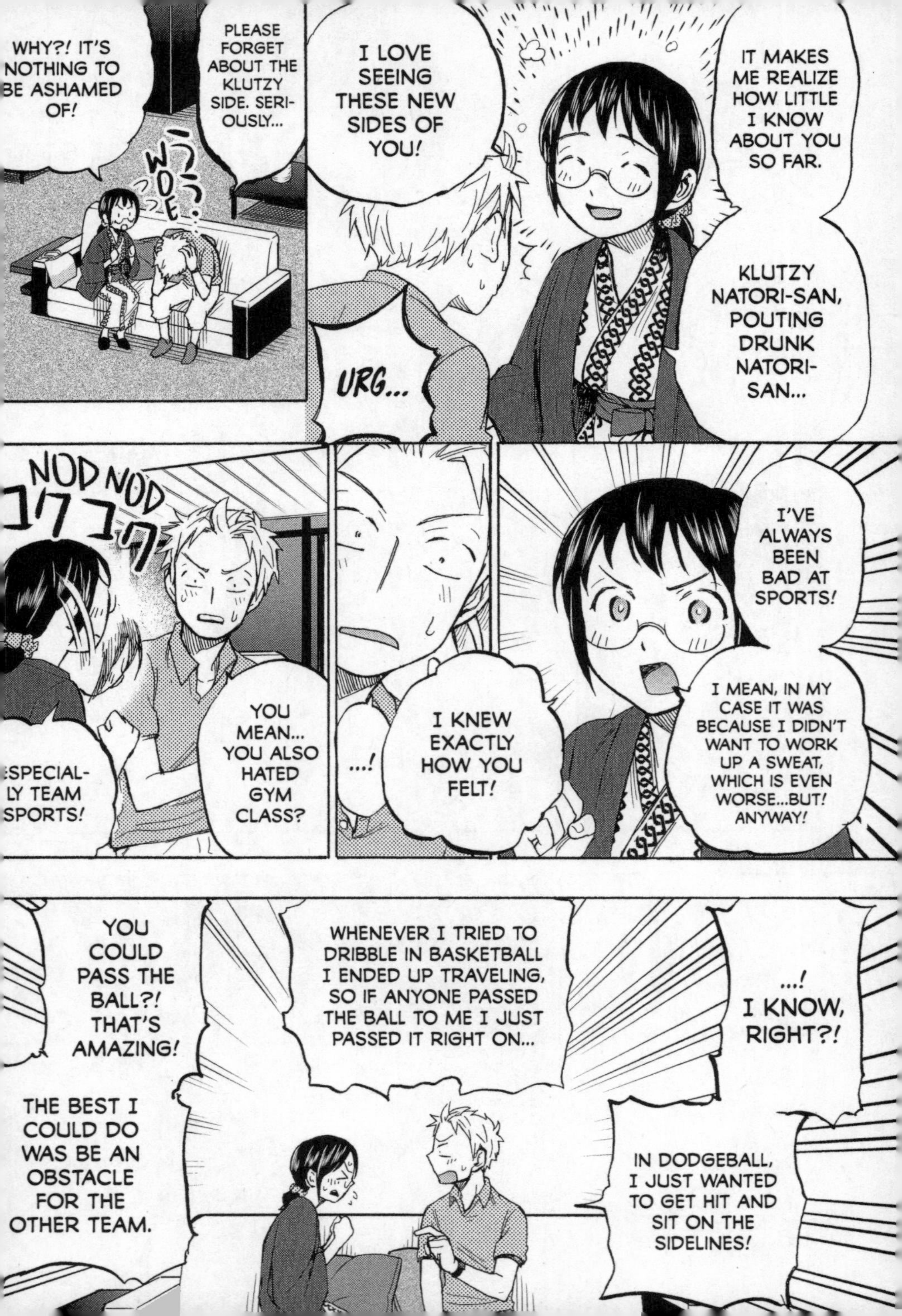
IT MAKES ME REALIZE HOW LITTLE I KNOW ABOUT YOU SO FAR.
KLUTZY NATORI-SAN, POUTING DRUNK NATORI-SAN...
I LOVE SEEING THESE NEW SIDES OF YOU!
URG...
PLEASE FORGET ABOUT THE KLUTZY SIDE. SERIOUSLY...
WHY?! IT'S NOTHING TO BE ASHAMED OF!
うう WOE
I'VE ALWAYS BEEN BAD AT SPORTS!
I MEAN, IN MY CASE IT WAS BECAUSE I DIDN'T WANT TO WORK UP A SWEAT, WHICH IS EVEN WORSE...BUT! ANYWAY!
...!
I KNEW EXACTLY HOW YOU FELT!
YOU MEAN... YOU ALSO HATED GYM CLASS?
NOD NOD コクコク
SPECIALLY TEAM SPORTS!
...! I KNOW, RIGHT?!
IN DODGEBALL, I JUST WANTED TO GET HIT AND SIT ON THE SIDELINES!
WHENEVER I TRIED TO DRIBBLE IN BASKETBALL I ENDED UP TRAVELING, SO IF ANYONE PASSED THE BALL TO ME I JUST PASSED IT RIGHT ON...
YOU COULD PASS THE BALL?! THAT'S AMAZING!
THE BEST I COULD DO WAS BE AN OBSTACLE FOR THE OTHER TEAM.

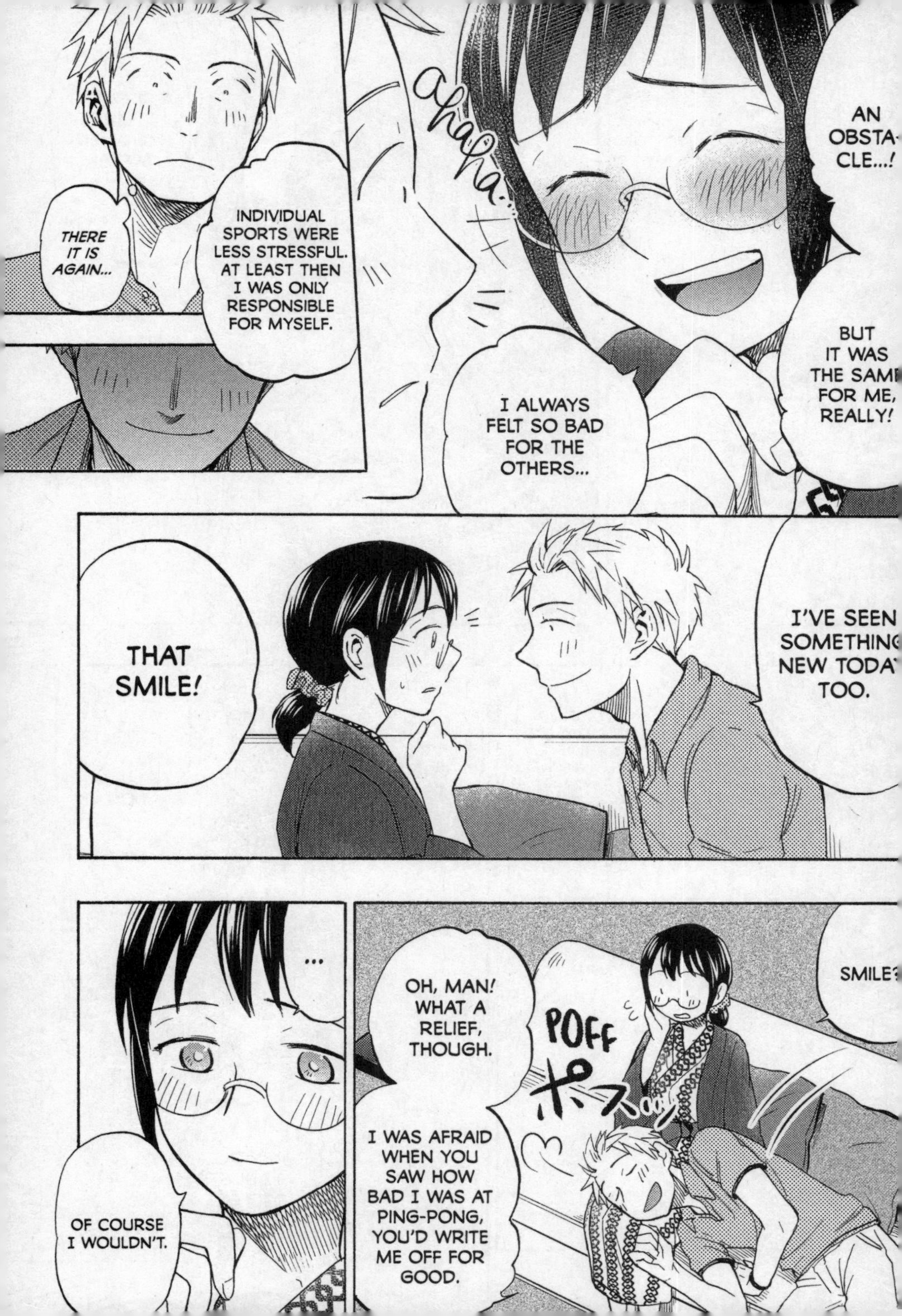
AN OBSTA-CLE...!
ahaha...
BUT IT WAS THE SAM FOR ME, REALLY!
I ALWAYS FELT SO BAD FOR THE OTHERS...
INDIVIDUAL SPORTS WERE LESS STRESSFUL. AT LEAST THEN I WAS ONLY RESPONSIBLE FOR MYSELF.
THERE IT IS AGAIN...
I'VE SEEN SOMETHING NEW TODA TOO.
THAT SMILE!
SMILE?
POFF
OH, MAN! WHAT A RELIEF, THOUGH.
I WAS AFRAID WHEN YOU SAW HOW BAD I WAS AT PING-PONG, YOU'D WRITE ME OFF FOR GOOD.
...
OF COURSE I WOULDN'T.

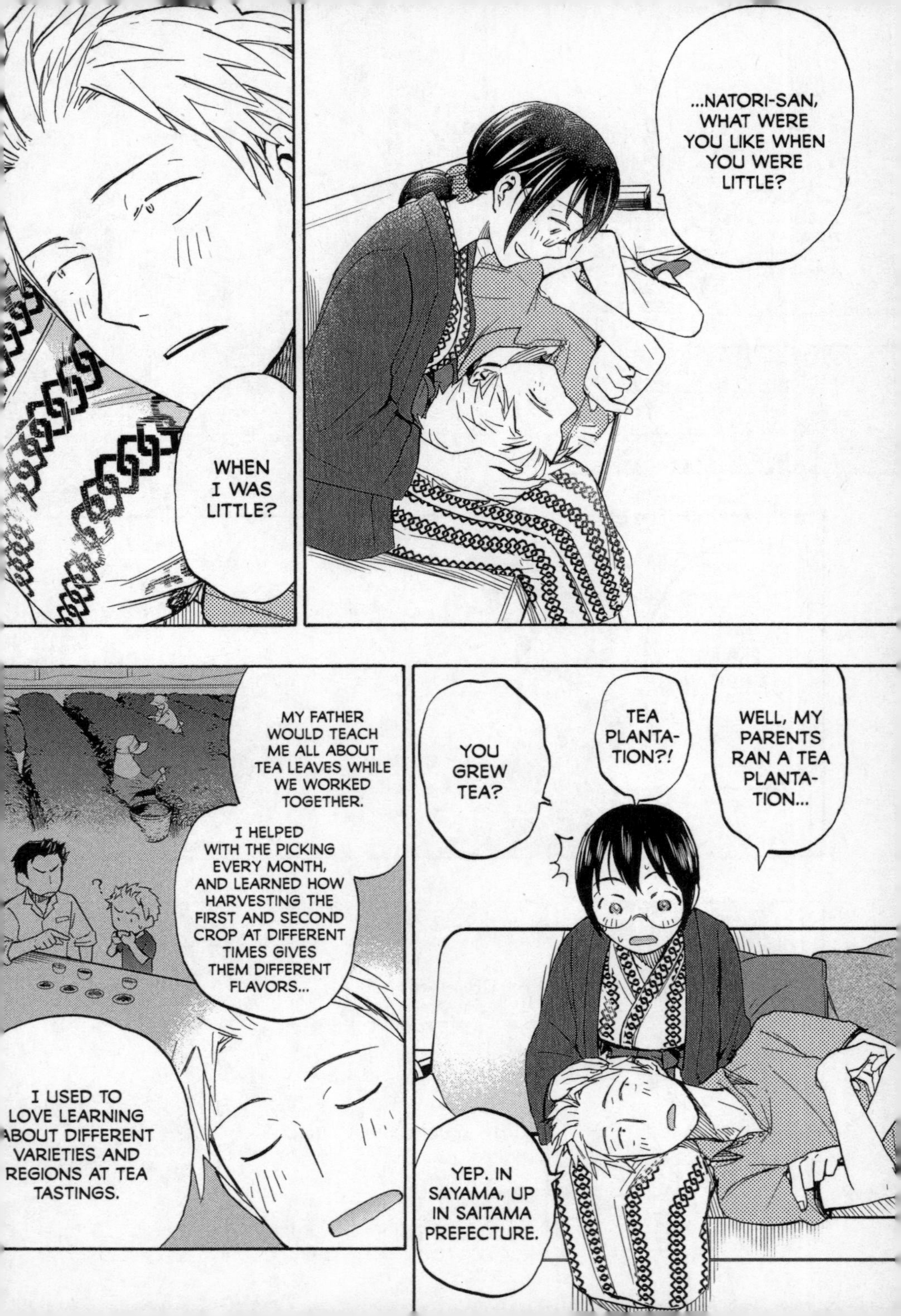
...NATORI-SAN, WHAT WERE YOU LIKE WHEN YOU WERE LITTLE?
WHEN I WAS LITTLE?
WELL, MY PARENTS RAN A TEA PLANTA-TION...
TEA PLANTA-TION?!
YOU GREW TEA?
YEP. IN SAYAMA, UP IN SAITAMA PREFECTURE.
MY FATHER WOULD TEACH ME ALL ABOUT TEA LEAVES WHILE WE WORKED TOGETHER.
I HELPED WITH THE PICKING EVERY MONTH, AND LEARNED HOW HARVESTING THE FIRST AND SECOND CROP AT DIFFERENT TIMES GIVES THEM DIFFERENT FLAVORS...
I USED TO LOVE LEARNING ABOUT DIFFERENT VARIETIES AND REGIONS AT TEA TASTINGS.

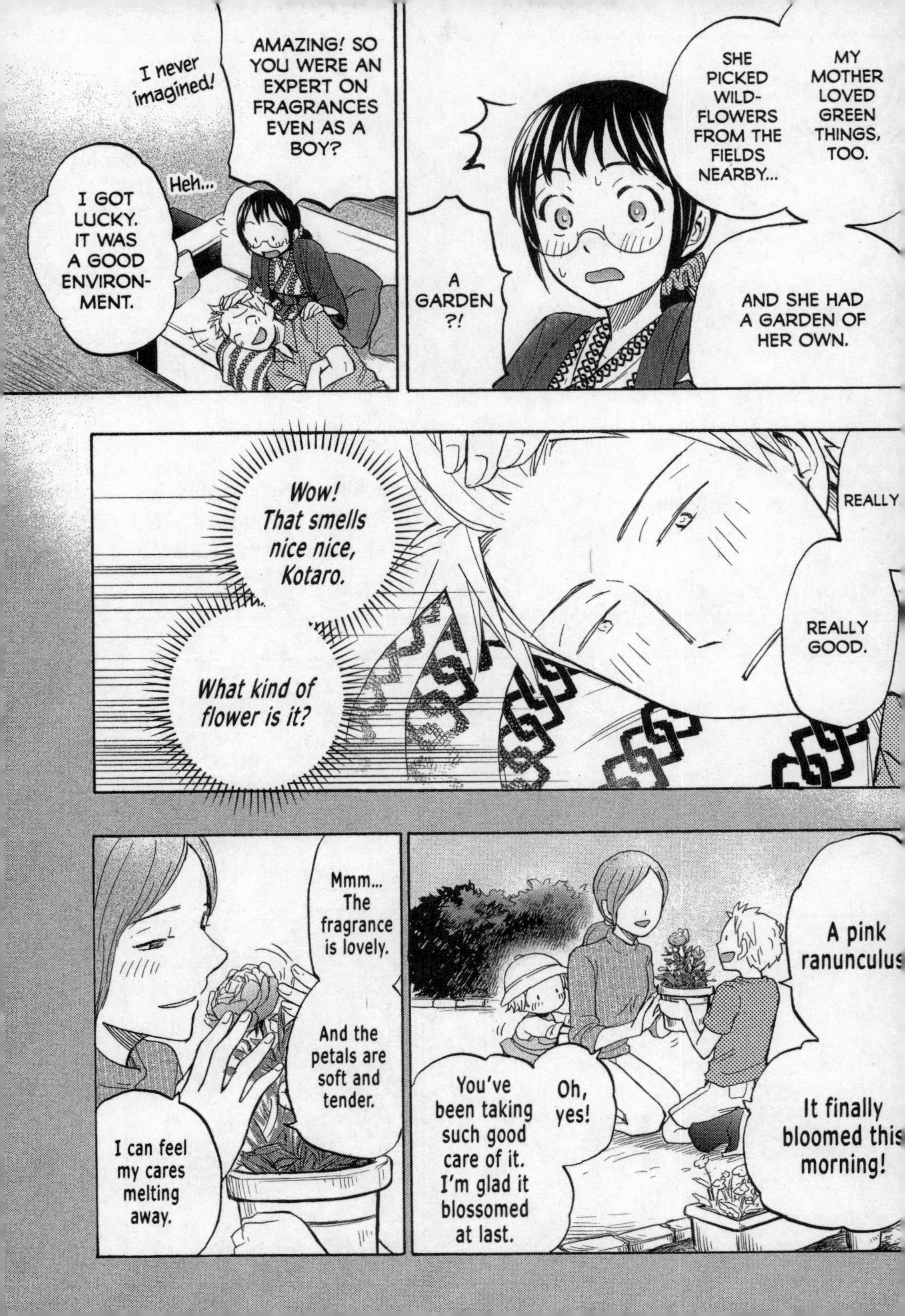
MY MOTHER LOVED GREEN THINGS, TOO.
SHE PICKED WILD-FLOWERS FROM THE FIELDS NEARBY...
AND SHE HAD A GARDEN OF HER OWN.
A GARDEN?!
AMAZING! SO YOU WERE AN EXPERT ON FRAGRANCES EVEN AS A BOY?
I never imagined!
Heh...
I GOT LUCKY. IT WAS A GOOD ENVIRON-MENT.
REALLY
REALLY GOOD.
Wow! That smells nice nice, Kotaro.
What kind of flower is it?
A pink ranunculus
It finally bloomed this morning!
Oh, yes!
You've been taking such good care of it. I'm glad it blossomed at last.
Mmm... The fragrance is lovely.
And the petals are soft and tender.
I can feel my cares melting away.

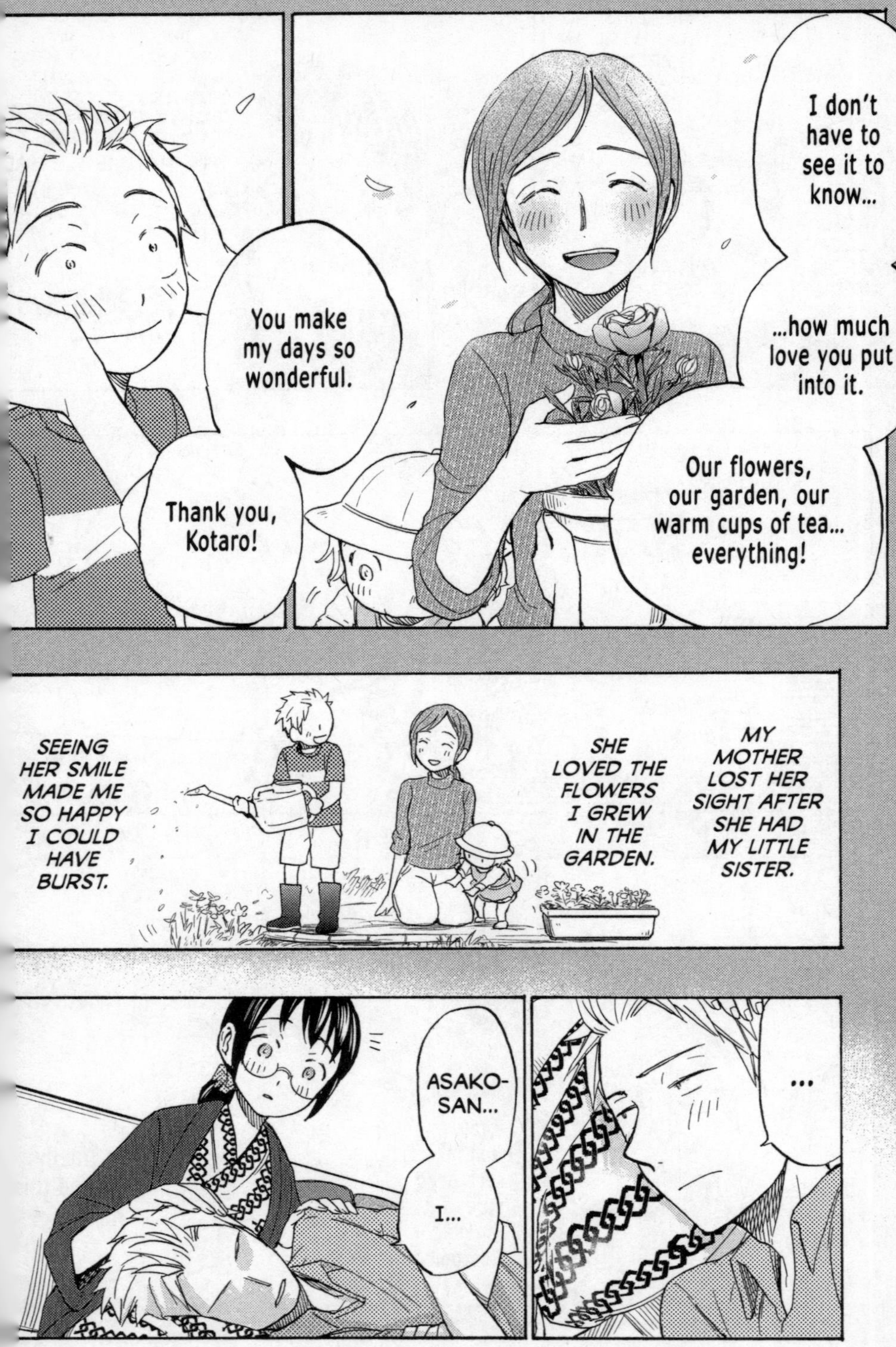
I don't have to see it to know...
...how much love you put into it.
Our flowers, our garden, our warm cups of tea... everything!
You make my days so wonderful.
Thank you, Kotaro!
MY MOTHER LOST HER SIGHT AFTER SHE HAD MY LITTLE SISTER.
SHE LOVED THE FLOWERS I GREW IN THE GARDEN.
SEEING HER SMILE MADE ME SO HAPPY I COULD HAVE BURST.
...
ASAKO-SAN...
I...

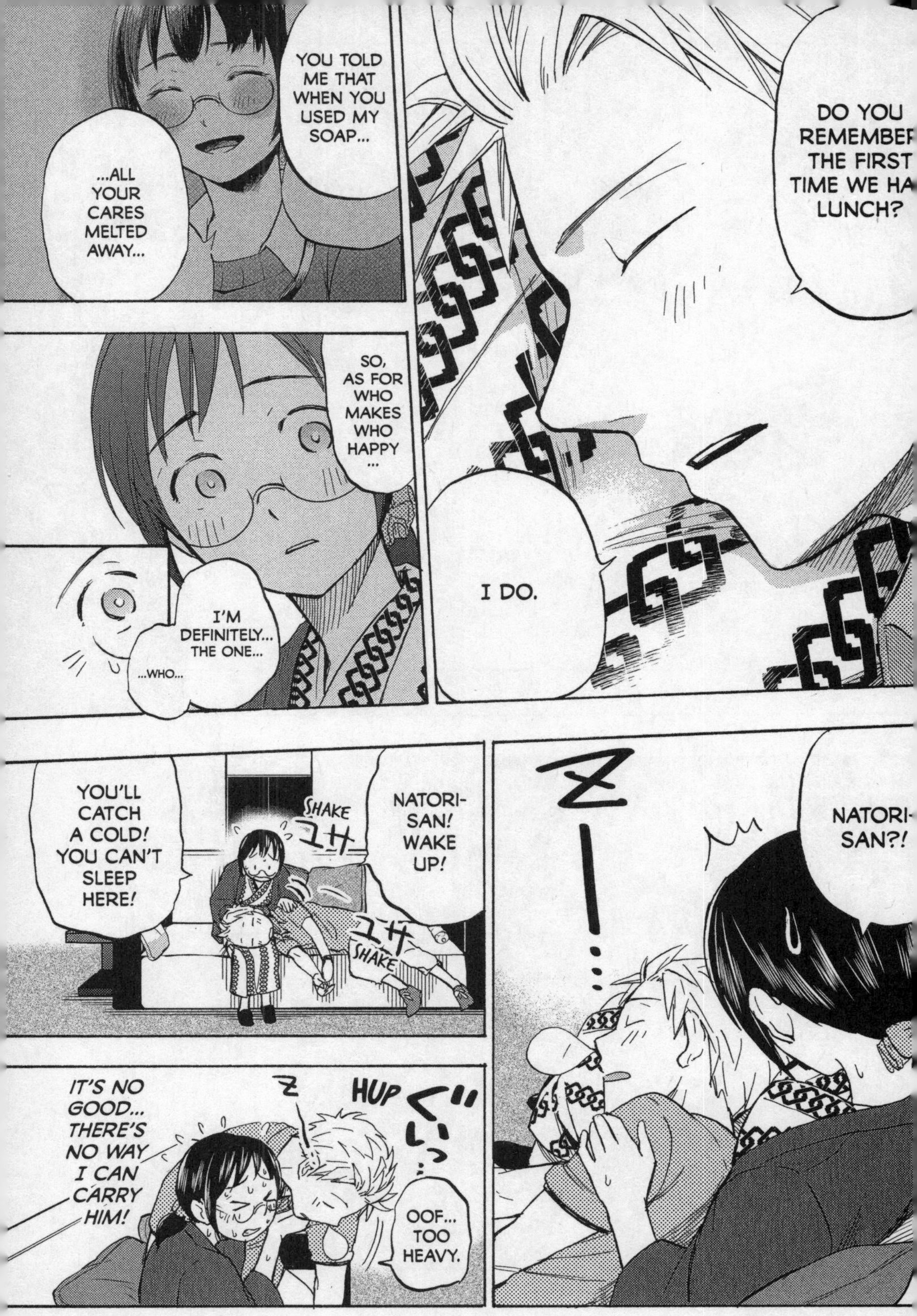
DO YOU REMEMBER THE FIRST TIME WE HA LUNCH?
I DO.
YOU TOLD ME THAT WHEN YOU USED MY SOAP...
...ALL YOUR CARES MELTED AWAY...
SO, AS FOR WHO MAKES WHO HAPPY ...
I'M DEFINITELY... THE ONE...
...WHO...
NATORI-SAN?!
Z
NATORI-SAN! WAKE UP!
SHAKE
YOU'LL CATCH A COLD! YOU CAN'T SLEEP HERE!
SHAKE
HUP
Z
OOF... TOO HEAVY.
IT'S NO GOOD... THERE'S NO WAY I CAN CARRY HIM!

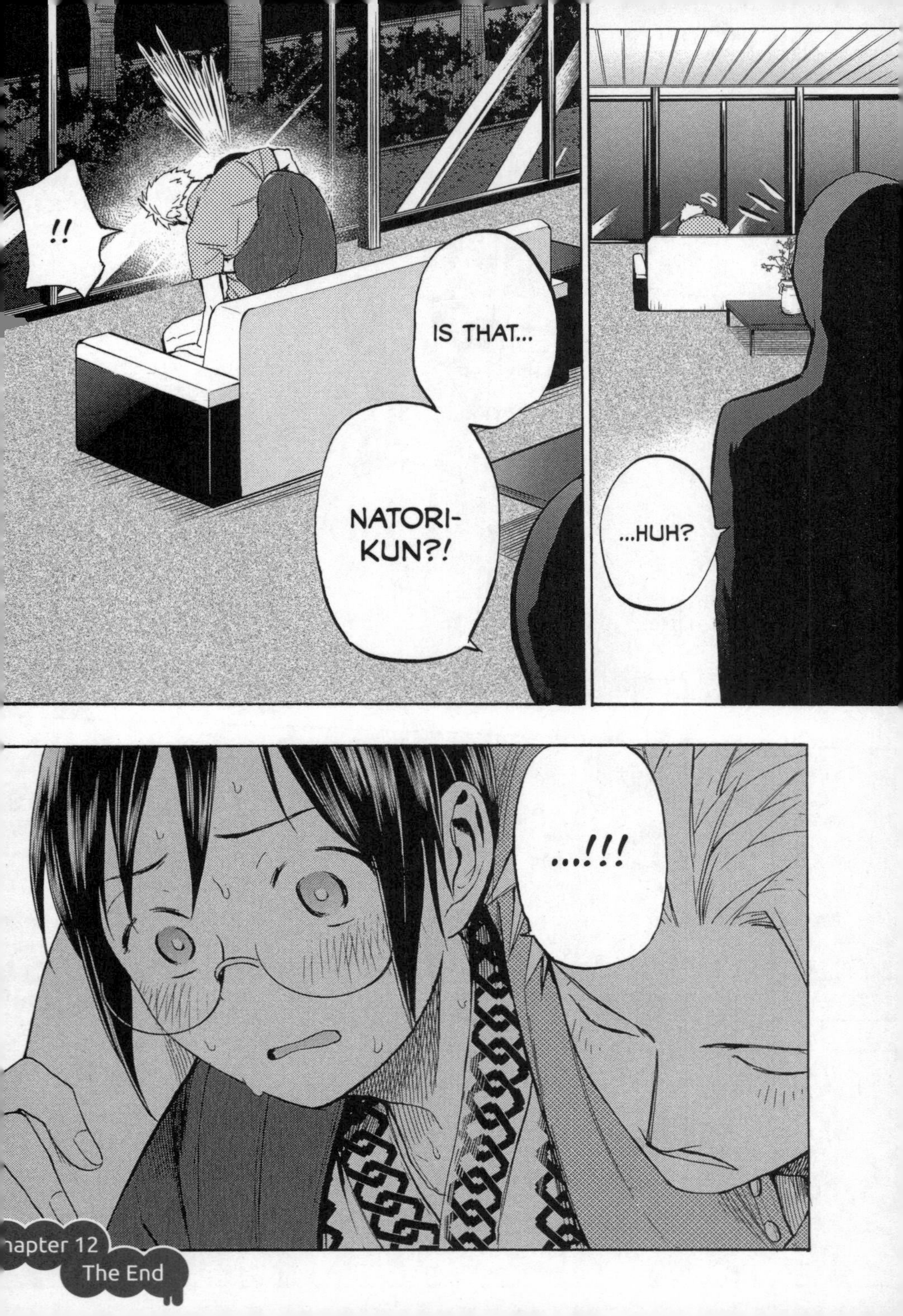
...HUH?
!!
IS THAT...
NATORI-KUN?!
...!!!
hapter 12
The End

BONUS! ROUGH DRAFT THEATER! NATORI-SAN PROTOTYPE

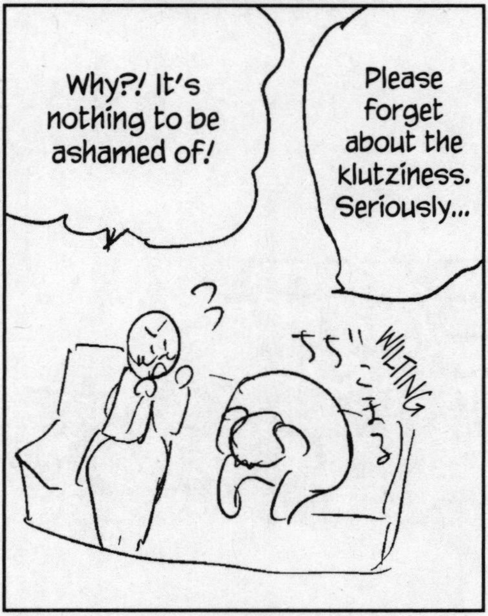
Please forget about the klutziness. Seriously...
Why?! It's nothing to be ashamed of!
WILTING
ちぢこまる

SWEAT AND SOAP

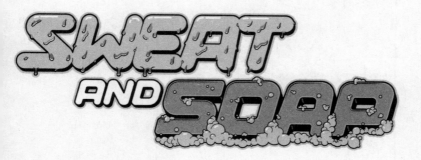

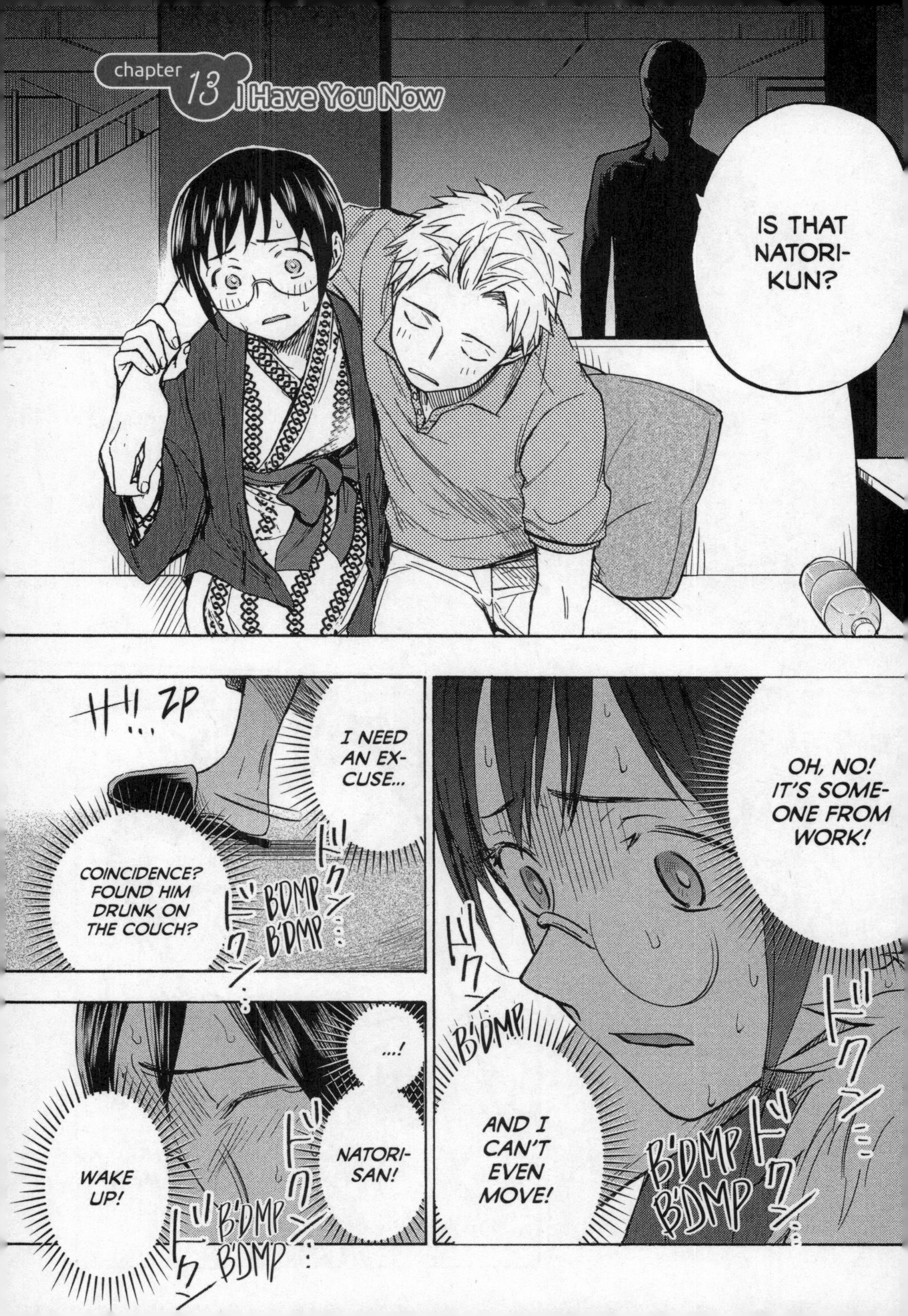
chapter 13 I Have You Now
IS THAT NATORI-KUN?
OH, NO! IT'S SOME-ONE FROM WORK!
B'DMP
AND I CAN'T EVEN MOVE!
B'DMP B'DMP
ZP
I NEED AN EX-CUSE...
COINCIDENCE? FOUND HIM DRUNK ON THE COUCH?
B'DMP B'DMP
...!
NATORI-SAN!
WAKE UP!
B'DMP B'DMP

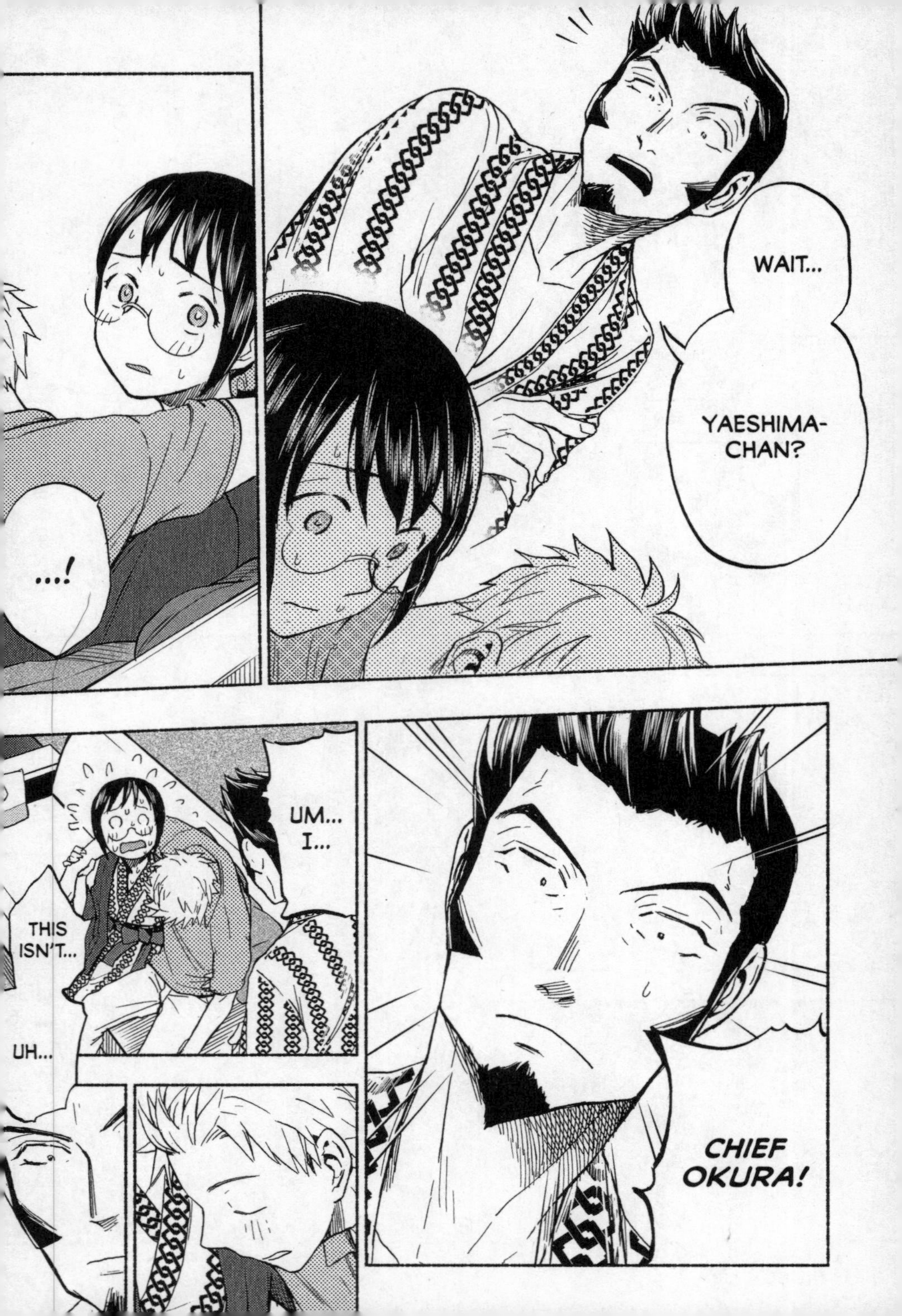
WAIT...
YAESHIMA-CHAN?
...!
CHIEF OKURA!
UM... I...
THIS ISN'T...
UH...

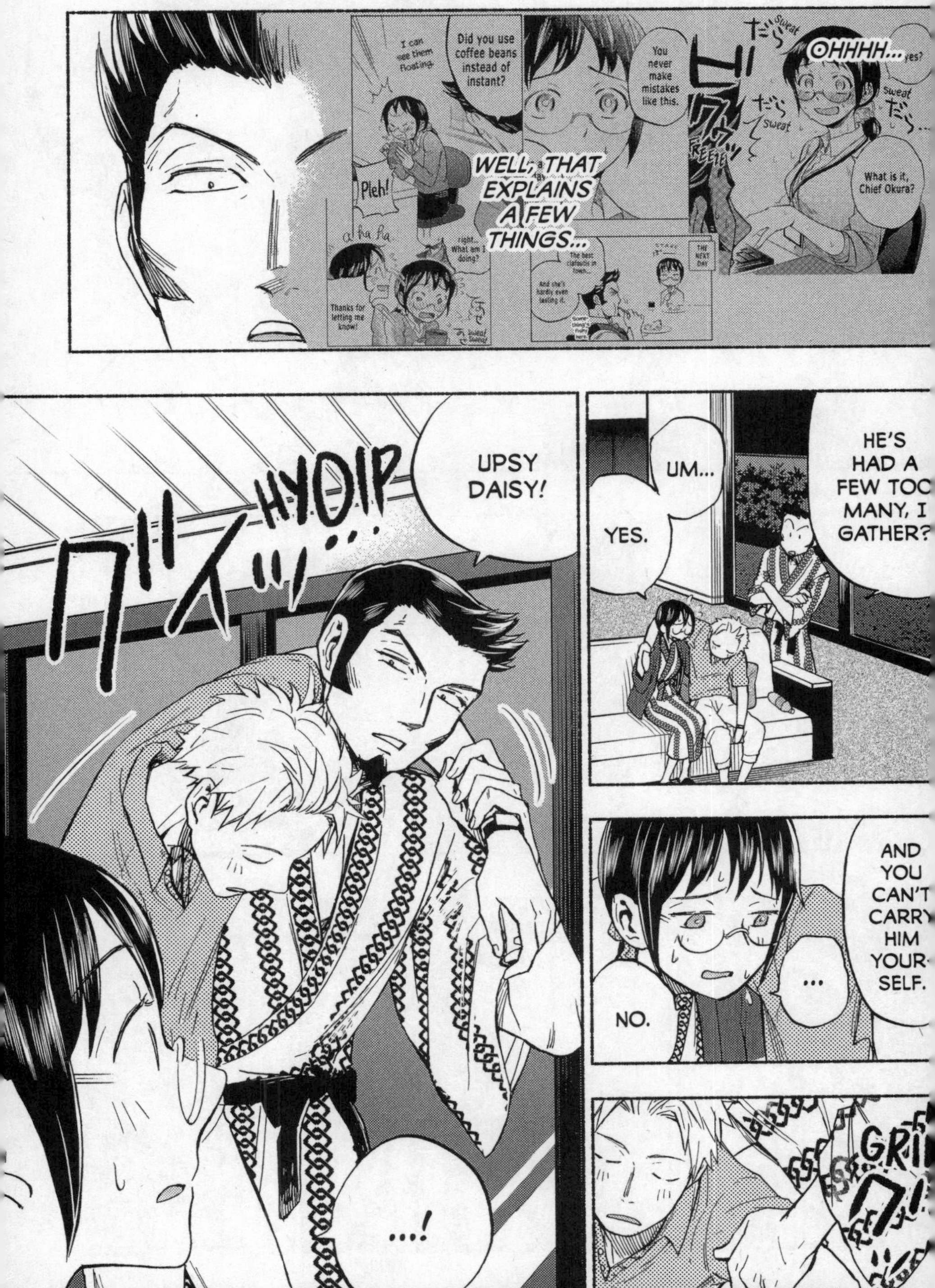
OHHHH...
yes?
Sweat
Sweat
Sweat
What is it, Chief Okura?
FREEZE
You never make mistakes like this.
Did you use coffee beans instead of instant?
I can see them floating.
Pleh!
THE NEXT DAY
The best clafoutis in town...
And she's hardly even tasting it.
Something's fishy here.
right... What am I doing?
a ha ha
Thanks for letting me know!
Sweat Sweat
WELL, THAT EXPLAINS A FEW THINGS...
HE'S HAD A FEW TOO MANY, I GATHER?
UM...
YES.
AND YOU CAN'T CARRY HIM YOURSELF.
...
NO.
UPSY DAISY!
HYOIP
...!
GRIP

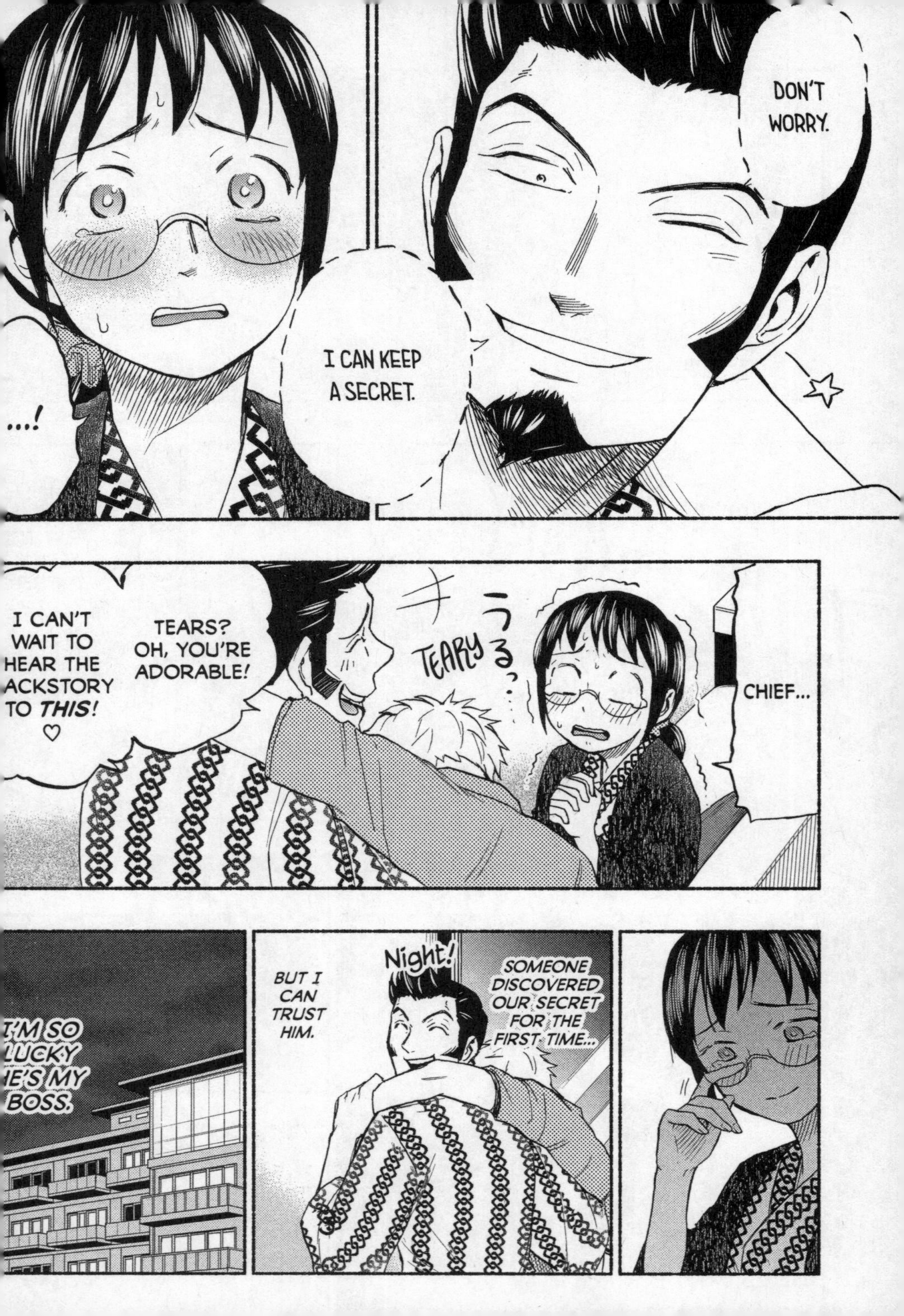
DON'T WORRY.
I CAN KEEP A SECRET.
...!
CHIEF...
うるっ
TEARY
TEARS? OH, YOU'RE ADORABLE!
I CAN'T WAIT TO HEAR THE ACKSTORY TO THIS! ♡
Night!
SOMEONE DISCOVERED OUR SECRET FOR THE FIRST TIME...
BUT I CAN TRUST HIM.
I'M SO LUCKY HE'S MY BOSS.

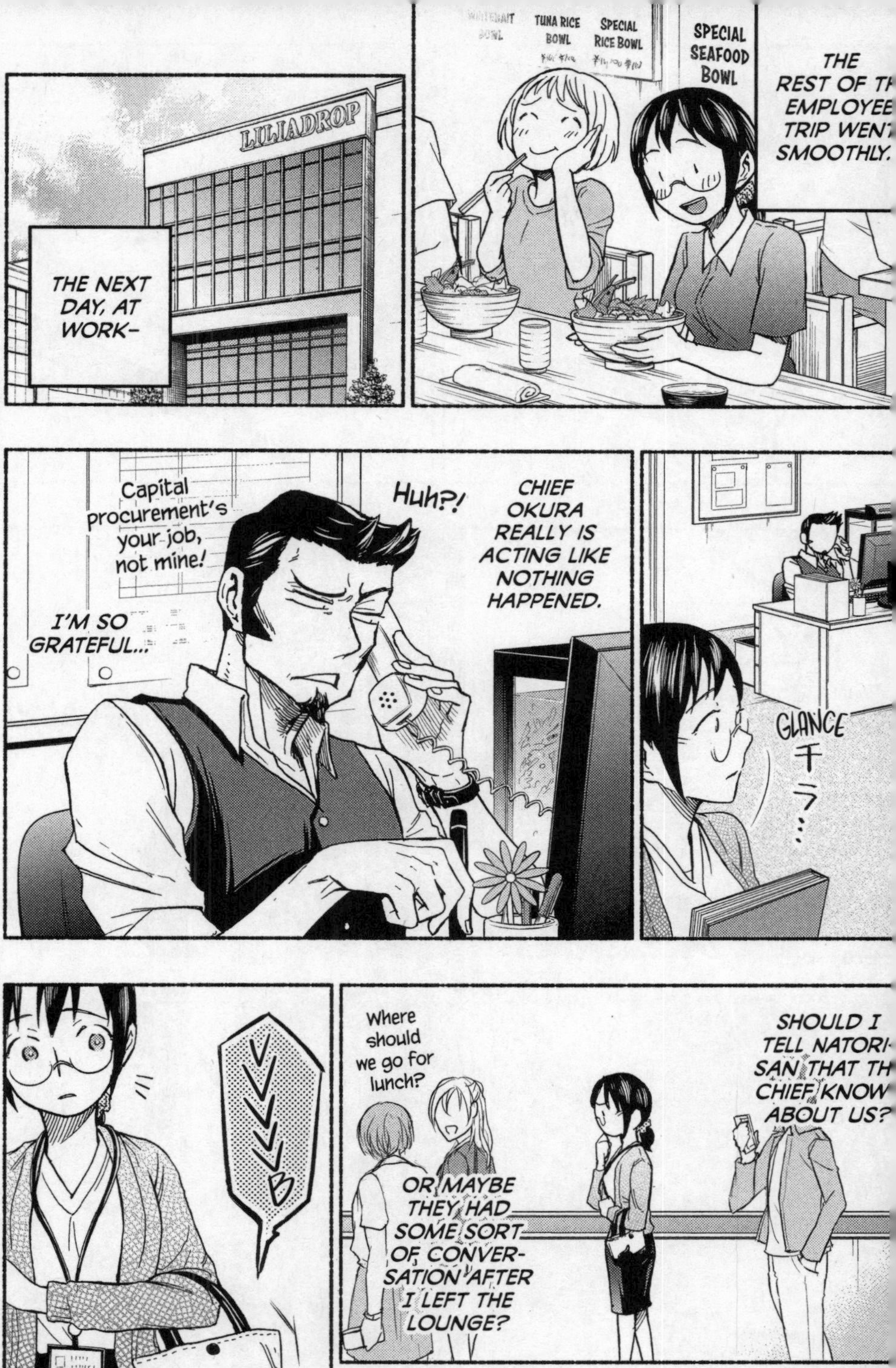
WHITEBAIT BOWL
TUNA RICE BOWL
SPECIAL RICE BOWL
SPECIAL SEAFOOD BOWL
THE REST OF TH EMPLOYEE TRIP WENT SMOOTHLY.
LILIADROP
THE NEXT DAY, AT WORK–
GLANCE
チラ…
CHIEF OKURA REALLY IS ACTING LIKE NOTHING HAPPENED.
Huh?!
Capital procurement's your job, not mine!
I'M SO GRATEFUL...
SHOULD I TELL NATORI-SAN THAT TH CHIEF KNOW ABOUT US?
Where should we go for lunch?
OR MAYBE THEY HAD SOME SORT OF CONVER-SATION AFTER I LEFT THE LOUNGE?
VVVVVB

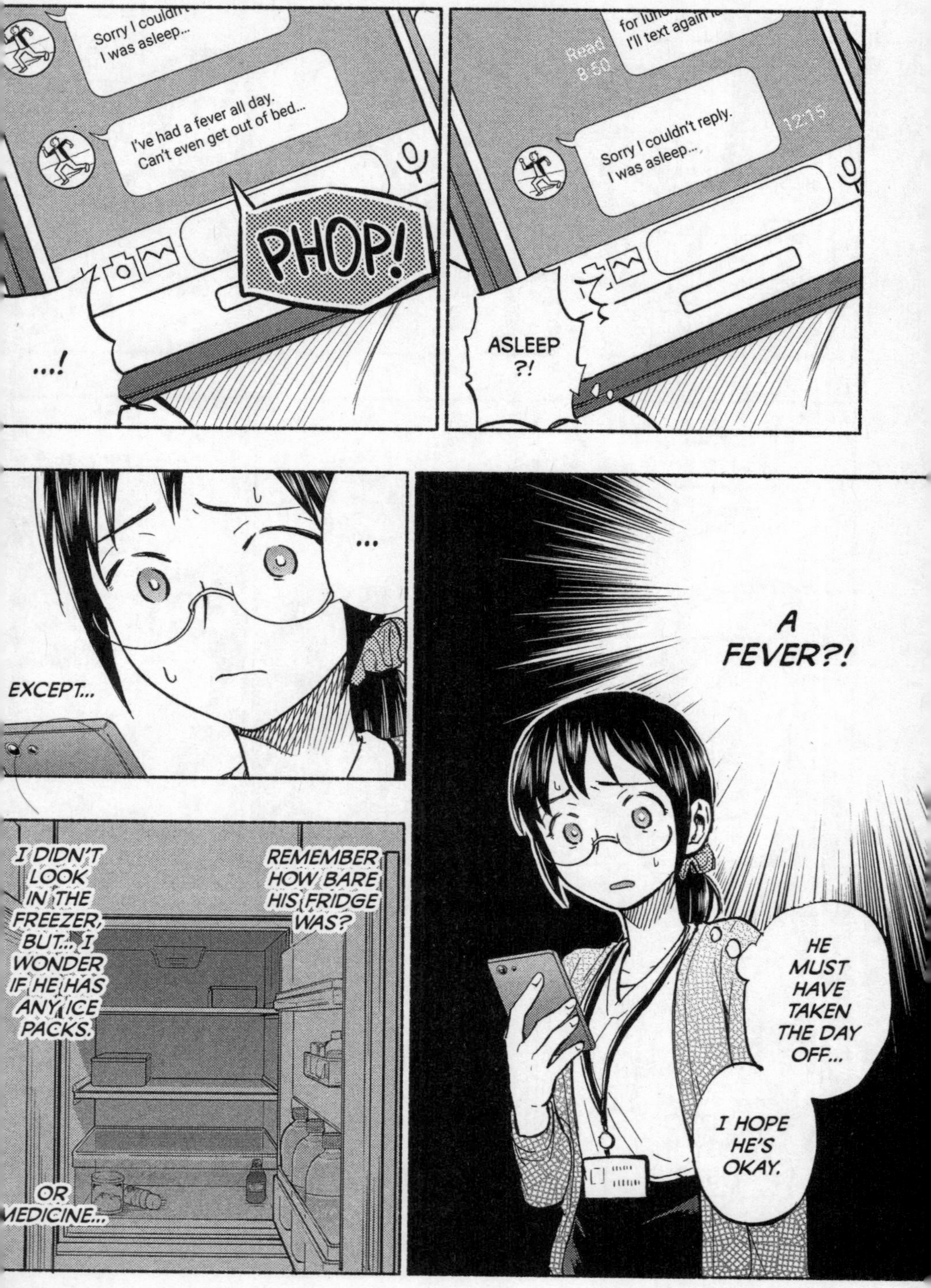
Read 8:50
I'll text again
Sorry I couldn't reply. I was asleep...
12:15
ASLEEP ?!
I was asleep...
I've had a fever all day. Can't even get out of bed...
PHOP!
...!
A FEVER?!
HE MUST HAVE TAKEN THE DAY OFF...
I HOPE HE'S OKAY.
...
EXCEPT...
REMEMBER HOW BARE HIS FRIDGE WAS?
I DIDN'T LOOK IN THE FREEZER, BUT... I WONDER IF HE HAS ANY ICE PACKS.
OR MEDICINE...

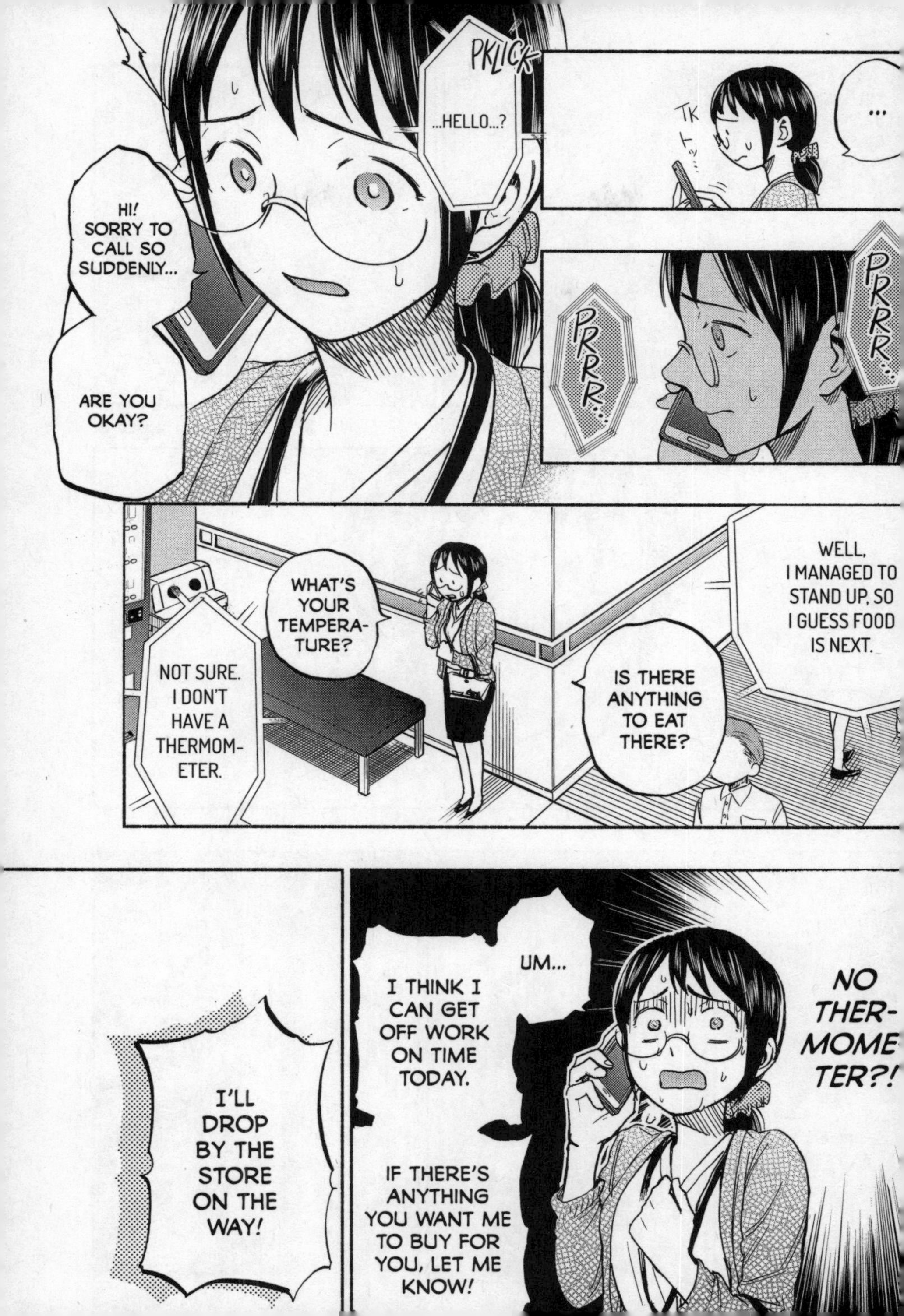
...
TK
PRRR
PRRR
PKLICK
...HELLO...?
HI! SORRY TO CALL SO SUDDENLY...
ARE YOU OKAY?
WELL, I MANAGED TO STAND UP, SO I GUESS FOOD IS NEXT.
IS THERE ANYTHING TO EAT THERE?
WHAT'S YOUR TEMPERA-TURE?
NOT SURE. I DON'T HAVE A THERMOM-ETER.
NO THER-MOMETER?!
UM...
I THINK I CAN GET OFF WORK ON TIME TODAY.
IF THERE'S ANYTHING YOU WANT ME TO BUY FOR YOU, LET ME KNOW!
I'LL DROP BY THE STORE ON THE WAY!

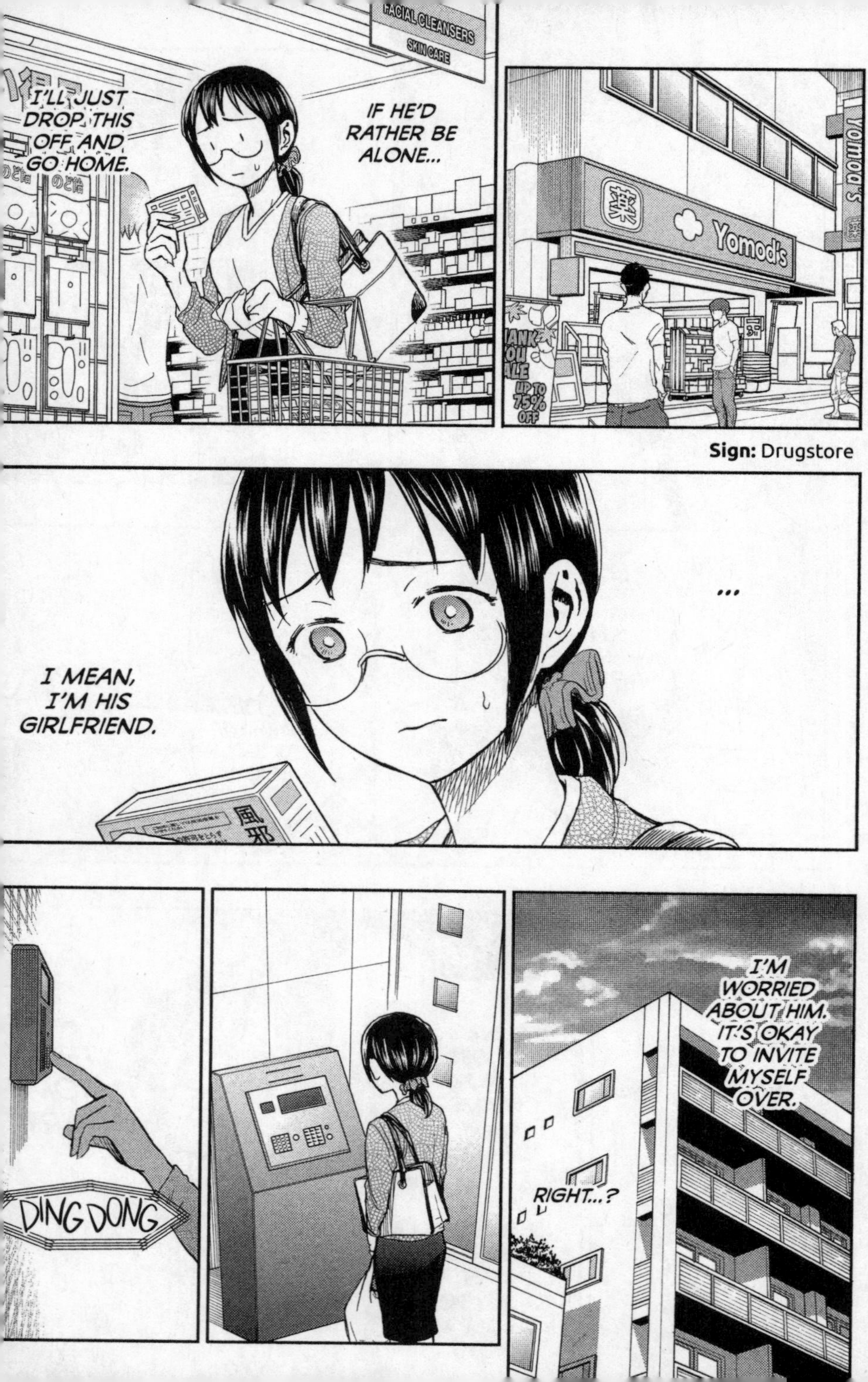

薬
Yomod's
Yomod's
UP TO 75% OFF
FACIAL CLEANSERS
SKIN CARE
IF HE'D RATHER BE ALONE...
I'LL JUST DROP THIS OFF AND GO HOME.
...
I MEAN, I'M HIS GIRLFRIEND.
風邪
I'M WORRIED ABOUT HIM. IT'S OKAY TO INVITE MYSELF OVER.
RIGHT...?
DING DONG

Sign: Drugstore

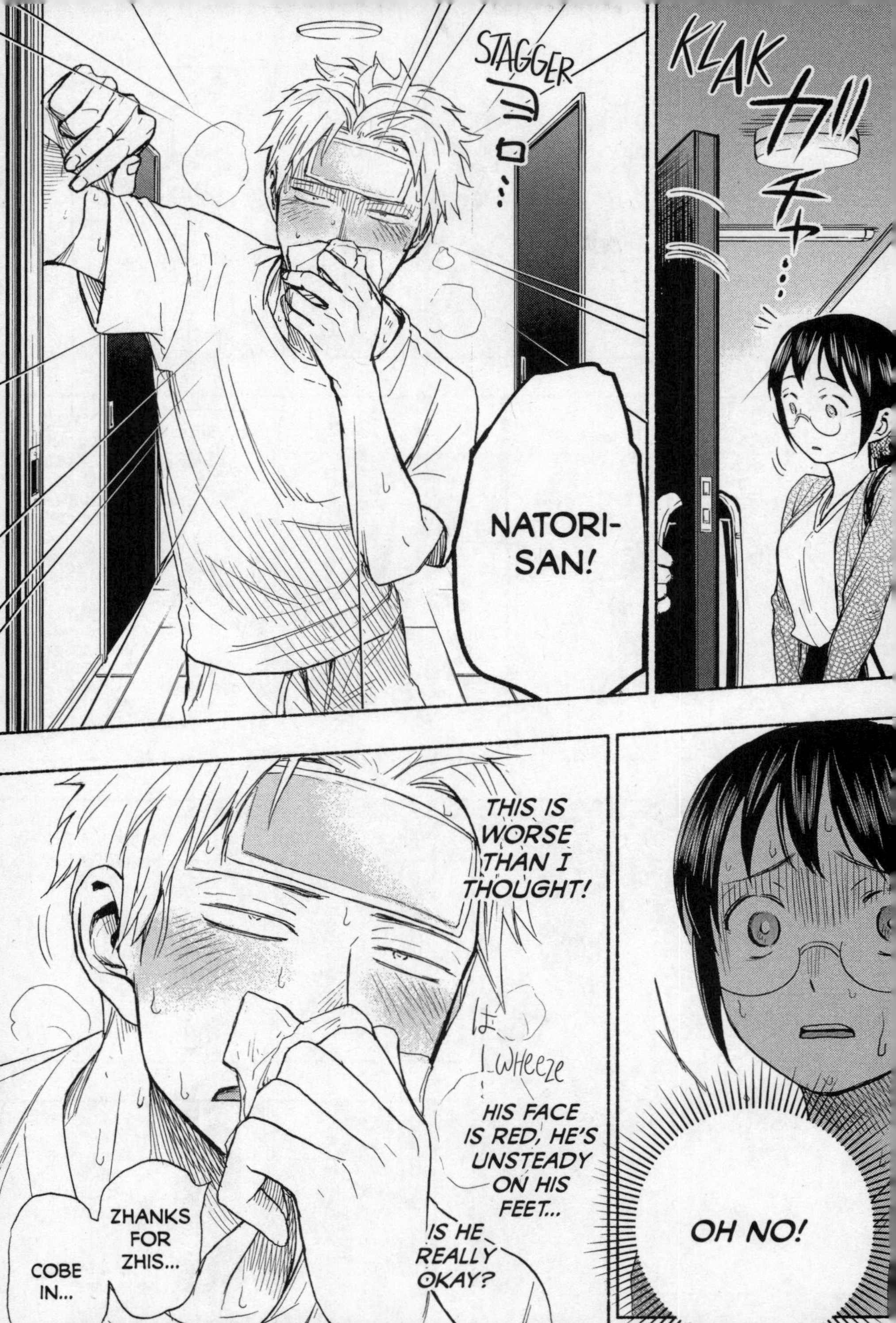
KLAK
カチャ…
STAGGER
ヨロ…
NATORI-SAN!
OH NO!
THIS IS WORSE THAN I THOUGHT!
は
WHEEZE
HIS FACE IS RED, HE'S UNSTEADY ON HIS FEET...
IS HE REALLY OKAY?
ZHANKS FOR ZHIS...
COBE IN...

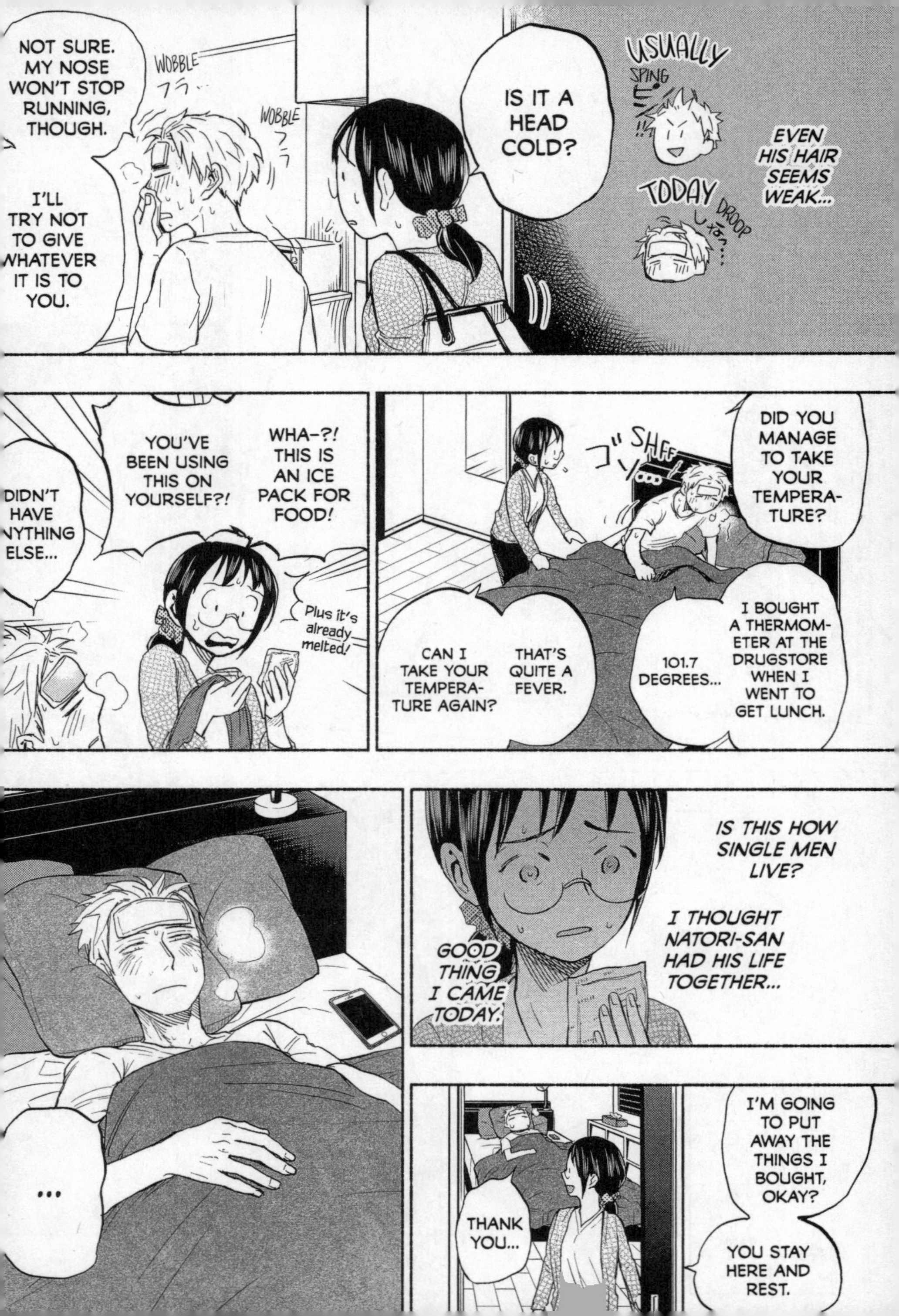
USUALLY
SPING
TODAY
DROOP
EVEN HIS HAIR SEEMS WEAK...
IS IT A HEAD COLD?
NOT SURE. MY NOSE WON'T STOP RUNNING, THOUGH.
WOBBLE
WOBBLE
I'LL TRY NOT TO GIVE WHATEVER IT IS TO YOU.
DID YOU MANAGE TO TAKE YOUR TEMPERA-TURE?
SHFF
I BOUGHT A THERMOM-ETER AT THE DRUGSTORE WHEN I WENT TO GET LUNCH.
101.7 DEGREES...
THAT'S QUITE A FEVER.
CAN I TAKE YOUR TEMPERA-TURE AGAIN?
WHA-?! THIS IS AN ICE PACK FOR FOOD!
YOU'VE BEEN USING THIS ON YOURSELF?!
DIDN'T HAVE NYTHING ELSE...
Plus it's already melted!
IS THIS HOW SINGLE MEN LIVE?
I THOUGHT NATORI-SAN HAD HIS LIFE TOGETHER...
GOOD THING I CAME TODAY.
I'M GOING TO PUT AWAY THE THINGS I BOUGHT, OKAY?
YOU STAY HERE AND REST.
THANK YOU...
...

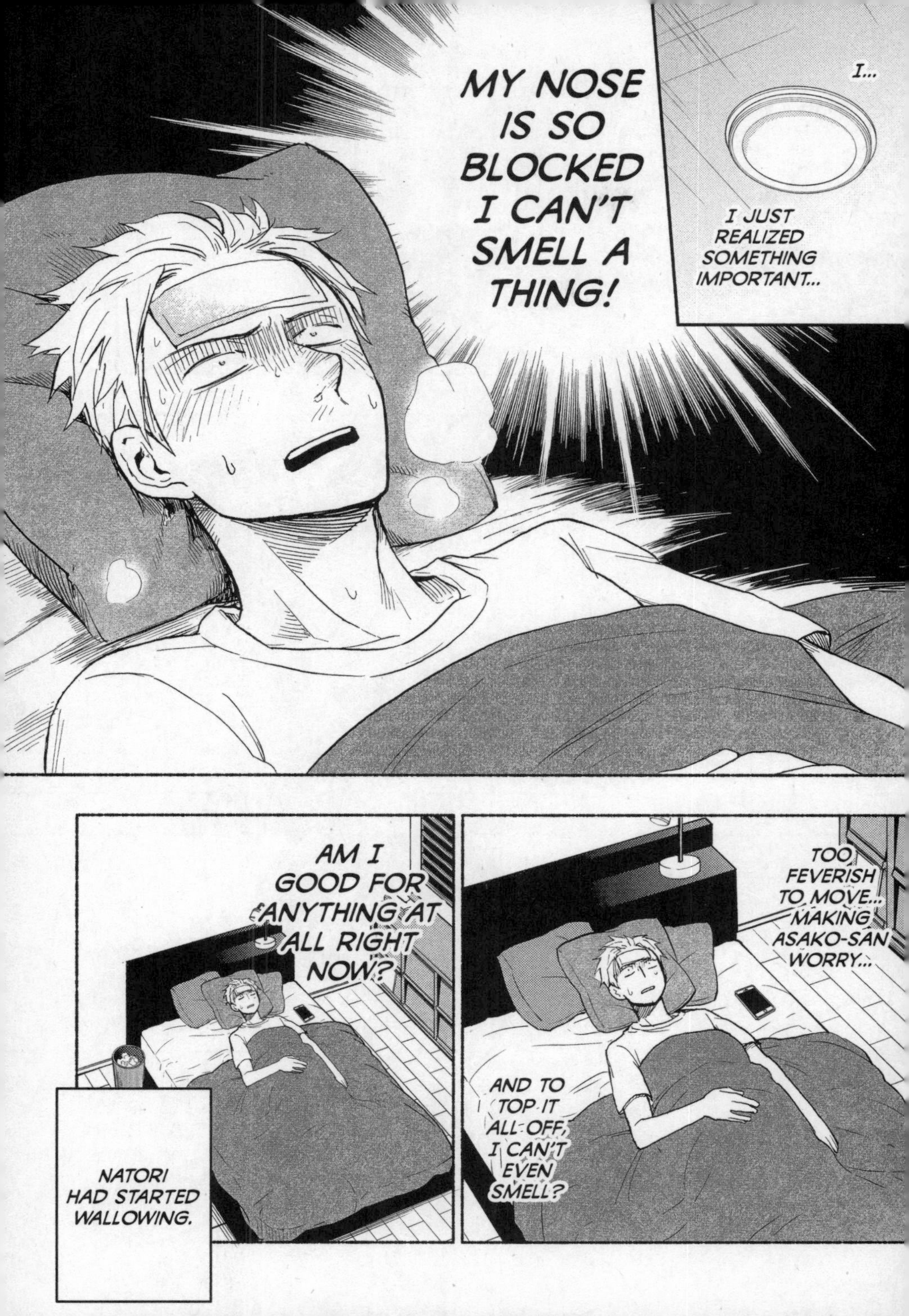
I...
I JUST REALIZED SOMETHING IMPORTANT...
MY NOSE IS SO BLOCKED I CAN'T SMELL A THING!
TOO FEVERISH TO MOVE... MAKING ASAKO-SAN WORRY...
AND TO TOP IT ALL OFF, I CAN'T EVEN SMELL?
AM I GOOD FOR ANYTHING AT ALL RIGHT NOW?
NATORI HAD STARTED WALLOWING.

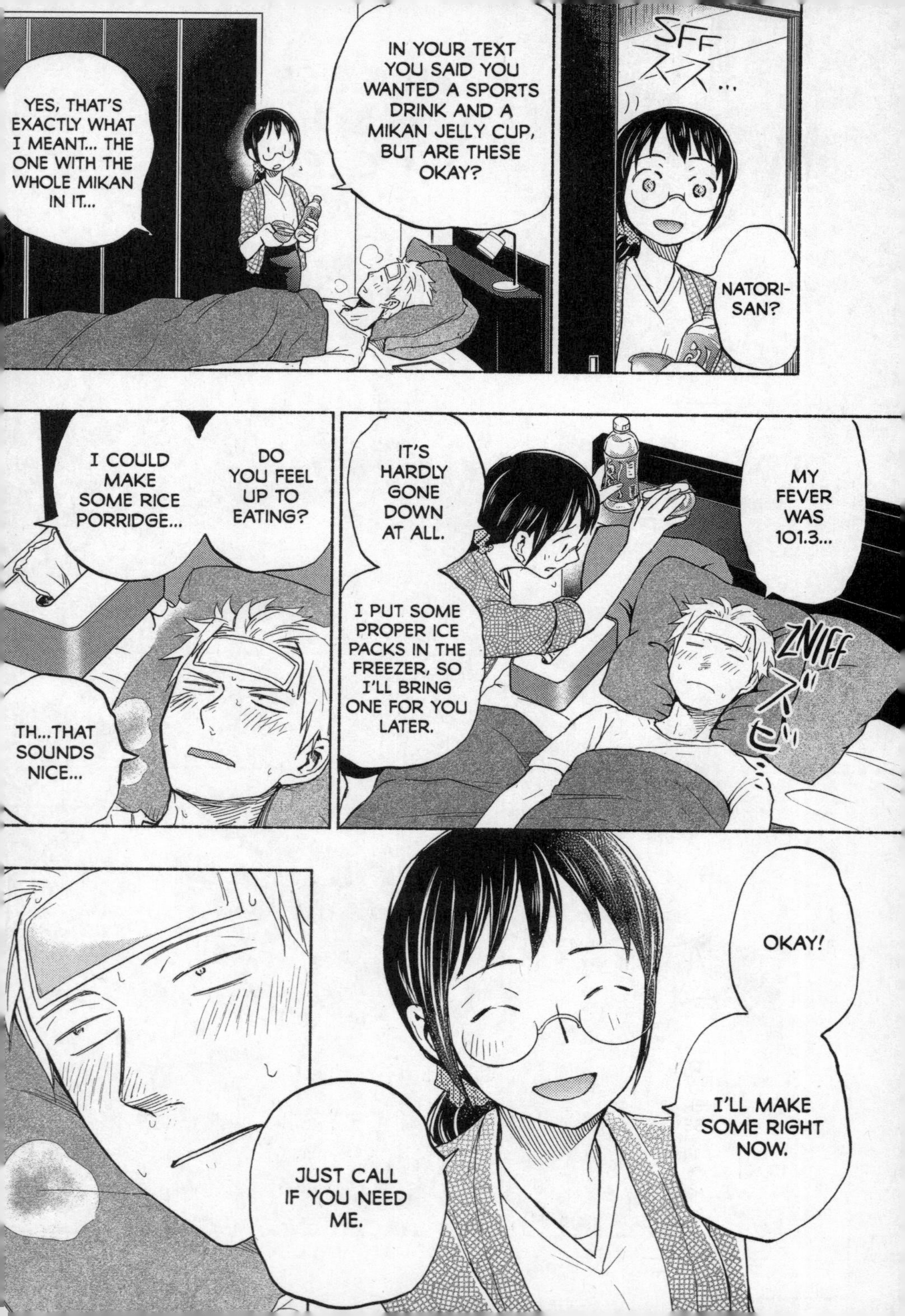

SFF
NATORI-SAN?
IN YOUR TEXT YOU SAID YOU WANTED A SPORTS DRINK AND A MIKAN JELLY CUP, BUT ARE THESE OKAY?
YES, THAT'S EXACTLY WHAT I MEANT... THE ONE WITH THE WHOLE MIKAN IN IT...
MY FEVER WAS 101.3...
ZNIFF
IT'S HARDLY GONE DOWN AT ALL.
I PUT SOME PROPER ICE PACKS IN THE FREEZER, SO I'LL BRING ONE FOR YOU LATER.
DO YOU FEEL UP TO EATING?
I COULD MAKE SOME RICE PORRIDGE...
TH...THAT SOUNDS NICE...
OKAY!
I'LL MAKE SOME RIGHT NOW.
JUST CALL IF YOU NEED ME.

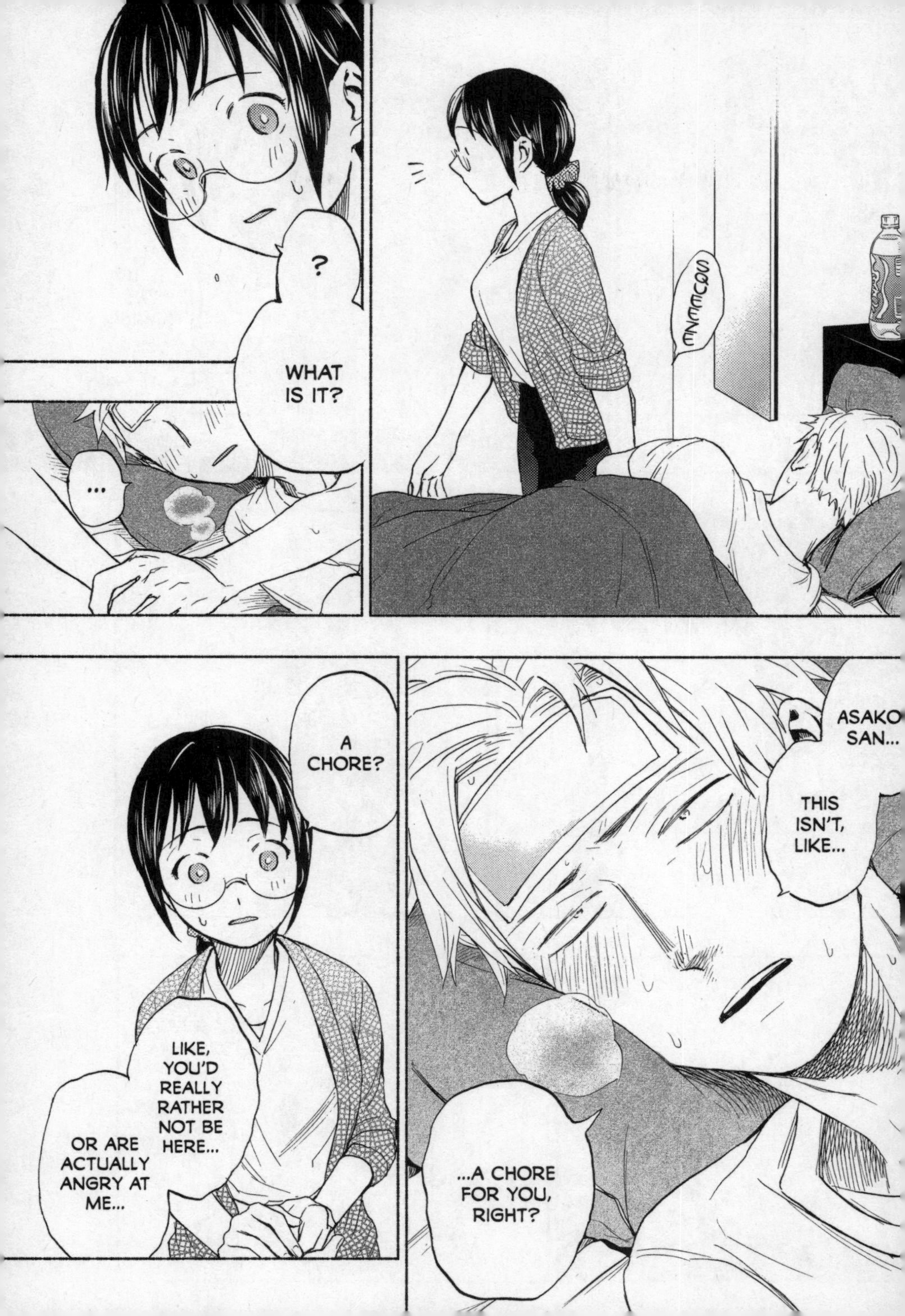
SQUEEEEE
?
WHAT IS IT?
...
ASAKO SAN...
THIS ISN'T, LIKE...
...A CHORE FOR YOU, RIGHT?
A CHORE?
LIKE, YOU'D REALLY RATHER NOT BE HERE...
OR ARE ACTUALLY ANGRY AT ME...

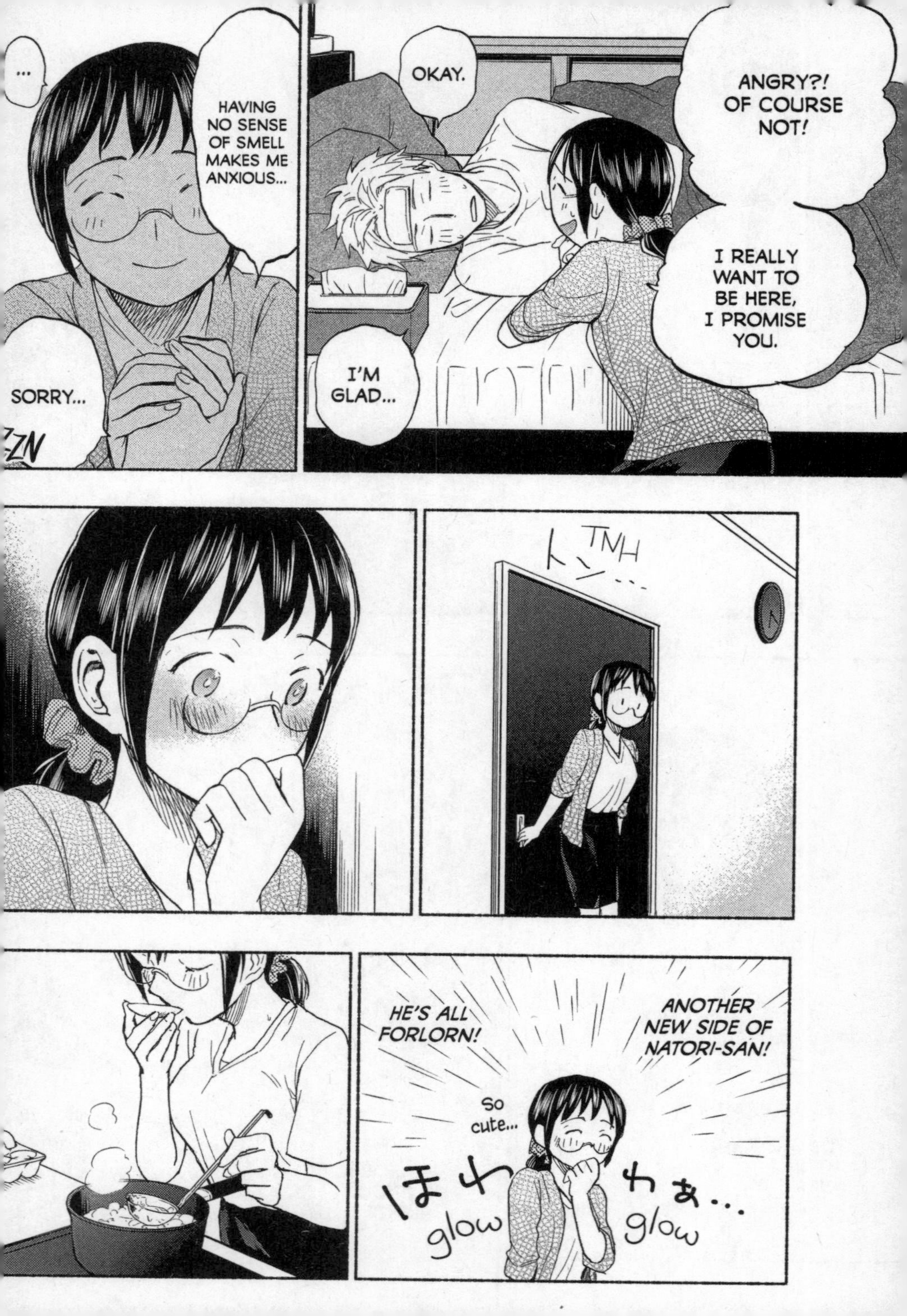
ANGRY?! OF COURSE NOT!
I REALLY WANT TO BE HERE, I PROMISE YOU.
OKAY.
I'M GLAD...
...
HAVING NO SENSE OF SMELL MAKES ME ANXIOUS...
SORRY...
ZZN
トン...
TNH
ANOTHER NEW SIDE OF NATORI-SAN!
HE'S ALL FORLORN!
So cute...
ほわ わぁ...
glow glow

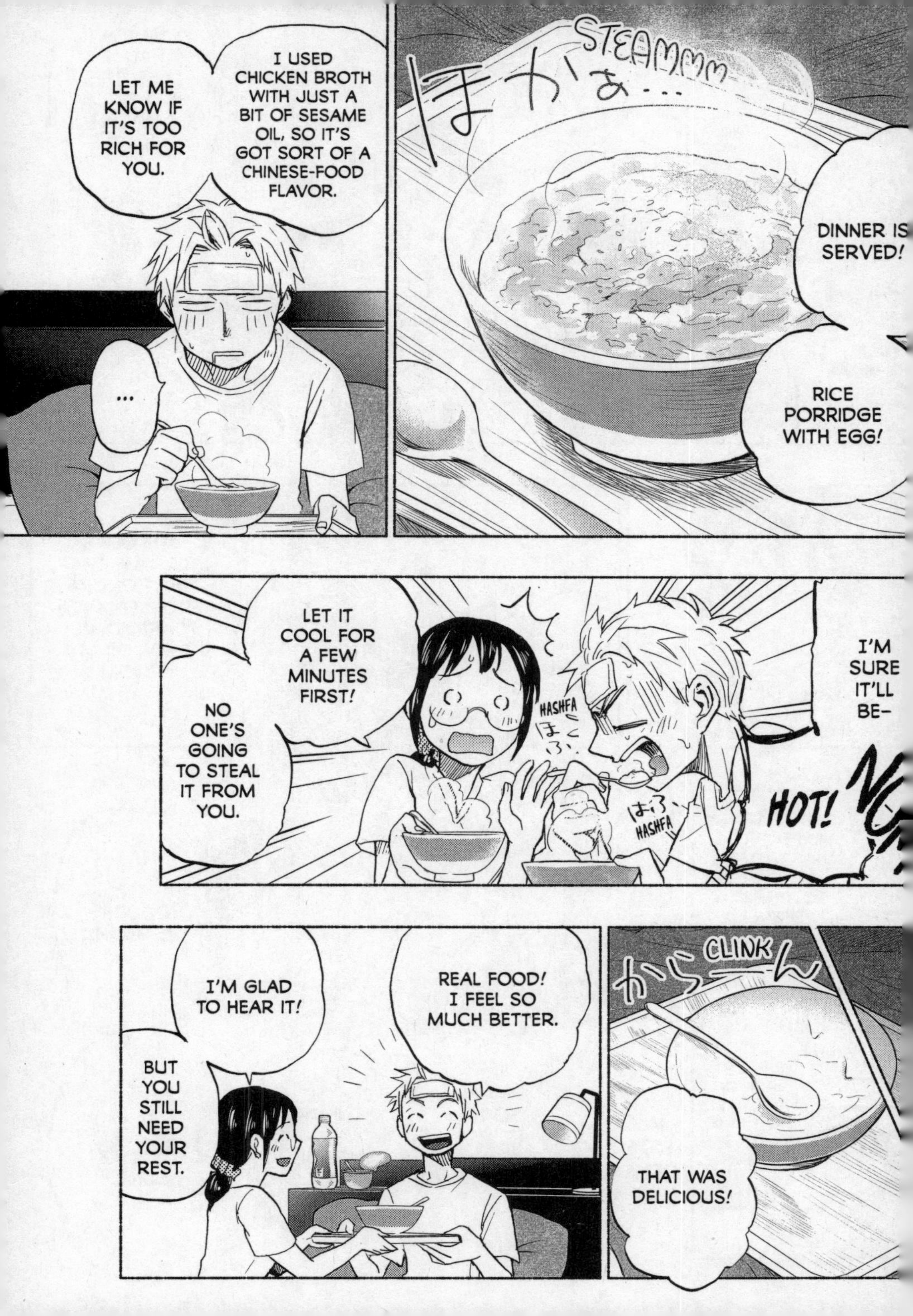
STEAMMM
ほかぁ…
DINNER IS SERVED!
RICE PORRIDGE WITH EGG!
I USED CHICKEN BROTH WITH JUST A BIT OF SESAME OIL, SO IT'S GOT SORT OF A CHINESE-FOOD FLAVOR.
LET ME KNOW IF IT'S TOO RICH FOR YOU.
...
I'M SURE IT'LL BE–
HOT!
HASHFA
HASHFA
LET IT COOL FOR A FEW MINUTES FIRST!
NO ONE'S GOING TO STEAL IT FROM YOU.
CLINK
THAT WAS DELICIOUS!
REAL FOOD! I FEEL SO MUCH BETTER.
I'M GLAD TO HEAR IT!
BUT YOU STILL NEED YOUR REST.

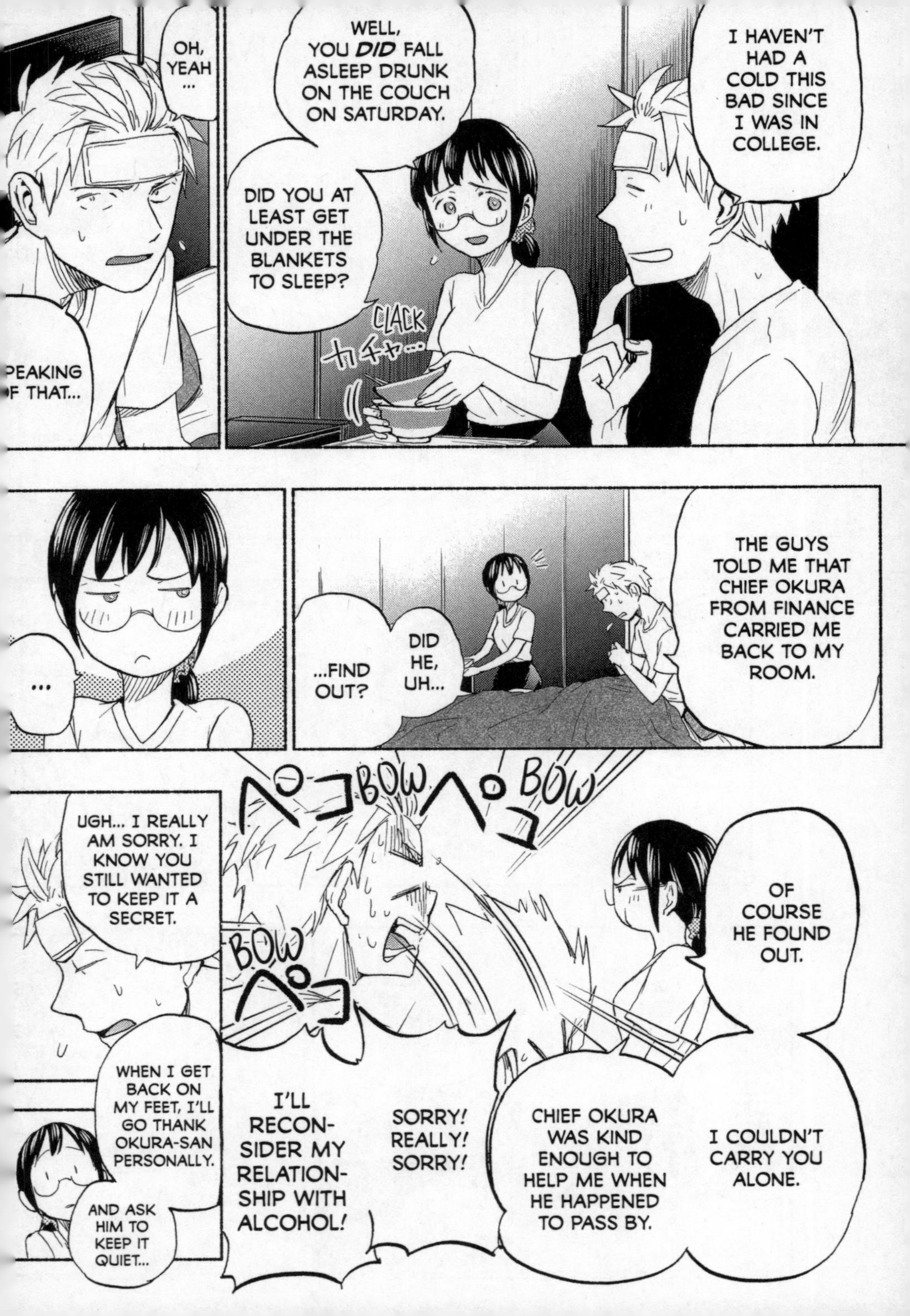
I HAVEN'T HAD A COLD THIS BAD SINCE I WAS IN COLLEGE.
WELL, YOU *DID* FALL ASLEEP DRUNK ON THE COUCH ON SATURDAY.
DID YOU AT LEAST GET UNDER THE BLANKETS TO SLEEP?
CLACK カチャ…
OH, YEAH …
PEAKING OF THAT…
THE GUYS TOLD ME THAT CHIEF OKURA FROM FINANCE CARRIED ME BACK TO MY ROOM.
DID HE, UH…
…FIND OUT?
…
OF COURSE HE FOUND OUT.
ペコ BOW ペコ BOW
I COULDN'T CARRY YOU ALONE.
CHIEF OKURA WAS KIND ENOUGH TO HELP ME WHEN HE HAPPENED TO PASS BY.
SORRY! REALLY! SORRY!
I'LL RECON-SIDER MY RELATION-SHIP WITH ALCOHOL!
BOW ペコ
UGH… I REALLY AM SORRY. I KNOW YOU STILL WANTED TO KEEP IT A SECRET.
WHEN I GET BACK ON MY FEET, I'LL GO THANK OKURA-SAN PERSONALLY.
AND ASK HIM TO KEEP IT QUIET…

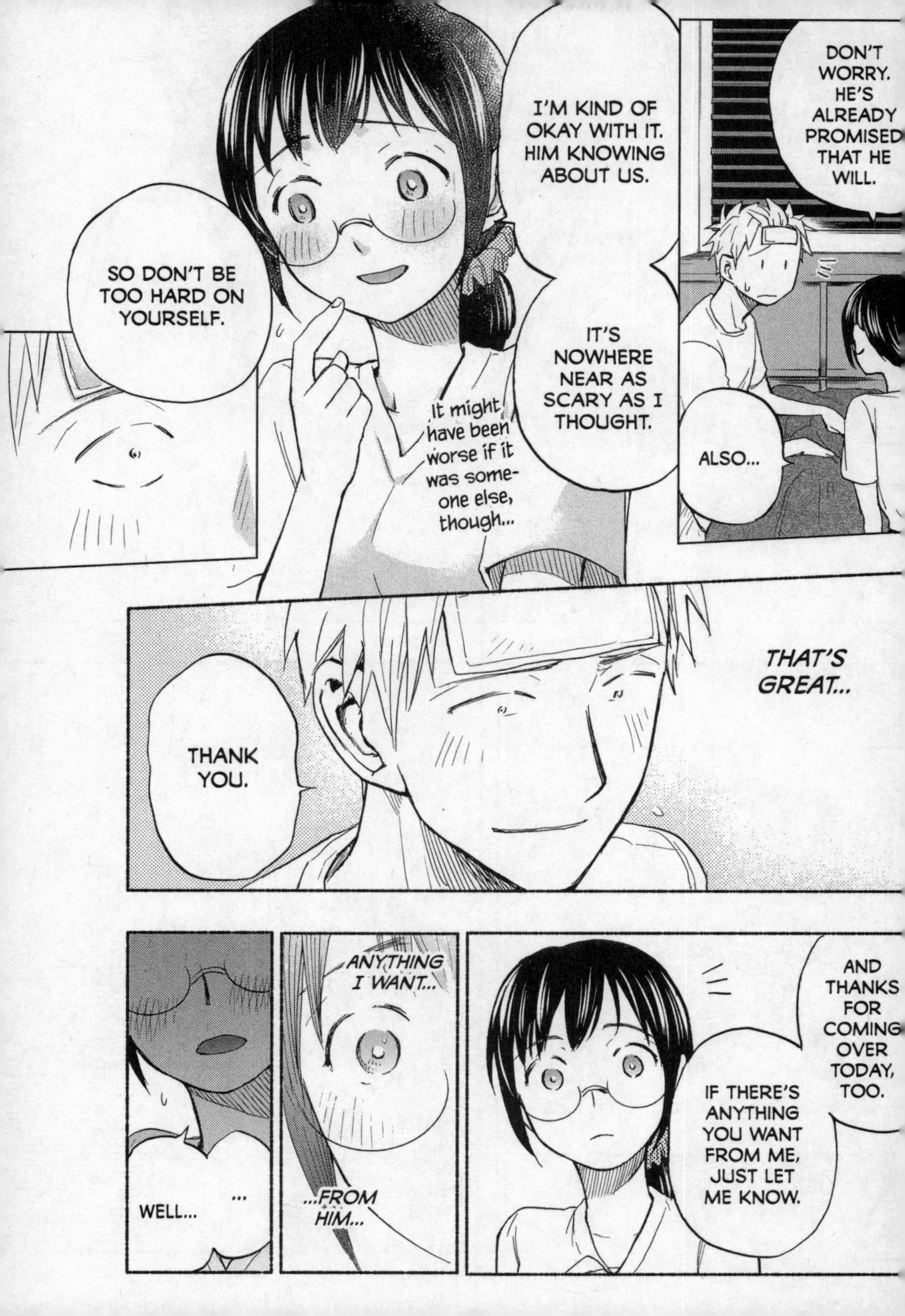
DON'T WORRY. HE'S ALREADY PROMISED THAT HE WILL.
ALSO...
I'M KIND OF OKAY WITH IT. HIM KNOWING ABOUT US.
IT'S NOWHERE NEAR AS SCARY AS I THOUGHT.
It might have been worse if it was some-one else, though...
SO DON'T BE TOO HARD ON YOURSELF.
THAT'S GREAT...
THANK YOU.
AND THANKS FOR COMING OVER TODAY, TOO.
IF THERE'S ANYTHING YOU WANT FROM ME, JUST LET ME KNOW.
ANYTHING I WANT...
...FROM HIM...
...
WELL...

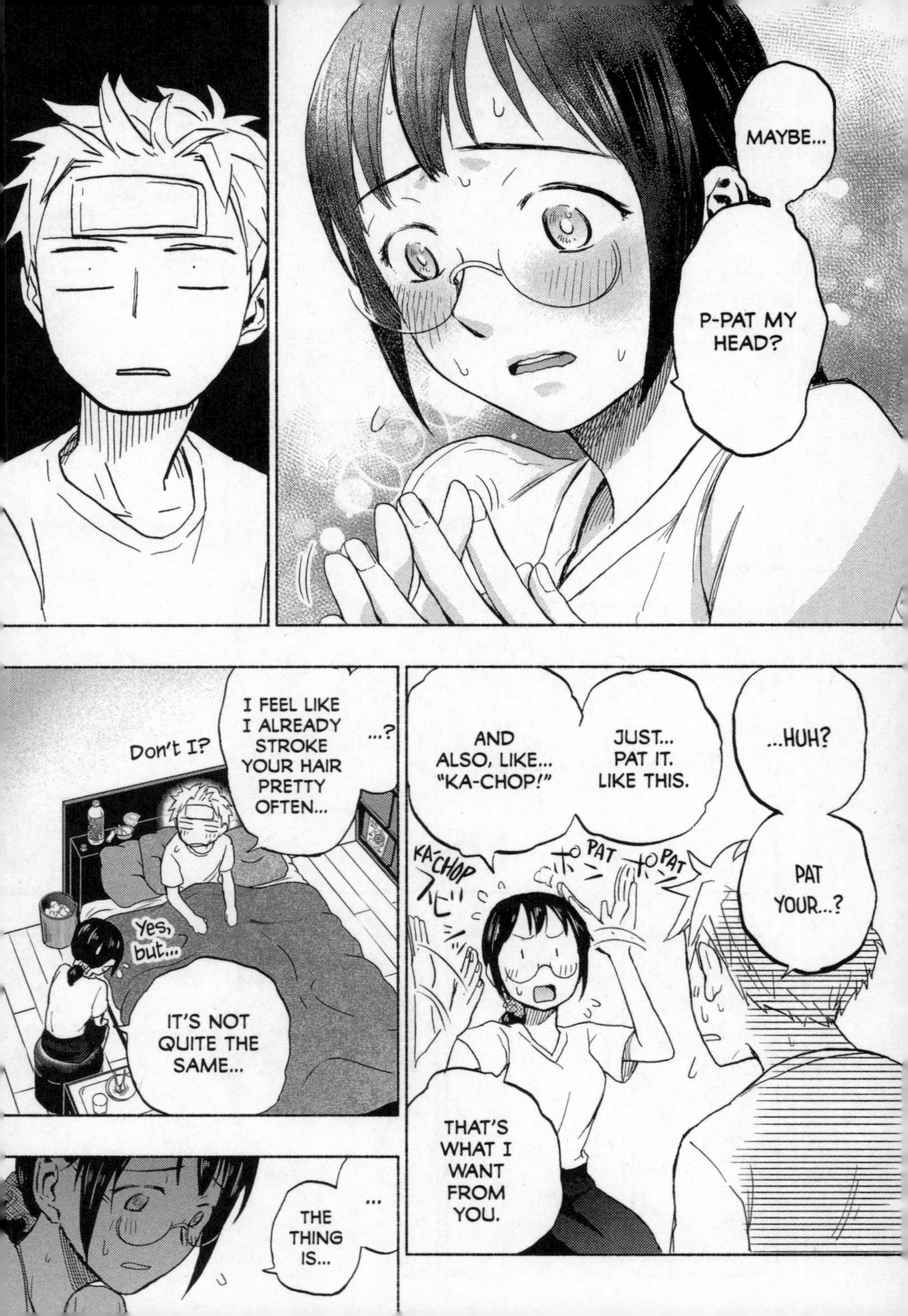
MAYBE...
P-PAT MY HEAD?
...HUH?
PAT YOUR...?
JUST... PAT IT. LIKE THIS.
PAT PAT
AND ALSO, LIKE... "KA-CHOP!"
KA-CHOP
THAT'S WHAT I WANT FROM YOU.
...?
I FEEL LIKE I ALREADY STROKE YOUR HAIR PRETTY OFTEN...
Don't I?
Yes, but...
IT'S NOT QUITE THE SAME...
...
THE THING IS...

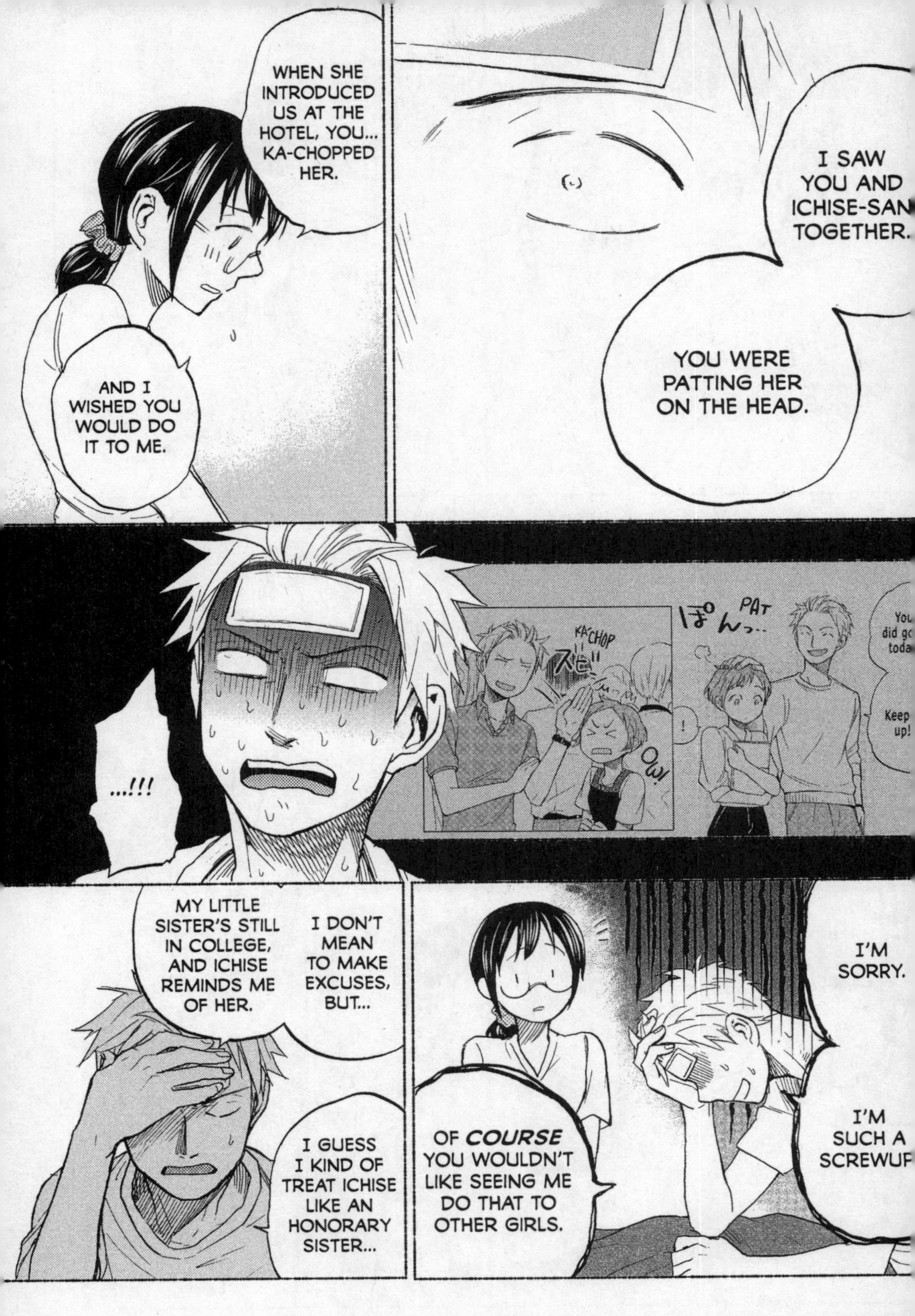

I SAW YOU AND ICHISE-SAN TOGETHER.
YOU WERE PATTING HER ON THE HEAD.
WHEN SHE INTRODUCED US AT THE HOTEL, YOU... KA-CHOPPED HER.
AND I WISHED YOU WOULD DO IT TO ME.
You did go toda
Keep up!
ぽんっ
PAT
!
KA-CHOP
ズビ
OW!
...!!!
I'M SORRY.
I'M SUCH A SCREWU
OF *COURSE* YOU WOULDN'T LIKE SEEING ME DO THAT TO OTHER GIRLS.
I DON'T MEAN TO MAKE EXCUSES, BUT...
MY LITTLE SISTER'S STILL IN COLLEGE, AND ICHISE REMINDS ME OF HER.
I GUESS I KIND OF TREAT ICHISE LIKE AN HONORARY SISTER...

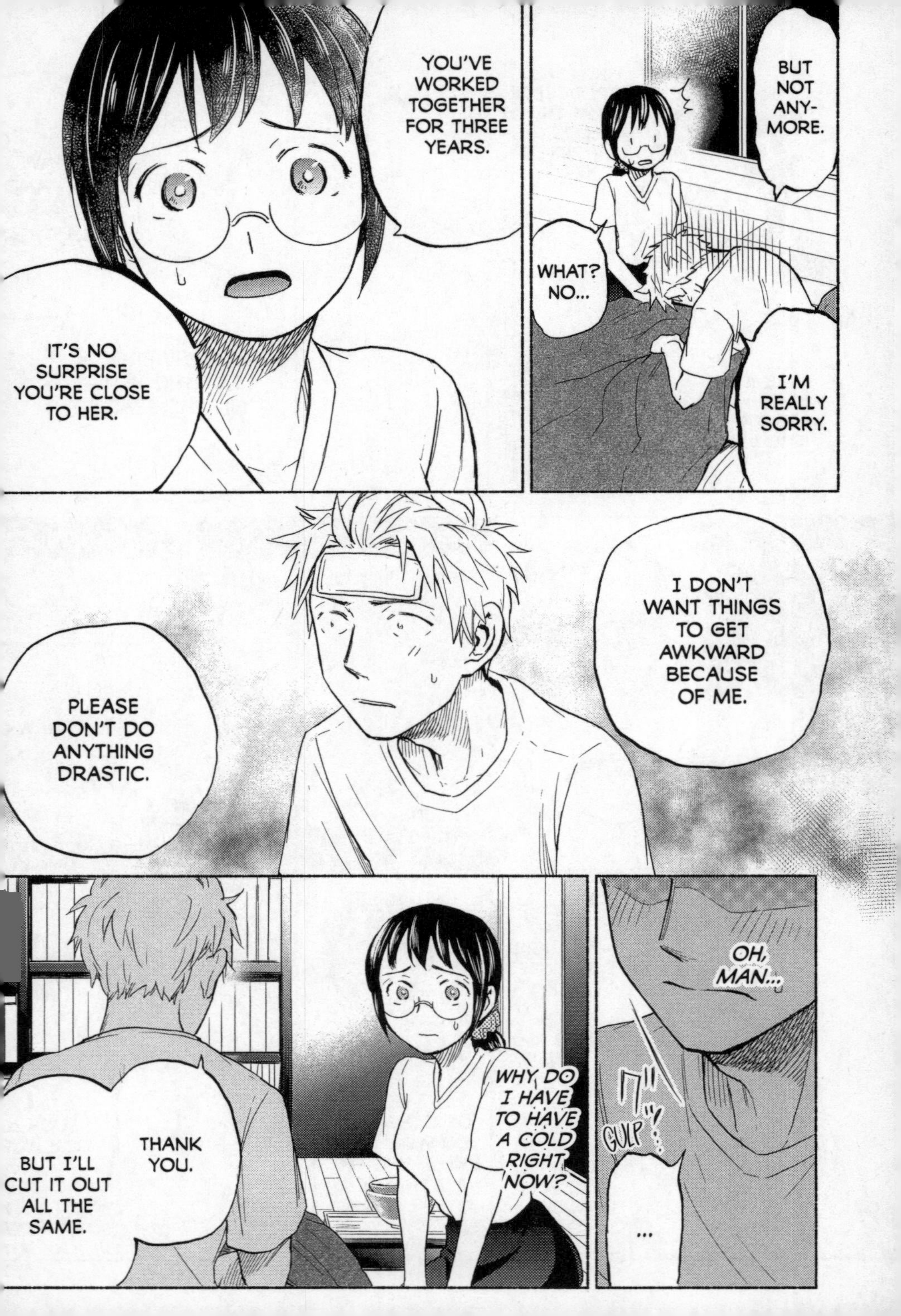
BUT NOT ANY-MORE.
WHAT? NO...
I'M REALLY SORRY.
YOU'VE WORKED TOGETHER FOR THREE YEARS.
IT'S NO SURPRISE YOU'RE CLOSE TO HER.
I DON'T WANT THINGS TO GET AWKWARD BECAUSE OF ME.
PLEASE DON'T DO ANYTHING DRASTIC.
OH, MAN...
GULP
...
WHY DO I HAVE TO HAVE A COLD RIGHT NOW?
THANK YOU.
BUT I'LL CUT IT OUT ALL THE SAME.

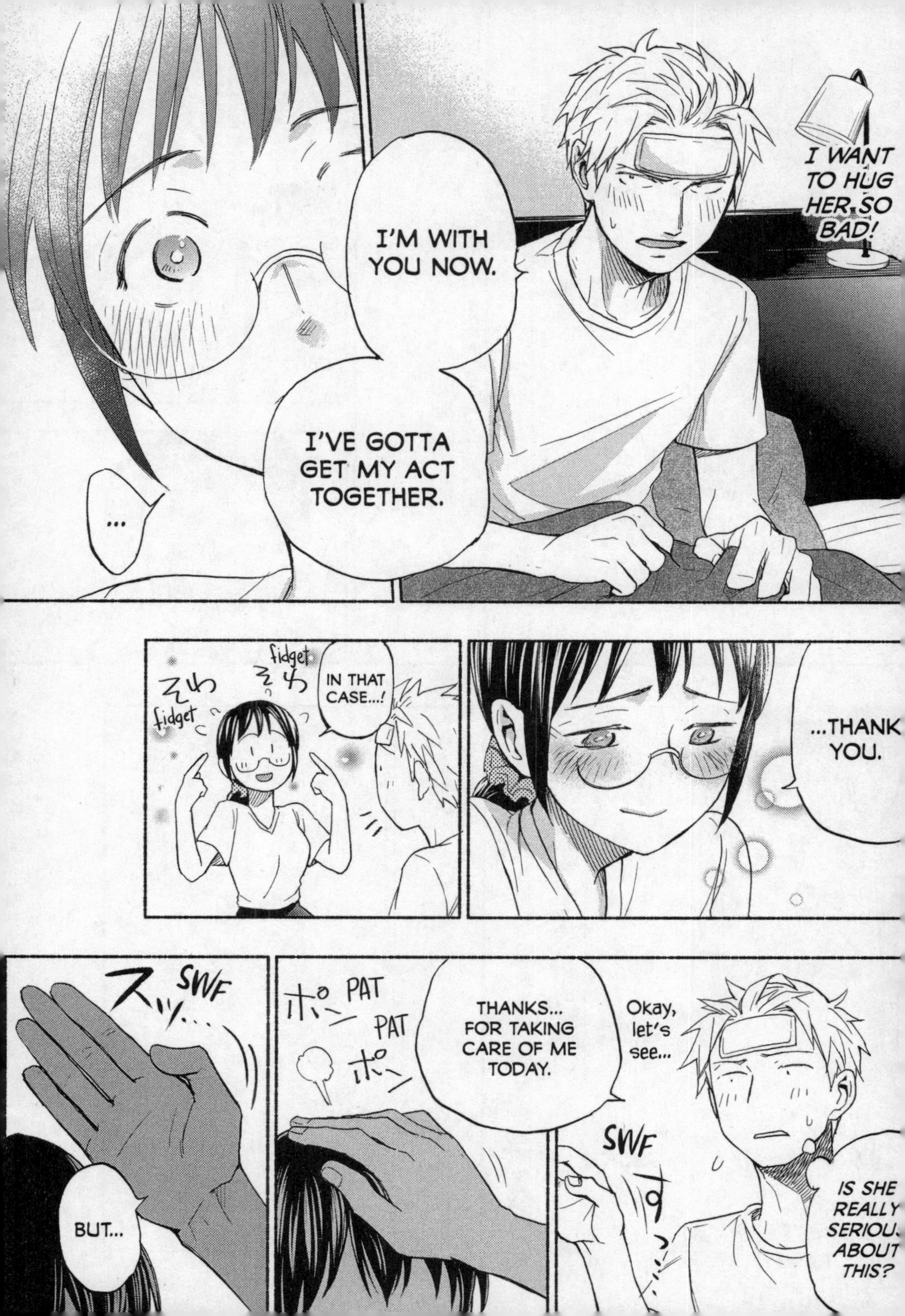
I WANT TO HUG HER SO BAD!
I'M WITH YOU NOW.
I'VE GOTTA GET MY ACT TOGETHER.
...
...THANK YOU.
fidget fidget
IN THAT CASE...!
Okay, let's see...
IS SHE REALLY SERIOU ABOUT THIS?
SWF
THANKS... FOR TAKING CARE OF ME TODAY.
PAT PAT
SWF
BUT...

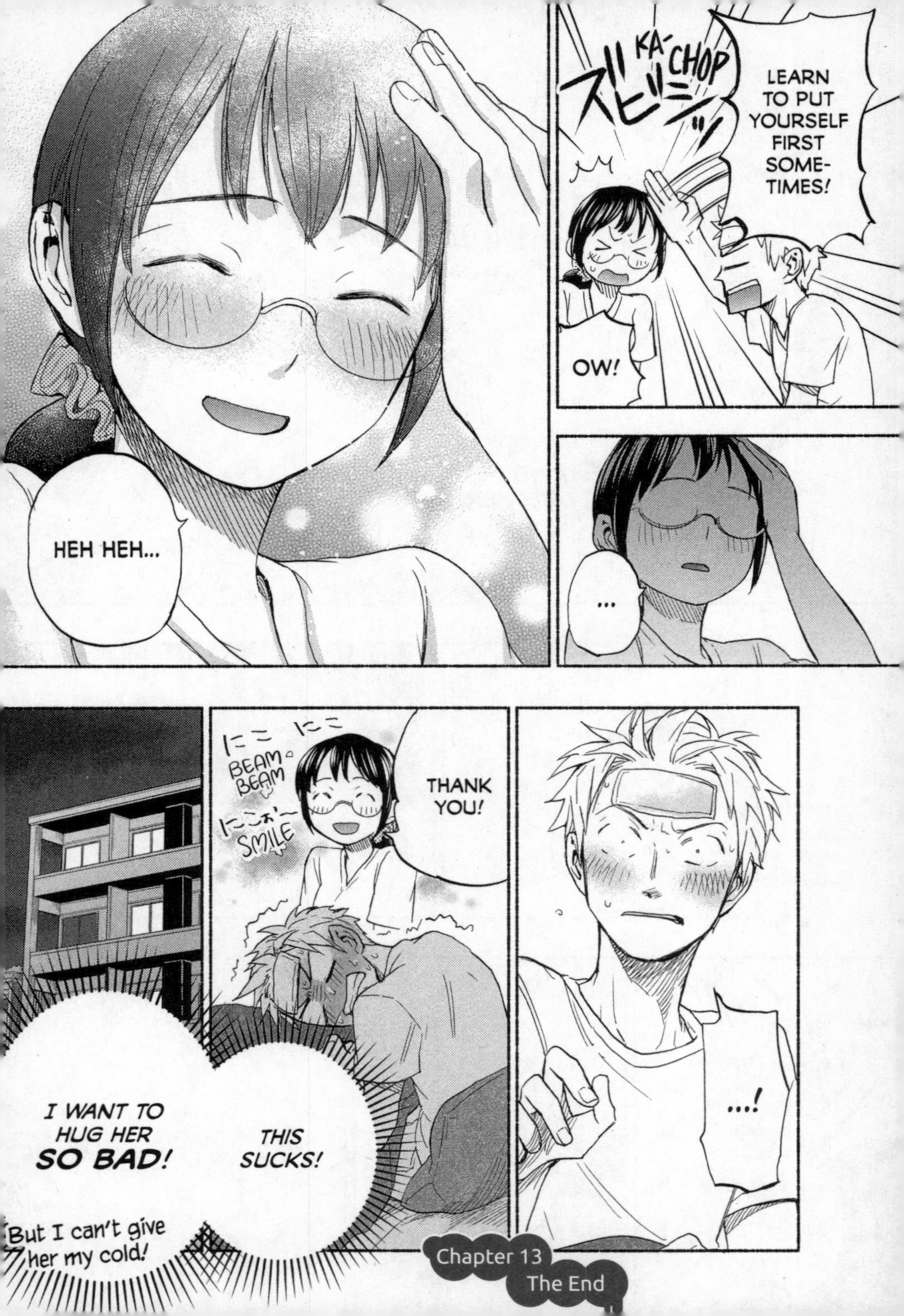
KA-CHOP
LEARN TO PUT YOURSELF FIRST SOME-TIMES!
OW!
...
HEH HEH...
...!
にこ にこ
BEAM BEAM
SMILE
THANK YOU!
THIS SUCKS!
I WANT TO HUG HER SO BAD!
But I can't give her my cold!
Chapter 13 The End

SMELT THIEF

A NAUGHTY BLACK CAT WHO LIVES TO STEAL SMELT. THIS IS THE CHARACTER ON THE MINI-BAG ASAKO-SAN HAD IN CHAPTER 13. APPARENTLY ALSO AVAILABLE ON T-SHIRTS, NOTE-PADS, AND OTHER MERCHANDISE.

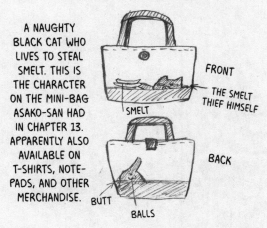

FRONT

THE SMELT THIEF HIMSELF

SMELT

BACK

BUTT

BALLS

SWEAT AND SOAP

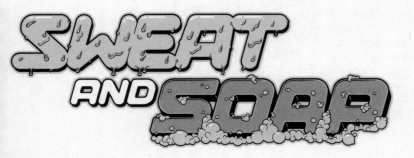

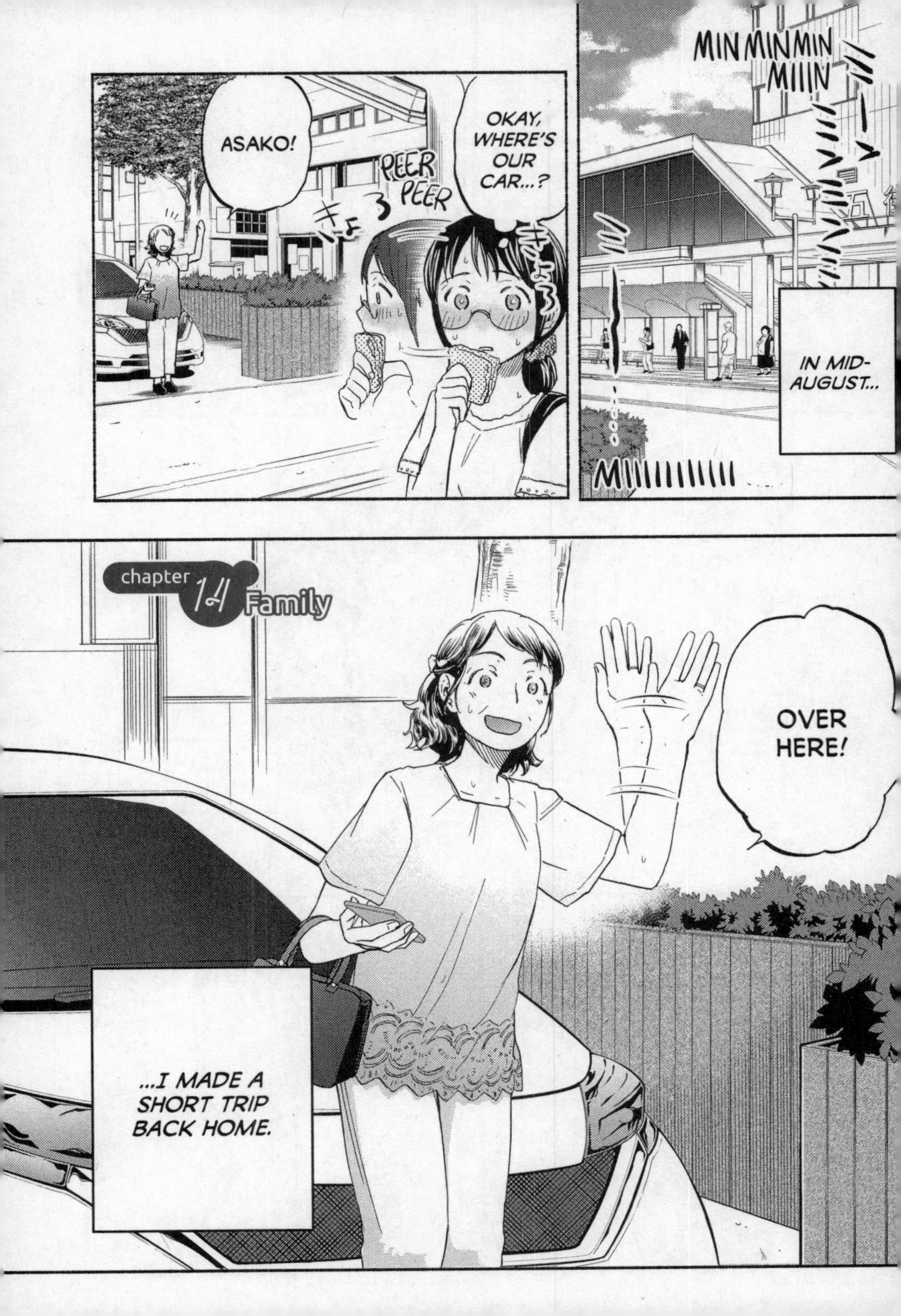
MIN MINMIN
MIIIN
IN MID-AUGUST...
MIIIIIIIII
OKAY, WHERE'S OUR CAR...?
PEER PEER
ASAKO!
chapter 14 Family
OVER HERE!
...I MADE A SHORT TRIP BACK HOME.

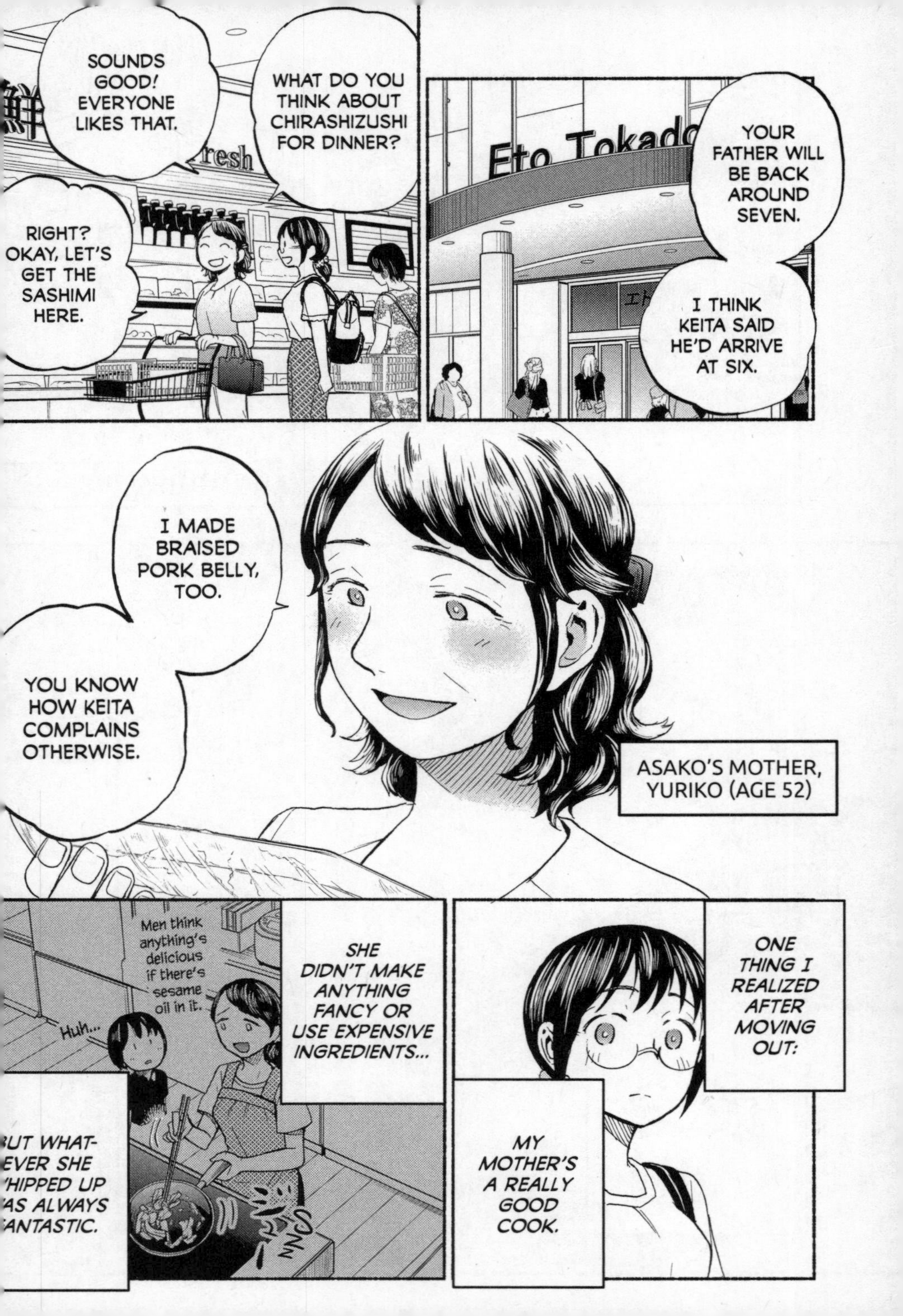
YOUR FATHER WILL BE BACK AROUND SEVEN.
I THINK KEITA SAID HE'D ARRIVE AT SIX.
WHAT DO YOU THINK ABOUT CHIRASHIZUSHI FOR DINNER?
SOUNDS GOOD! EVERYONE LIKES THAT.
RIGHT? OKAY, LET'S GET THE SASHIMI HERE.
I MADE BRAISED PORK BELLY, TOO.
YOU KNOW HOW KEITA COMPLAINS OTHERWISE.
ASAKO'S MOTHER, YURIKO (AGE 52)
ONE THING I REALIZED AFTER MOVING OUT:
MY MOTHER'S A REALLY GOOD COOK.
SHE DIDN'T MAKE ANYTHING FANCY OR USE EXPENSIVE INGREDIENTS...
Men think anything's delicious if there's sesame oil in it.
Huh...
UT WHAT-EVER SHE HIPPED UP AS ALWAYS ANTASTIC.

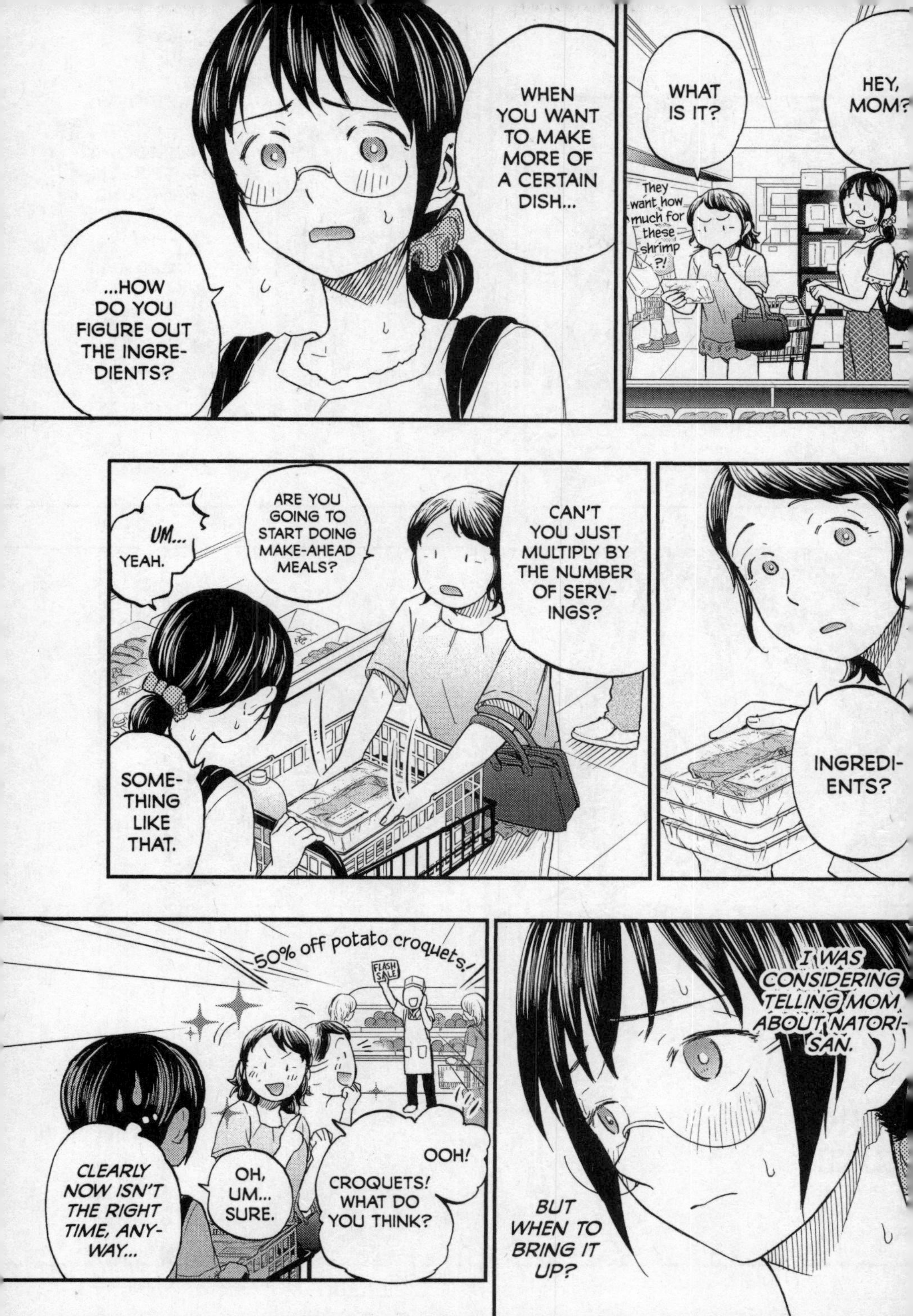
HEY, MOM?
WHAT IS IT?
They want how much for these shrimp ?!
WHEN YOU WANT TO MAKE MORE OF A CERTAIN DISH...
...HOW DO YOU FIGURE OUT THE INGREDIENTS?
INGREDIENTS?
CAN'T YOU JUST MULTIPLY BY THE NUMBER OF SERVINGS?
ARE YOU GOING TO START DOING MAKE-AHEAD MEALS?
UM... YEAH.
SOMETHING LIKE THAT.
I WAS CONSIDERING TELLING MOM ABOUT NATORI-SAN.
BUT WHEN TO BRING IT UP?
50% off potato croquets!
FLASH SALE
OOH!
CROQUETS! WHAT DO YOU THINK?
OH, UM... SURE.
CLEARLY NOW ISN'T THE RIGHT TIME, ANYWAY...

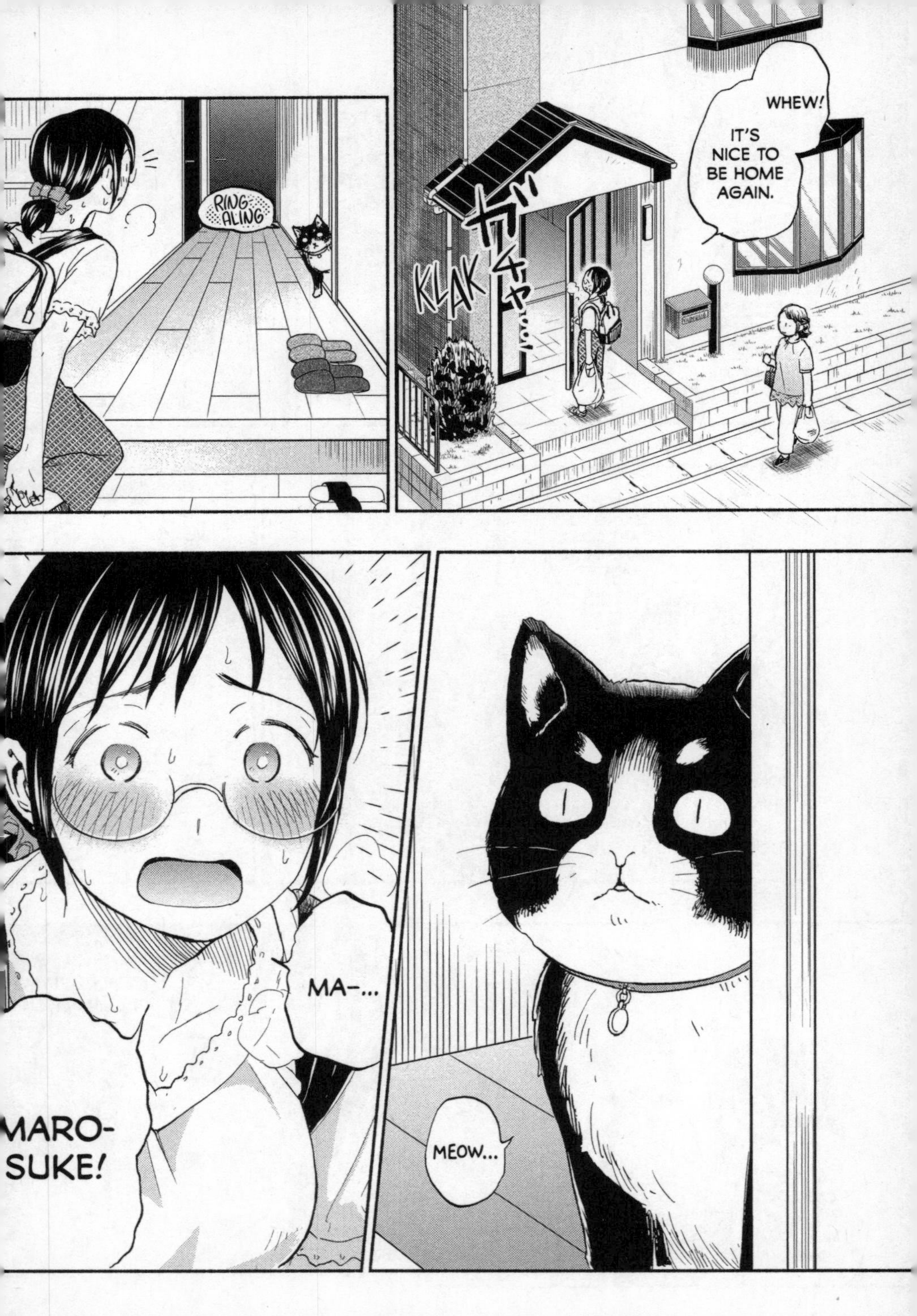
WHEW!
IT'S NICE TO BE HOME AGAIN.
KLAK
ガチャ…
RING ALING
MEOW…
MA-…
MARO-SUKE!

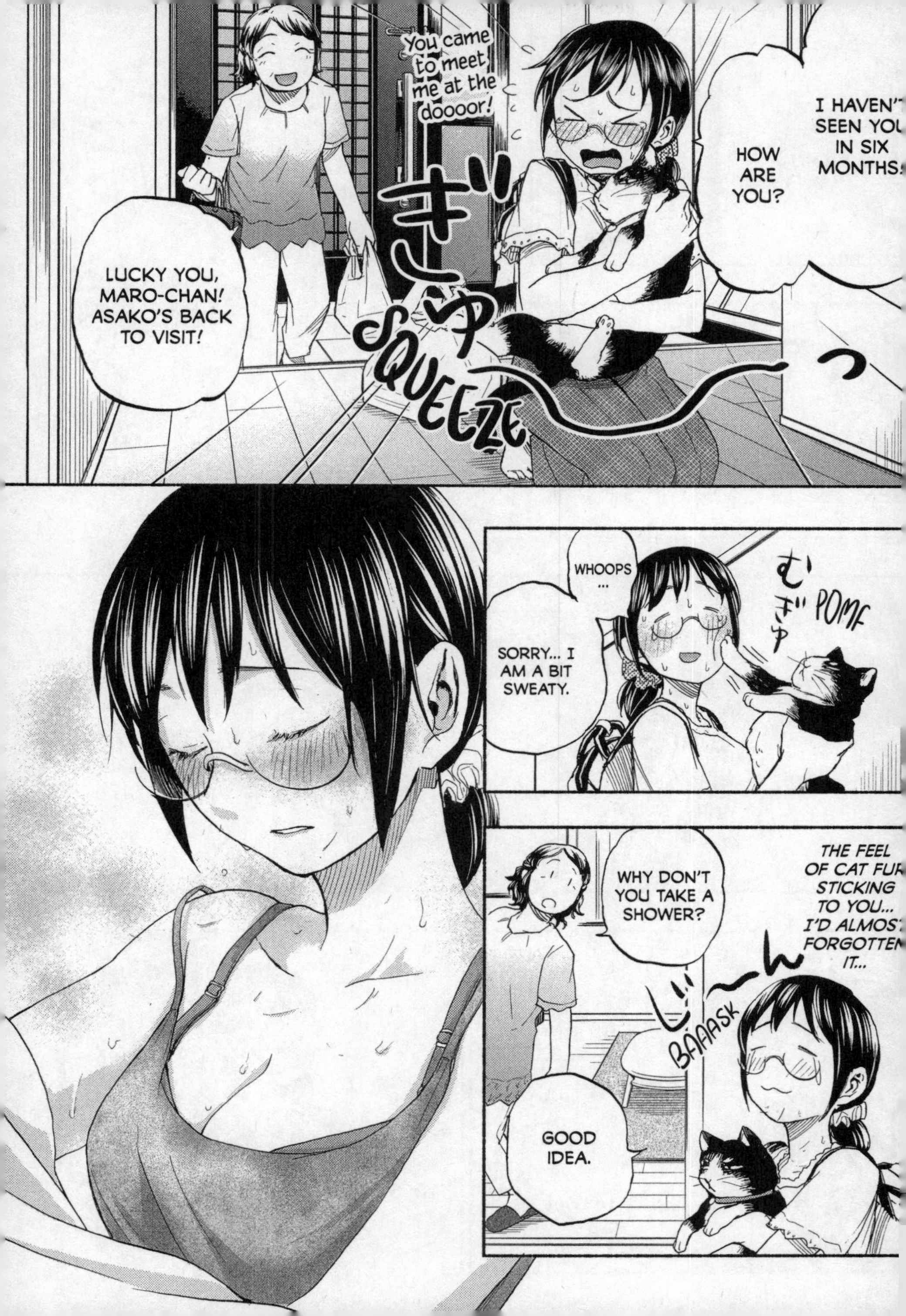
I HAVEN'T SEEN YOU IN SIX MONTHS!
HOW ARE YOU?
You came to meet me at the doooor!
ぎゅ
SQUEEZE
LUCKY YOU, MARO-CHAN! ASAKO'S BACK TO VISIT!
WHOOPS ...
むぎゅ
POMF
SORRY... I AM A BIT SWEATY.
THE FEEL OF CAT FUR STICKING TO YOU... I'D ALMOST FORGOTTEN IT...
WHY DON'T YOU TAKE A SHOWER?
じ~ん
BAAASK
GOOD IDEA.

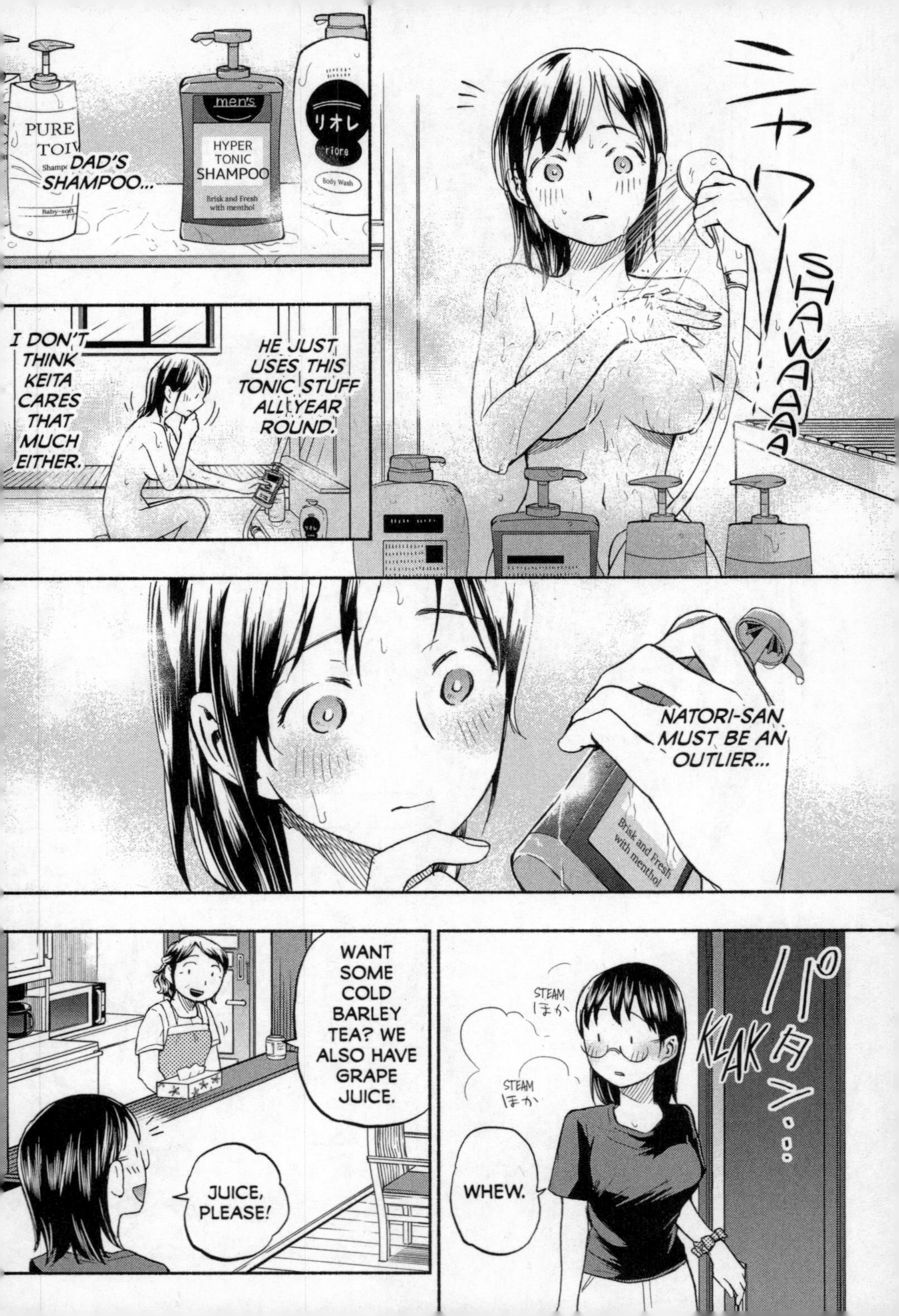
SHAWAAAAA
PURE TOI
Shampoo
Baby-soft
men's
HYPER TONIC SHAMPOO
Brisk and Fresh with menthol
リオレ
riore
Body Wash
DAD'S SHAMPOO...
HE JUST USES THIS TONIC STUFF ALL YEAR ROUND.
I DON'T THINK KEITA CARES THAT MUCH EITHER.
NATORI-SAN MUST BE AN OUTLIER...
Brisk and Fresh with menthol
KLAK
STEAM
STEAM
WHEW.
WANT SOME COLD BARLEY TEA? WE ALSO HAVE GRAPE JUICE.
JUICE, PLEASE!

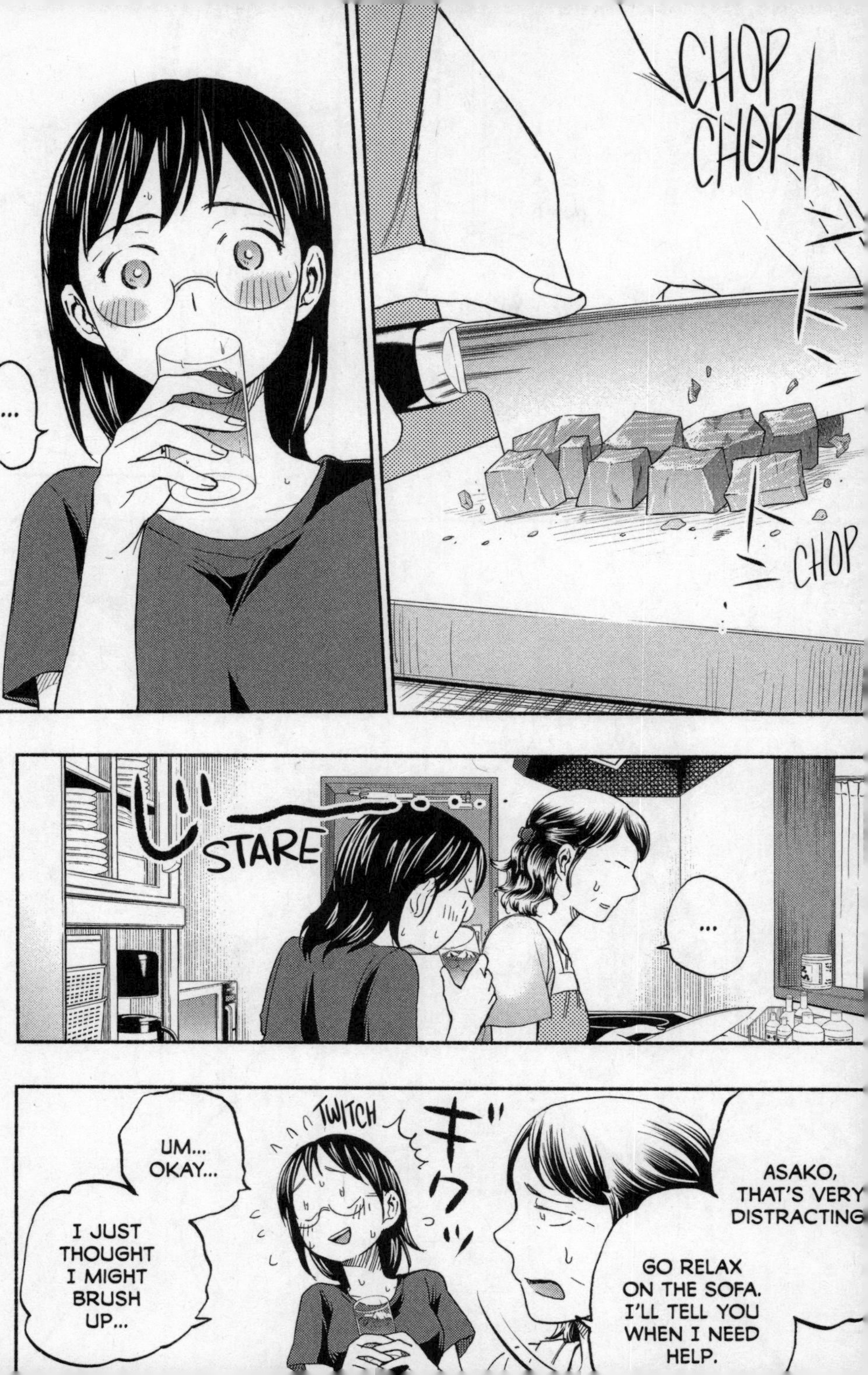
CHOP CHOP
CHOP
...
STARE
...
ASAKO, THAT'S VERY DISTRACTING.
GO RELAX ON THE SOFA. I'LL TELL YOU WHEN I NEED HELP.
TWITCH
UM... OKAY...
I JUST THOUGHT I MIGHT BRUSH UP...

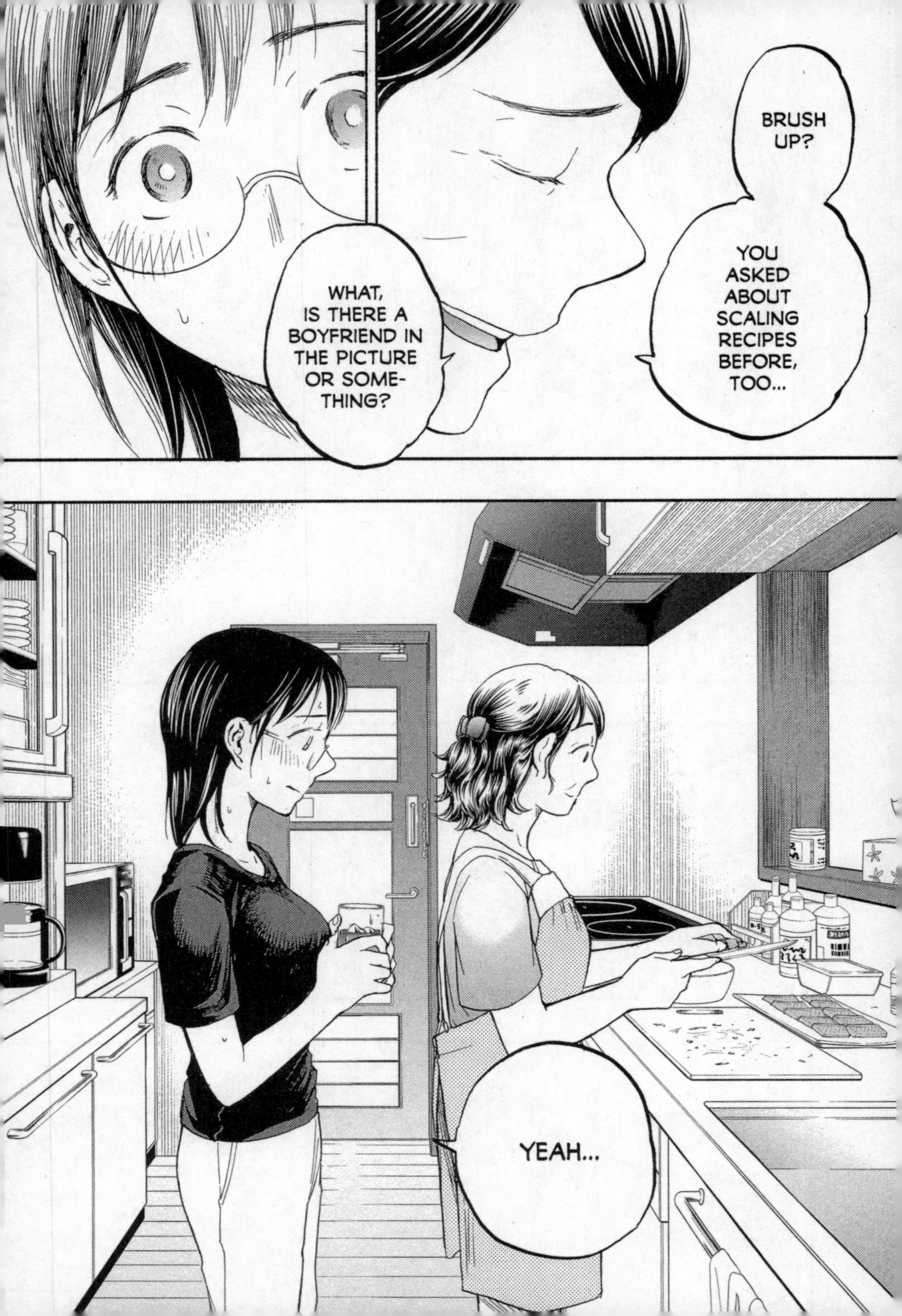
BRUSH UP?
YOU ASKED ABOUT SCALING RECIPES BEFORE, TOO...
WHAT, IS THERE A BOYFRIEND IN THE PICTURE OR SOME-THING?
YEAH...

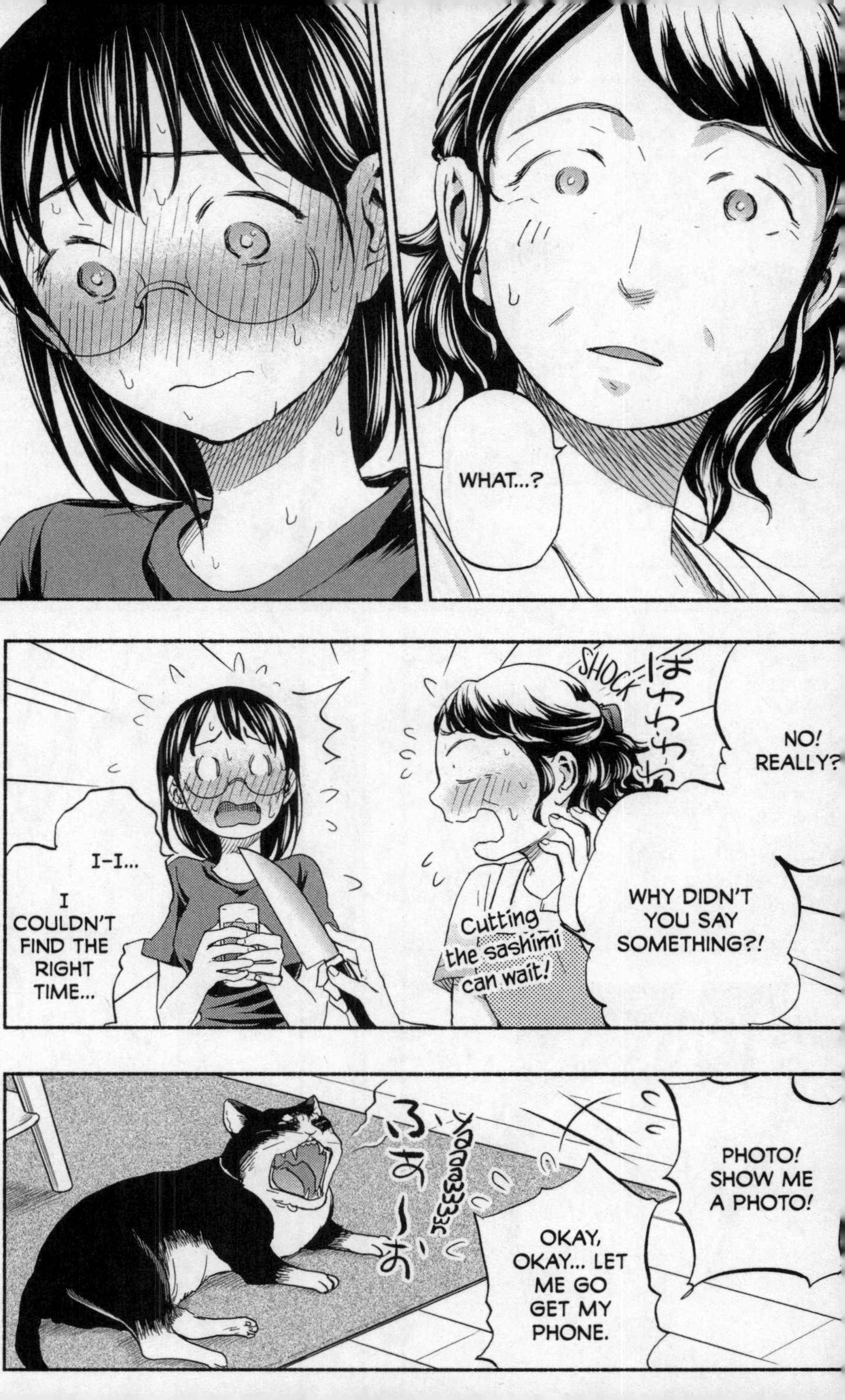
WHAT...?
NO! REALLY?
SHOCK
はわわわ
WHY DIDN'T YOU SAY SOMETHING?!
Cutting the sashimi can wait!
I-I...
I COULDN'T FIND THE RIGHT TIME...
PHOTO! SHOW ME A PHOTO!
OKAY, OKAY... LET ME GO GET MY PHONE.
ふあ～お

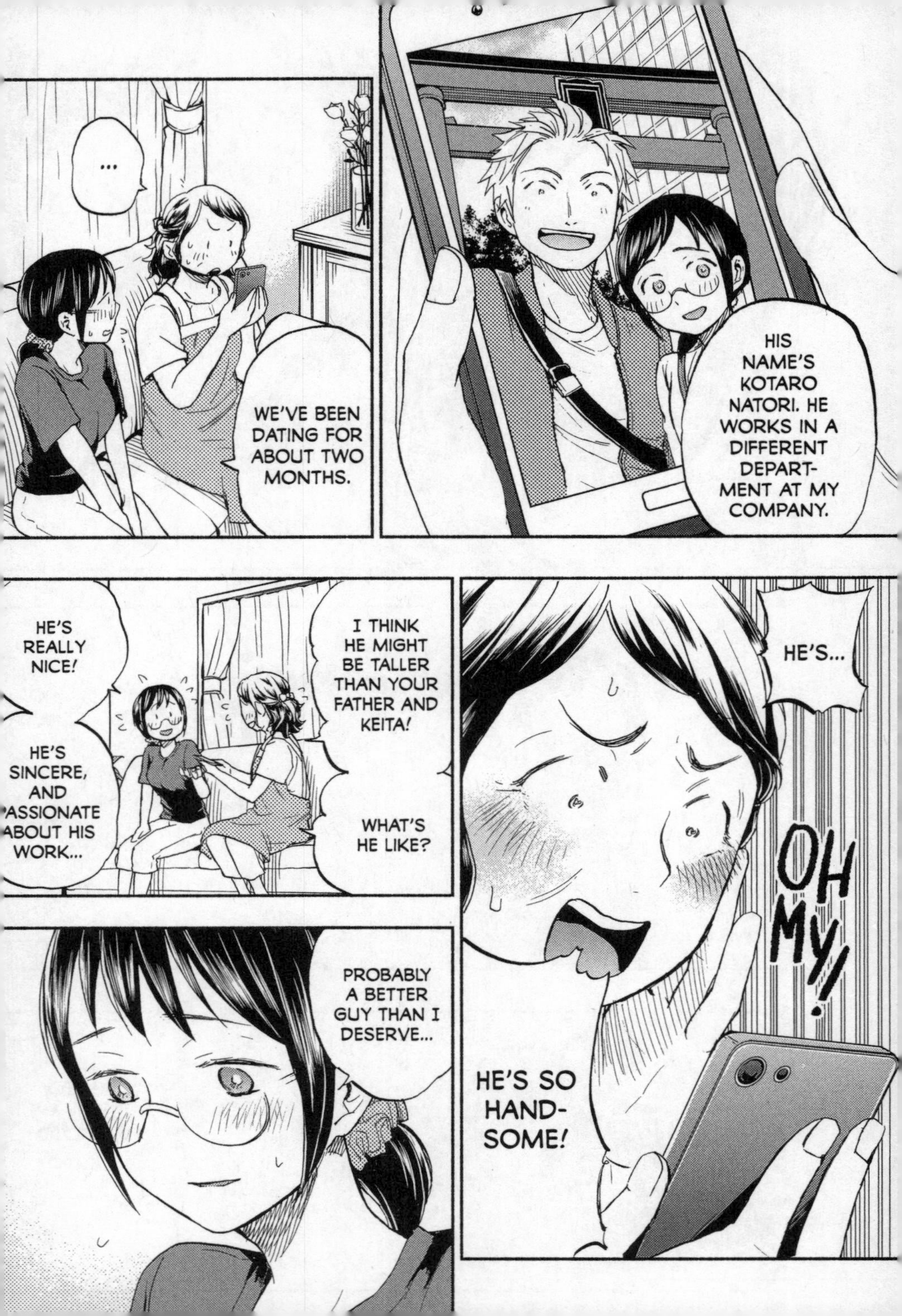
HIS NAME'S KOTARO NATORI. HE WORKS IN A DIFFERENT DEPART-MENT AT MY COMPANY.
WE'VE BEEN DATING FOR ABOUT TWO MONTHS.
...
HE'S...
OH MY!
HE'S SO HAND-SOME!
I THINK HE MIGHT BE TALLER THAN YOUR FATHER AND KEITA!
WHAT'S HE LIKE?
HE'S REALLY NICE!
HE'S SINCERE, AND PASSIONATE ABOUT HIS WORK...
PROBABLY A BETTER GUY THAN I DESERVE...

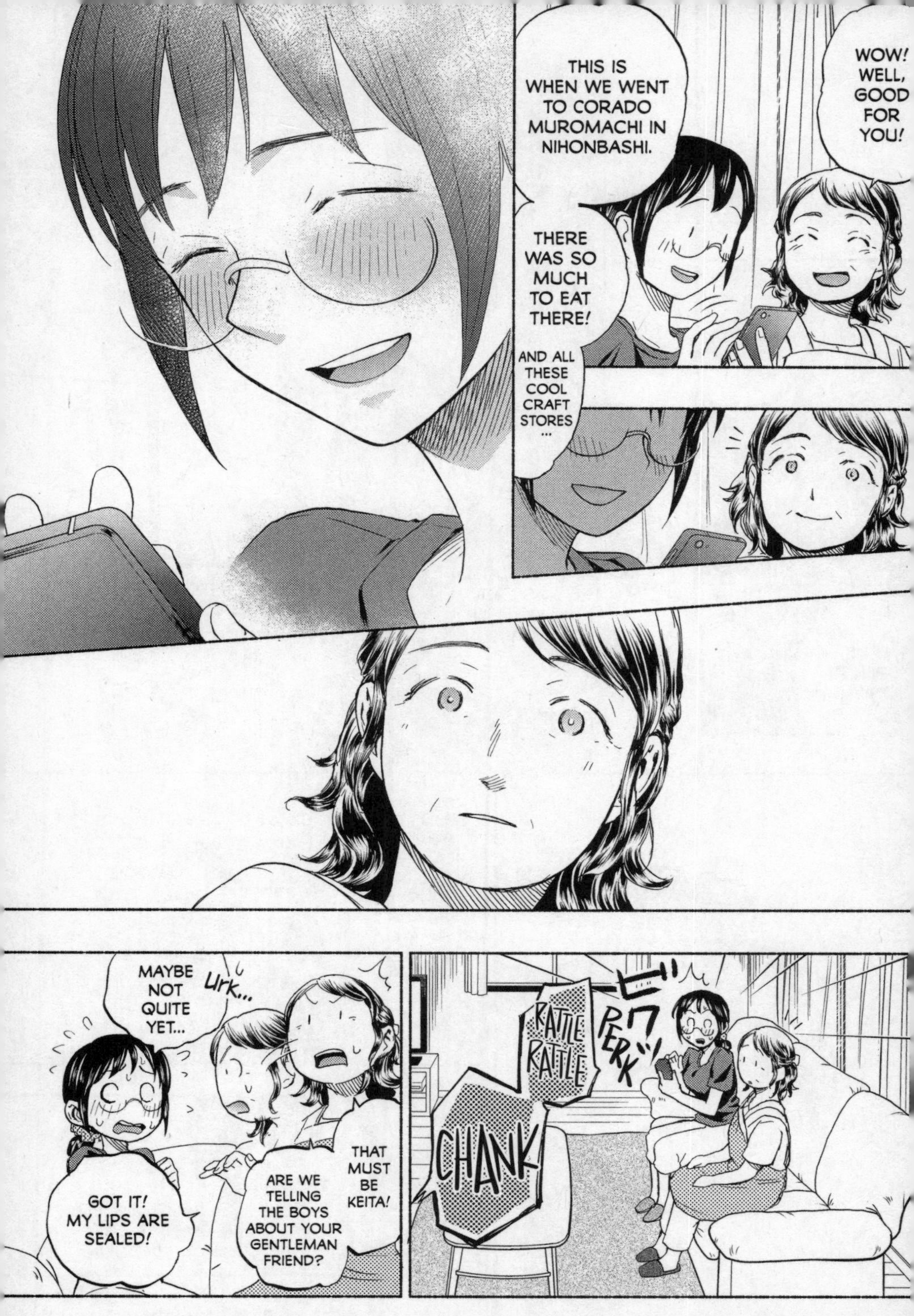

WOW! WELL, GOOD FOR YOU!
THIS IS WHEN WE WENT TO CORADO MUROMACHI IN NIHONBASHI.
THERE WAS SO MUCH TO EAT THERE!
AND ALL THESE COOL CRAFT STORES...
PERK
RATTLE RATTLE
CHANK
THAT MUST BE KEITA!
ARE WE TELLING THE BOYS ABOUT YOUR GENTLEMAN FRIEND?
Urk...
MAYBE NOT QUITE YET...
GOT IT! MY LIPS ARE SEALED!

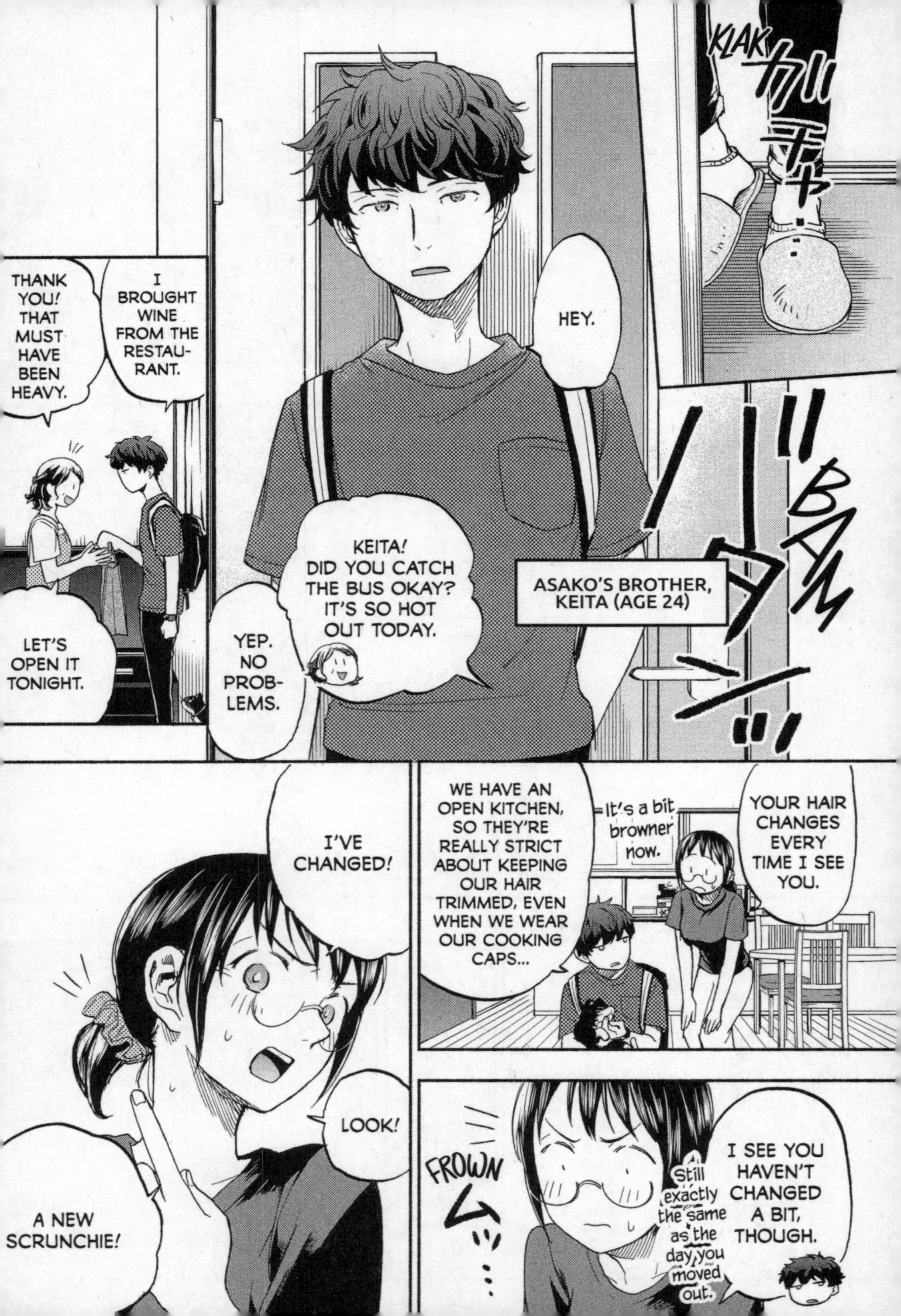
KLAK
BAM
HEY.
ASAKO'S BROTHER, KEITA (AGE 24)
KEITA! DID YOU CATCH THE BUS OKAY? IT'S SO HOT OUT TODAY.
YEP. NO PROB-LEMS.
I BROUGHT WINE FROM THE RESTAU-RANT.
THANK YOU! THAT MUST HAVE BEEN HEAVY.
LET'S OPEN IT TONIGHT.
YOUR HAIR CHANGES EVERY TIME I SEE YOU.
It's a bit browner now.
WE HAVE AN OPEN KITCHEN, SO THEY'RE REALLY STRICT ABOUT KEEPING OUR HAIR TRIMMED, EVEN WHEN WE WEAR OUR COOKING CAPS...
I SEE YOU HAVEN'T CHANGED A BIT, THOUGH.
Still exactly the same as the day you moved out.
FROWN
I'VE CHANGED!
LOOK!
A NEW SCRUNCHIE!

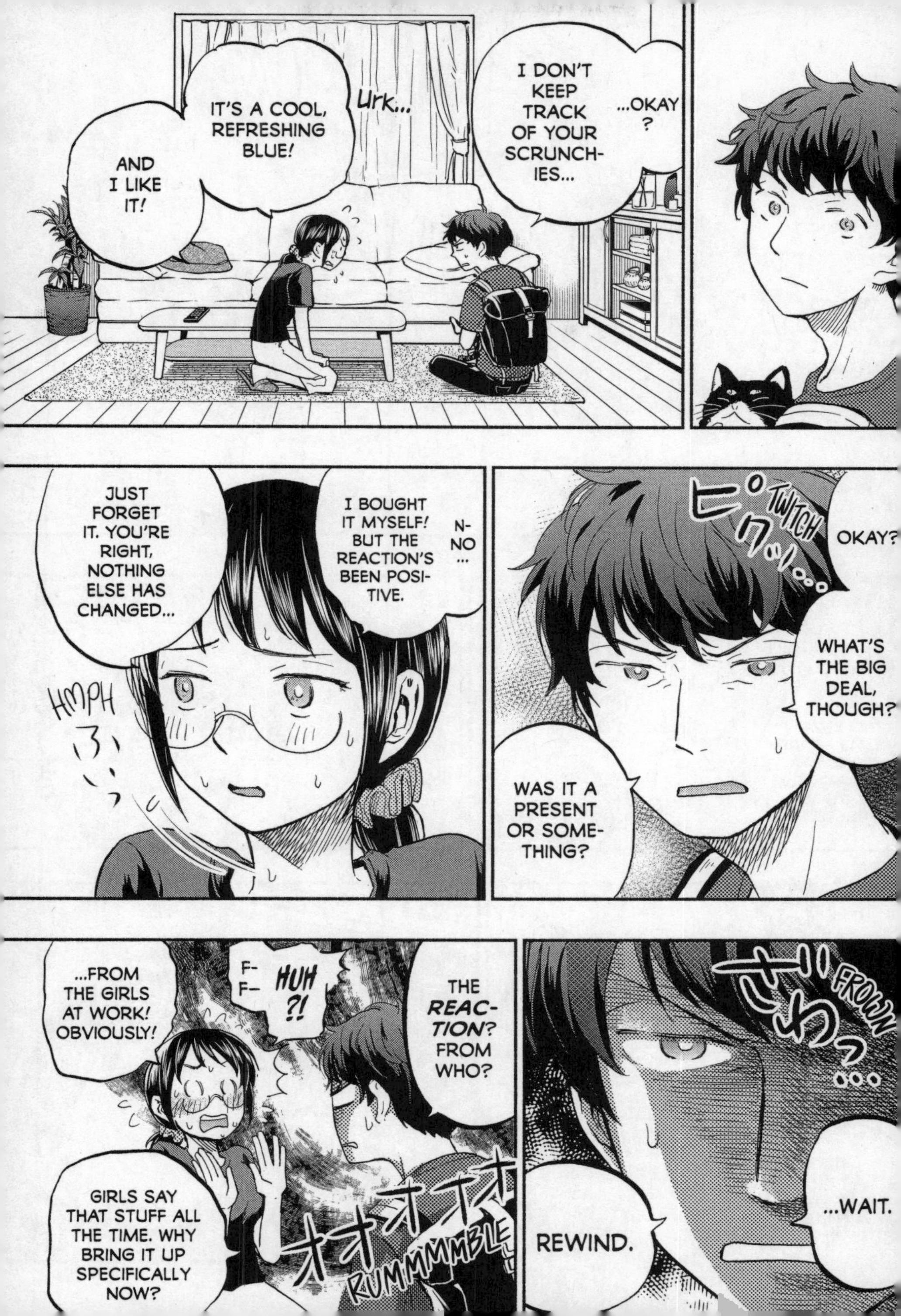
I DON'T KEEP TRACK OF YOUR SCRUNCH-IES...
...OKAY?
Urk...
IT'S A COOL, REFRESHING BLUE!
AND I LIKE IT!
OKAY?
TWITCH
WHAT'S THE BIG DEAL, THOUGH?
WAS IT A PRESENT OR SOME-THING?
N-NO...
I BOUGHT IT MYSELF! BUT THE REACTION'S BEEN POSI-TIVE.
JUST FORGET IT. YOU'RE RIGHT, NOTHING ELSE HAS CHANGED...
HMPH
FROWN
...WAIT.
REWIND.
THE *REAC-TION*? FROM WHO?
F-F— HUH?!
...FROM THE GIRLS AT WORK! OBVIOUSLY!
GIRLS SAY THAT STUFF ALL THE TIME. WHY BRING IT UP SPECIFICALLY NOW?
RUMMMMBLE

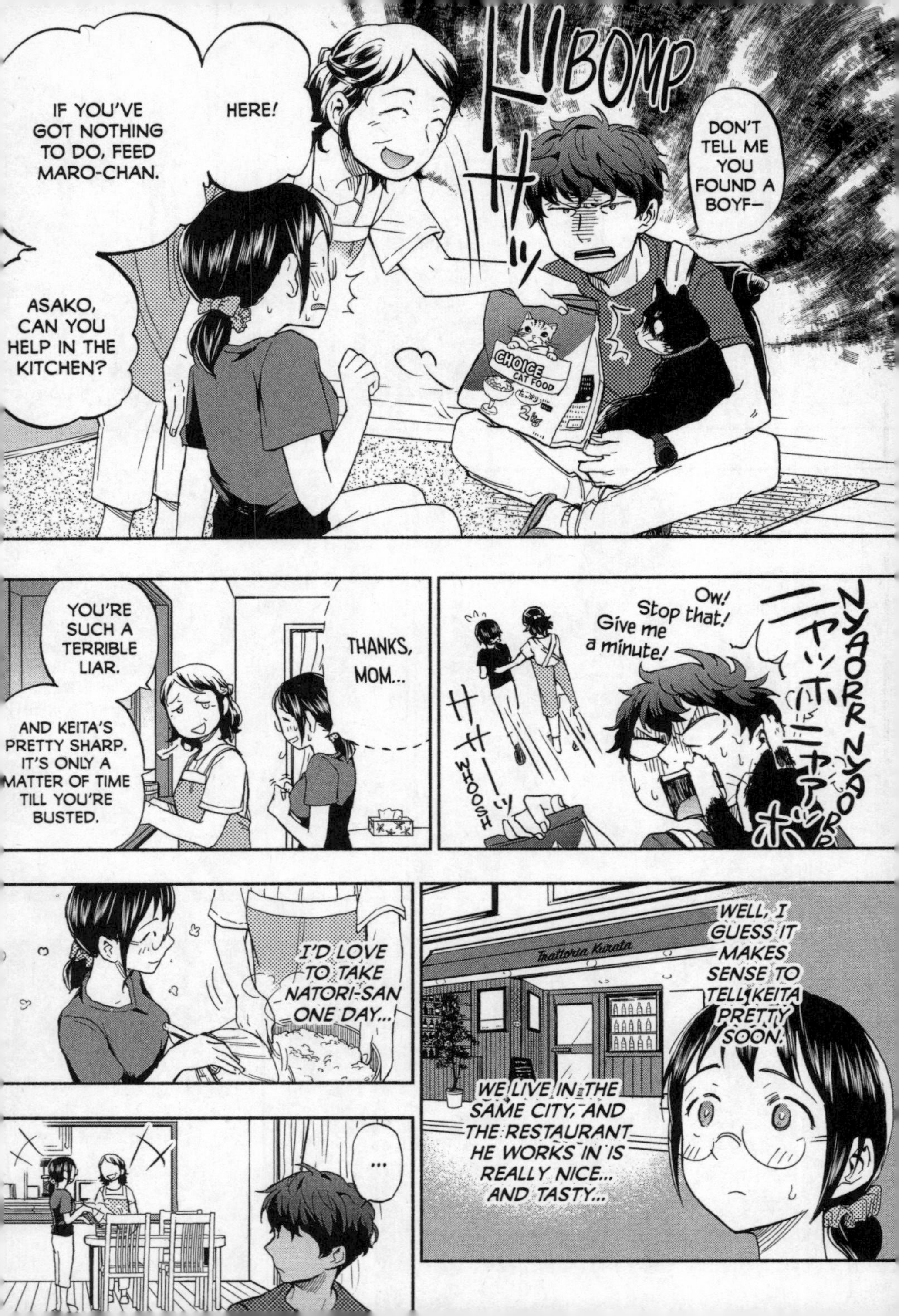
BOMP
DON'T TELL ME YOU FOUND A BOYF—
HERE!
IF YOU'VE GOT NOTHING TO DO, FEED MARO-CHAN.
ASAKO, CAN YOU HELP IN THE KITCHEN?
CHOICE CAT FOOD
2kg
NYAORR NYAORR
Ow! Stop that! Give me a minute!
WHOOSH
THANKS, MOM...
YOU'RE SUCH A TERRIBLE LIAR.
AND KEITA'S PRETTY SHARP. IT'S ONLY A MATTER OF TIME TILL YOU'RE BUSTED.
WELL, I GUESS IT MAKES SENSE TO TELL KEITA PRETTY SOON.
Trattoria Kurata
WE LIVE IN THE SAME CITY, AND THE RESTAURANT HE WORKS IN IS REALLY NICE... AND TASTY...
I'D LOVE TO TAKE NATORI-SAN ONE DAY...
...

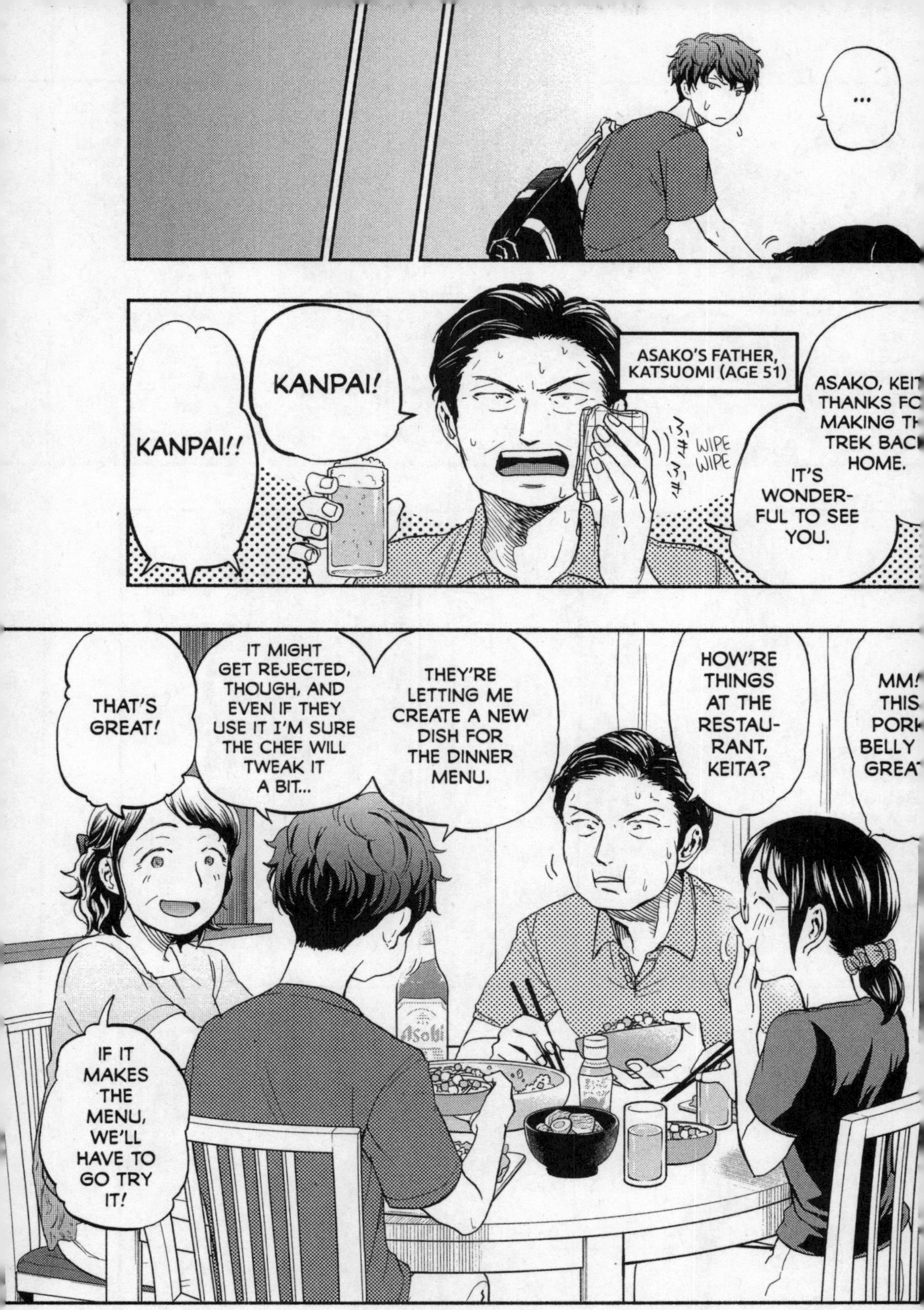
...
ASAKO'S FATHER, KATSUOMI (AGE 51)
ASAKO, KEIT THANKS FO MAKING TH TREK BAC HOME.
IT'S WONDER-FUL TO SEE YOU.
ふきふき WIPE WIPE
KANPAI!
KANPAI!!
MM! THIS PORK BELLY GREAT
HOW'RE THINGS AT THE RESTAU-RANT, KEITA?
THEY'RE LETTING ME CREATE A NEW DISH FOR THE DINNER MENU.
IT MIGHT GET REJECTED, THOUGH, AND EVEN IF THEY USE IT I'M SURE THE CHEF WILL TWEAK IT A BIT...
THAT'S GREAT!
IF IT MAKES THE MENU, WE'LL HAVE TO GO TRY IT!
Asobi

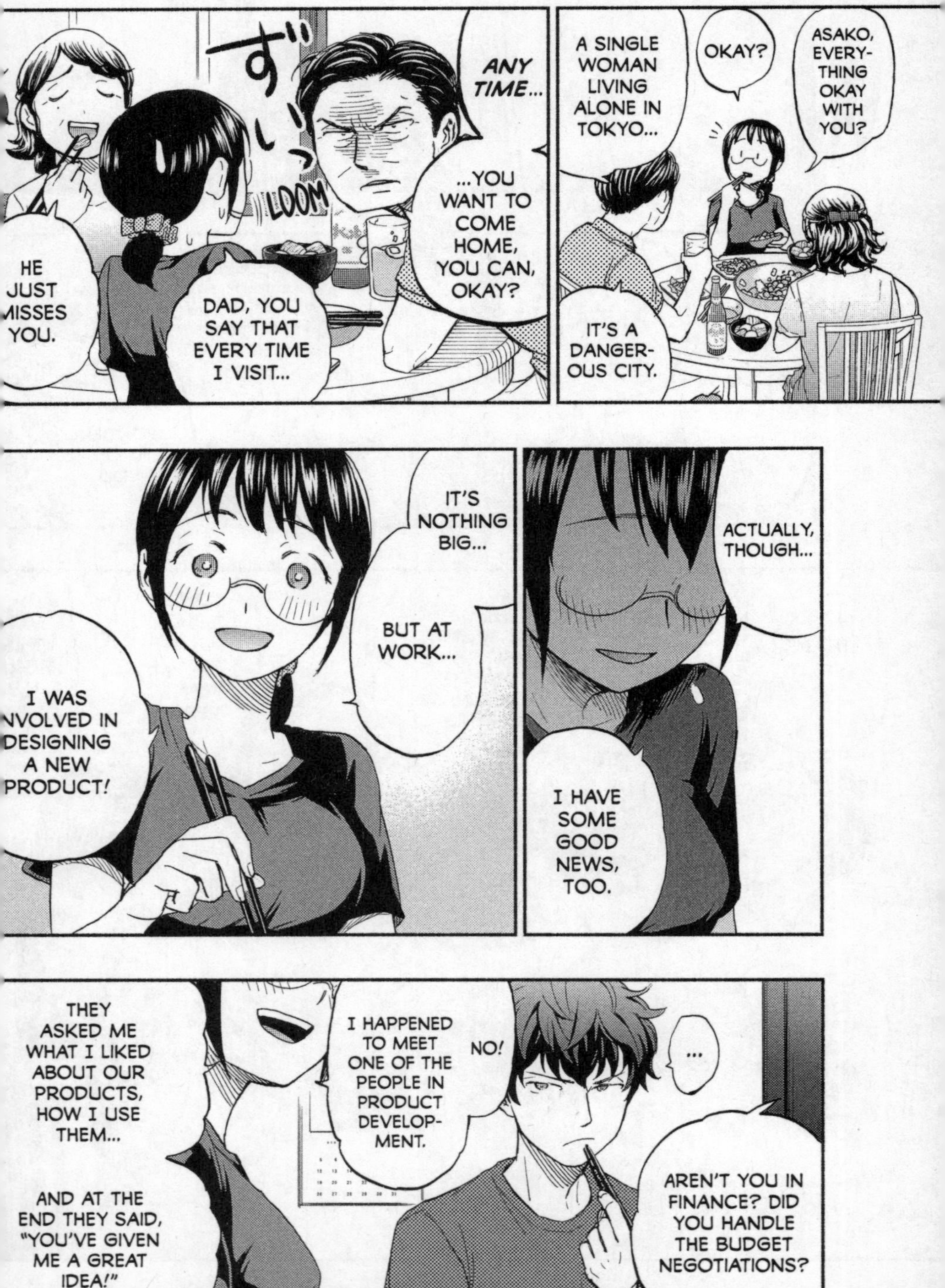
ASAKO, EVERYTHING OKAY WITH YOU?
OKAY?
A SINGLE WOMAN LIVING ALONE IN TOKYO...
IT'S A DANGEROUS CITY.
ANY TIME...
...YOU WANT TO COME HOME, YOU CAN, OKAY?
LOOM
DAD, YOU SAY THAT EVERY TIME I VISIT...
HE JUST MISSES YOU.
ACTUALLY, THOUGH...
I HAVE SOME GOOD NEWS, TOO.
IT'S NOTHING BIG...
BUT AT WORK...
I WAS NVOLVED IN DESIGNING A NEW PRODUCT!
...
AREN'T YOU IN FINANCE? DID YOU HANDLE THE BUDGET NEGOTIATIONS?
NO!
I HAPPENED TO MEET ONE OF THE PEOPLE IN PRODUCT DEVELOPMENT.
THEY ASKED ME WHAT I LIKED ABOUT OUR PRODUCTS, HOW I USE THEM...
AND AT THE END THEY SAID, "YOU'VE GIVEN ME A GREAT IDEA!"

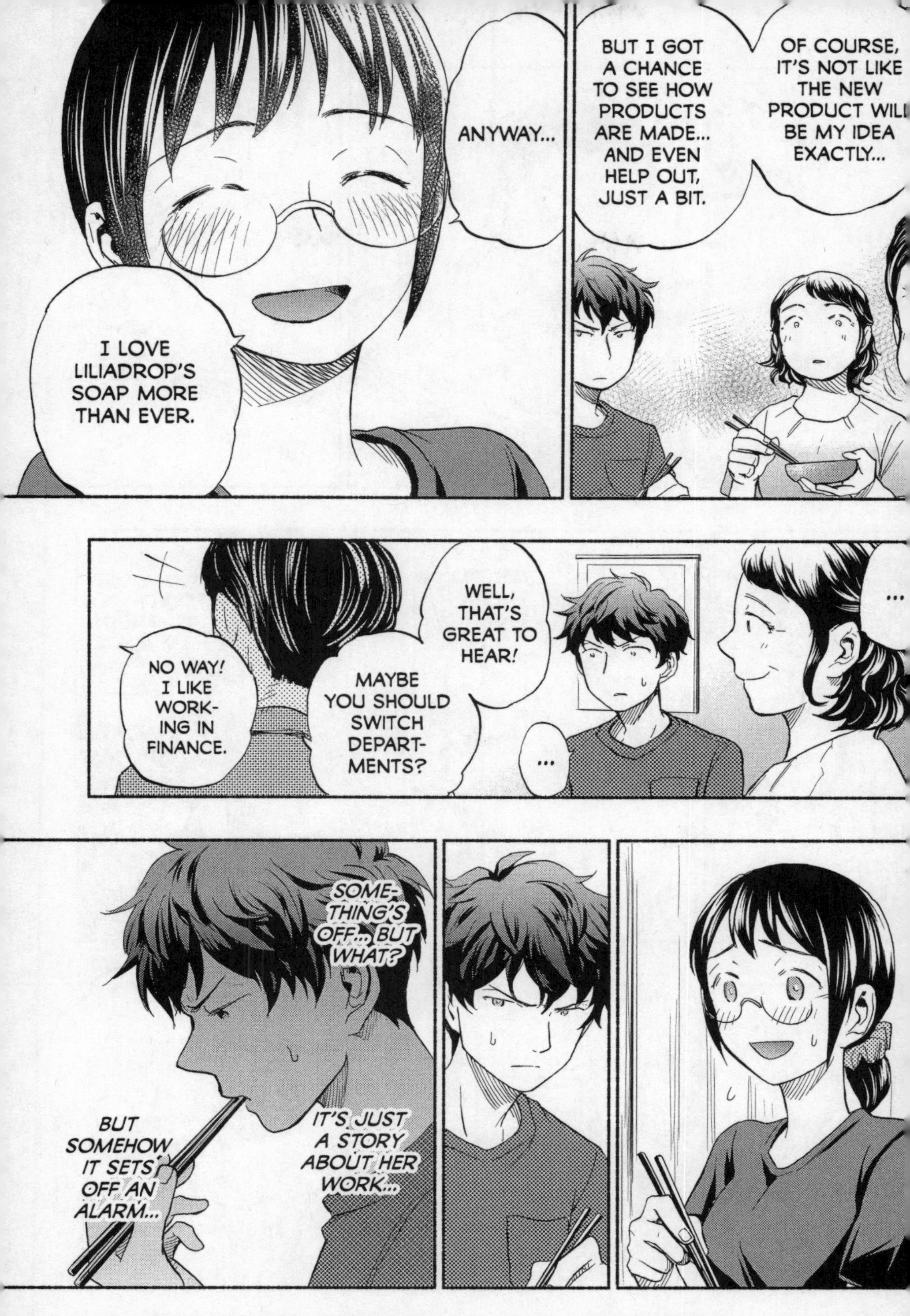
OF COURSE, IT'S NOT LIKE THE NEW PRODUCT WILL BE MY IDEA EXACTLY...
BUT I GOT A CHANCE TO SEE HOW PRODUCTS ARE MADE... AND EVEN HELP OUT, JUST A BIT.
ANYWAY...
I LOVE LILIADROP'S SOAP MORE THAN EVER.
...
WELL, THAT'S GREAT TO HEAR!
MAYBE YOU SHOULD SWITCH DEPART-MENTS?
...
NO WAY! I LIKE WORK-ING IN FINANCE.
SOME-THING'S OFF... BUT WHAT?
IT'S JUST A STORY ABOUT HER WORK...
BUT SOMEHOW IT SETS OFF AN ALARM...

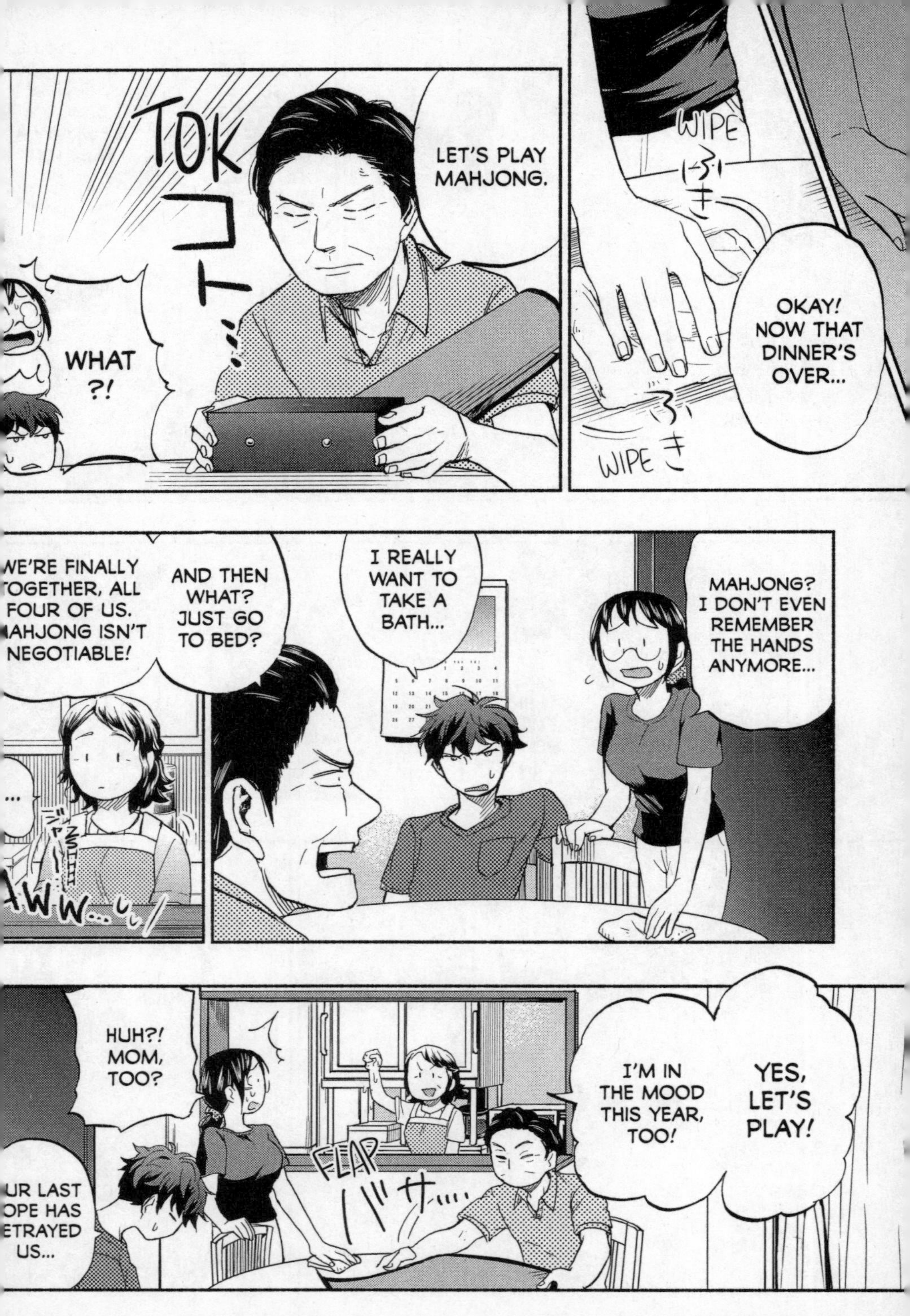
WIPE ふき
OKAY! NOW THAT DINNER'S OVER...
ふき WIPE
LET'S PLAY MAHJONG.
TOK コト
WHAT?!
MAHJONG? I DON'T EVEN REMEMBER THE HANDS ANYMORE...
I REALLY WANT TO TAKE A BATH...
AND THEN WHAT? JUST GO TO BED?
VE'RE FINALLY OGETHER, ALL FOUR OF US. AHJONG ISN'T NEGOTIABLE!
AWW...
YES, LET'S PLAY!
I'M IN THE MOOD THIS YEAR, TOO!
HUH?! MOM, TOO?
FLAP バサ…
UR LAST OPE HAS ETRAYED US...

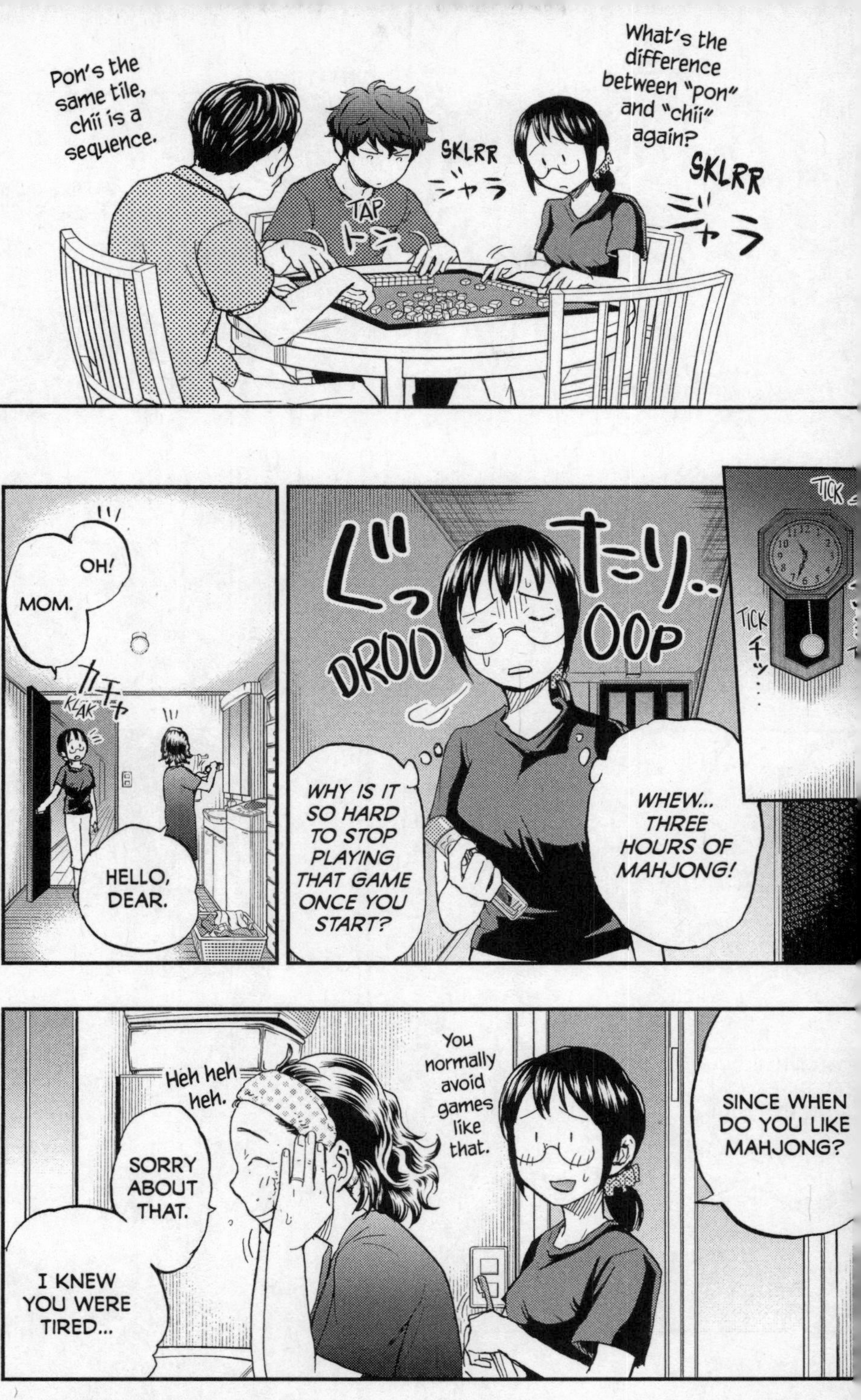
What's the difference between "pon" and "chii" again?
SKLRR
ジャラ
SKLRR
ジャラ
TAP
トン
Pon's the same tile, chii is a sequence.
TICK
TICK
チッ...
ぐったり..
DROOOP
WHEW... THREE HOURS OF MAHJONG!
WHY IS IT SO HARD TO STOP PLAYING THAT GAME ONCE YOU START?
OH! MOM.
KLAK
カチャ
HELLO, DEAR.
SINCE WHEN DO YOU LIKE MAHJONG?
You normally avoid games like that.
Heh heh heh.
SORRY ABOUT THAT.
I KNEW YOU WERE TIRED...

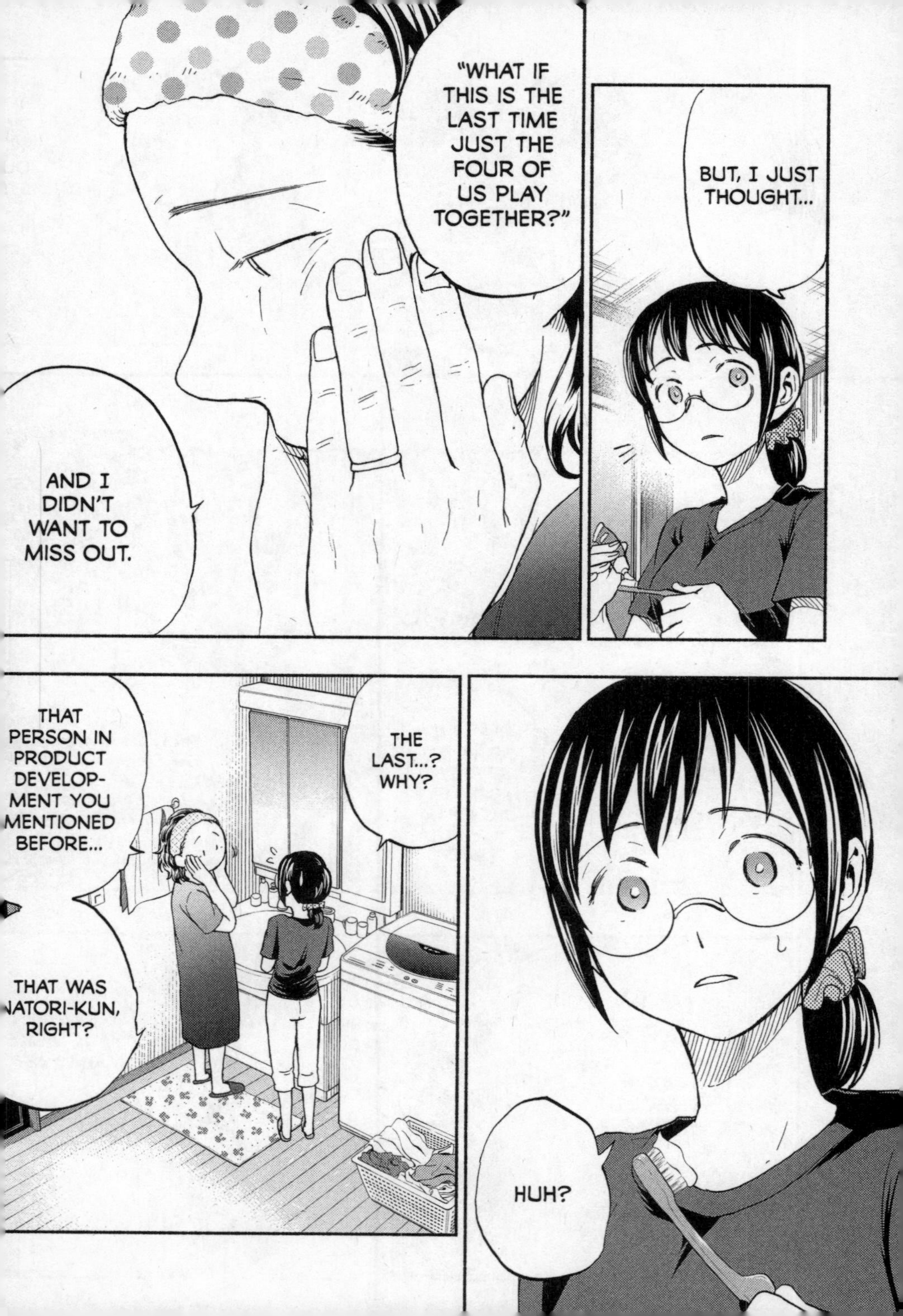
BUT, I JUST THOUGHT...
"WHAT IF THIS IS THE LAST TIME JUST THE FOUR OF US PLAY TOGETHER?"
AND I DIDN'T WANT TO MISS OUT.
HUH?
THE LAST...? WHY?
THAT PERSON IN PRODUCT DEVELOPMENT YOU MENTIONED BEFORE...
THAT WAS NATORI-KUN, RIGHT?

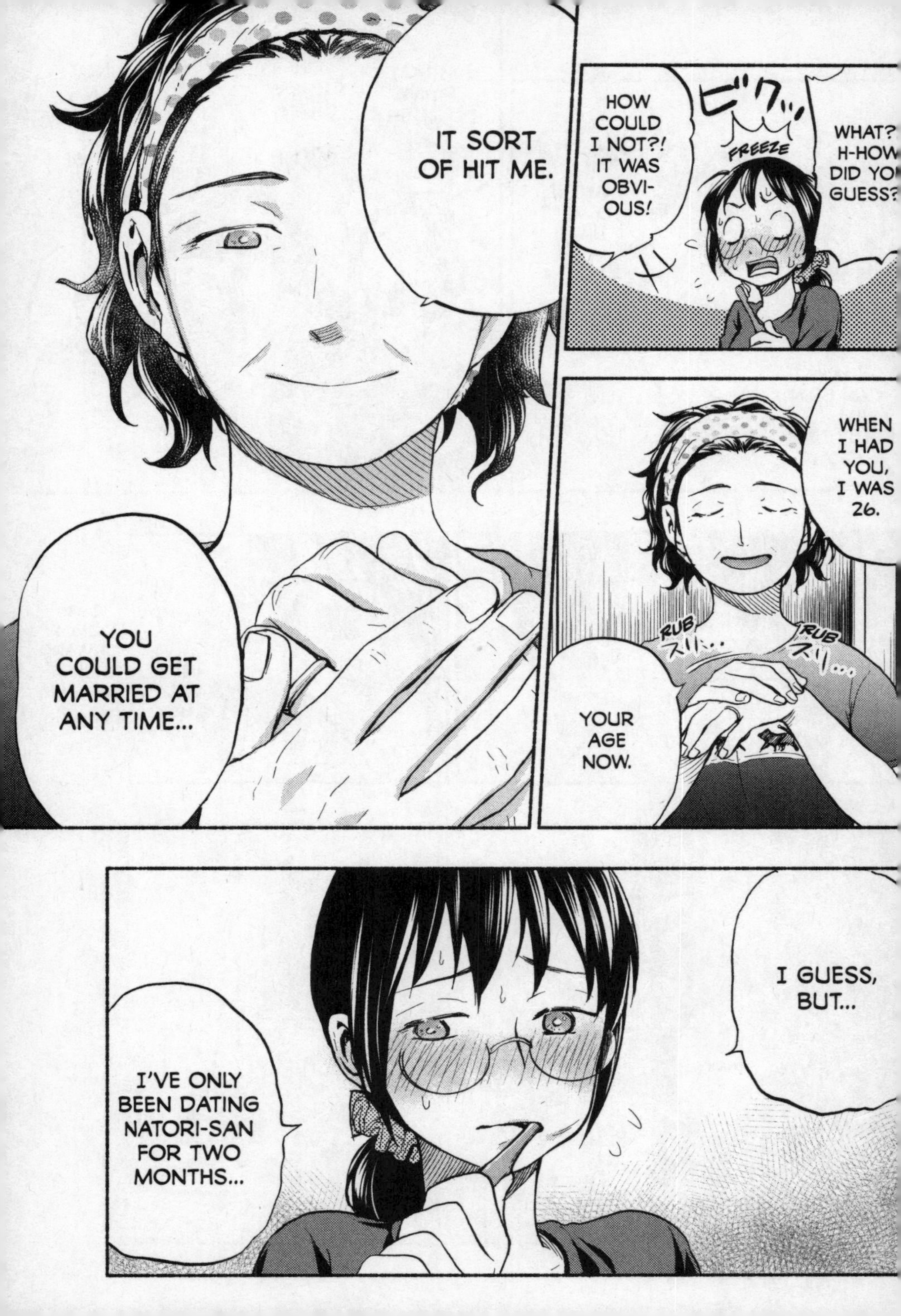
WHAT? H-HOW DID YO GUESS?
ビクッ
FREEZE
HOW COULD I NOT?! IT WAS OBVI-OUS!
WHEN I HAD YOU, I WAS 26.
RUB スリ…
RUB スリ…
YOUR AGE NOW.
IT SORT OF HIT ME.
YOU COULD GET MARRIED AT ANY TIME...
I GUESS, BUT...
I'VE ONLY BEEN DATING NATORI-SAN FOR TWO MONTHS...

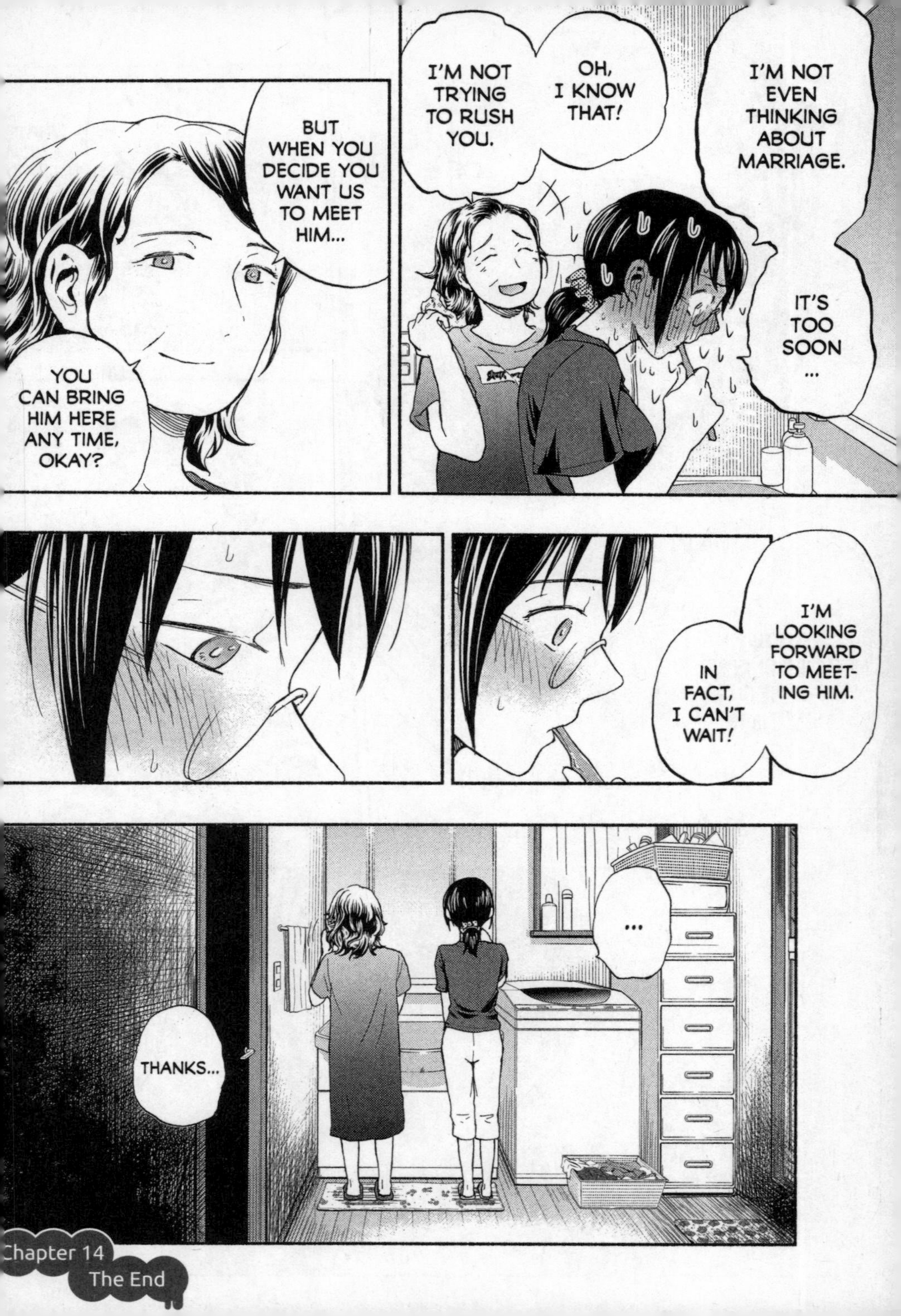
I'M NOT EVEN THINKING ABOUT MARRIAGE.
IT'S TOO SOON ...
OH, I KNOW THAT!
I'M NOT TRYING TO RUSH YOU.
BUT WHEN YOU DECIDE YOU WANT US TO MEET HIM...
YOU CAN BRING HIM HERE ANY TIME, OKAY?
I'M LOOKING FORWARD TO MEET-ING HIM.
IN FACT, I CAN'T WAIT!
...
THANKS...
Chapter 14 The End

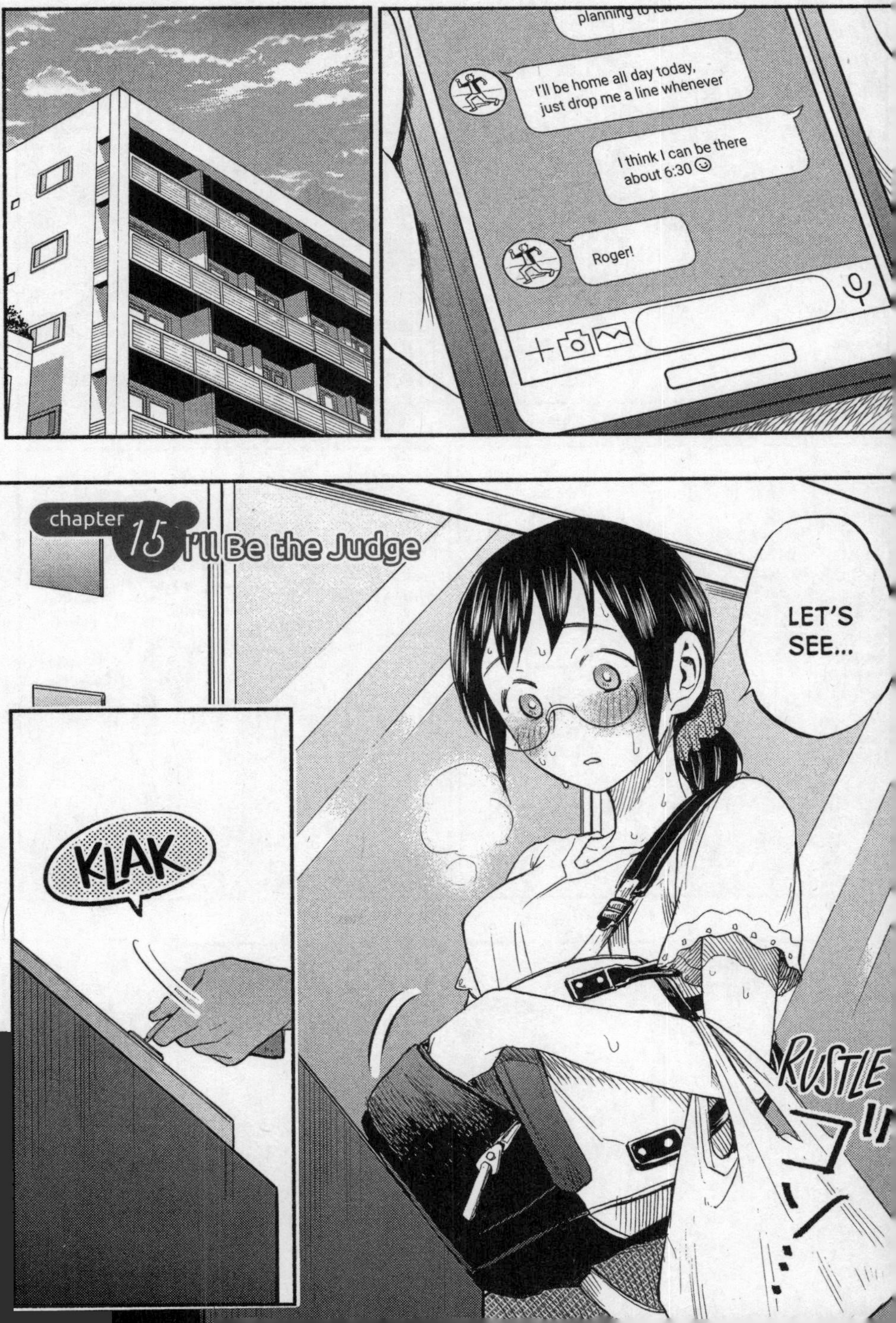
I'll be home all day today, just drop me a line whenever
I think I can be there about 6:30 ☺
Roger!
chapter 15 I'll Be the Judge
LET'S SEE...
RUSTLE
KLAK

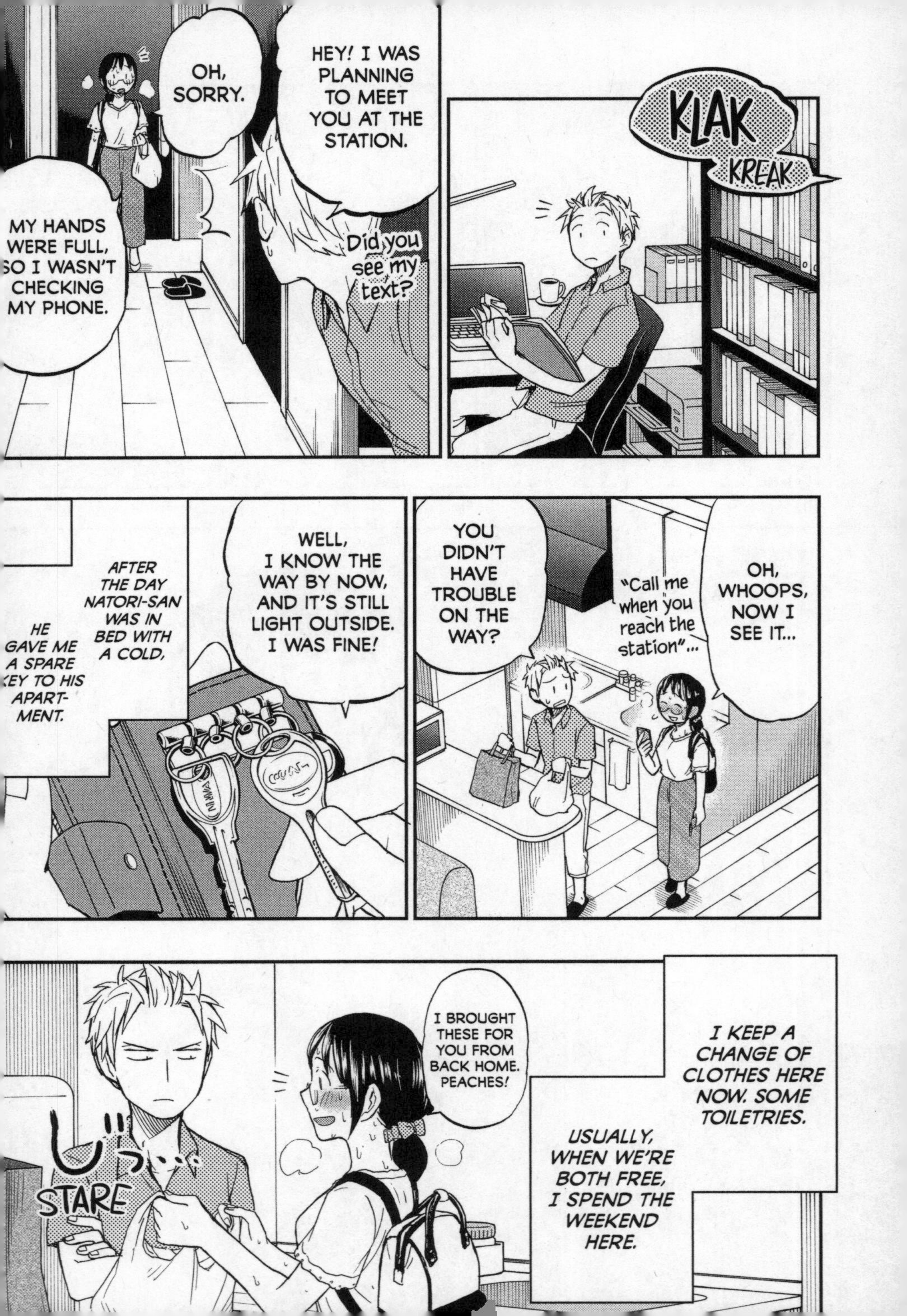
KLAK
KREAK
HEY! I WAS PLANNING TO MEET YOU AT THE STATION.
OH, SORRY.
Did you see my text?
MY HANDS WERE FULL, SO I WASN'T CHECKING MY PHONE.
OH, WHOOPS, NOW I SEE IT...
"Call me when you reach the station"...
YOU DIDN'T HAVE TROUBLE ON THE WAY?
WELL, I KNOW THE WAY BY NOW, AND IT'S STILL LIGHT OUTSIDE. I WAS FINE!
AFTER THE DAY NATORI-SAN WAS IN BED WITH A COLD,
HE GAVE ME A SPARE KEY TO HIS APARTMENT.
I KEEP A CHANGE OF CLOTHES HERE NOW. SOME TOILETRIES.
USUALLY, WHEN WE'RE BOTH FREE, I SPEND THE WEEKEND HERE.
I BROUGHT THESE FOR YOU FROM BACK HOME. PEACHES!
STARE

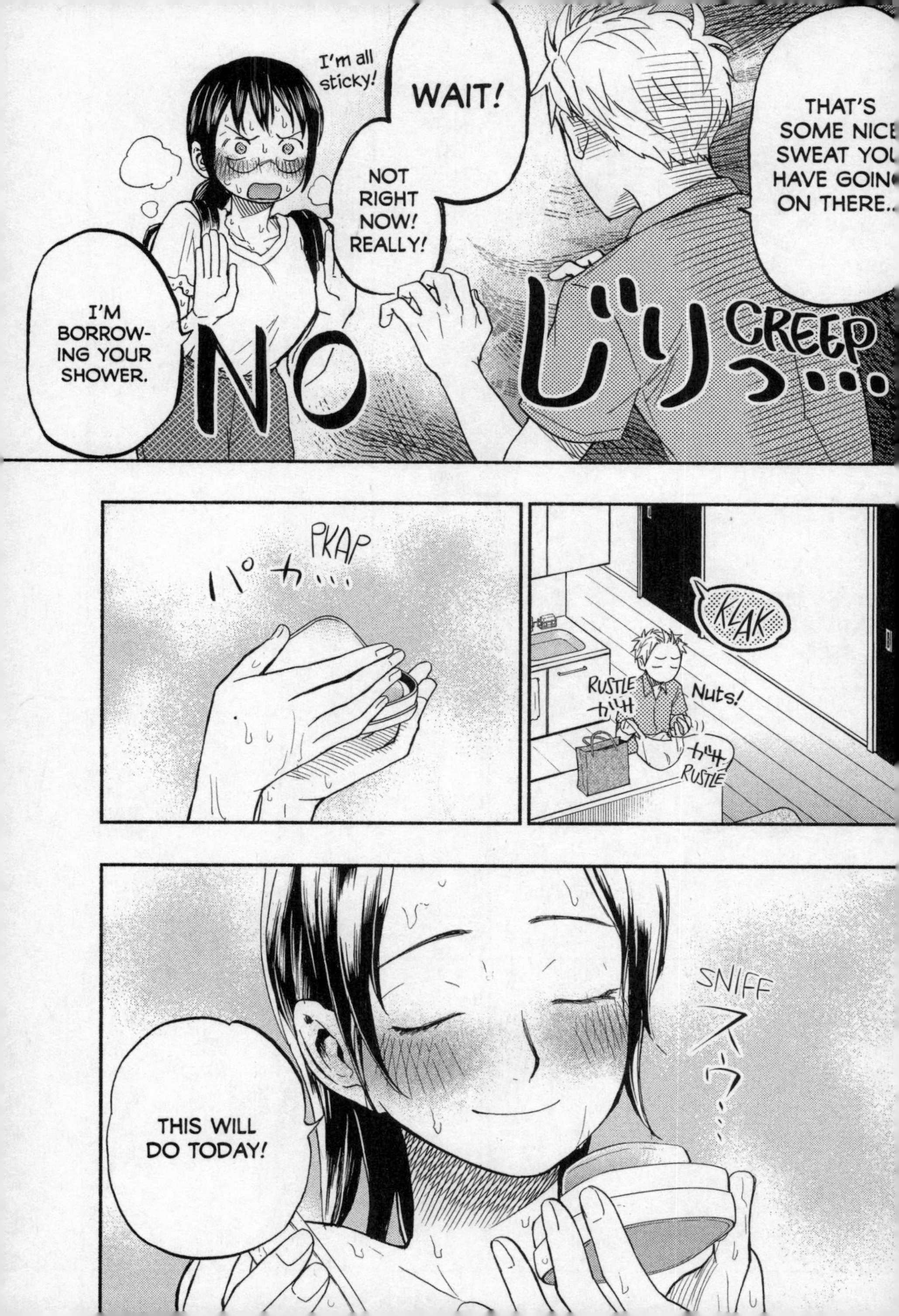
THAT'S SOME NICE SWEAT YOU HAVE GOING ON THERE...
じりっ…
CREEP
WAIT!
NOT RIGHT NOW! REALLY!
I'm all sticky!
NO
I'M BORROWING YOUR SHOWER.
KLAK
Nuts!
ガサ
RUSTLE
ガサ
RUSTLE
パカ…
PKAP
スーッ…
SNIFF
THIS WILL DO TODAY!

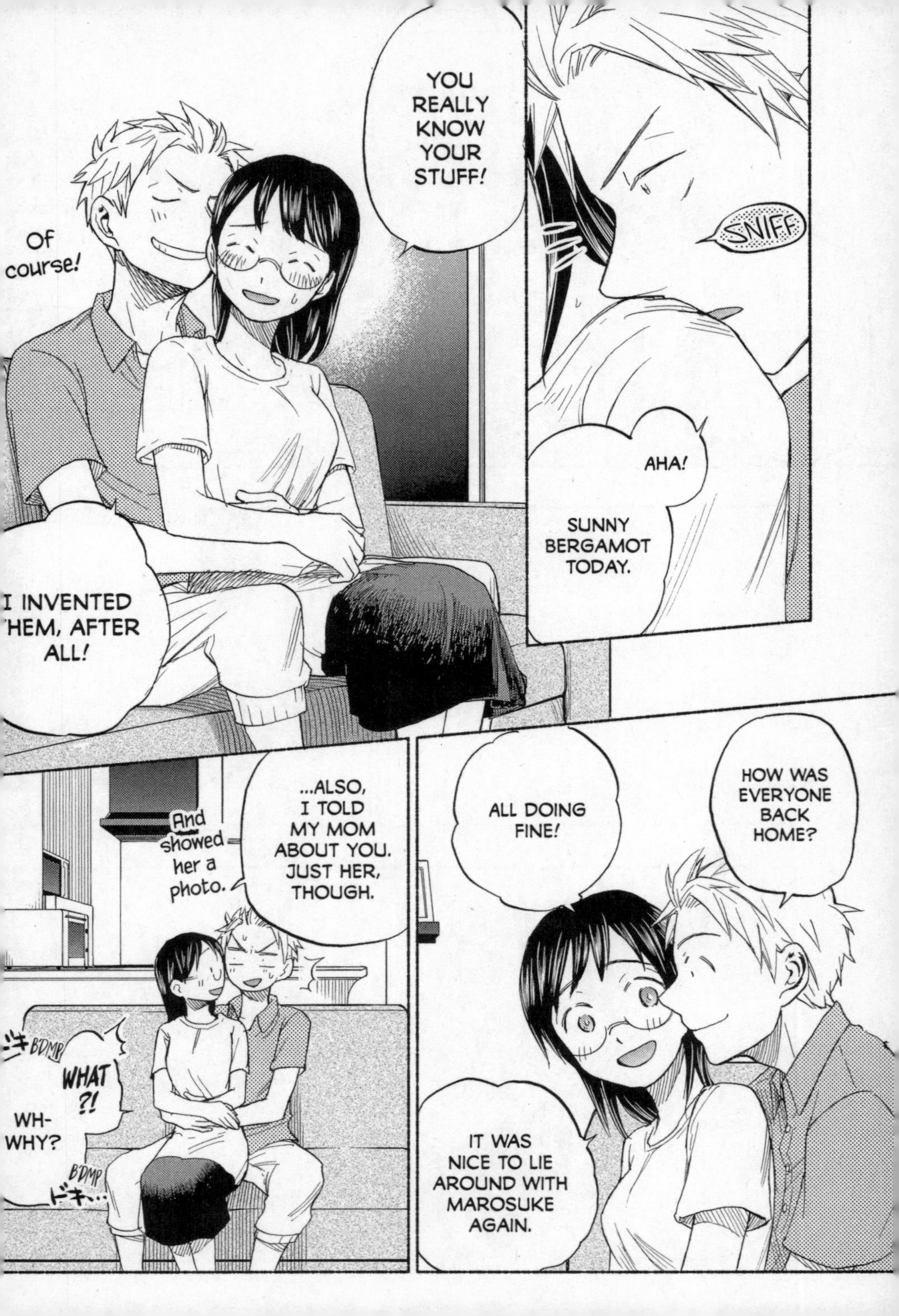
SNIFF
AHA!
SUNNY BERGAMOT TODAY.
YOU REALLY KNOW YOUR STUFF!
Of course!
I INVENTED THEM, AFTER ALL!
HOW WAS EVERYONE BACK HOME?
ALL DOING FINE!
IT WAS NICE TO LIE AROUND WITH MAROSUKE AGAIN.
...ALSO, I TOLD MY MOM ABOUT YOU. JUST HER, THOUGH.
And showed her a photo.
B'DMP
WHAT?!
WH- WHY?
B'DMP
ドキ…

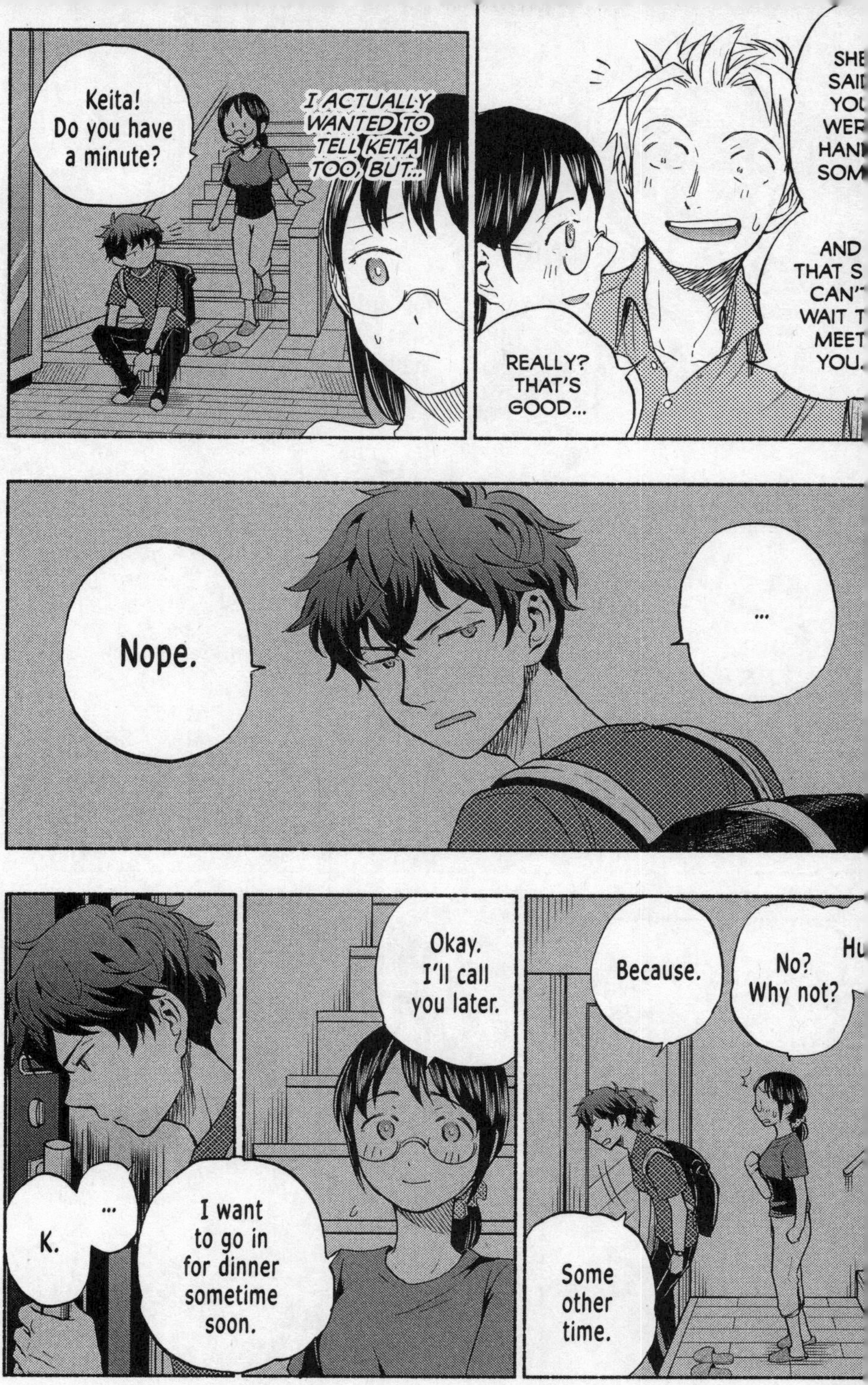

SHE SAID YOU WER HAN SOM
AND THAT S CAN'T WAIT T MEET YOU.
REALLY? THAT'S GOOD...
I ACTUALLY WANTED TO TELL KEITA TOO, BUT...
Keita! Do you have a minute?
...
Nope.
Hu
No? Why not?
Because.
Some other time.
Okay. I'll call you later.
I want to go in for dinner sometime soon.
...
K.

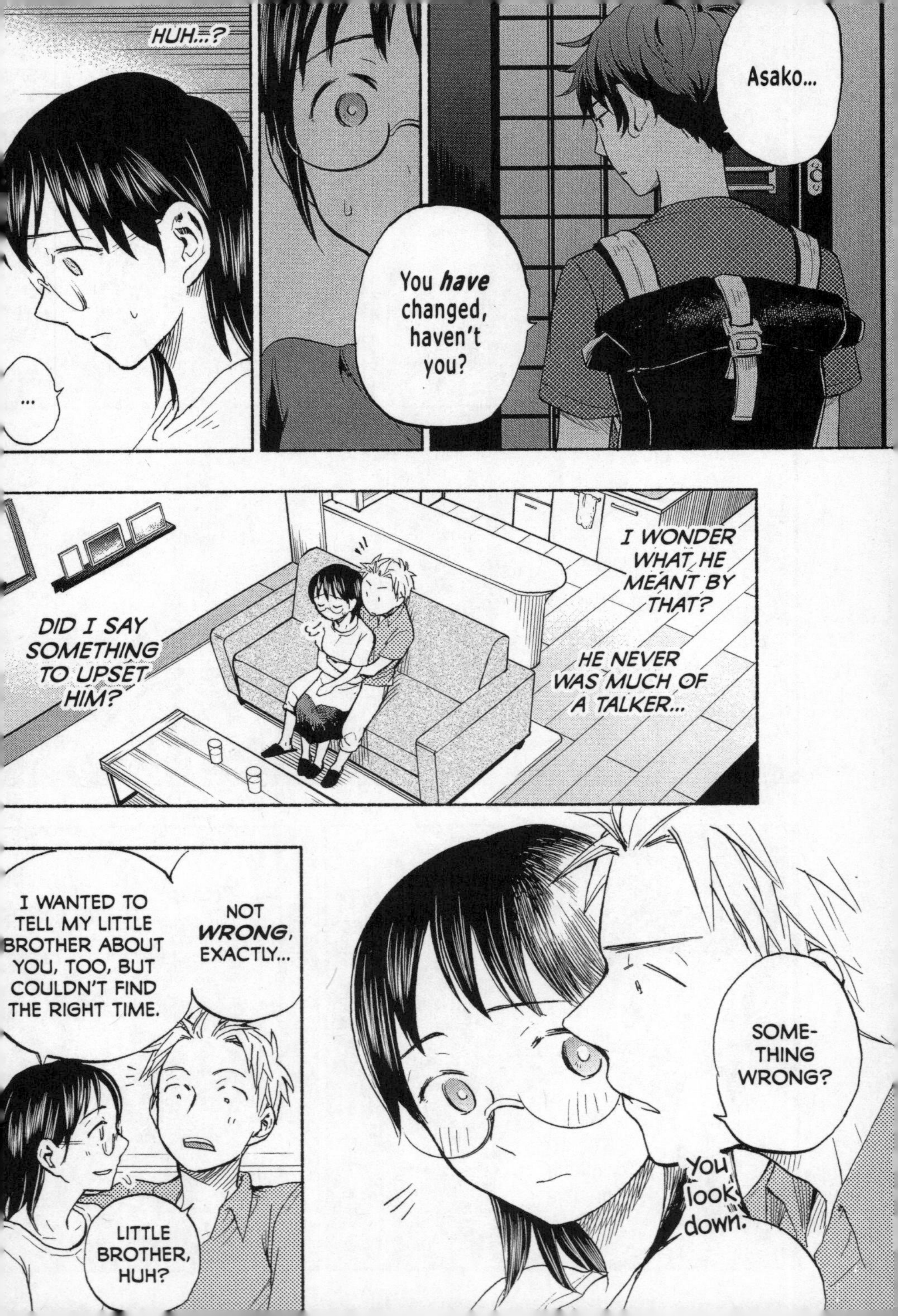

Asako...
You *have* changed, haven't you?
HUH...?
...
I WONDER WHAT HE MEANT BY THAT?
HE NEVER WAS MUCH OF A TALKER...
DID I SAY SOMETHING TO UPSET HIM?
SOME-THING WRONG?
You look down.
NOT *WRONG*, EXACTLY...
I WANTED TO TELL MY LITTLE BROTHER ABOUT YOU, TOO, BUT COULDN'T FIND THE RIGHT TIME.
LITTLE BROTHER, HUH?

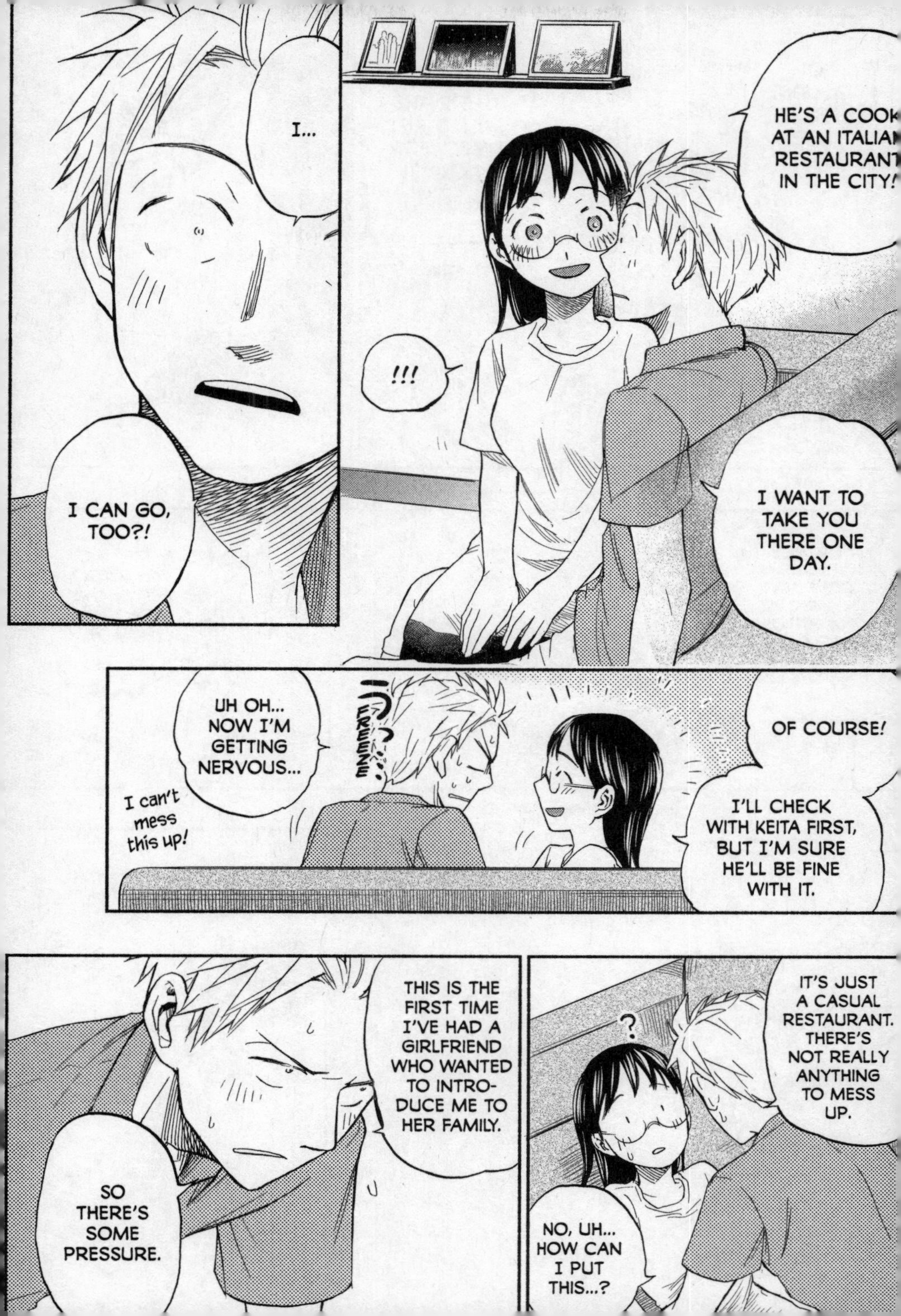
HE'S A COOK AT AN ITALIAN RESTAURANT IN THE CITY!
I WANT TO TAKE YOU THERE ONE DAY.
!!!
I...
I CAN GO, TOO?!
OF COURSE!
I'LL CHECK WITH KEITA FIRST, BUT I'M SURE HE'LL BE FINE WITH IT.
FREEZE
UH OH... NOW I'M GETTING NERVOUS...
I can't mess this up!
IT'S JUST A CASUAL RESTAURANT. THERE'S NOT REALLY ANYTHING TO MESS UP.
?
NO, UH... HOW CAN I PUT THIS...?
THIS IS THE FIRST TIME I'VE HAD A GIRLFRIEND WHO WANTED TO INTRO-DUCE ME TO HER FAMILY.
SO THERE'S SOME PRESSURE.

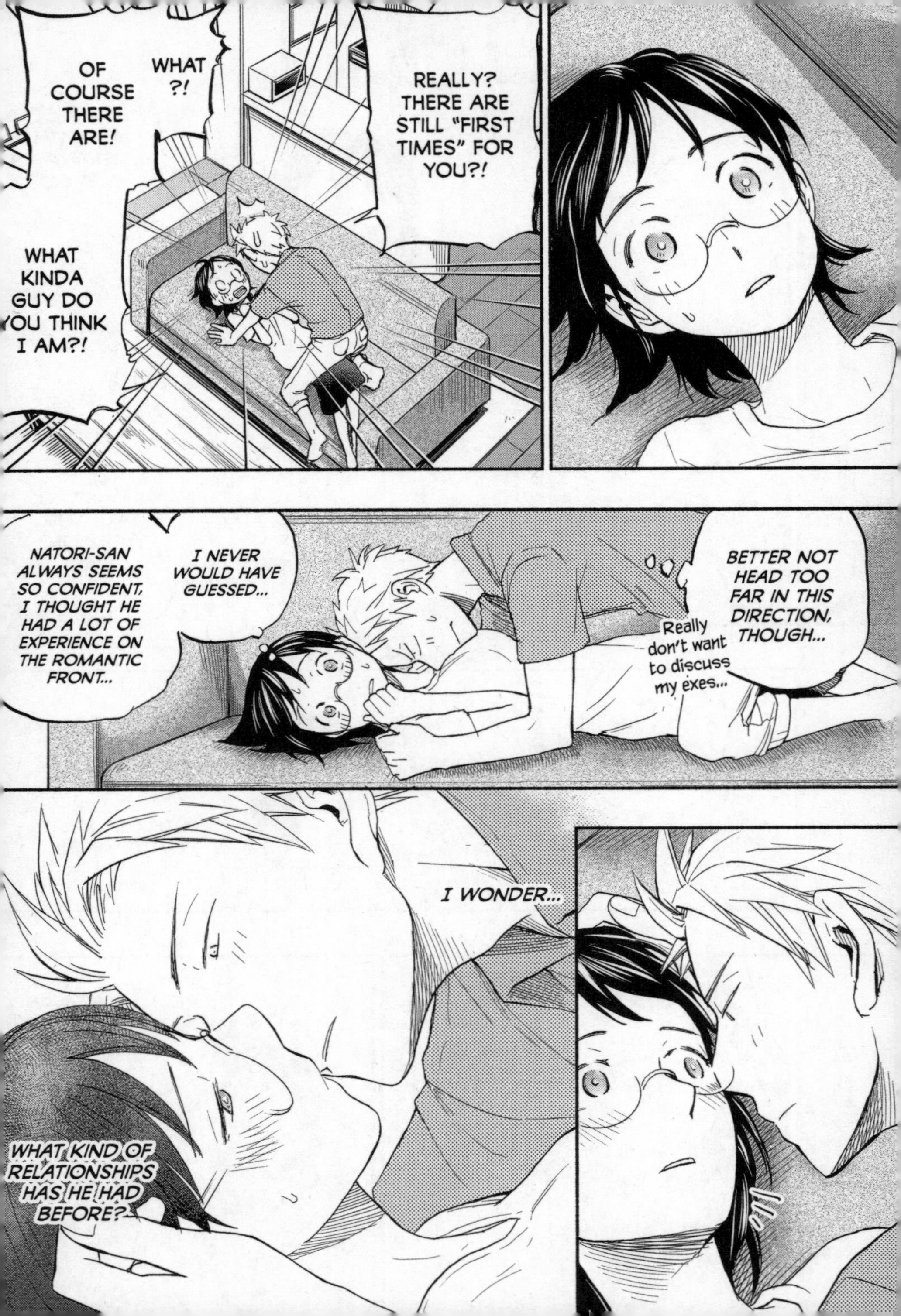
REALLY? THERE ARE STILL "FIRST TIMES" FOR YOU?!
WHAT ?!
OF COURSE THERE ARE!
WHAT KINDA GUY DO YOU THINK I AM?!
BETTER NOT HEAD TOO FAR IN THIS DIRECTION, THOUGH...
Really don't want to discuss my exes...
I NEVER WOULD HAVE GUESSED...
NATORI-SAN ALWAYS SEEMS SO CONFIDENT, I THOUGHT HE HAD A LOT OF EXPERIENCE ON THE ROMANTIC FRONT...
I WONDER...
WHAT KIND OF RELATIONSHIPS HAS HE HAD BEFORE?

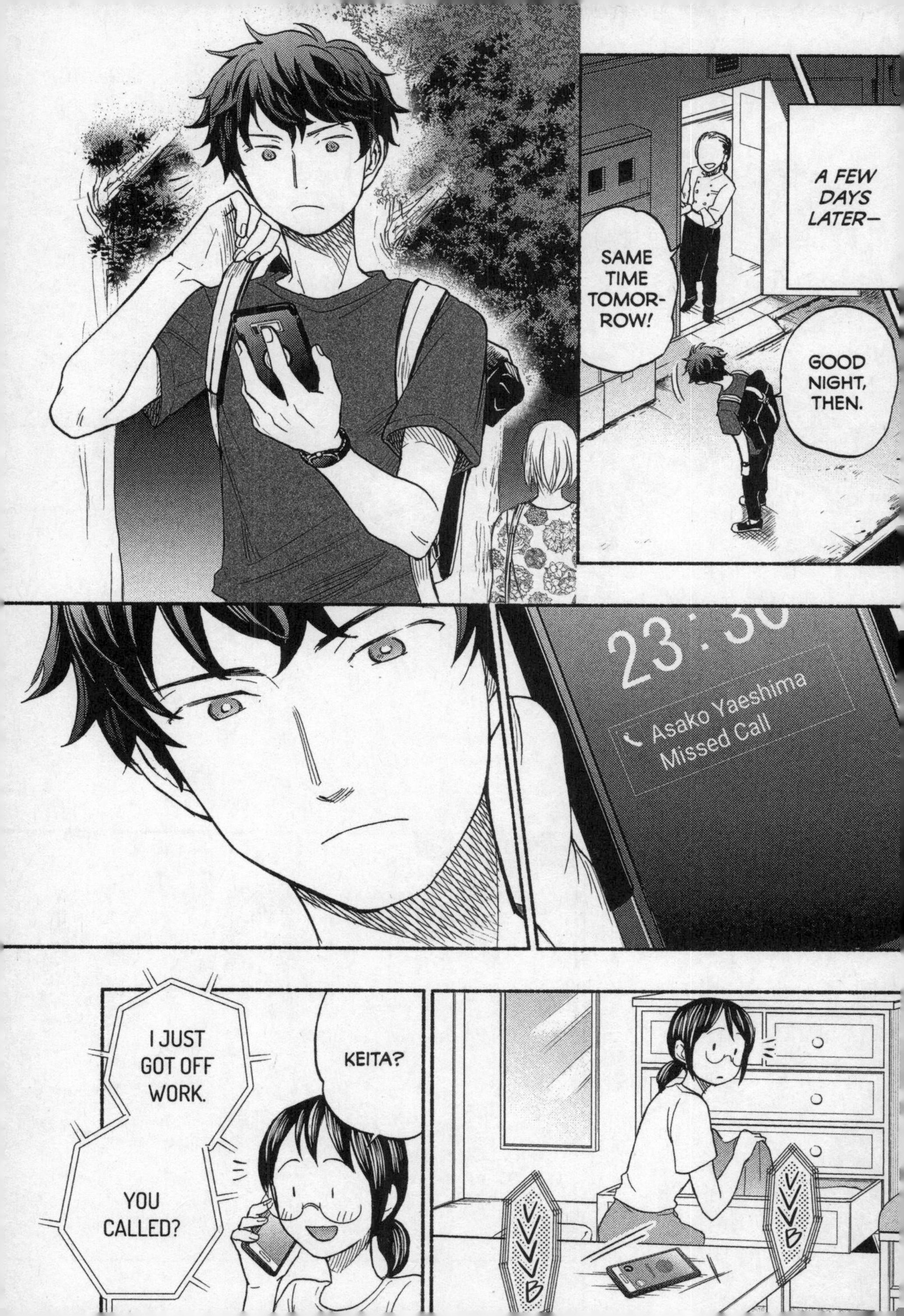
A FEW DAYS LATER—
SAME TIME TOMORROW!
GOOD NIGHT, THEN.
23 : 30
Asako Yaeshima Missed Call
VVVB
VVVB
KEITA?
I JUST GOT OFF WORK.
YOU CALLED?

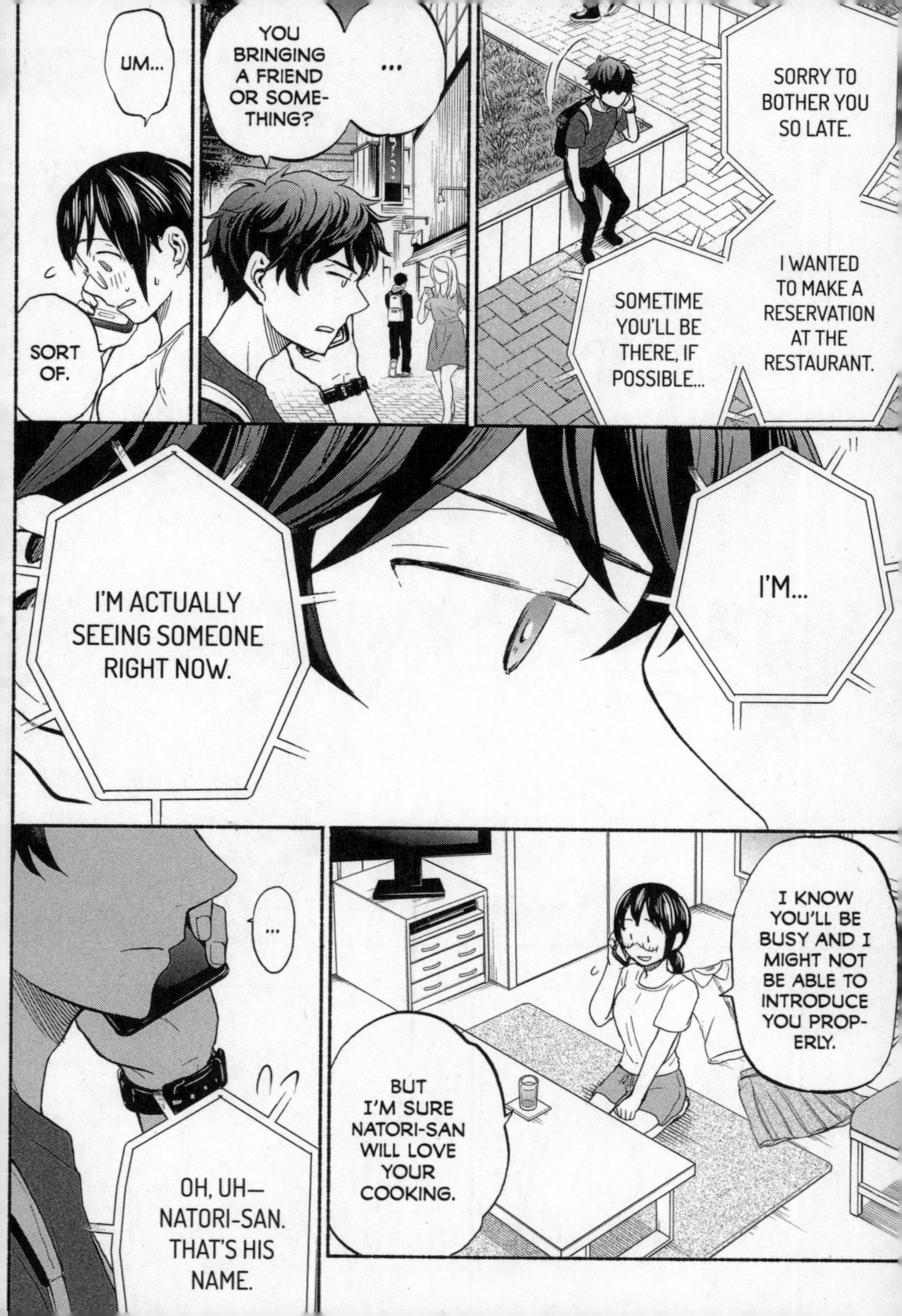
SORRY TO BOTHER YOU SO LATE.
I WANTED TO MAKE A RESERVATION AT THE RESTAURANT.
SOMETIME YOU'LL BE THERE, IF POSSIBLE...
YOU BRINGING A FRIEND OR SOMETHING?
...
UM...
SORT OF.
I'M...
I'M ACTUALLY SEEING SOMEONE RIGHT NOW.
I KNOW YOU'LL BE BUSY AND I MIGHT NOT BE ABLE TO INTRODUCE YOU PROPERLY.
BUT I'M SURE NATORI-SAN WILL LOVE YOUR COOKING.
...
OH, UH— NATORI-SAN. THAT'S HIS NAME.

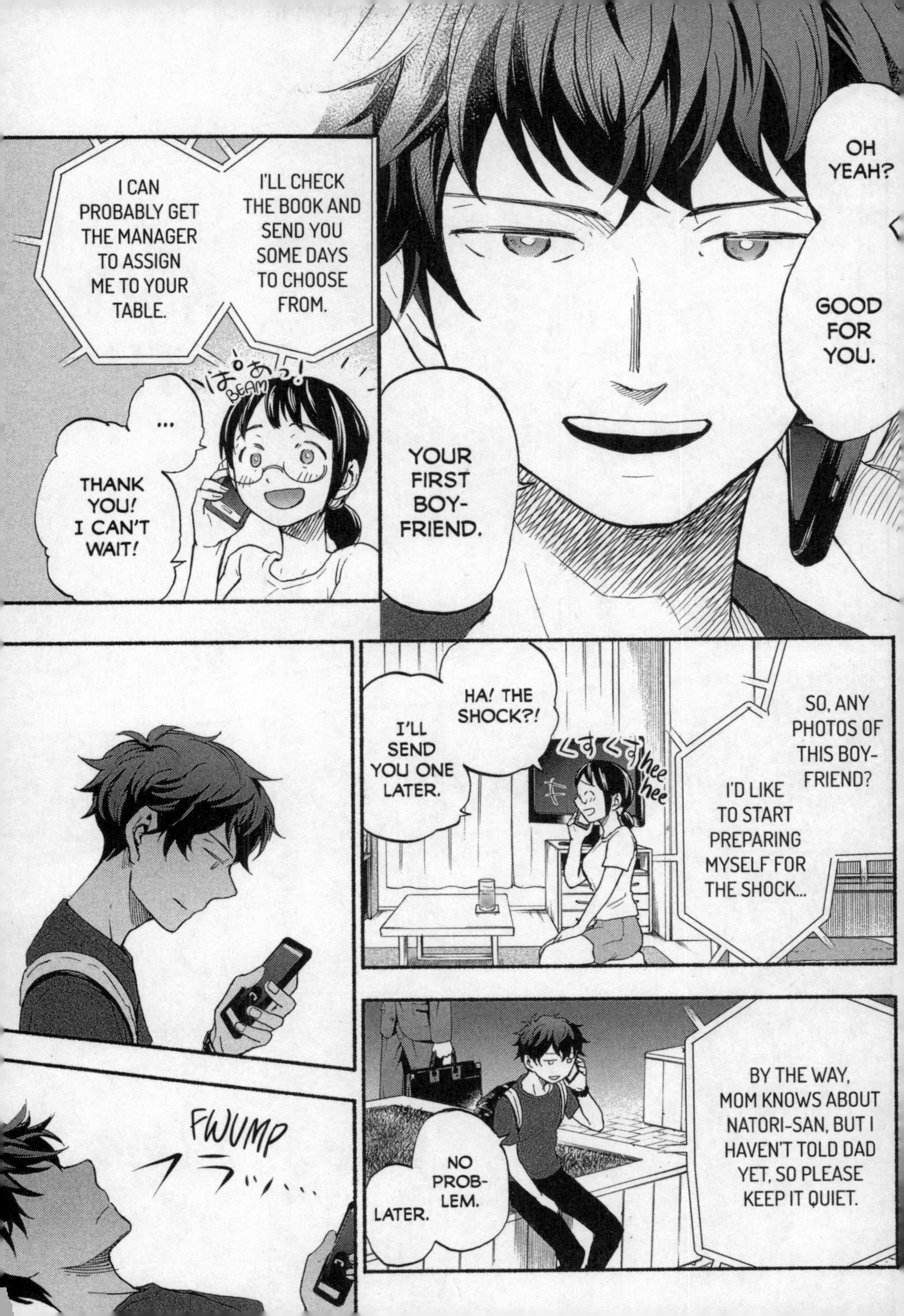
OH YEAH?
GOOD FOR YOU.
YOUR FIRST BOY-FRIEND.
I'LL CHECK THE BOOK AND SEND YOU SOME DAYS TO CHOOSE FROM.
I CAN PROBABLY GET THE MANAGER TO ASSIGN ME TO YOUR TABLE.
BEAM
...
THANK YOU! I CAN'T WAIT!
SO, ANY PHOTOS OF THIS BOY-FRIEND?
I'D LIKE TO START PREPARING MYSELF FOR THE SHOCK...
HA! THE SHOCK?!
I'LL SEND YOU ONE LATER.
hee hee
BY THE WAY, MOM KNOWS ABOUT NATORI-SAN, BUT I HAVEN'T TOLD DAD YET, SO PLEASE KEEP IT QUIET.
NO PROB-LEM.
LATER.
FWUMP

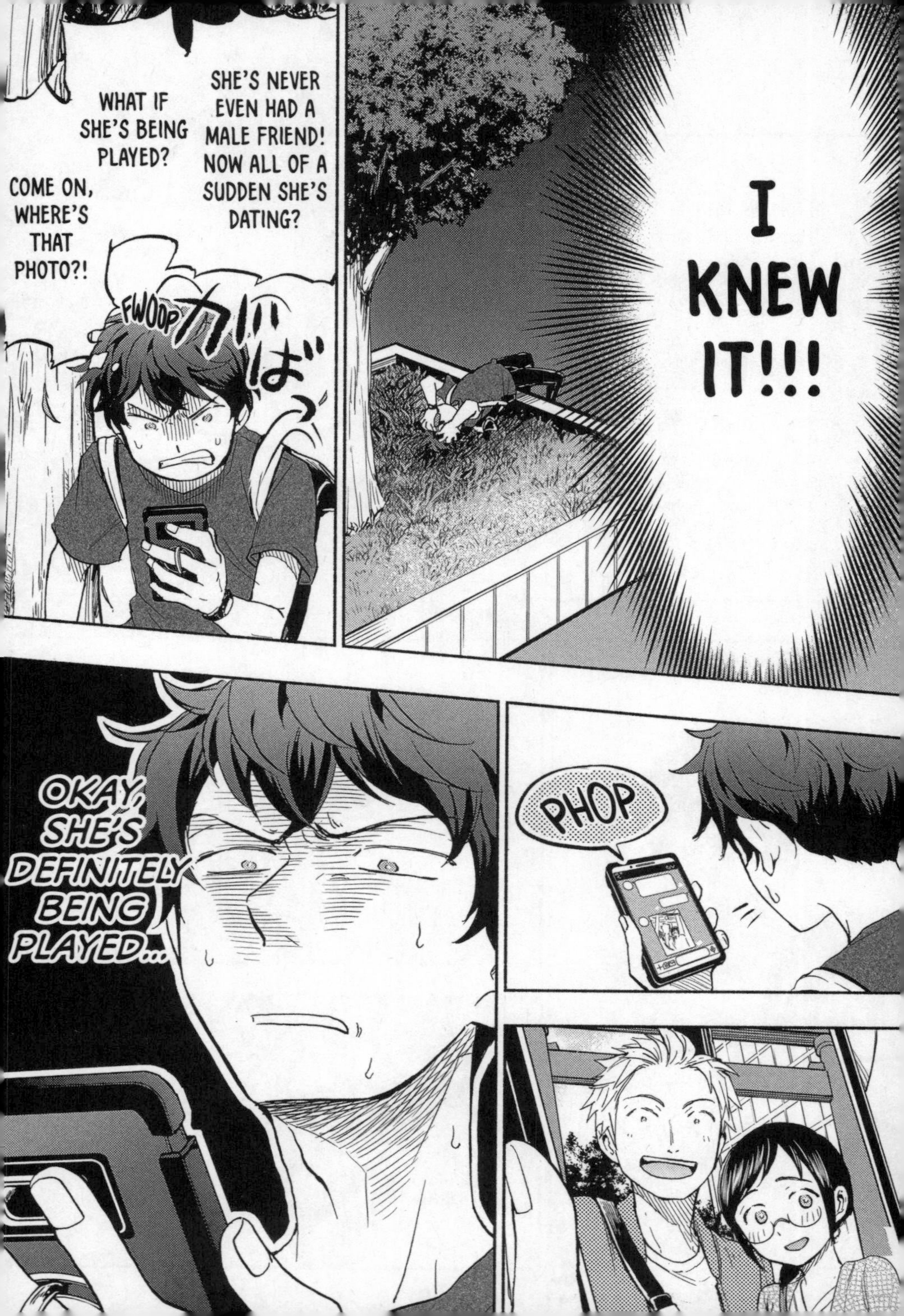
I KNEW IT!!!
SHE'S NEVER EVEN HAD A MALE FRIEND! NOW ALL OF A SUDDEN SHE'S DATING?
WHAT IF SHE'S BEING PLAYED?
COME ON, WHERE'S THAT PHOTO?!
FWOOP
カばっ
PHOP
OKAY, SHE'S DEFINITELY BEING PLAYED...

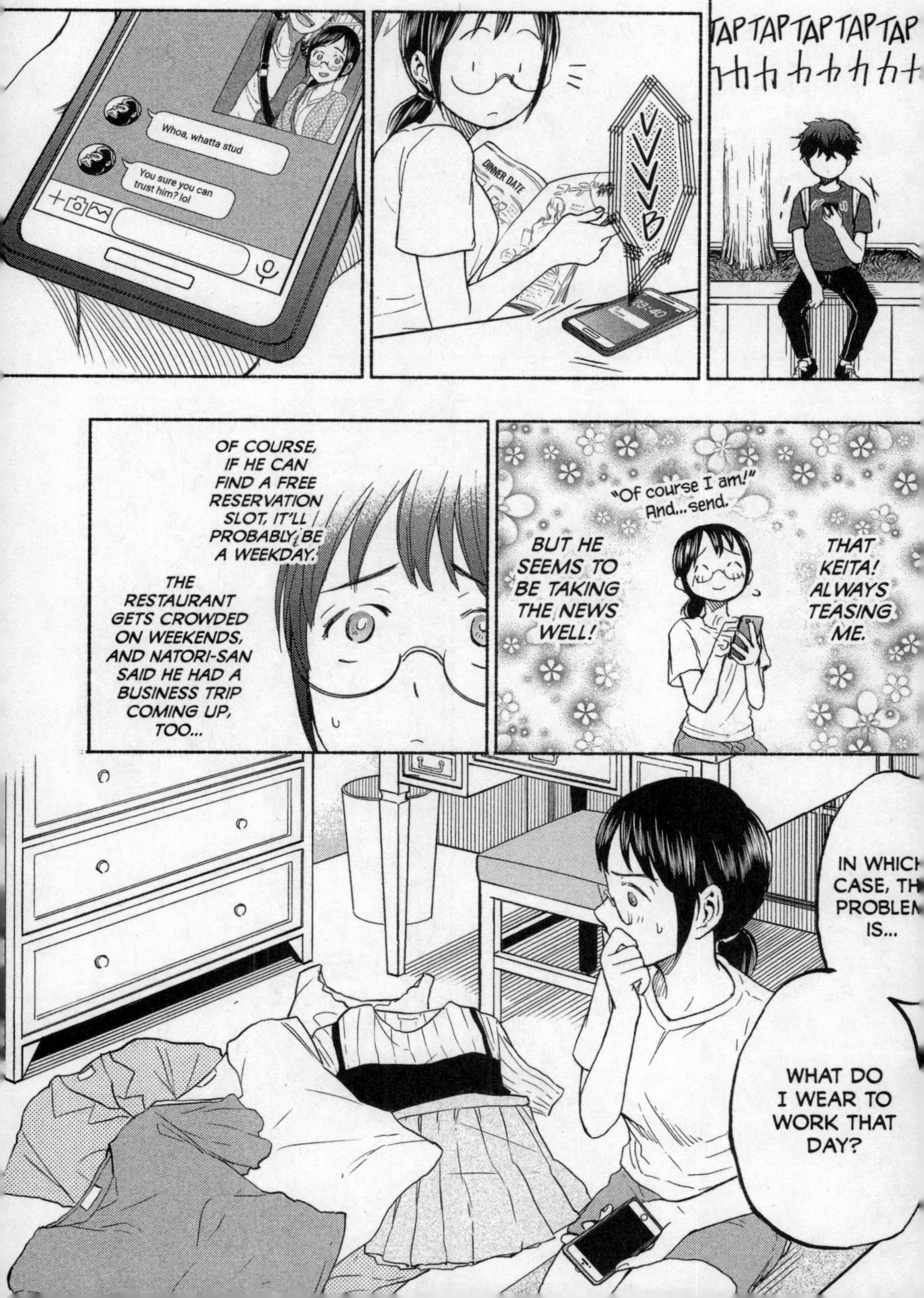
TAPTAPTAPTAPTAP
カカカカカカ
VVVVB
DINNER DATE
Whoa, whatta stud
You sure you can trust him? lol
"Of course I am!" And...send.
THAT KEITA! ALWAYS TEASING ME.
BUT HE SEEMS TO BE TAKING THE NEWS WELL!
OF COURSE, IF HE CAN FIND A FREE RESERVATION SLOT, IT'LL PROBABLY BE A WEEKDAY.
THE RESTAURANT GETS CROWDED ON WEEKENDS, AND NATORI-SAN SAID HE HAD A BUSINESS TRIP COMING UP, TOO...
IN WHIC CASE, TH PROBLEM IS...
WHAT DO I WEAR TO WORK THAT DAY?

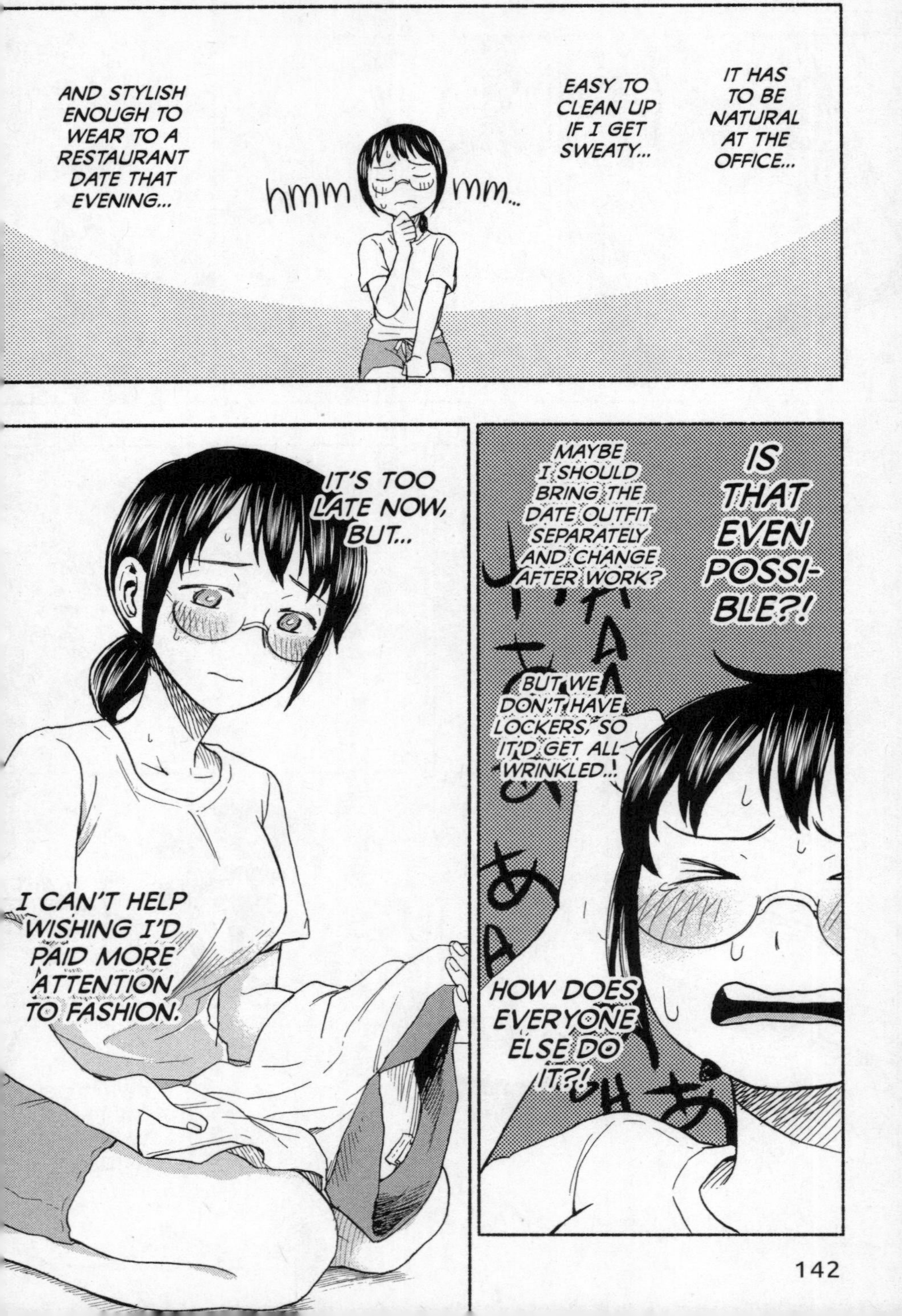

IT HAS TO BE NATURAL AT THE OFFICE...
EASY TO CLEAN UP IF I GET SWEATY...
hmm mm...
AND STYLISH ENOUGH TO WEAR TO A RESTAURANT DATE THAT EVENING...
IS THAT EVEN POSSI-BLE?!
MAYBE I SHOULD BRING THE DATE OUTFIT SEPARATELY AND CHANGE AFTER WORK?
BUT WE DON'T HAVE LOCKERS, SO IT'D GET ALL WRINKLED...
HOW DOES EVERYONE ELSE DO IT?!
IT'S TOO LATE NOW, BUT...
I CAN'T HELP WISHING I'D PAID MORE ATTENTION TO FASHION.

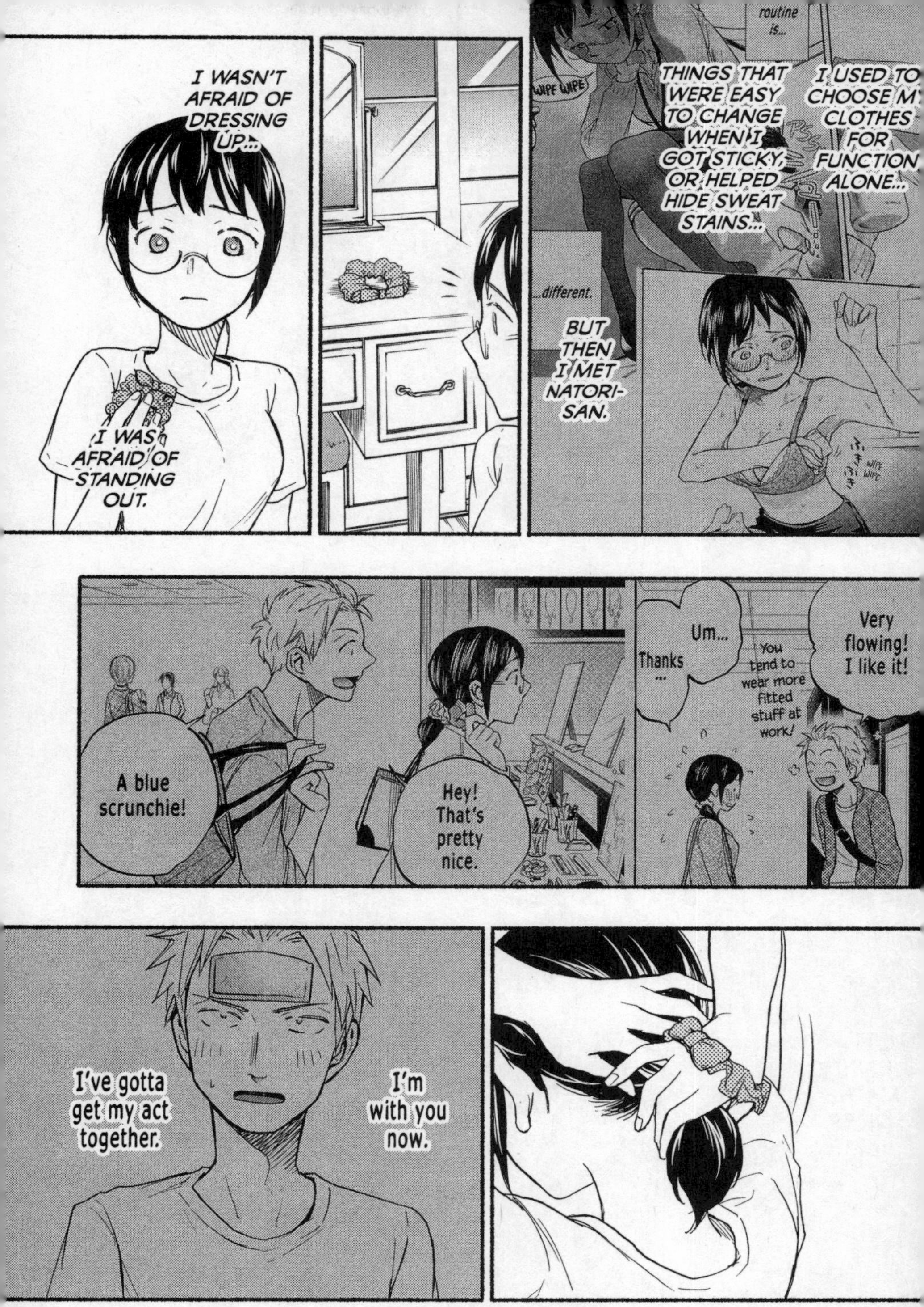
routine is...
I USED TO CHOOSE M CLOTHES FOR FUNCTION ALONE...
THINGS THAT WERE EASY TO CHANGE WHEN I GOT STICKY, OR HELPED HIDE SWEAT STAINS...
WIPE WIPE
...different.
BUT THEN I MET NATORI-SAN.
WIPE WIPE
I WASN'T AFRAID OF DRESSING UP...
I WAS AFRAID OF STANDING OUT.
Very flowing! I like it!
You tend to wear more fitted stuff at work!
Um...
Thanks...
Hey! That's pretty nice.
A blue scrunchie!
I'm with you now.
I've gotta get my act together.

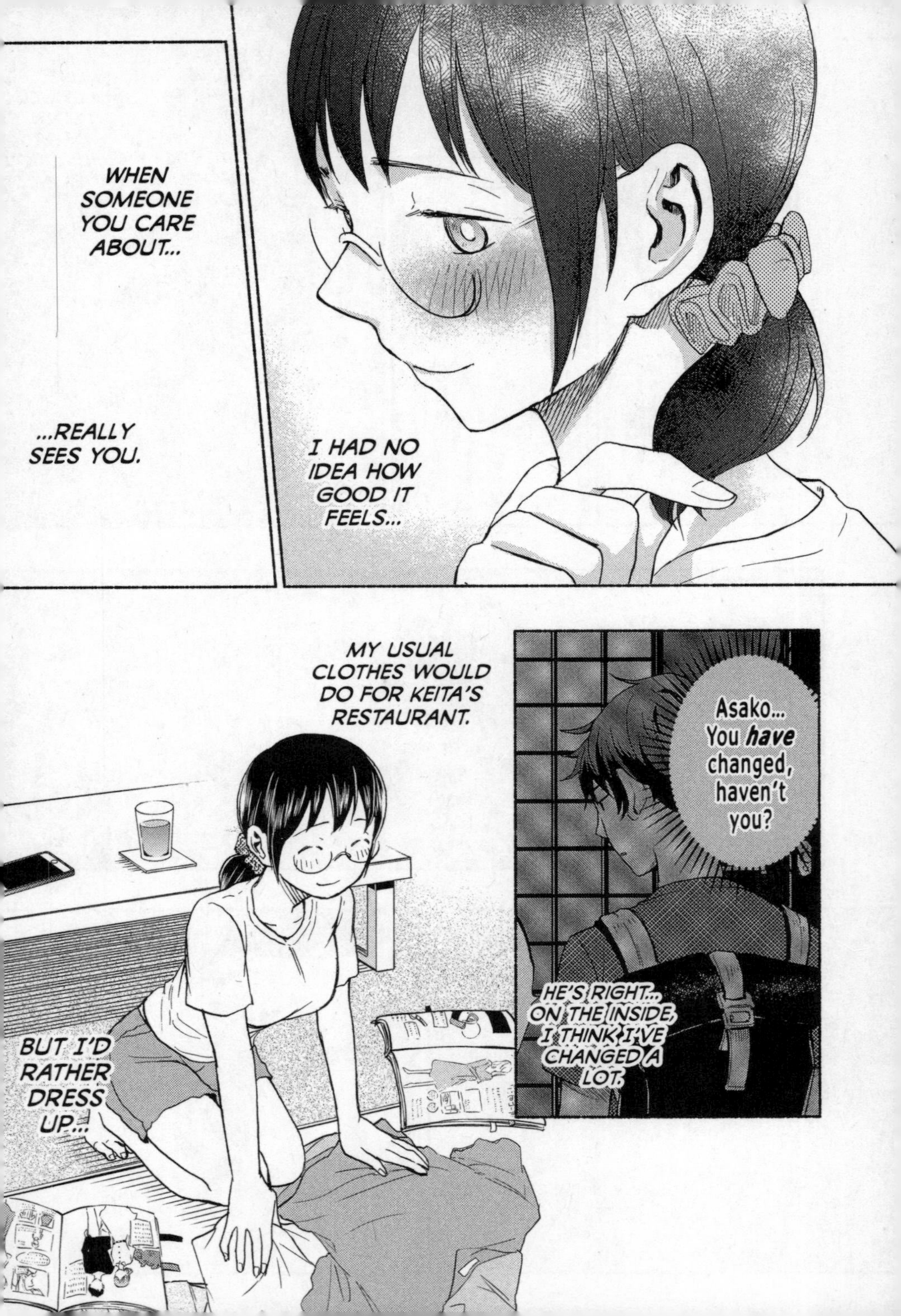
I HAD NO IDEA HOW GOOD IT FEELS...
WHEN SOMEONE YOU CARE ABOUT...
...REALLY SEES YOU.
Asako... You have changed, haven't you?
HE'S RIGHT... ON THE INSIDE, I THINK I'VE CHANGED A LOT.
MY USUAL CLOTHES WOULD DO FOR KEITA'S RESTAURANT.
BUT I'D RATHER DRESS UP...

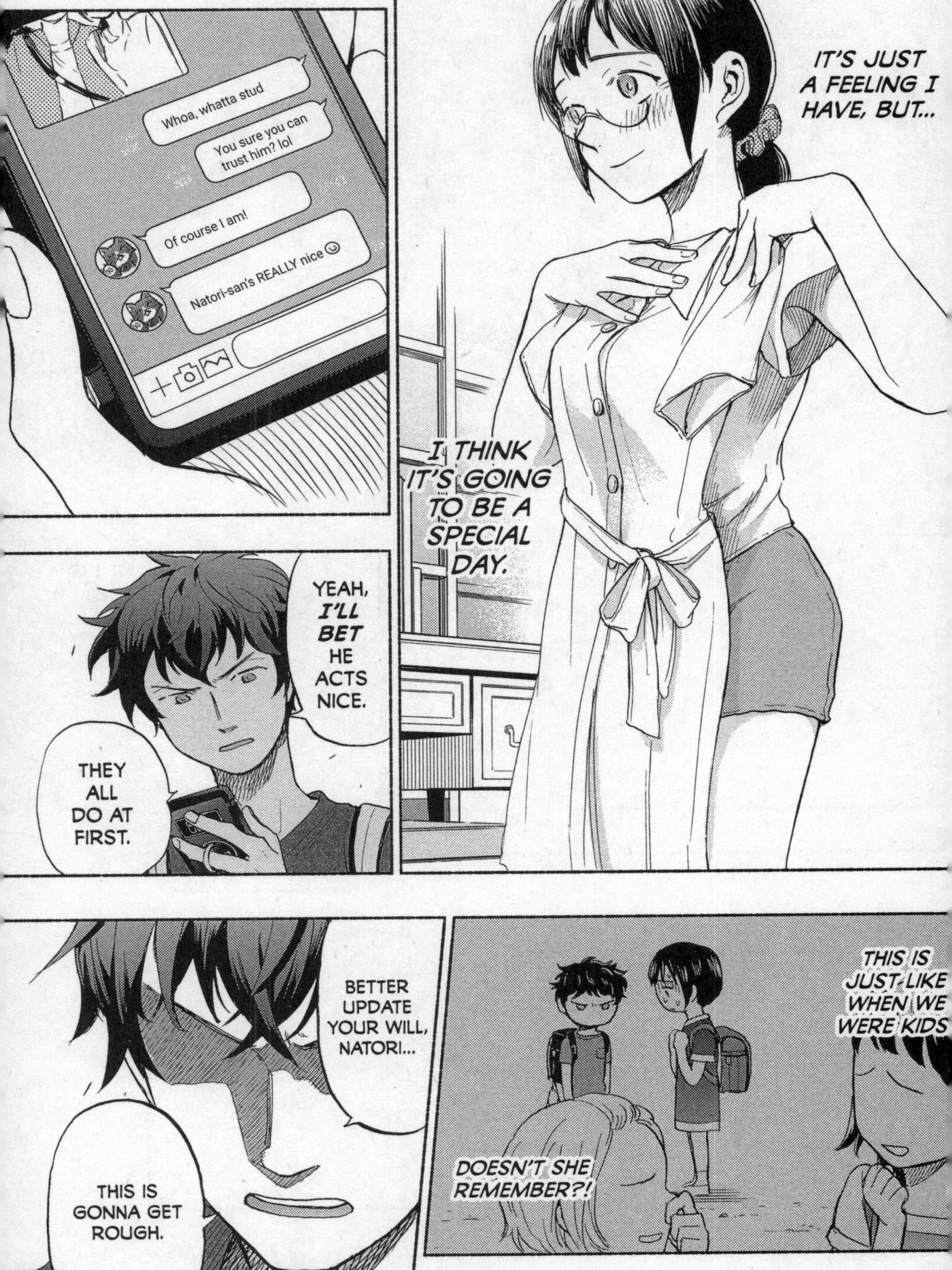
IT'S JUST A FEELING I HAVE, BUT...
I THINK IT'S GOING TO BE A SPECIAL DAY.
Whoa, whatta stud
You sure you can trust him? lol
Of course I am!
Natori-san's REALLY nice ☺
YEAH, *I'LL BET* HE ACTS NICE.
THEY ALL DO AT FIRST.
THIS IS JUST LIKE WHEN WE WERE KIDS
DOESN'T SHE REMEMBER?!
BETTER UPDATE YOUR WILL, NATORI...
THIS IS GONNA GET ROUGH.

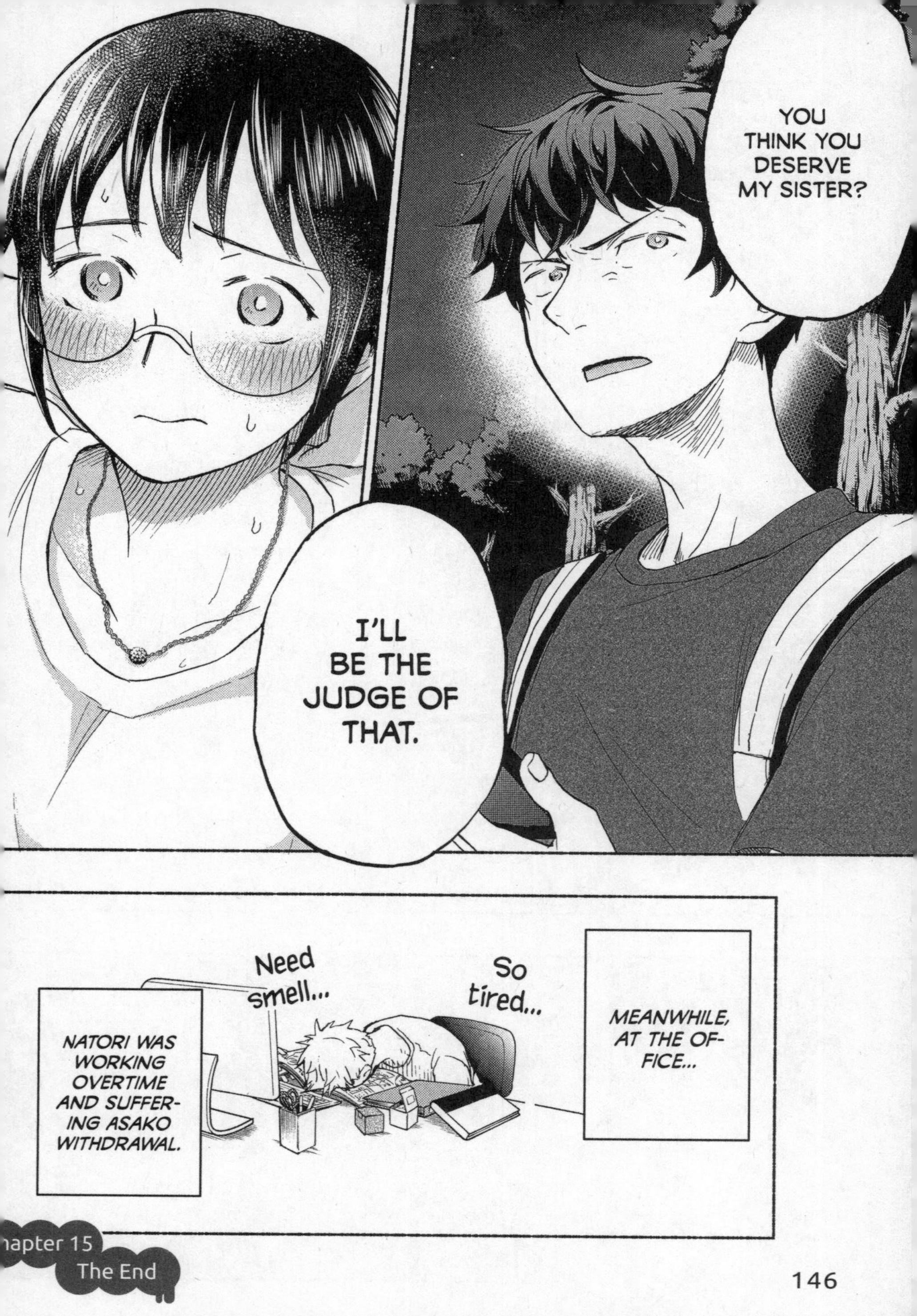
YOU THINK YOU DESERVE MY SISTER?
I'LL BE THE JUDGE OF THAT.
MEANWHILE, AT THE OF-FICE...
So tired...
Need smell...
NATORI WAS WORKING OVERTIME AND SUFFER-ING ASAKO WITHDRAWAL.
apter 15 The End

BONUS! ROUGH DRAFT THEATER!
NATORI-SAN PROTOTYPE II

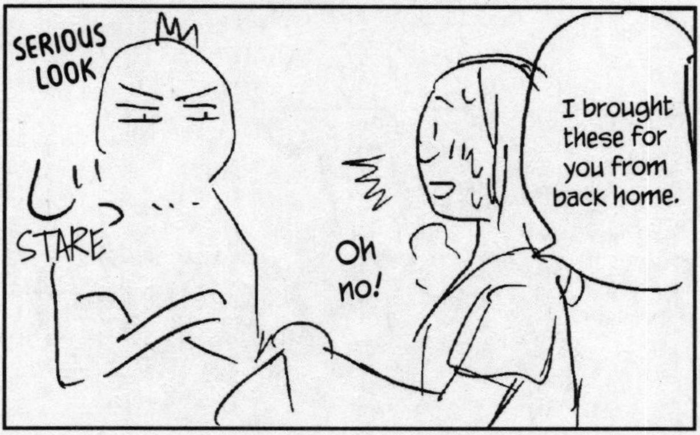
I brought these for you from back home.
Oh no!
SERIOUS LOOK
STARE

SWEAT AND SOAP

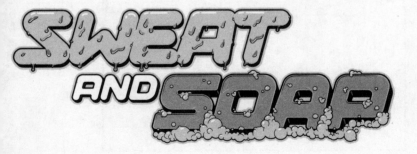

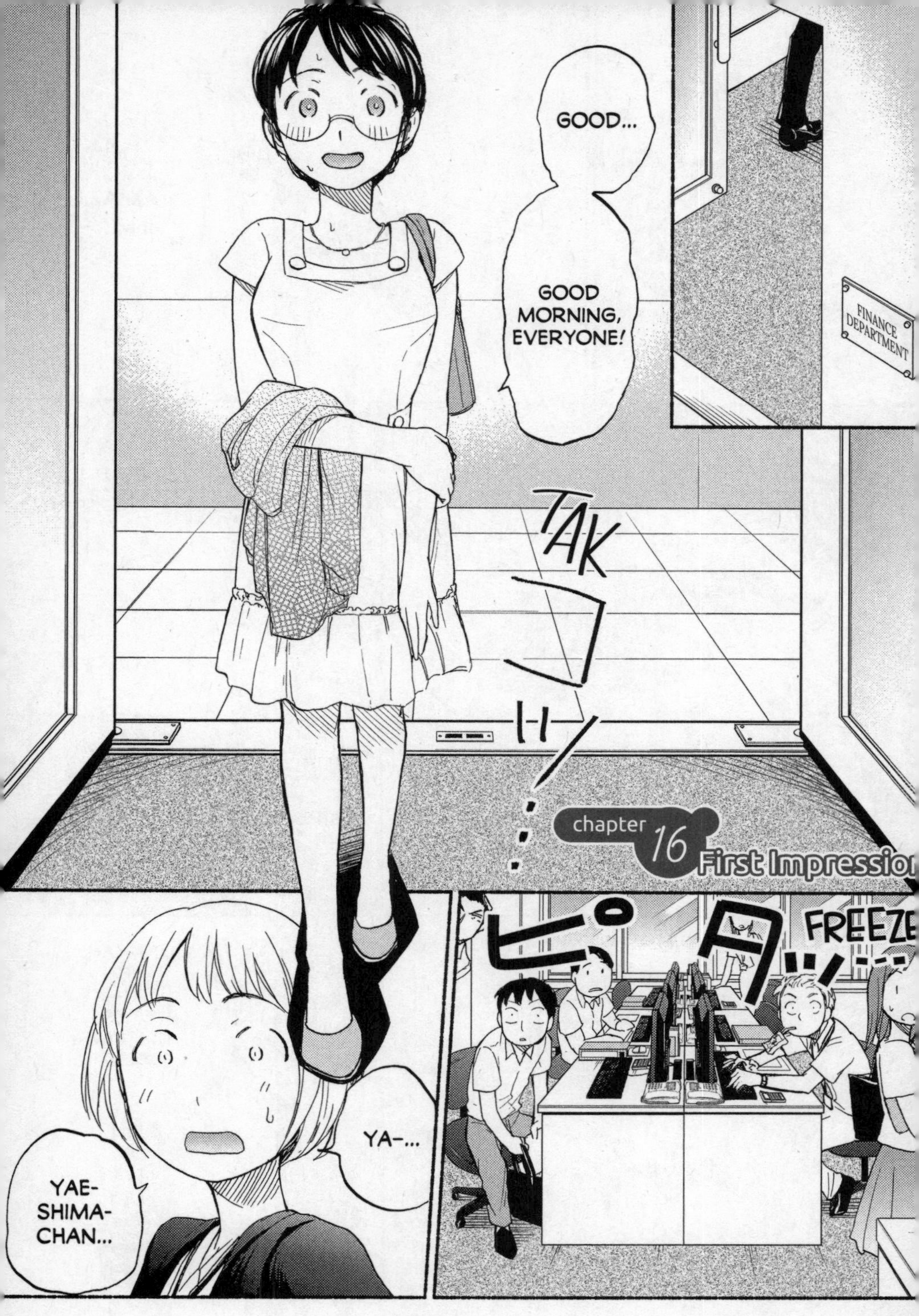
FINANCE DEPARTMENT
GOOD...
GOOD MORNING, EVERYONE!
TAK
chapter 16
First Impressio
FREEZE
YA-...
YAE-SHIMA-CHAN...

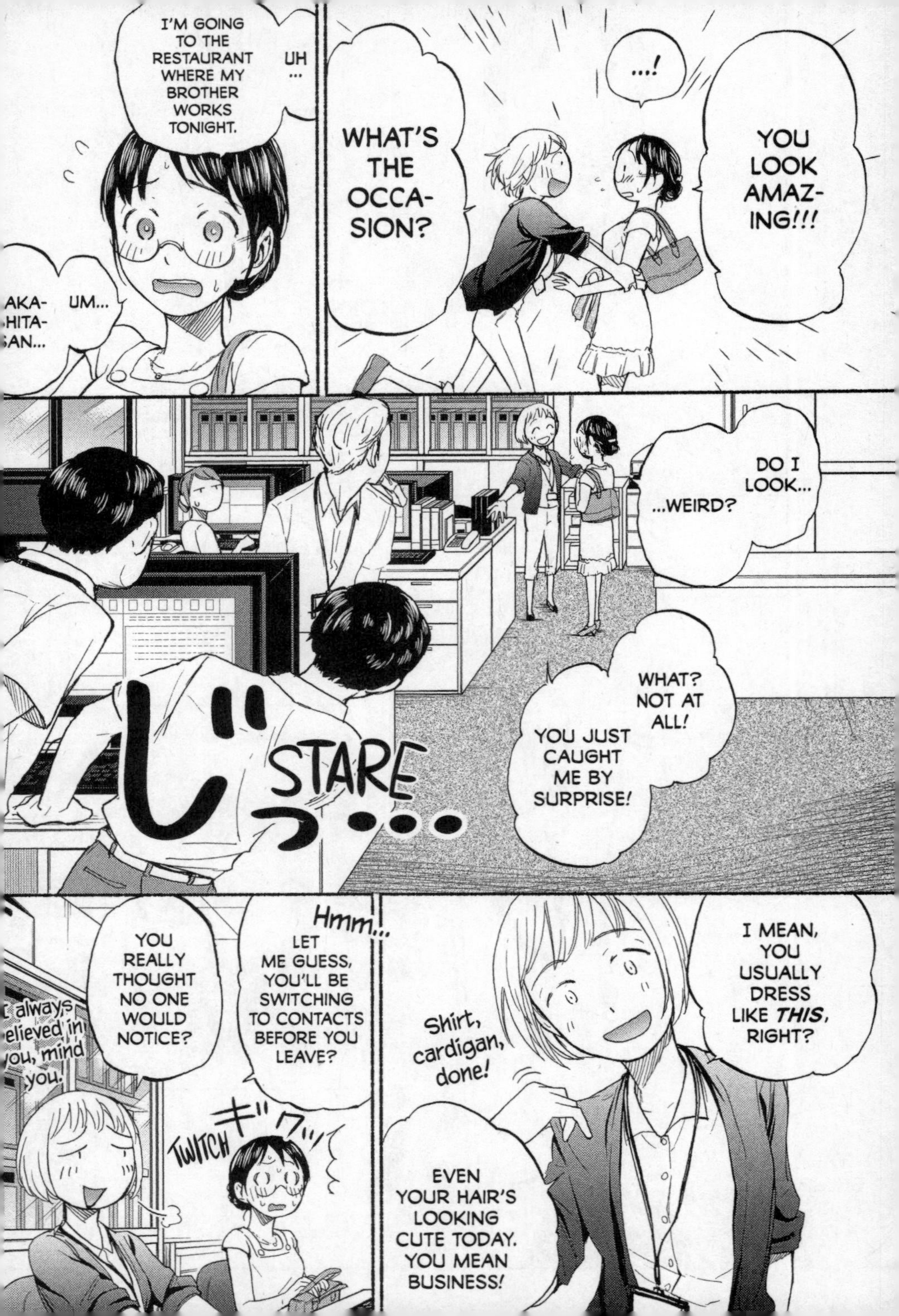
YOU LOOK AMAZING!!!
...!
WHAT'S THE OCCASION?
UH ...
I'M GOING TO THE RESTAURANT WHERE MY BROTHER WORKS TONIGHT.
UM...
AKA-HITA-SAN...
DO I LOOK... ...WEIRD?
WHAT? NOT AT ALL! YOU JUST CAUGHT ME BY SURPRISE!
じっ•••
STARE
I MEAN, YOU USUALLY DRESS LIKE *THIS*, RIGHT?
Shirt, cardigan, done!
EVEN YOUR HAIR'S LOOKING CUTE TODAY. YOU MEAN BUSINESS!
Hmm...
LET ME GUESS, YOU'LL BE SWITCHING TO CONTACTS BEFORE YOU LEAVE?
YOU REALLY THOUGHT NO ONE WOULD NOTICE?
always elieved in ou, mind you.
ギクッ
TWITCH

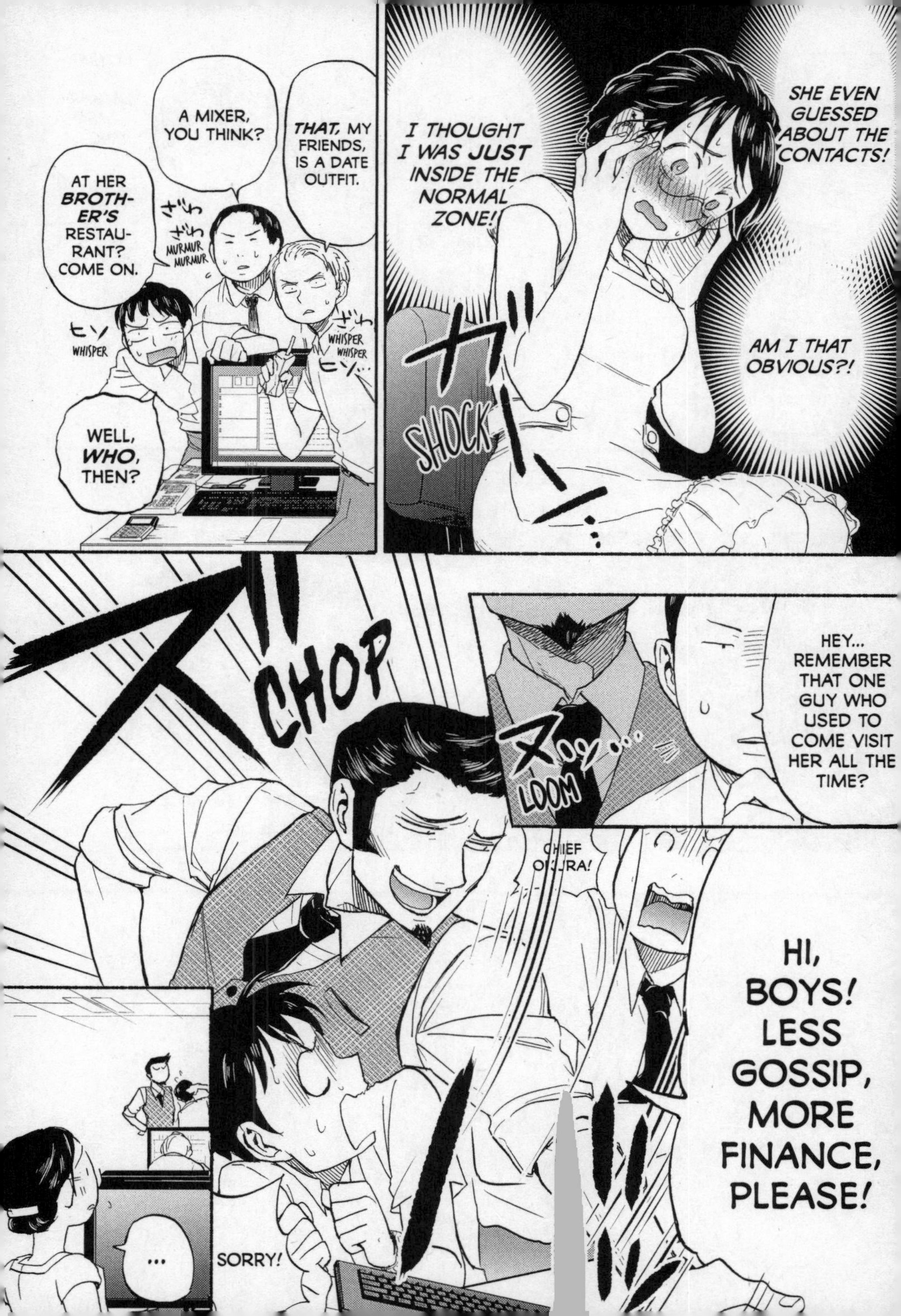
SHE EVEN GUESSED ABOUT THE CONTACTS!
I THOUGHT I WAS JUST INSIDE THE NORMAL ZONE!
SHOCK
AM I THAT OBVIOUS?!
THAT, MY FRIENDS, IS A DATE OUTFIT.
A MIXER, YOU THINK?
ざわ ざわ
MURMUR MURMUR
AT HER BROTHER'S RESTAURANT? COME ON.
ざわ
WHISPER WHISPER
ヒソ…
ヒソ
WHISPER
WELL, WHO, THEN?
HEY... REMEMBER THAT ONE GUY WHO USED TO COME VISIT HER ALL THE TIME?
LOOM
CHOP
HI, BOYS! LESS GOSSIP, MORE FINANCE, PLEASE!
CHIEF
SORRY!
...

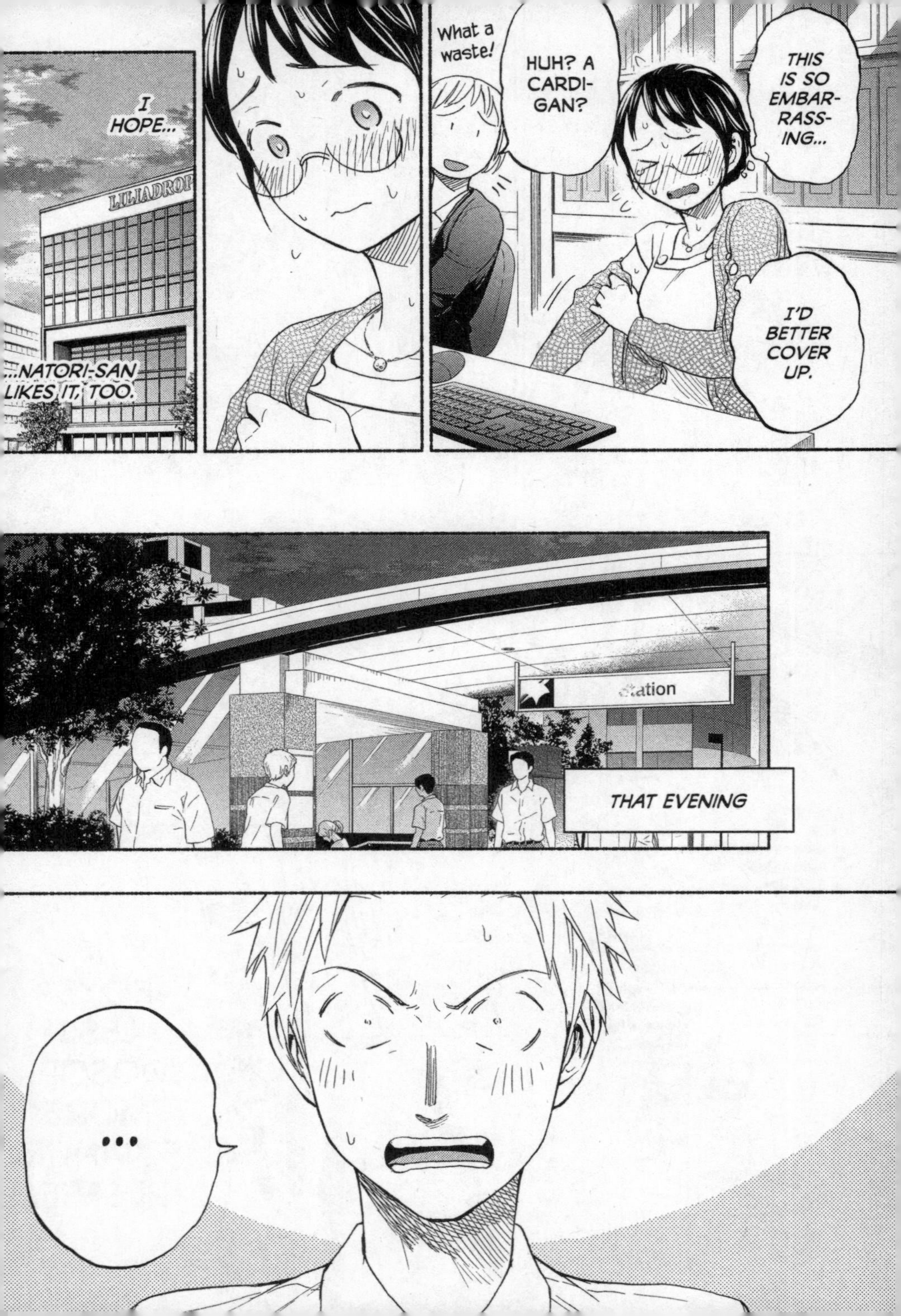
THIS IS SO EMBARRASSING...
I'D BETTER COVER UP.
HUH? A CARDIGAN?
What a waste!
I HOPE...
...NATORI-SAN LIKES IT, TOO.
station
THAT EVENING
...

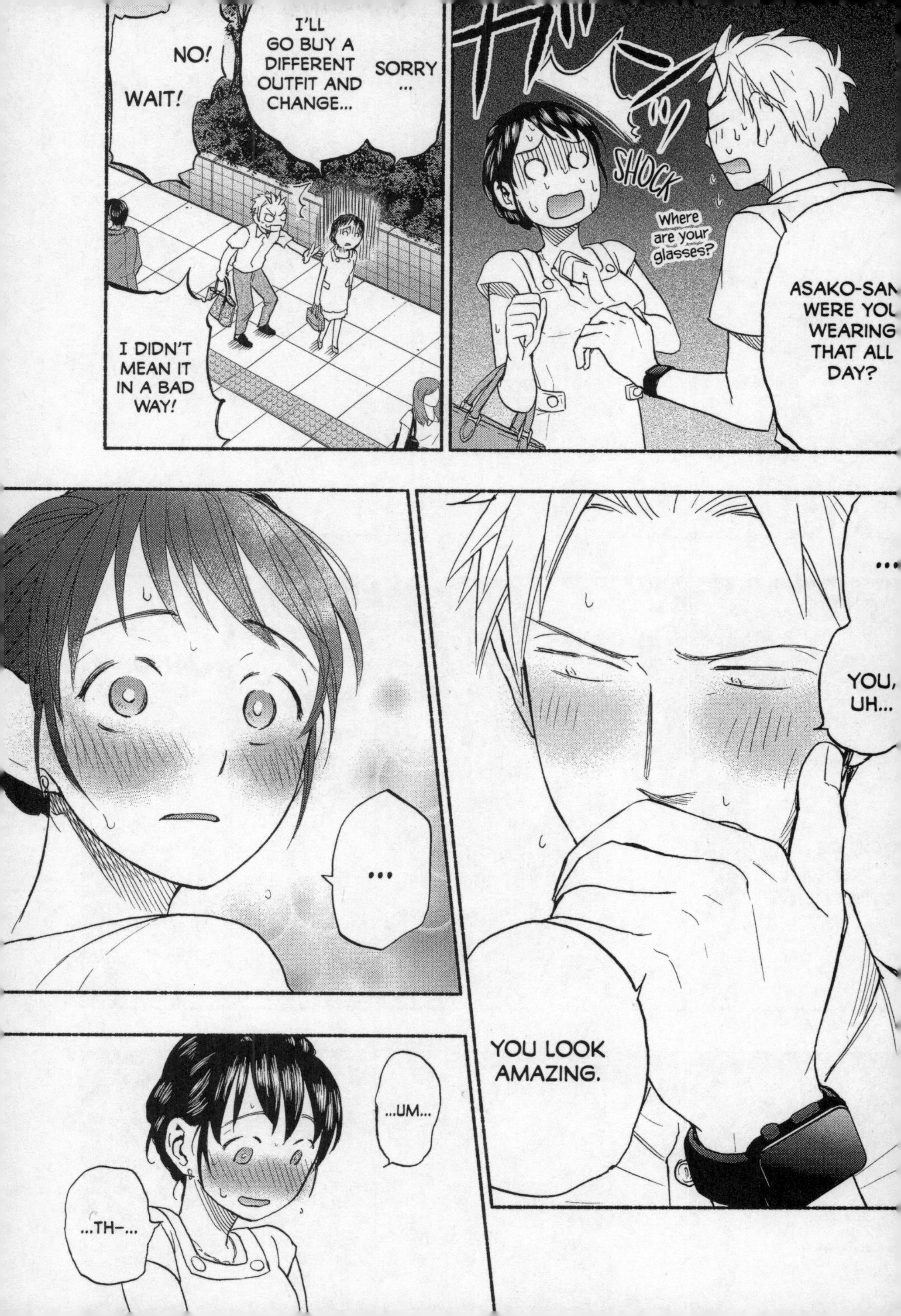
SHOCK
Where are your glasses?
ASAKO-SAN WERE YOU WEARING THAT ALL DAY?
SORRY ...
I'LL GO BUY A DIFFERENT OUTFIT AND CHANGE...
NO!
WAIT!
I DIDN'T MEAN IT IN A BAD WAY!
...
YOU, UH...
YOU LOOK AMAZING.
...
...UM...
...TH-...

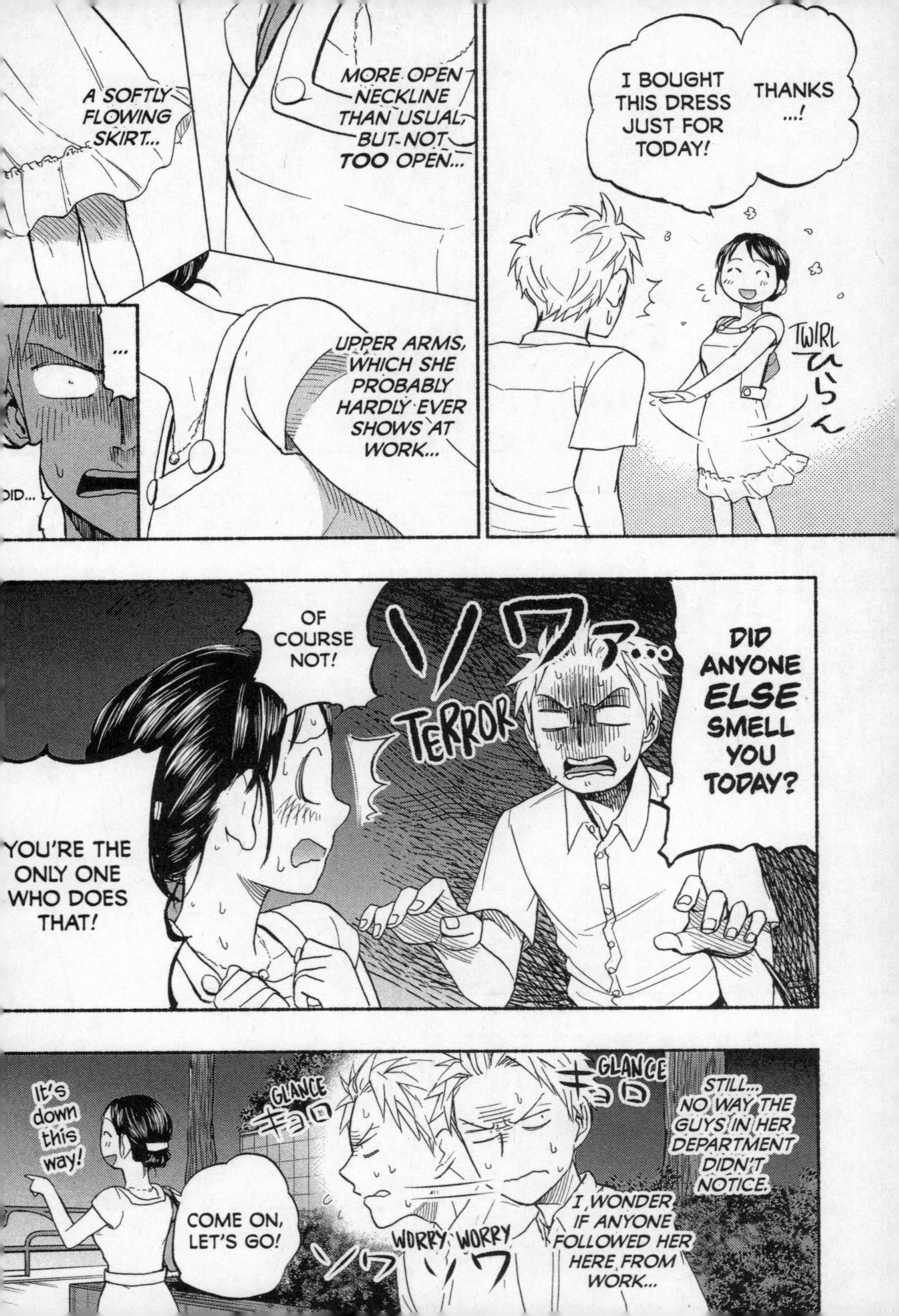
I BOUGHT THIS DRESS JUST FOR TODAY!
THANKS ...!
TWIRL
ひらん
MORE OPEN NECKLINE THAN USUAL, BUT NOT TOO OPEN...
A SOFTLY FLOWING SKIRT...
UPPER ARMS, WHICH SHE PROBABLY HARDLY EVER SHOWS AT WORK...
...
ID...
DID ANYONE ELSE SMELL YOU TODAY?
ゾワァ...
TERROR
OF COURSE NOT!
YOU'RE THE ONLY ONE WHO DOES THAT!
STILL... NO WAY THE GUYS IN HER DEPARTMENT DIDN'T NOTICE.
GLANCE
キョロ
I WONDER IF ANYONE FOLLOWED HER HERE FROM WORK...
GLANCE
キョロ
WORRY WORRY
ソワソワ
COME ON, LET'S GO!
It's down this way!

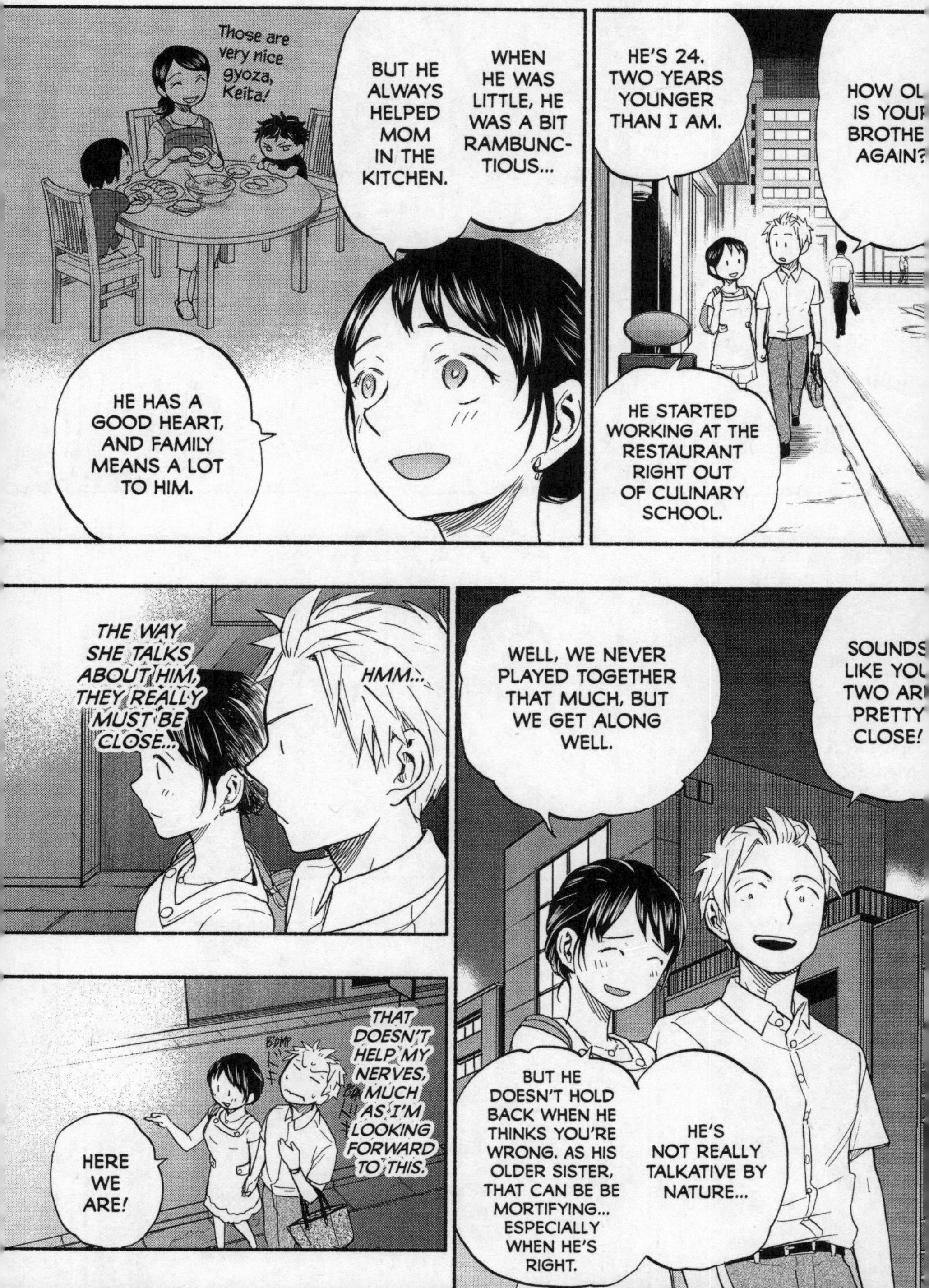
HOW OL IS YOUR BROTHE AGAIN?
HE'S 24. TWO YEARS YOUNGER THAN I AM.
HE STARTED WORKING AT THE RESTAURANT RIGHT OUT OF CULINARY SCHOOL.
WHEN HE WAS LITTLE, HE WAS A BIT RAMBUNC-TIOUS...
BUT HE ALWAYS HELPED MOM IN THE KITCHEN.
Those are very nice gyoza, Keita!
HE HAS A GOOD HEART, AND FAMILY MEANS A LOT TO HIM.
SOUNDS LIKE YOU TWO AR PRETTY CLOSE!
WELL, WE NEVER PLAYED TOGETHER THAT MUCH, BUT WE GET ALONG WELL.
HE'S NOT REALLY TALKATIVE BY NATURE...
BUT HE DOESN'T HOLD BACK WHEN HE THINKS YOU'RE WRONG. AS HIS OLDER SISTER, THAT CAN BE BE MORTIFYING... ESPECIALLY WHEN HE'S RIGHT.
HMM...
THE WAY SHE TALKS ABOUT HIM, THEY REALLY MUST BE CLOSE...
THAT DOESN'T HELP MY NERVES, MUCH AS I'M LOOKING FORWARD TO THIS.
HERE WE ARE!

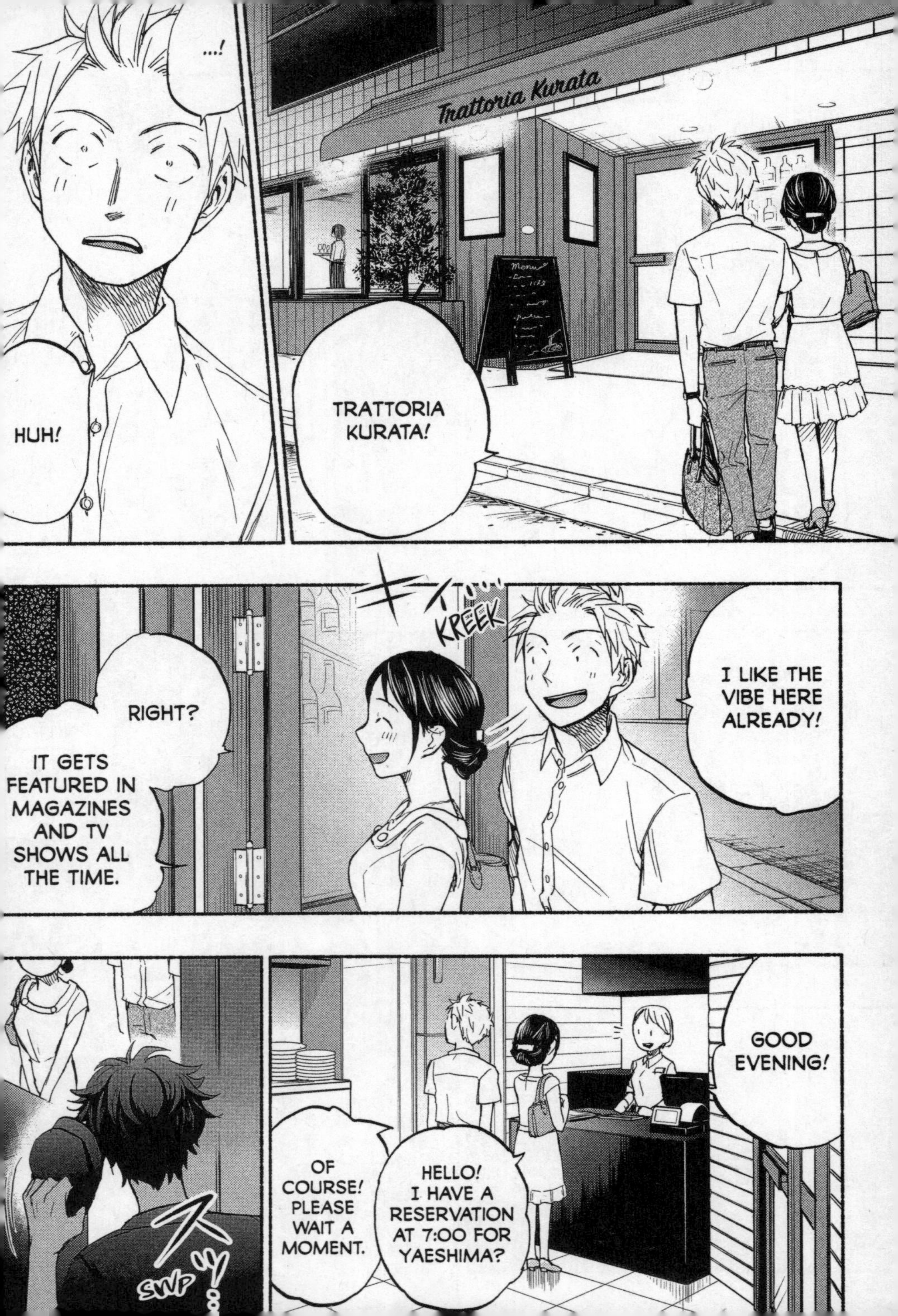

Trattoria Kurata
TRATTORIA KURATA!
...!
HUH!
KREEK
I LIKE THE VIBE HERE ALREADY!
RIGHT?
IT GETS FEATURED IN MAGAZINES AND TV SHOWS ALL THE TIME.
GOOD EVENING!
HELLO! I HAVE A RESERVATION AT 7:00 FOR YAESHIMA?
OF COURSE! PLEASE WAIT A MOMENT.
SWP

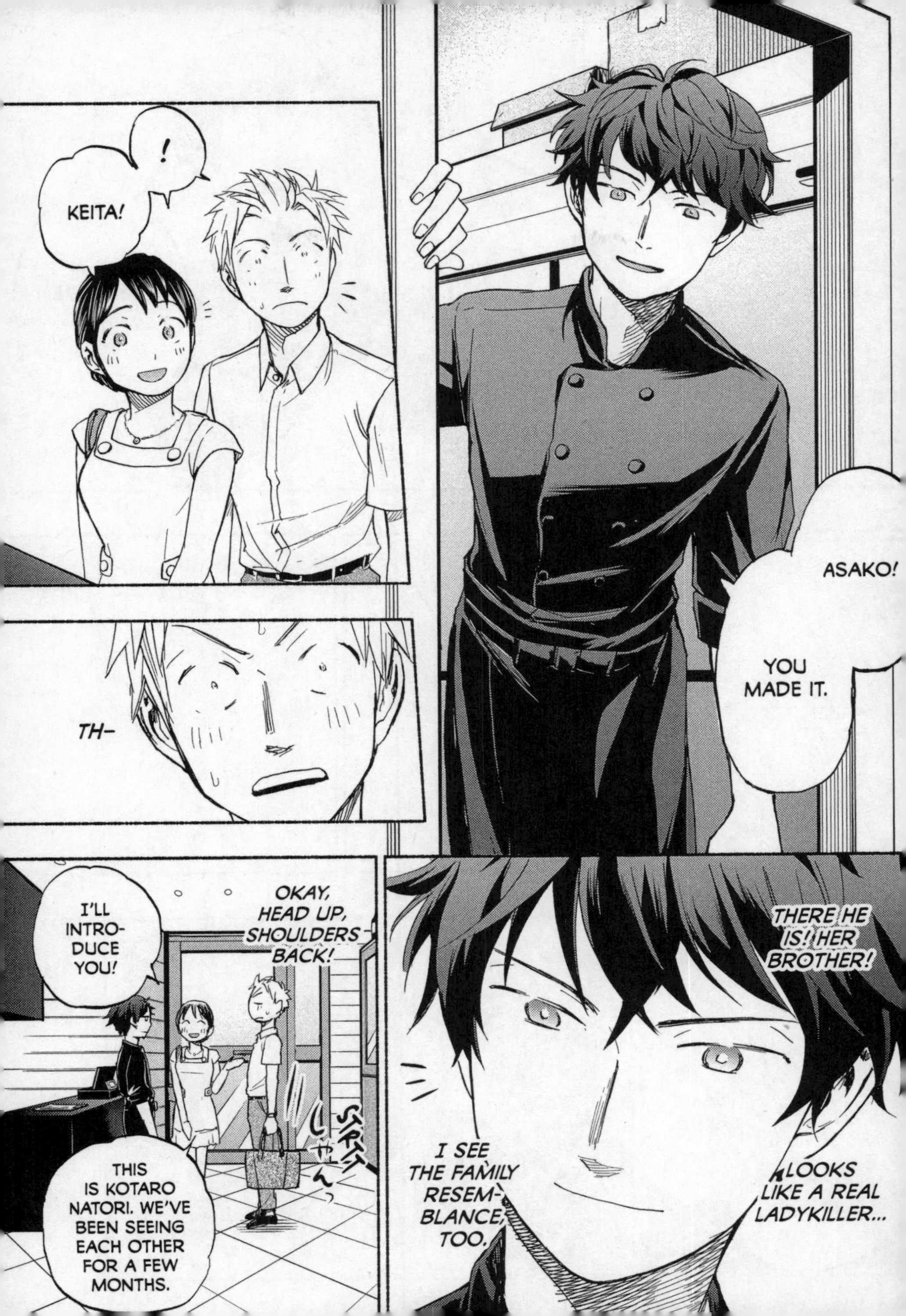
ASAKO!
YOU MADE IT.
!
KEITA!
TH–
THERE HE IS! HER BROTHER!
LOOKS LIKE A REAL LADYKILLER...
I SEE THE FAMILY RESEMBLANCE, TOO.
OKAY, HEAD UP, SHOULDERS BACK!
I'LL INTRODUCE YOU!
STRTT
THIS IS KOTARO NATORI. WE'VE BEEN SEEING EACH OTHER FOR A FEW MONTHS.

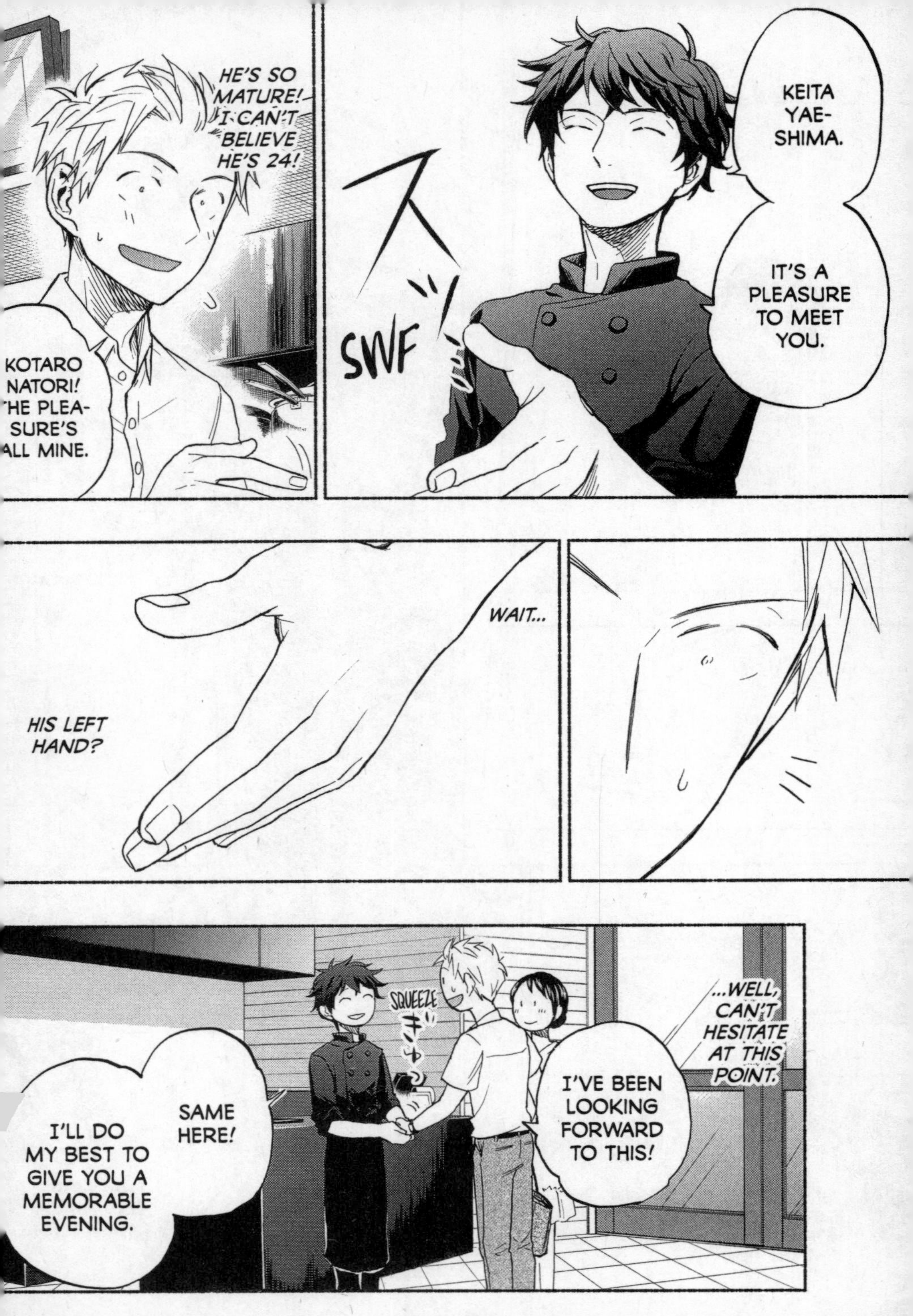
KEITA YAE-SHIMA.
IT'S A PLEASURE TO MEET YOU.
SWF
HE'S SO MATURE! I CAN'T BELIEVE HE'S 24!
KOTARO NATORI! THE PLEA-SURE'S ALL MINE.
WAIT...
HIS LEFT HAND?
...WELL, CAN'T HESITATE AT THIS POINT.
I'VE BEEN LOOKING FORWARD TO THIS!
SQUEEZE
SAME HERE!
I'LL DO MY BEST TO GIVE YOU A MEMORABLE EVENING.

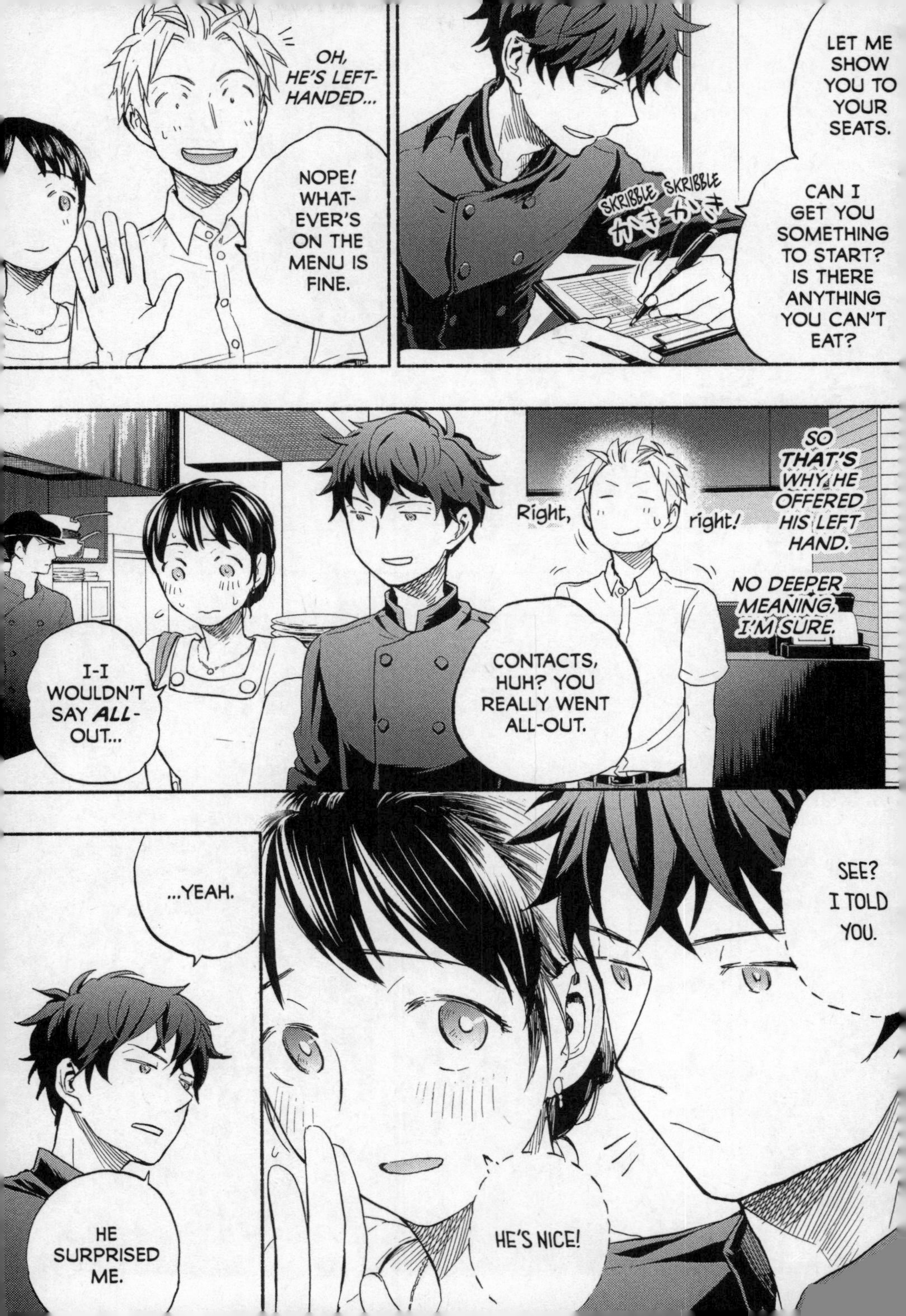
LET ME SHOW YOU TO YOUR SEATS.
SKRIBBLE SKRIBBLE
かきかき
CAN I GET YOU SOMETHING TO START? IS THERE ANYTHING YOU CAN'T EAT?
OH, HE'S LEFT-HANDED...
NOPE! WHAT-EVER'S ON THE MENU IS FINE.
SO THAT'S WHY HE OFFERED HIS LEFT HAND.
NO DEEPER MEANING, I'M SURE.
Right, right!
CONTACTS, HUH? YOU REALLY WENT ALL-OUT.
I-I WOULDN'T SAY ALL-OUT...
SEE? I TOLD YOU.
HE'S NICE!
...YEAH.
HE SURPRISED ME.

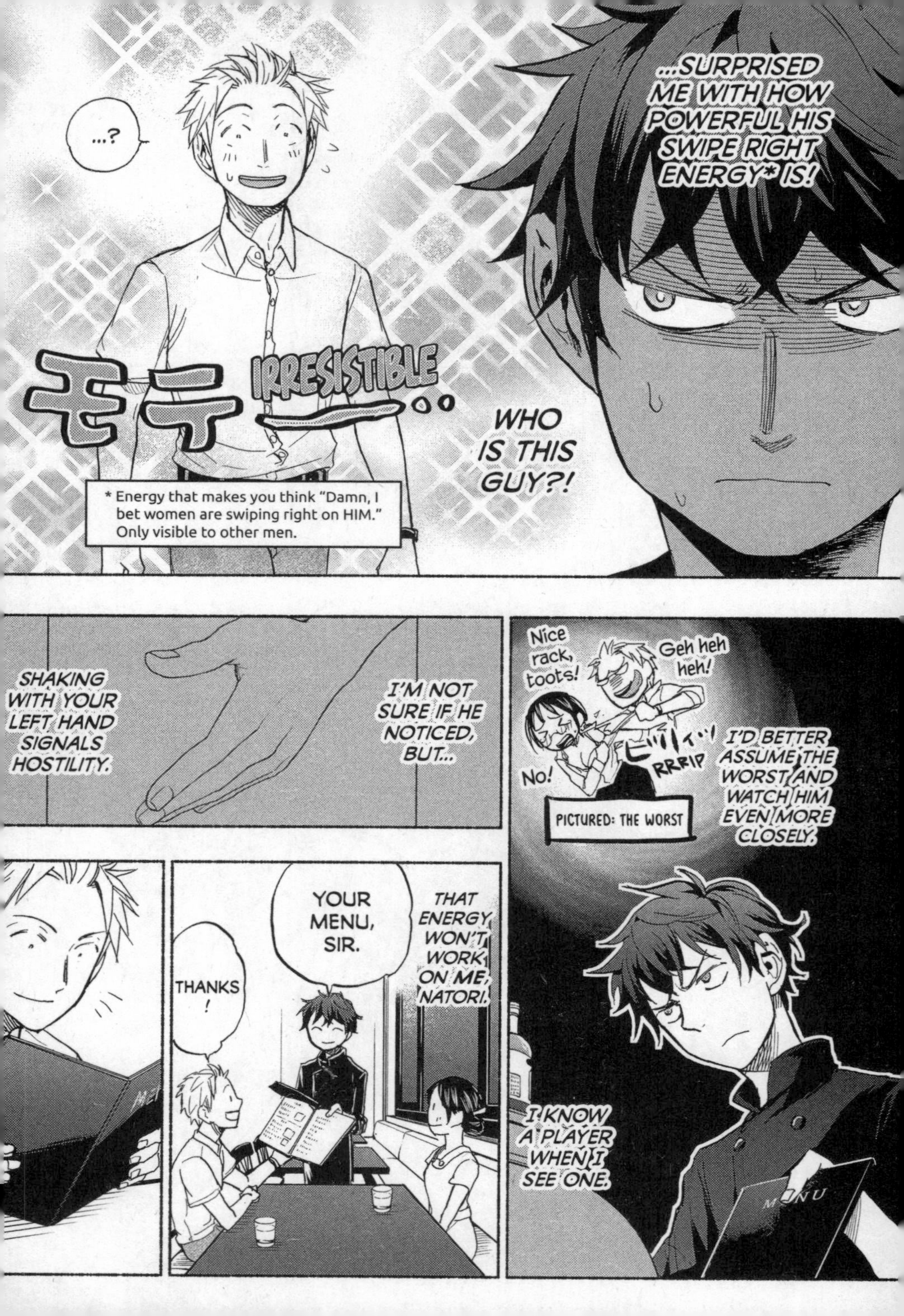
...SURPRISED ME WITH HOW POWERFUL HIS SWIPE RIGHT ENERGY* IS!
WHO IS THIS GUY?!
...?
モテー
IRRESISTIBLE
* Energy that makes you think "Damn, I bet women are swiping right on HIM." Only visible to other men.
Geh heh heh!
Nice rack, toots!
ビリィッ
RRRIP
No!
PICTURED: THE WORST
I'D BETTER ASSUME THE WORST AND WATCH HIM EVEN MORE CLOSELY.
I KNOW A PLAYER WHEN I SEE ONE.
I'M NOT SURE IF HE NOTICED, BUT...
SHAKING WITH YOUR LEFT HAND SIGNALS HOSTILITY.
THAT ENERGY WON'T WORK ON ME, NATORI.
YOUR MENU, SIR.
THANKS!

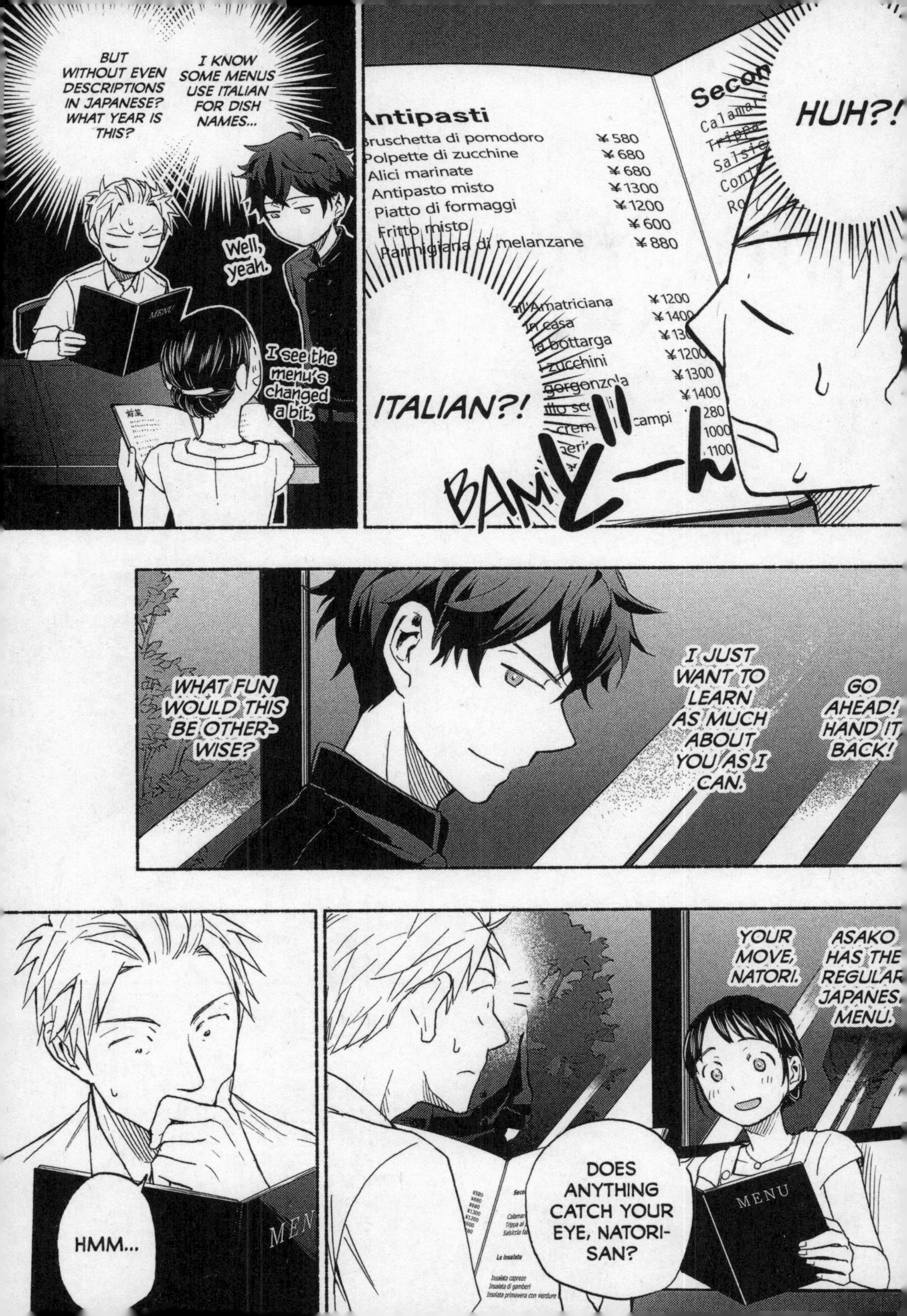
Antipasti
Bruschetta di pomodoro ¥580
Polpette di zucchine ¥680
Alici marinate ¥680
Antipasto misto ¥1300
Piatto di formaggi ¥1200
Fritto misto ¥600
Parmigiana di melanzane ¥880
Secon
HUH?!
ITALIAN?!
BAM
I KNOW SOME MENUS USE ITALIAN FOR DISH NAMES...
BUT WITHOUT EVEN DESCRIPTIONS IN JAPANESE? WHAT YEAR IS THIS?
Well, yeah.
I see the menu's changed a bit.
GO AHEAD! HAND IT BACK!
I JUST WANT TO LEARN AS MUCH ABOUT YOU AS I CAN.
WHAT FUN WOULD THIS BE OTHER-WISE?
ASAKO HAS THE REGULAR JAPANES MENU.
YOUR MOVE, NATORI.
DOES ANYTHING CATCH YOUR EYE, NATORI-SAN?
HMM...

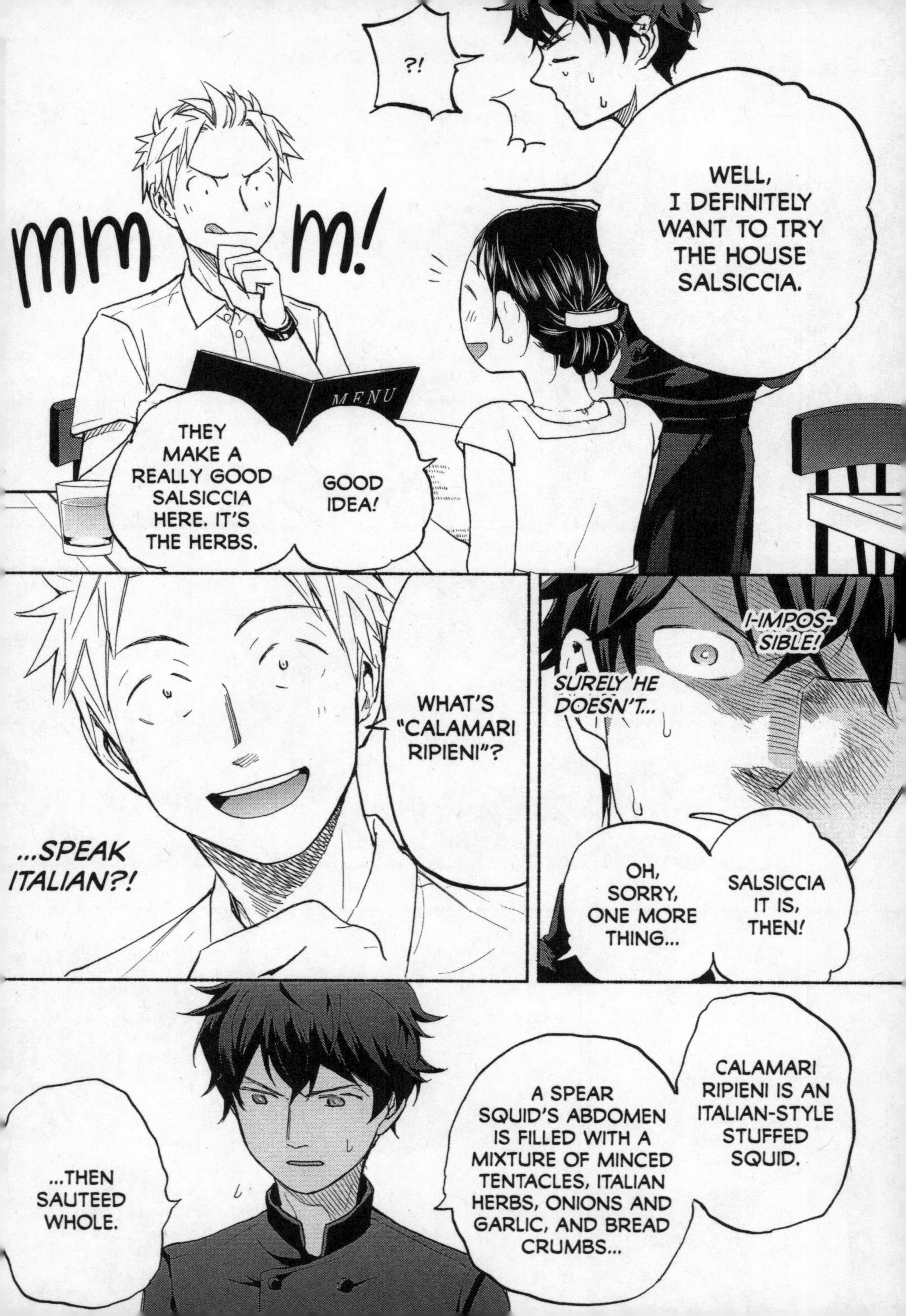
?!
WELL, I DEFINITELY WANT TO TRY THE HOUSE SALSICCIA.
MM M!
MENU
GOOD IDEA!
THEY MAKE A REALLY GOOD SALSICCIA HERE. IT'S THE HERBS.
I-IMPOSSIBLE!
SURELY HE DOESN'T...
SALSICCIA IT IS, THEN!
OH, SORRY, ONE MORE THING...
WHAT'S "CALAMARI RIPIENI"?
...SPEAK ITALIAN?!
CALAMARI RIPIENI IS AN ITALIAN-STYLE STUFFED SQUID.
A SPEAR SQUID'S ABDOMEN IS FILLED WITH A MIXTURE OF MINCED TENTACLES, ITALIAN HERBS, ONIONS AND GARLIC, AND BREAD CRUMBS...
...THEN SAUTEED WHOLE.

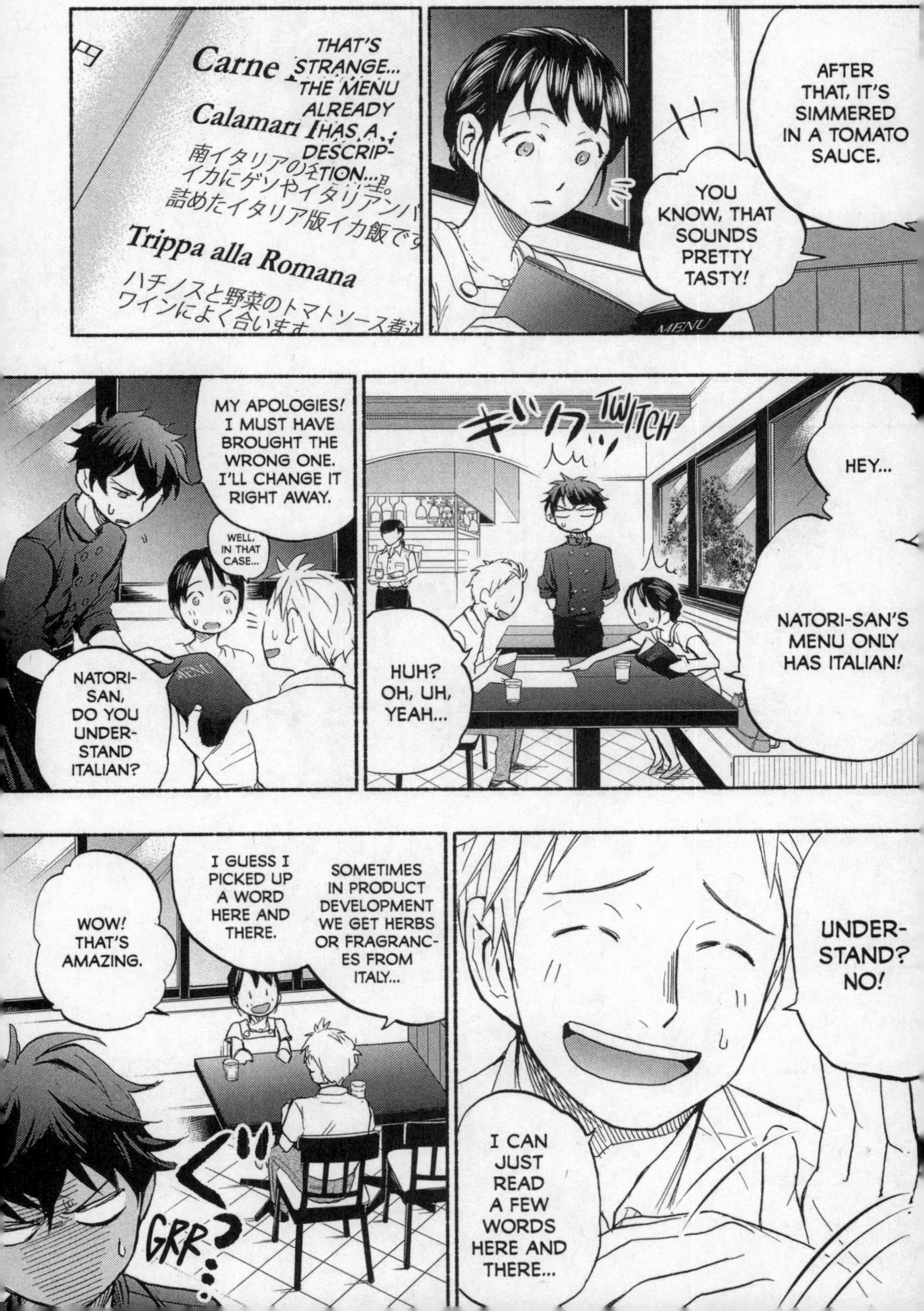
AFTER THAT, IT'S SIMMERED IN A TOMATO SAUCE.
YOU KNOW, THAT SOUNDS PRETTY TASTY!
THAT'S STRANGE... THE MENU ALREADY HAS A DESCRIPTION...
Carne
Calamari I
Trippa alla Romana
ハチノスと野菜のトマトソース煮
ワインによく合います
MENU
HEY...
NATORI-SAN'S MENU ONLY HAS ITALIAN!
TWITCH
HUH? OH, UH, YEAH...
MY APOLOGIES! I MUST HAVE BROUGHT THE WRONG ONE. I'LL CHANGE IT RIGHT AWAY.
WELL, IN THAT CASE...
NATORI-SAN, DO YOU UNDERSTAND ITALIAN?
UNDERSTAND? NO!
I CAN JUST READ A FEW WORDS HERE AND THERE...
SOMETIMES IN PRODUCT DEVELOPMENT WE GET HERBS OR FRAGRANCES FROM ITALY...
I GUESS I PICKED UP A WORD HERE AND THERE.
WOW! THAT'S AMAZING.
GRR...

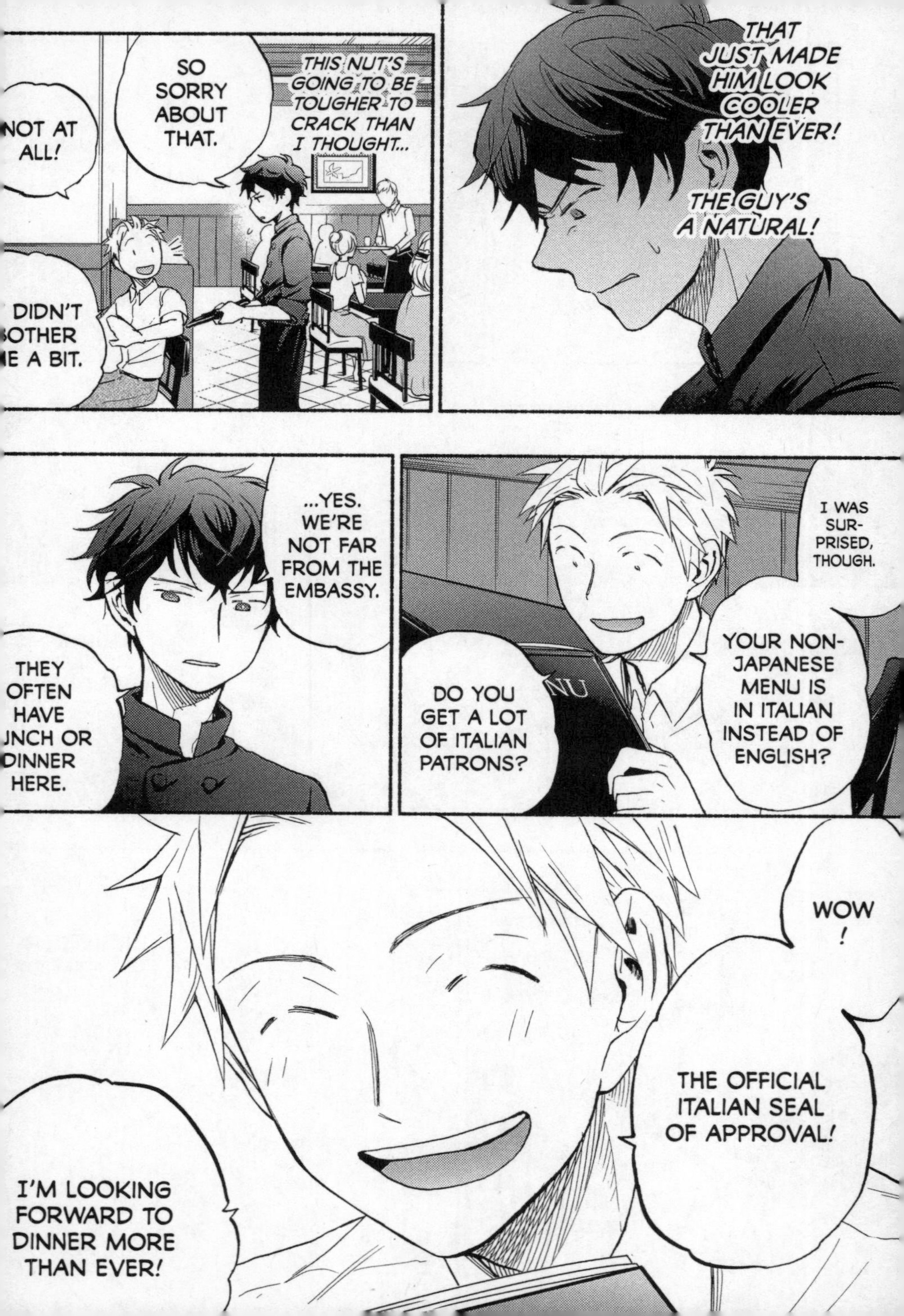
THAT JUST MADE HIM LOOK COOLER THAN EVER!
THE GUY'S A NATURAL!
THIS NUT'S GOING TO BE TOUGHER TO CRACK THAN I THOUGHT...
SO SORRY ABOUT THAT.
NOT AT ALL!
DIDN'T OTHER E A BIT.
I WAS SUR-PRISED, THOUGH.
YOUR NON-JAPANESE MENU IS IN ITALIAN INSTEAD OF ENGLISH?
DO YOU GET A LOT OF ITALIAN PATRONS?
NU
...YES. WE'RE NOT FAR FROM THE EMBASSY.
THEY OFTEN HAVE NCH OR DINNER HERE.
WOW!
THE OFFICIAL ITALIAN SEAL OF APPROVAL!
I'M LOOKING FORWARD TO DINNER MORE THAN EVER!

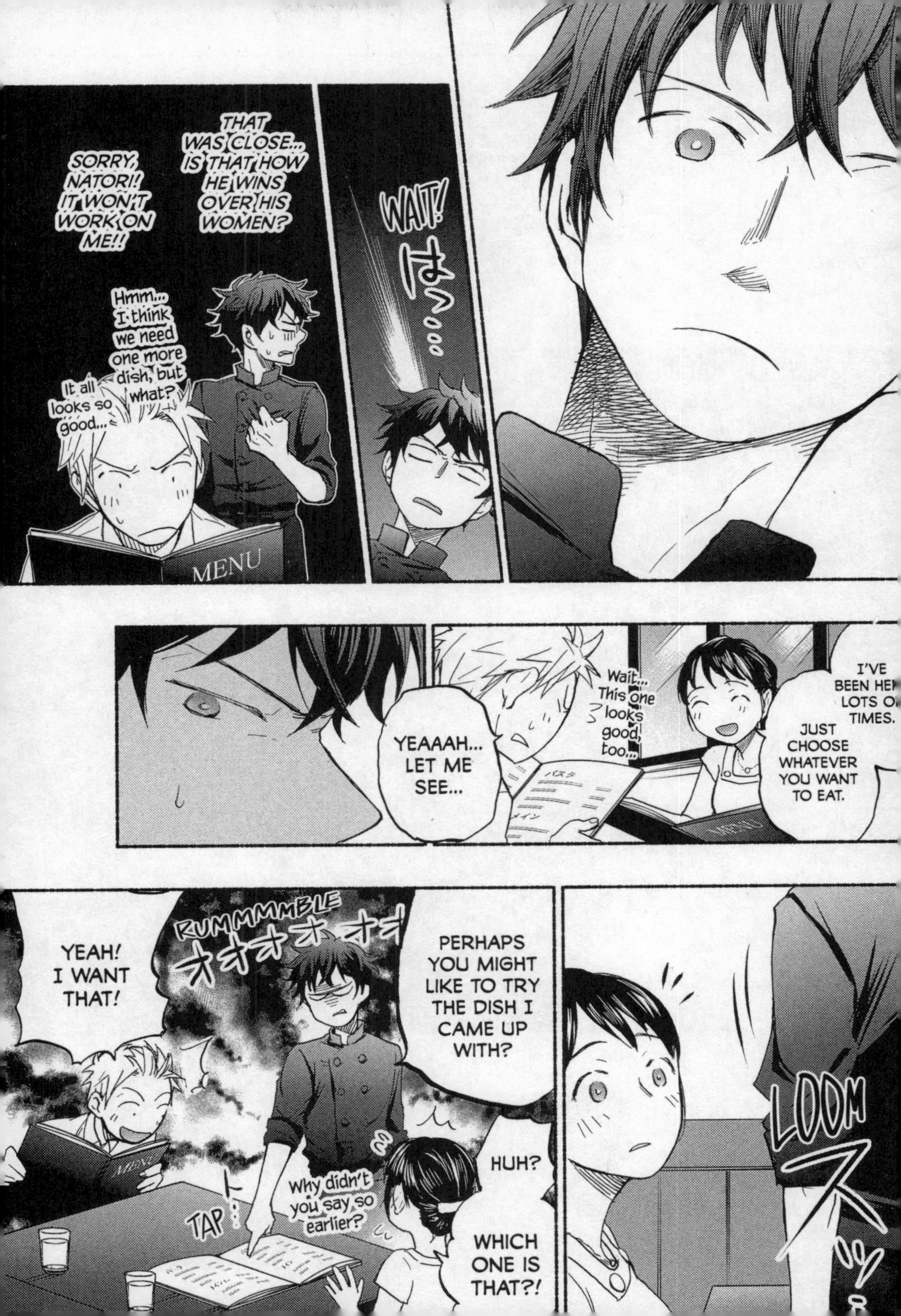
WAIT! はっ...
THAT WAS CLOSE... IS THAT HOW HE WINS OVER HIS WOMEN?
SORRY, NATORI! IT WON'T WORK ON ME!!
Hmm... I think we need one more dish, but what?
It all looks so good...
MENU
I'VE BEEN HE LOTS O TIMES.
JUST CHOOSE WHATEVER YOU WANT TO EAT.
Wait... This one looks good, too...
MENU
YEAAAH... LET ME SEE...
LOOM
PERHAPS YOU MIGHT LIKE TO TRY THE DISH I CAME UP WITH?
HUH?
WHICH ONE IS THAT?!
RUMMMMBLE オオオオオ
YEAH! I WANT THAT!
MENU
Why didn't you say so earlier?
TAP ト...

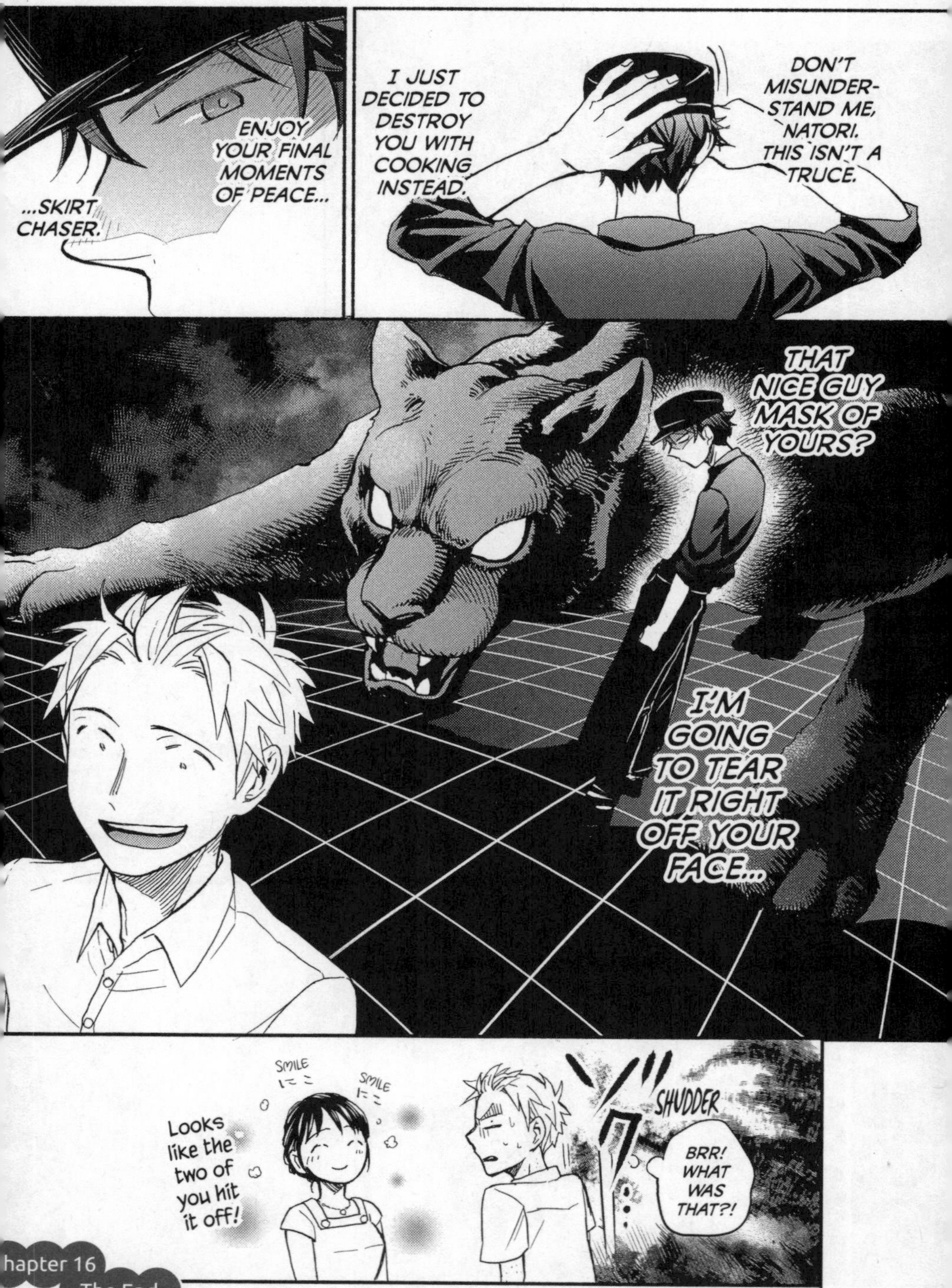
DON'T MISUNDER-STAND ME, NATORI. THIS ISN'T A TRUCE.
I JUST DECIDED TO DESTROY YOU WITH COOKING INSTEAD.
ENJOY YOUR FINAL MOMENTS OF PEACE...
...SKIRT CHASER.
THAT NICE GUY MASK OF YOURS?
I'M GOING TO TEAR IT RIGHT OFF YOUR FACE...
SHUDDER
BRR! WHAT WAS THAT?!
SMILE
にこ
SMILE
にこ
Looks like the two of you hit it off!

hapter 16
The End

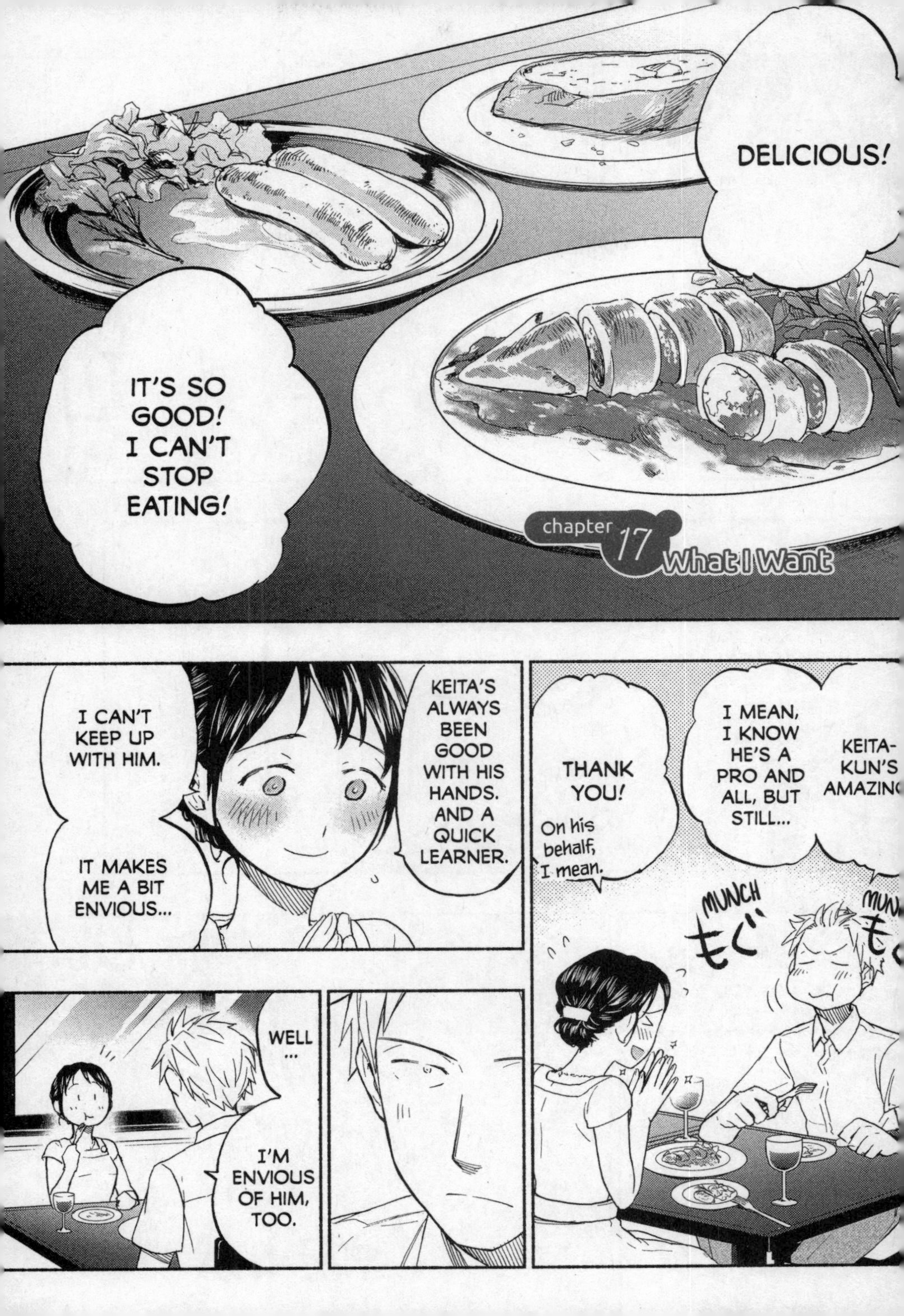
DELICIOUS!
IT'S SO GOOD! I CAN'T STOP EATING!
chapter 17 What I Want
KEITA-KUN'S AMAZIN
I MEAN, I KNOW HE'S A PRO AND ALL, BUT STILL...
THANK YOU!
On his behalf, I mean.
MUN
MUNCH
KEITA'S ALWAYS BEEN GOOD WITH HIS HANDS. AND A QUICK LEARNER.
I CAN'T KEEP UP WITH HIM.
IT MAKES ME A BIT ENVIOUS...
WELL...
I'M ENVIOUS OF HIM, TOO.

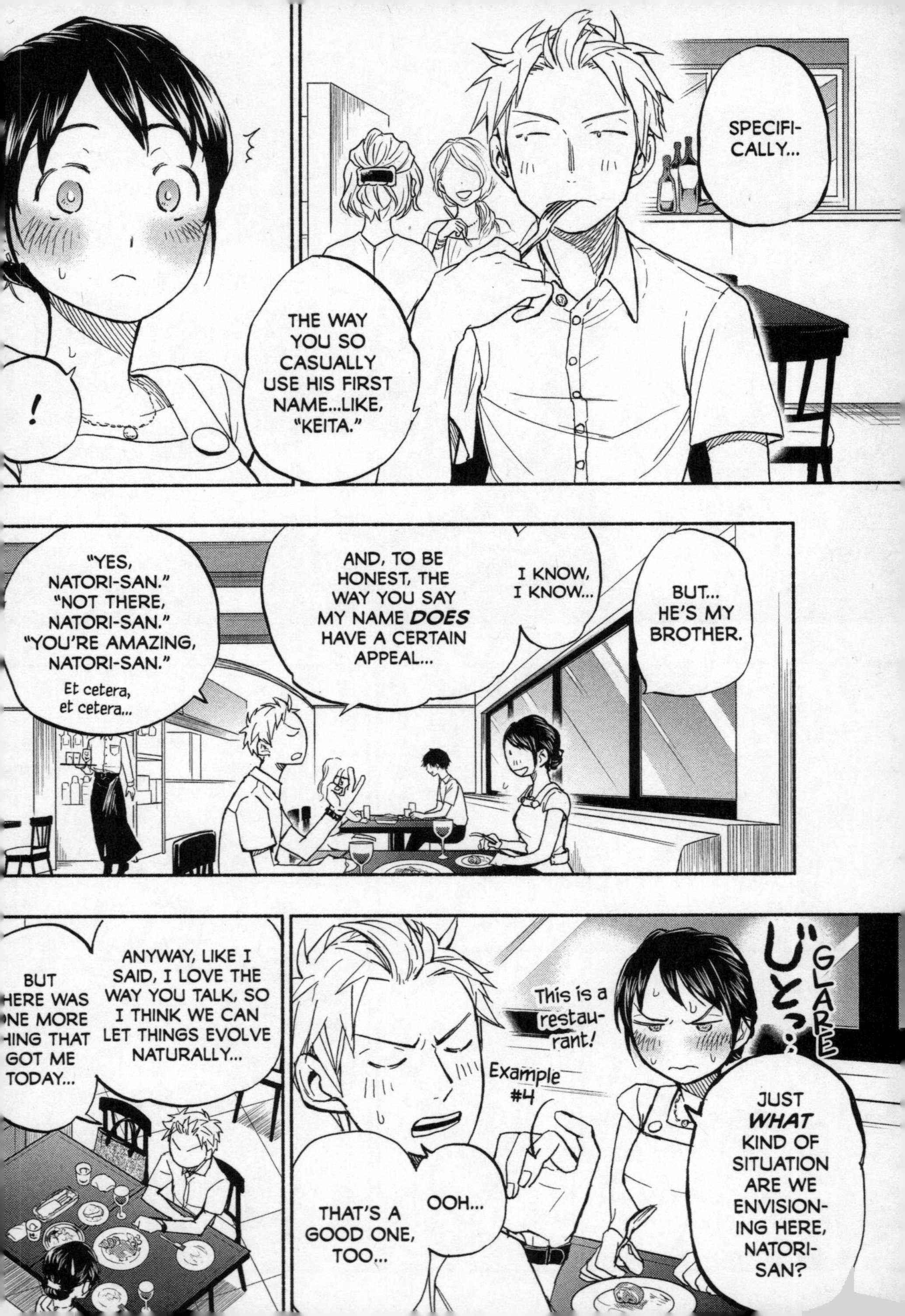
SPECIFI-CALLY...
THE WAY YOU SO CASUALLY USE HIS FIRST NAME...LIKE, "KEITA."
!
BUT... HE'S MY BROTHER.
I KNOW, I KNOW...
AND, TO BE HONEST, THE WAY YOU SAY MY NAME ***DOES*** HAVE A CERTAIN APPEAL...
"YES, NATORI-SAN." "NOT THERE, NATORI-SAN." "YOU'RE AMAZING, NATORI-SAN."
Et cetera, et cetera...
じとっ GLARE
This is a restaurant!
JUST ***WHAT*** KIND OF SITUATION ARE WE ENVISIONING HERE, NATORI-SAN?
Example #4
OOH...
THAT'S A GOOD ONE, TOO...
ANYWAY, LIKE I SAID, I LOVE THE WAY YOU TALK, SO I THINK WE CAN LET THINGS EVOLVE NATURALLY...
BUT HERE WAS NE MORE HING THAT GOT ME TODAY...

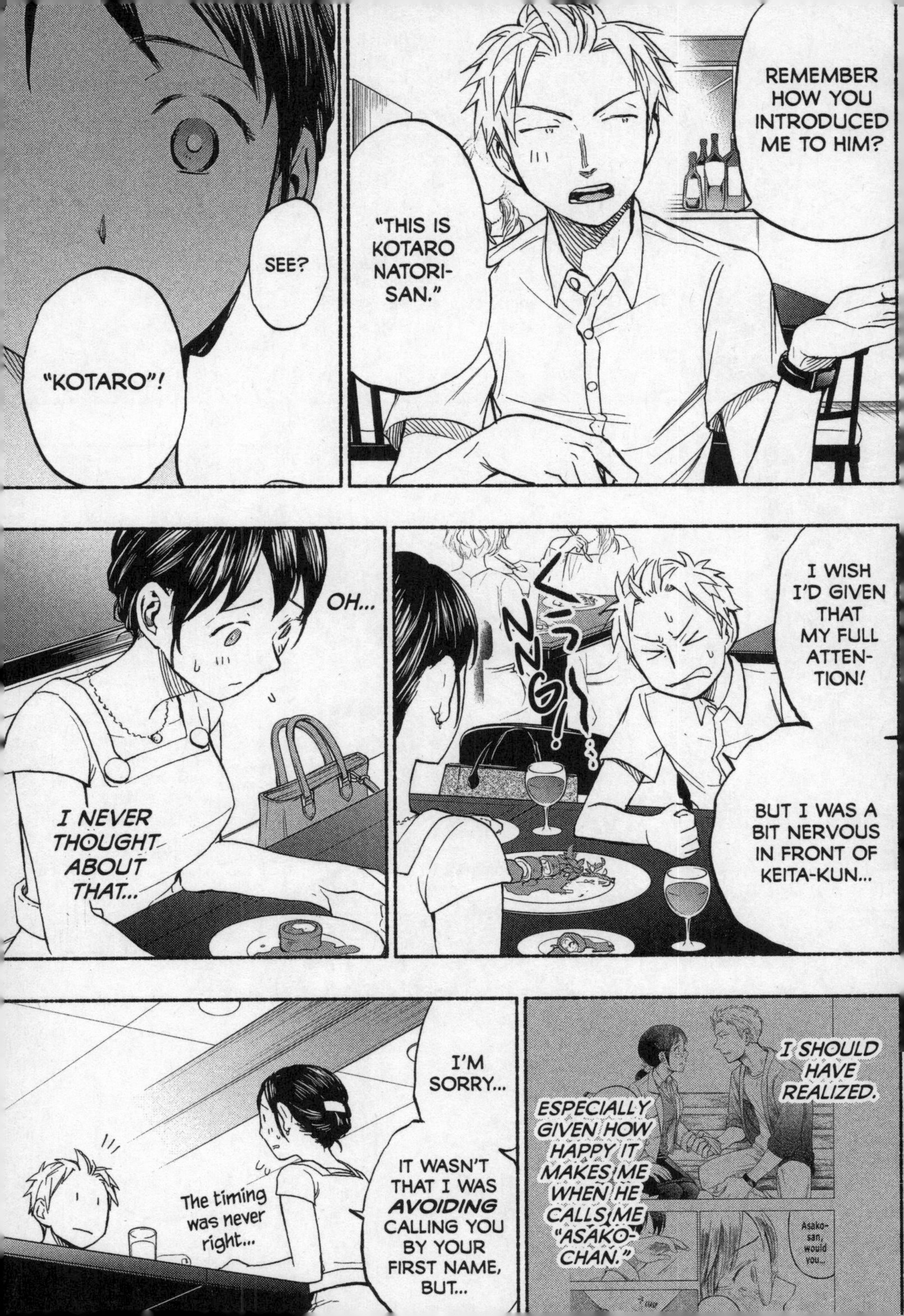
REMEMBER HOW YOU INTRODUCED ME TO HIM?
"THIS IS KOTARO NATORI-SAN."
SEE?
"KOTARO"!
I WISH I'D GIVEN THAT MY FULL ATTEN-TION!
NNG!
BUT I WAS A BIT NERVOUS IN FRONT OF KEITA-KUN...
OH...
I NEVER THOUGHT ABOUT THAT...
I SHOULD HAVE REALIZED.
ESPECIALLY GIVEN HOW HAPPY IT MAKES ME WHEN HE CALLS ME "ASAKO-CHAN."
Asako-san, would you...
I'M SORRY...
IT WASN'T THAT I WAS *AVOIDING* CALLING YOU BY YOUR FIRST NAME, BUT...
The timing was never right...

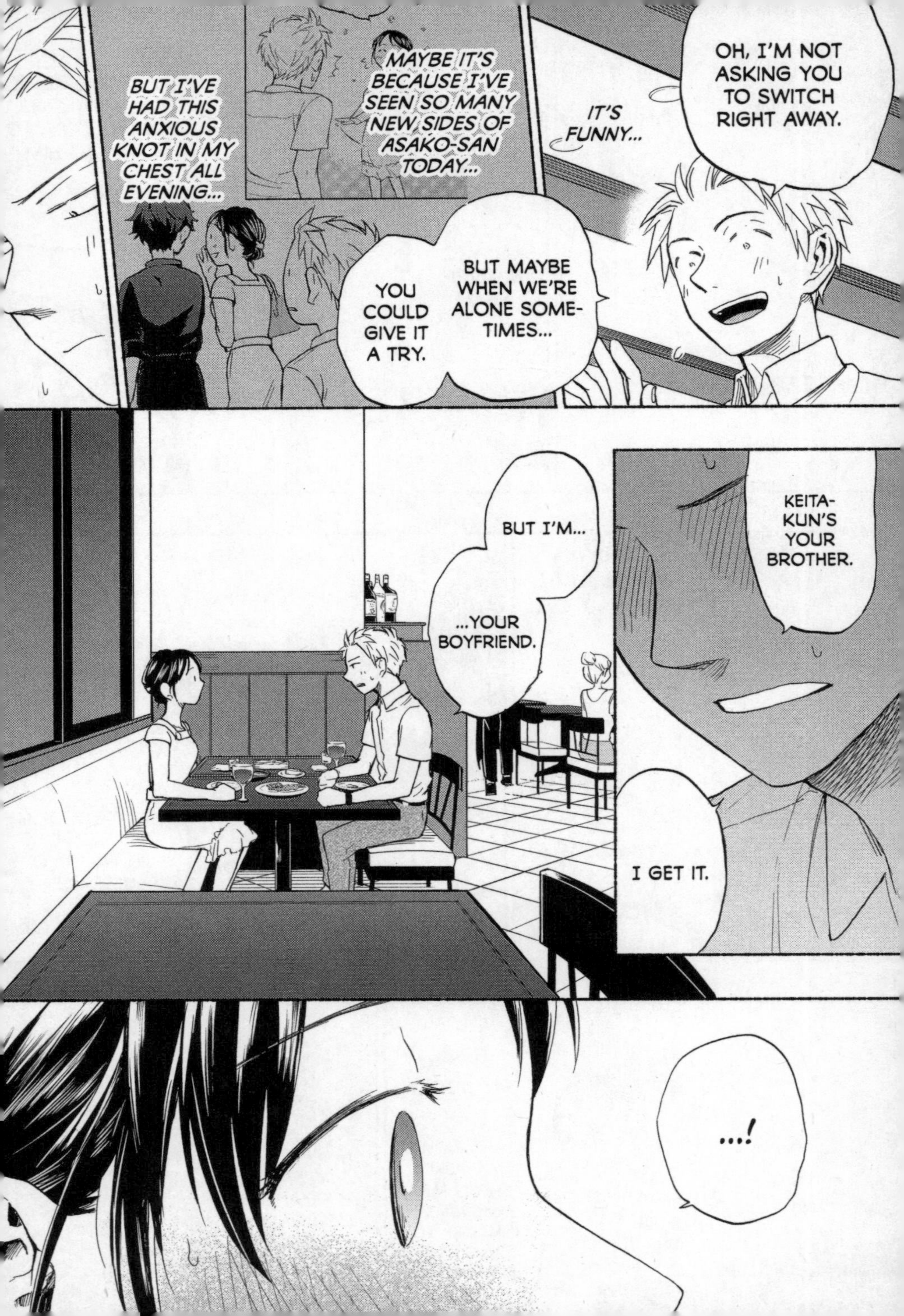
OH, I'M NOT ASKING YOU TO SWITCH RIGHT AWAY.
IT'S FUNNY...
BUT MAYBE WHEN WE'RE ALONE SOME-TIMES...
YOU COULD GIVE IT A TRY.
MAYBE IT'S BECAUSE I'VE SEEN SO MANY NEW SIDES OF ASAKO-SAN TODAY...
BUT I'VE HAD THIS ANXIOUS KNOT IN MY CHEST ALL EVENING...
KEITA-KUN'S YOUR BROTHER.
I GET IT.
BUT I'M...
...YOUR BOYFRIEND.
...!

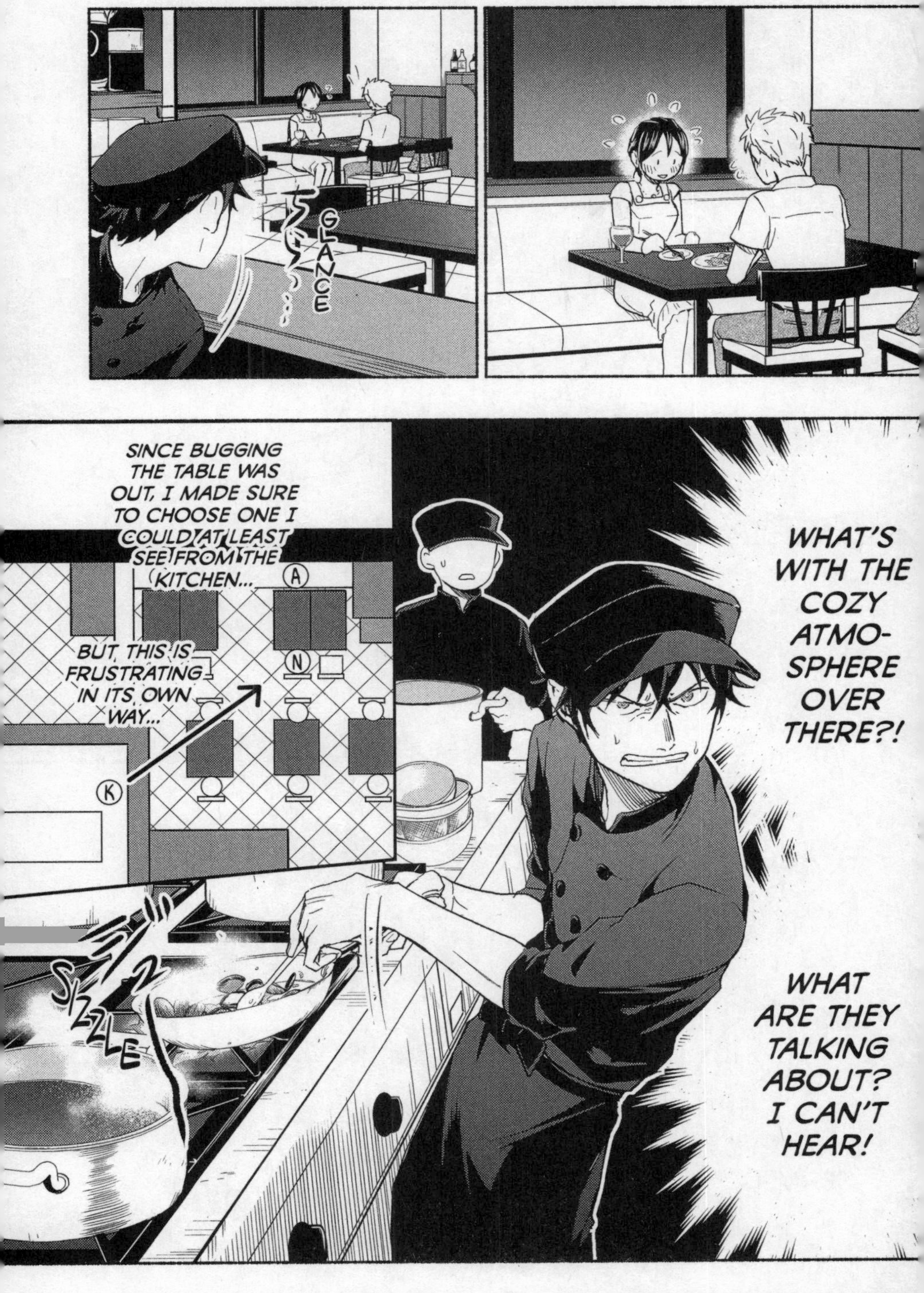
GLANCE
WHAT'S WITH THE COZY ATMOSPHERE OVER THERE?!
WHAT ARE THEY TALKING ABOUT? I CAN'T HEAR!
SINCE BUGGING THE TABLE WAS OUT, I MADE SURE TO CHOOSE ONE I COULD AT LEAST SEE FROM THE KITCHEN...
A
N
K
BUT THIS IS FRUSTRATING IN ITS OWN WAY...
SIZZLE

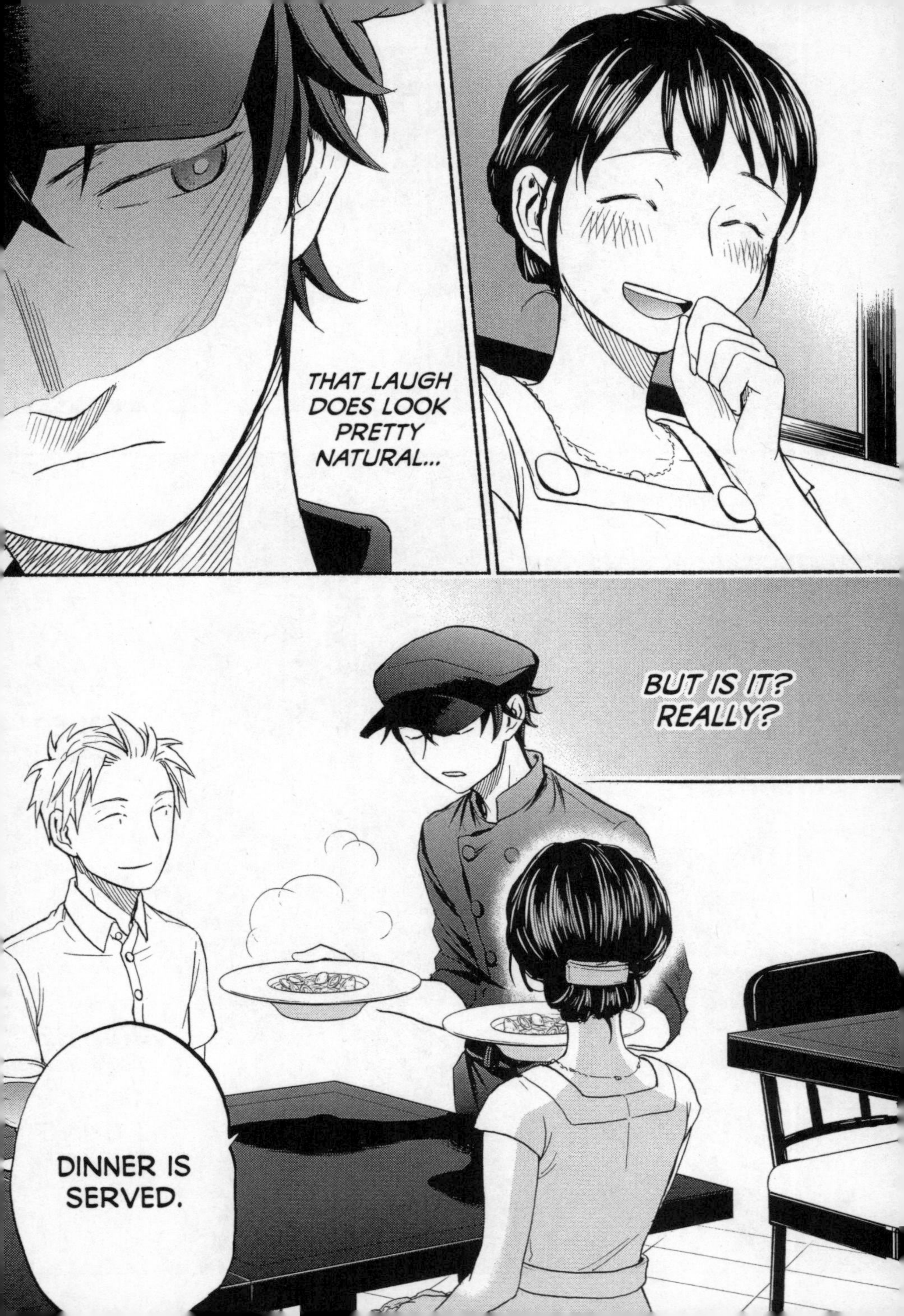
THAT LAUGH DOES LOOK PRETTY NATURAL...
BUT IS IT? REALLY?
DINNER IS SERVED.

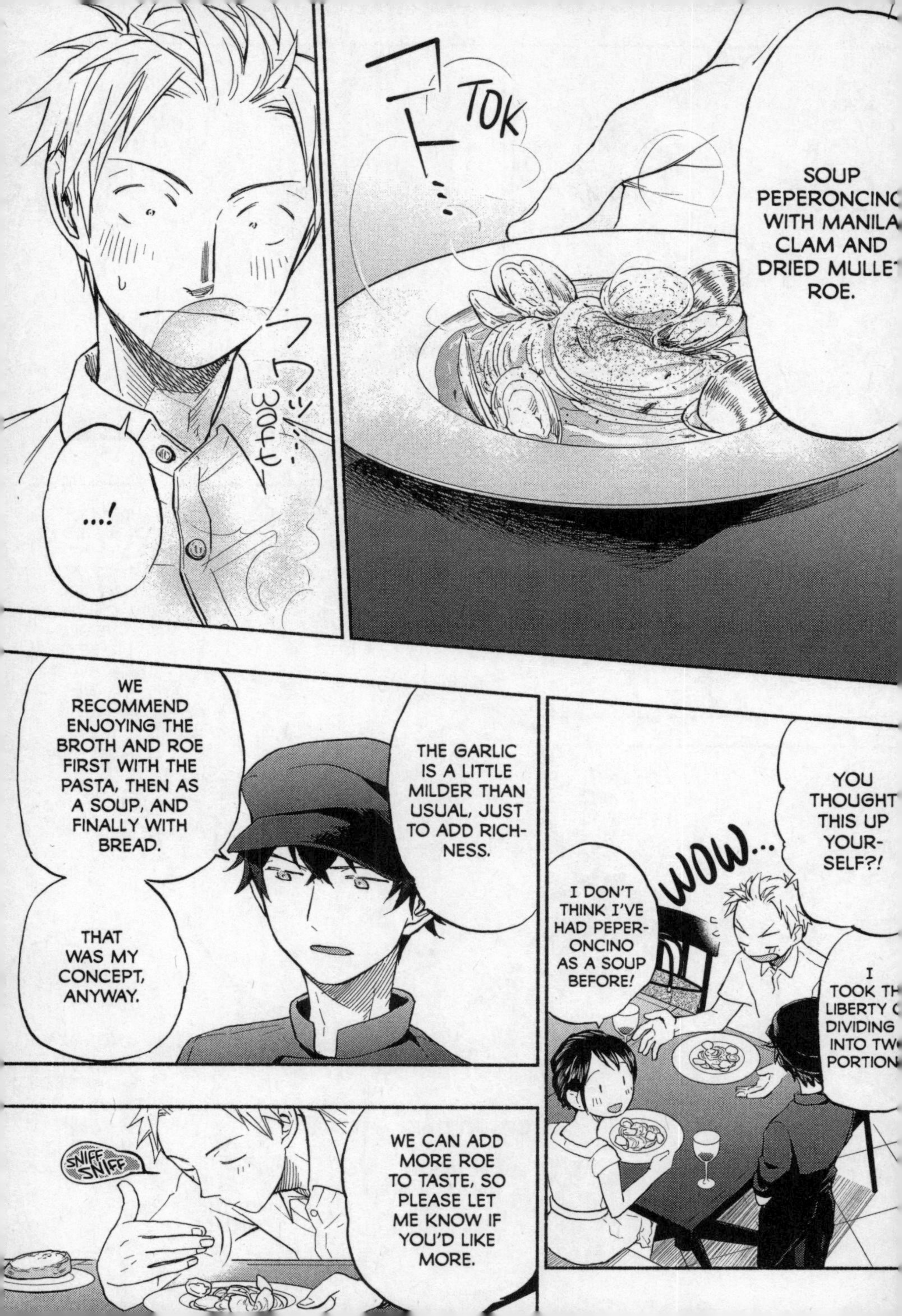
TOK
SOUP PEPERONCINO WITH MANILA CLAM AND DRIED MULLET ROE.
...!
YOU THOUGHT THIS UP YOURSELF?!
WOW...
I DON'T THINK I'VE HAD PEPERONCINO AS A SOUP BEFORE!
I TOOK THE LIBERTY OF DIVIDING INTO TWO PORTIONS
THE GARLIC IS A LITTLE MILDER THAN USUAL, JUST TO ADD RICHNESS.
WE RECOMMEND ENJOYING THE BROTH AND ROE FIRST WITH THE PASTA, THEN AS A SOUP, AND FINALLY WITH BREAD.
THAT WAS MY CONCEPT, ANYWAY.
WE CAN ADD MORE ROE TO TASTE, SO PLEASE LET ME KNOW IF YOU'D LIKE MORE.
SNIFF SNIFF

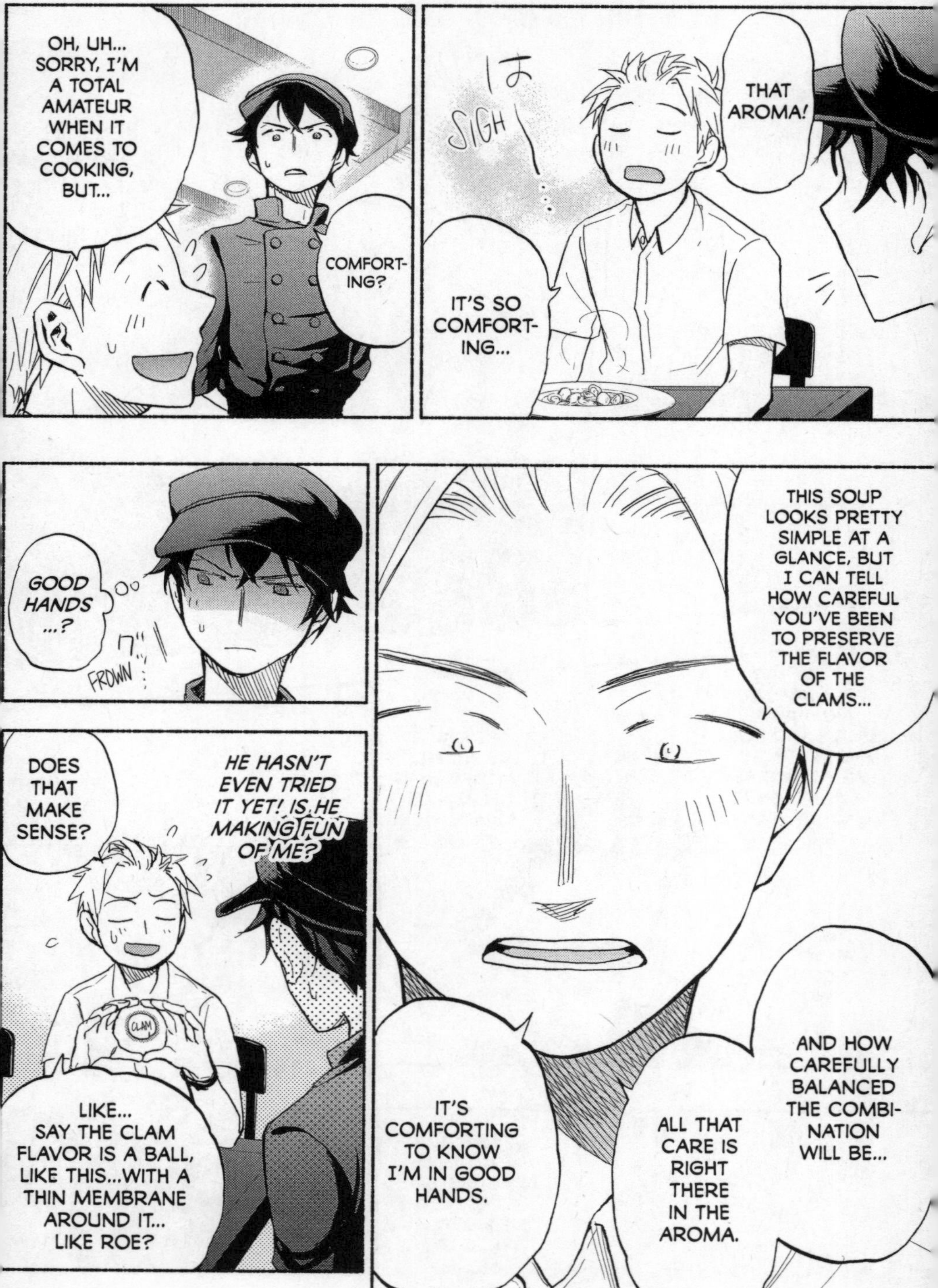
THAT AROMA!
は
SIGH
IT'S SO COMFORTING...
COMFORTING?
OH, UH... SORRY, I'M A TOTAL AMATEUR WHEN IT COMES TO COOKING, BUT...
THIS SOUP LOOKS PRETTY SIMPLE AT A GLANCE, BUT I CAN TELL HOW CAREFUL YOU'VE BEEN TO PRESERVE THE FLAVOR OF THE CLAMS...
AND HOW CAREFULLY BALANCED THE COMBINATION WILL BE...
ALL THAT CARE IS RIGHT THERE IN THE AROMA.
IT'S COMFORTING TO KNOW I'M IN GOOD HANDS.
GOOD HANDS ...?
FROWN
HE HASN'T EVEN TRIED IT YET! IS HE MAKING FUN OF ME?
DOES THAT MAKE SENSE?
CLAM
LIKE... SAY THE CLAM FLAVOR IS A BALL, LIKE THIS...WITH A THIN MEMBRANE AROUND IT... LIKE ROE?

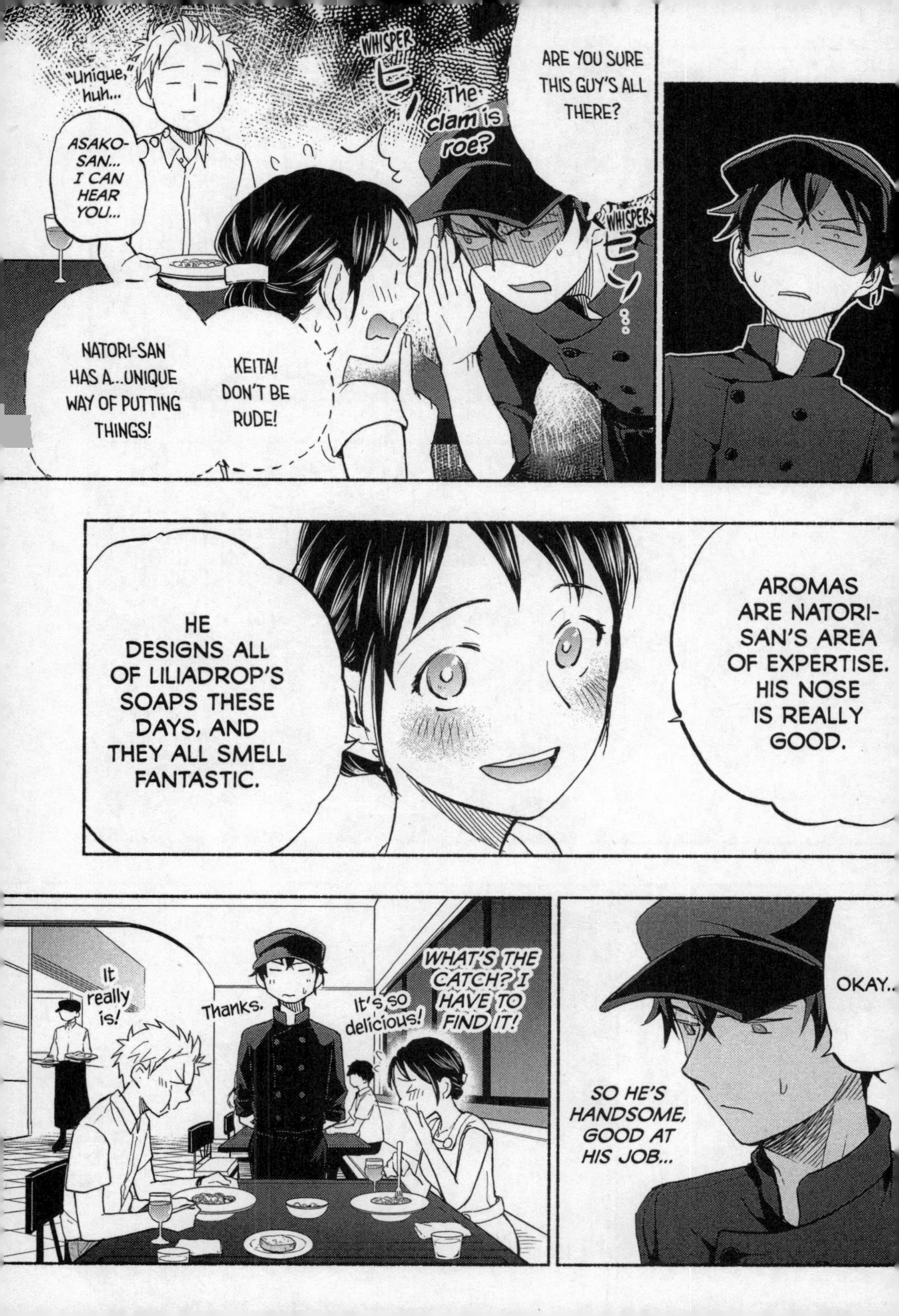
ARE YOU SURE THIS GUY'S ALL THERE?
WHISPER
The clam is roe?
WHISPER
KEITA! DON'T BE RUDE!
NATORI-SAN HAS A...UNIQUE WAY OF PUTTING THINGS!
"Unique," huh...
ASAKO-SAN... I CAN HEAR YOU...
AROMAS ARE NATORI-SAN'S AREA OF EXPERTISE. HIS NOSE IS REALLY GOOD.
HE DESIGNS ALL OF LILIADROP'S SOAPS THESE DAYS, AND THEY ALL SMELL FANTASTIC.
OKAY...
SO HE'S HANDSOME, GOOD AT HIS JOB...
WHAT'S THE CATCH? I HAVE TO FIND IT!
It's so delicious!
Thanks.
It really is!

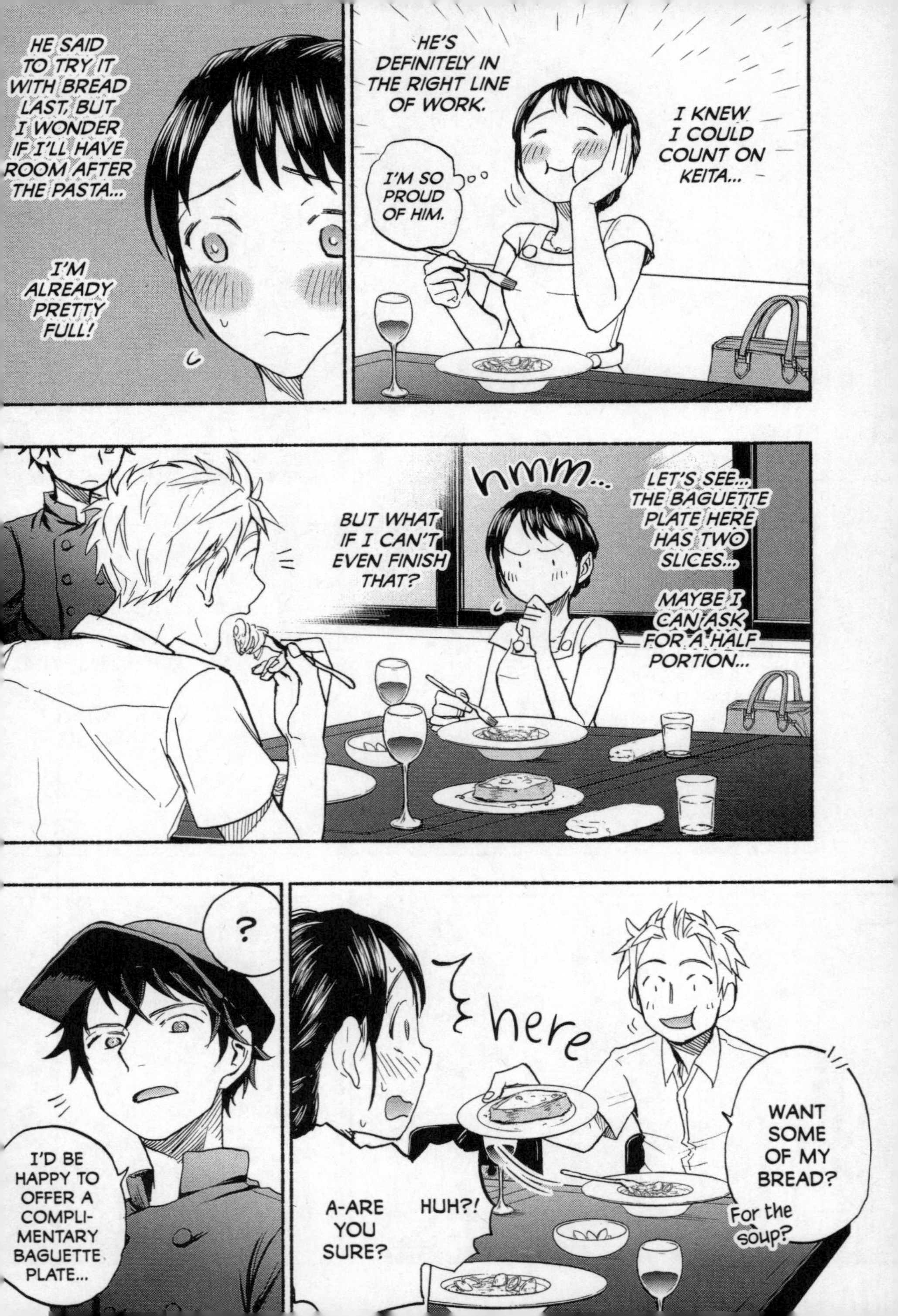
HE'S DEFINITELY IN THE RIGHT LINE OF WORK.
I KNEW I COULD COUNT ON KEITA...
I'M SO PROUD OF HIM.
HE SAID TO TRY IT WITH BREAD LAST, BUT I WONDER IF I'LL HAVE ROOM AFTER THE PASTA...
I'M ALREADY PRETTY FULL!
hmm...
LET'S SEE... THE BAGUETTE PLATE HERE HAS TWO SLICES...
MAYBE I CAN ASK FOR A HALF PORTION...
BUT WHAT IF I CAN'T EVEN FINISH THAT?
WANT SOME OF MY BREAD?
For the soup?
here
HUH?!
A-ARE YOU SURE?
?
I'D BE HAPPY TO OFFER A COMPLI-MENTARY BAGUETTE PLATE...

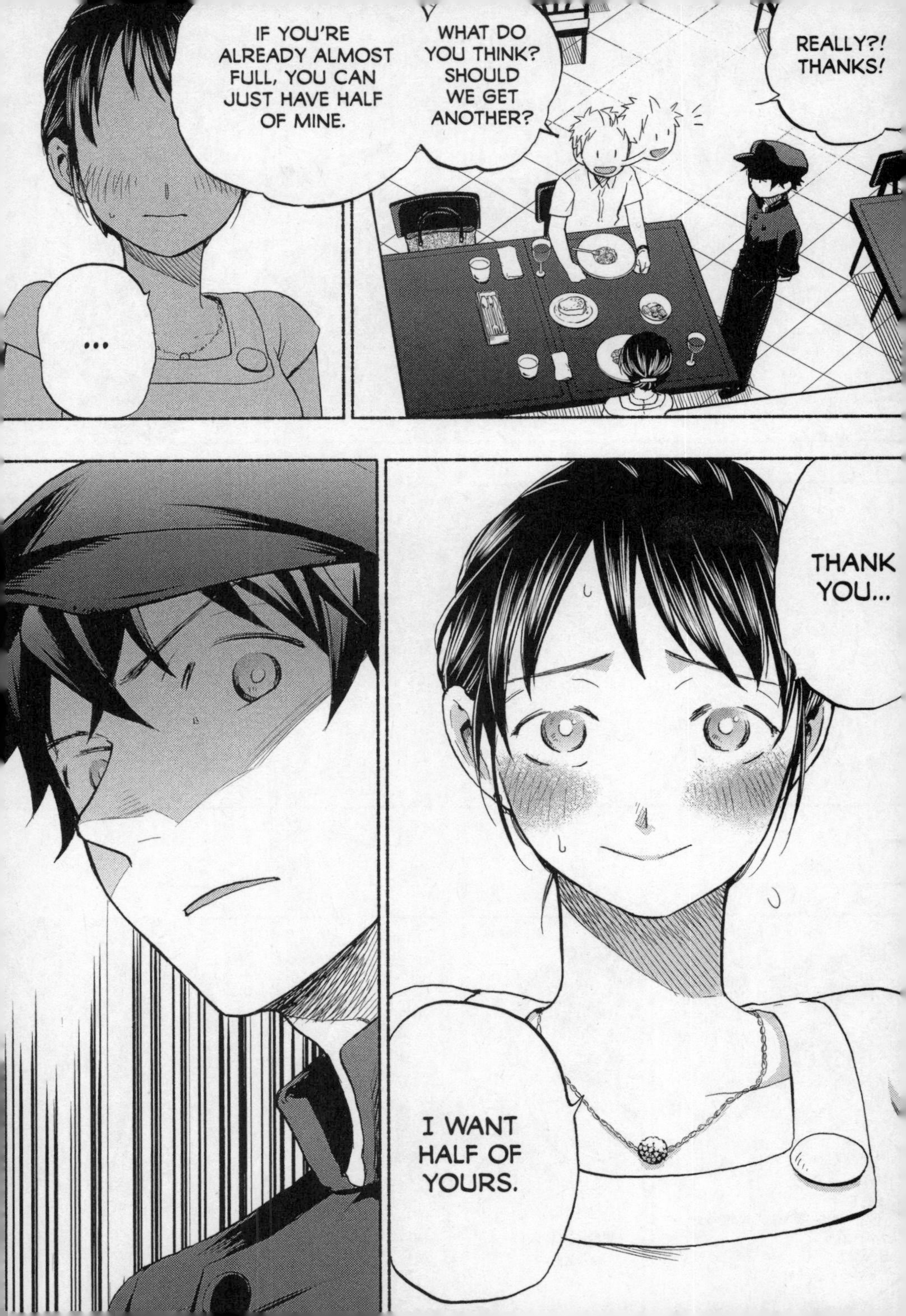
REALLY?! THANKS!
WHAT DO YOU THINK? SHOULD WE GET ANOTHER?
IF YOU'RE ALREADY ALMOST FULL, YOU CAN JUST HAVE HALF OF MINE.
...
THANK YOU...
I WANT HALF OF YOURS.

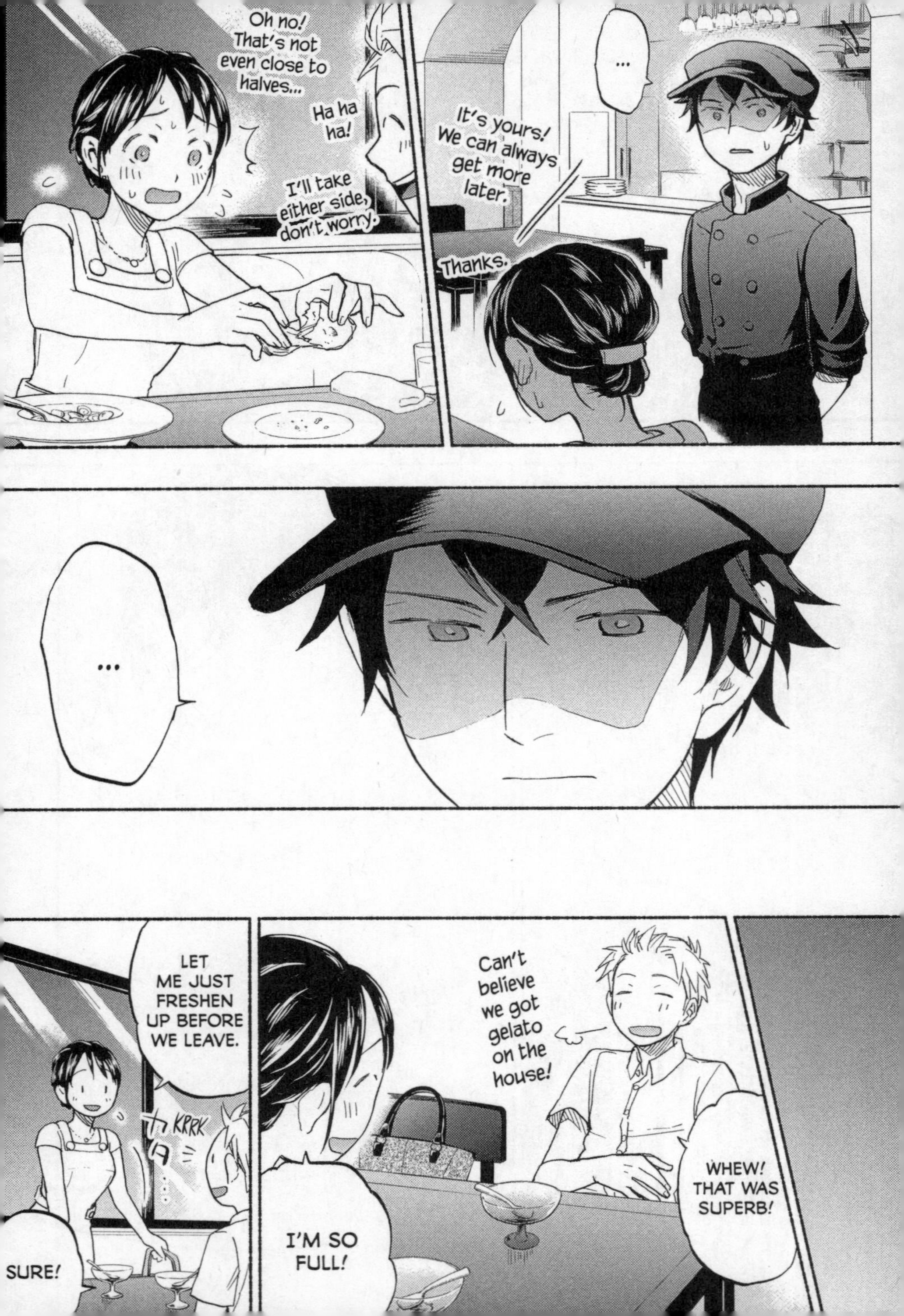
...
It's yours! We can always get more later.
Thanks.
Oh no! That's not even close to halves...
Ha ha ha!
I'll take either side, don't worry.
...
Can't believe we got gelato on the house!
WHEW! THAT WAS SUPERB!
I'M SO FULL!
LET ME JUST FRESHEN UP BEFORE WE LEAVE.
KRRK
SURE!

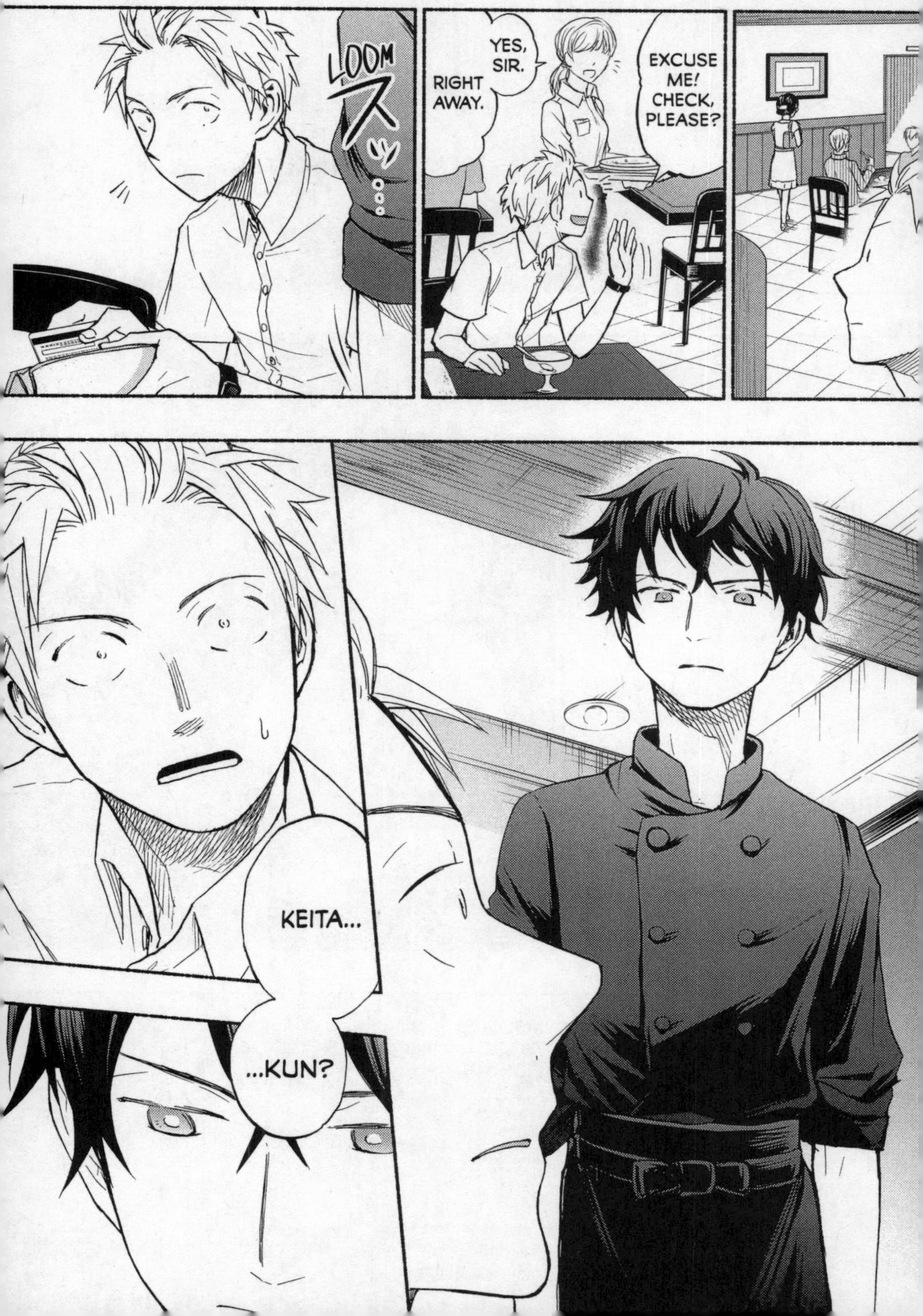
EXCUSE ME! CHECK, PLEASE?
YES, SIR. RIGHT AWAY.
LOOM
スッ
KEITA...
...KUN?

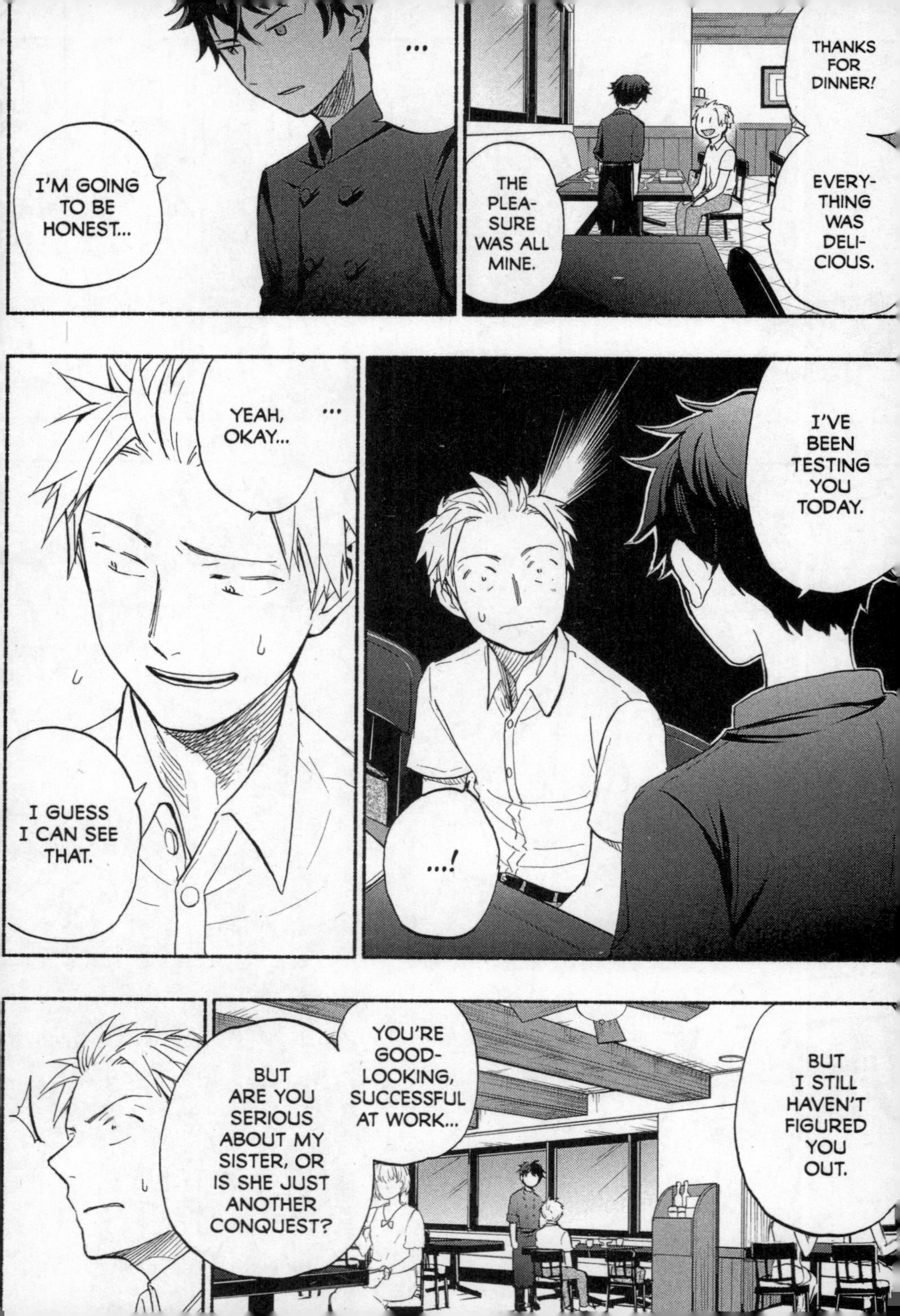
THANKS FOR DINNER!
EVERY-THING WAS DELI-CIOUS.
THE PLEA-SURE WAS ALL MINE.
...
I'M GOING TO BE HONEST...
I'VE BEEN TESTING YOU TODAY.
...!
YEAH, OKAY...
...
I GUESS I CAN SEE THAT.
BUT I STILL HAVEN'T FIGURED YOU OUT.
YOU'RE GOOD-LOOKING, SUCCESSFUL AT WORK...
BUT ARE YOU SERIOUS ABOUT MY SISTER, OR IS SHE JUST ANOTHER CONQUEST?

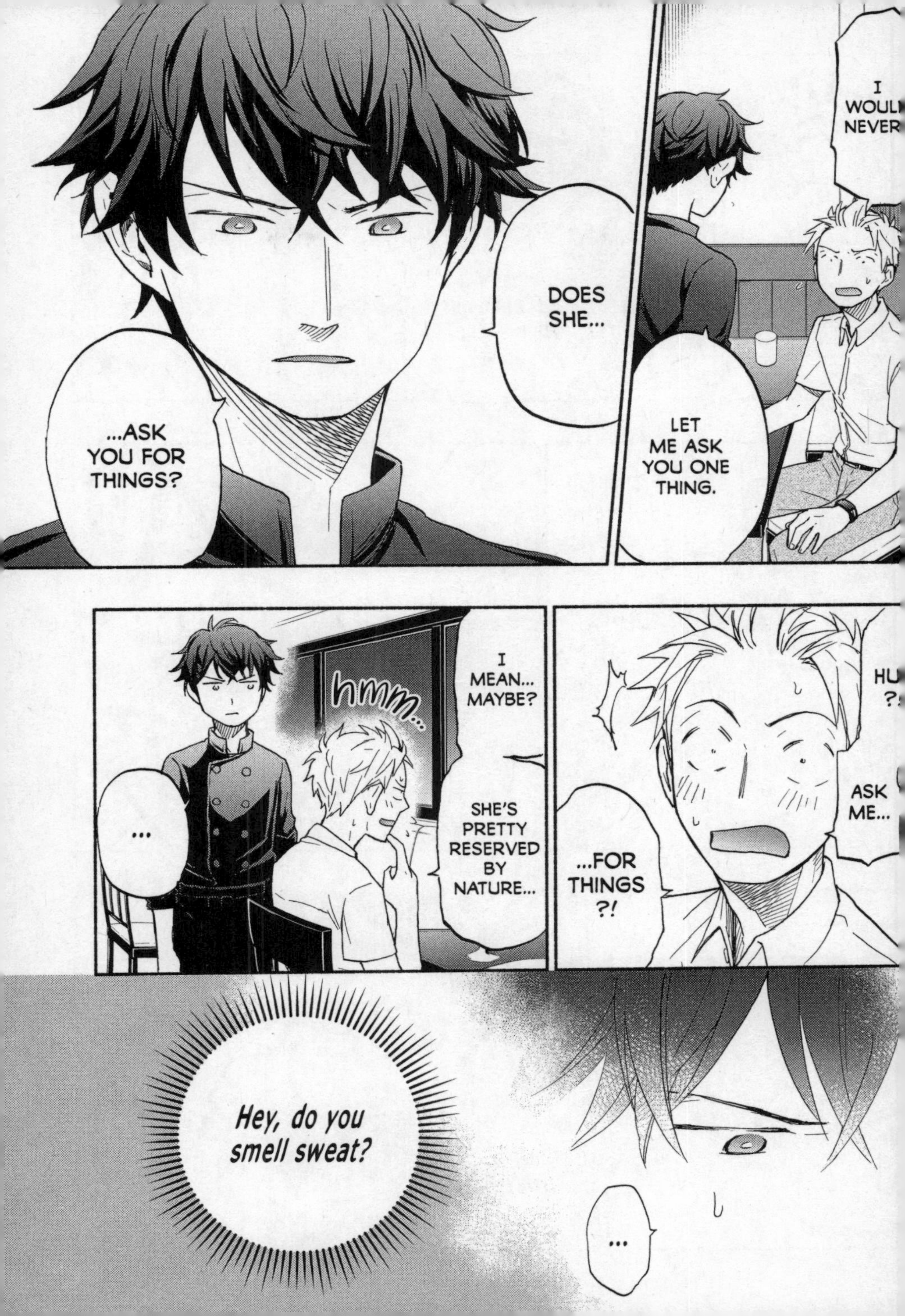
I WOUL NEVER
LET ME ASK YOU ONE THING.
DOES SHE...
...ASK YOU FOR THINGS?
HU ?
ASK ME...
...FOR THINGS ?!
I MEAN... MAYBE?
hmm...
SHE'S PRETTY RESERVED BY NATURE...
...
Hey, do you smell sweat?
...

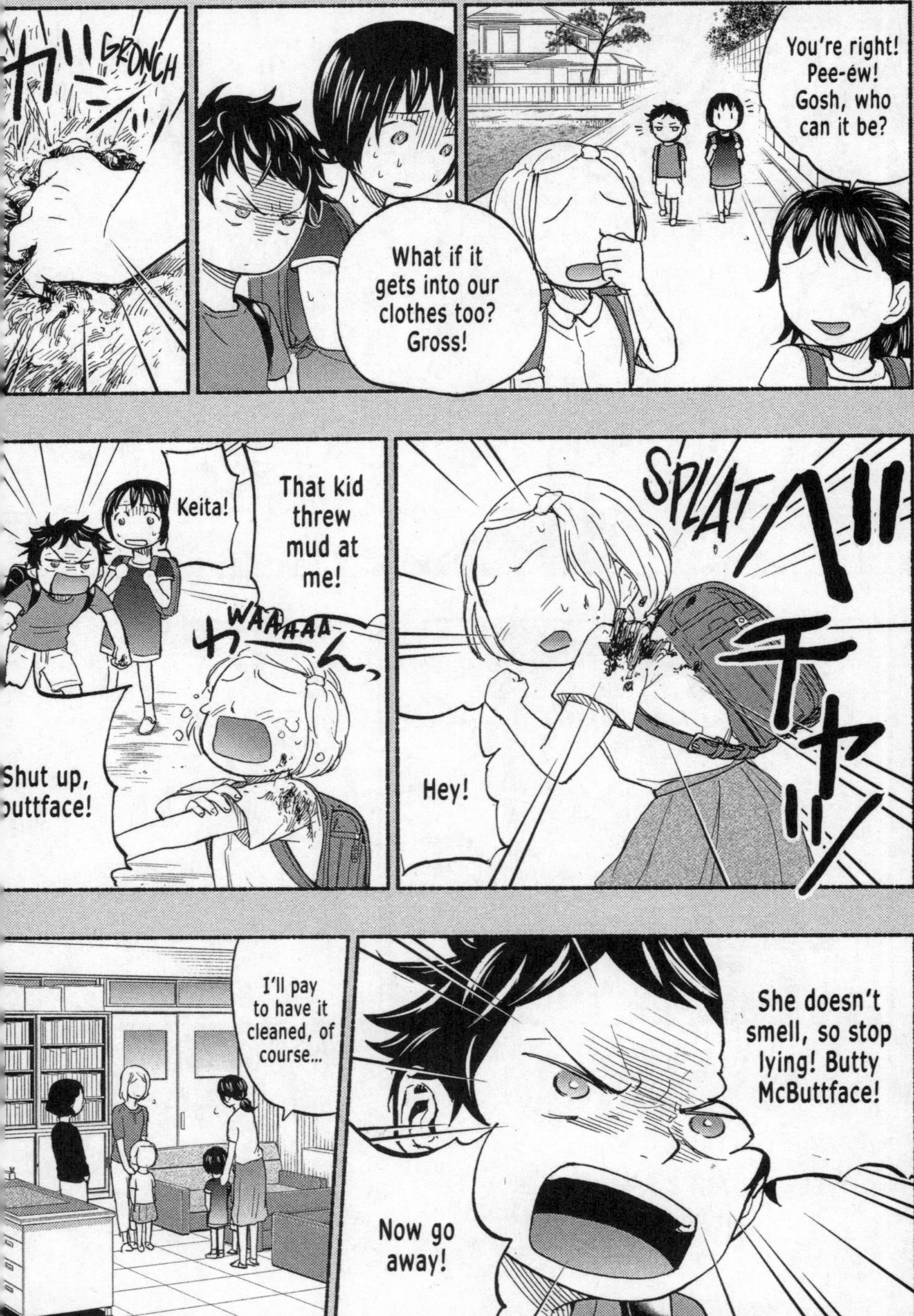
You're right! Pee-éw! Gosh, who can it be?
What if it gets into our clothes too? Gross!
GRONCH
SPLAT
ベチャッ
Hey!
Keita!
That kid threw mud at me!
WAAAAA
わ〜ん
Shut up,
uttface!
She doesn't smell, so stop lying! Butty McButtface!
Now go away!
I'll pay to have it cleaned, of course...

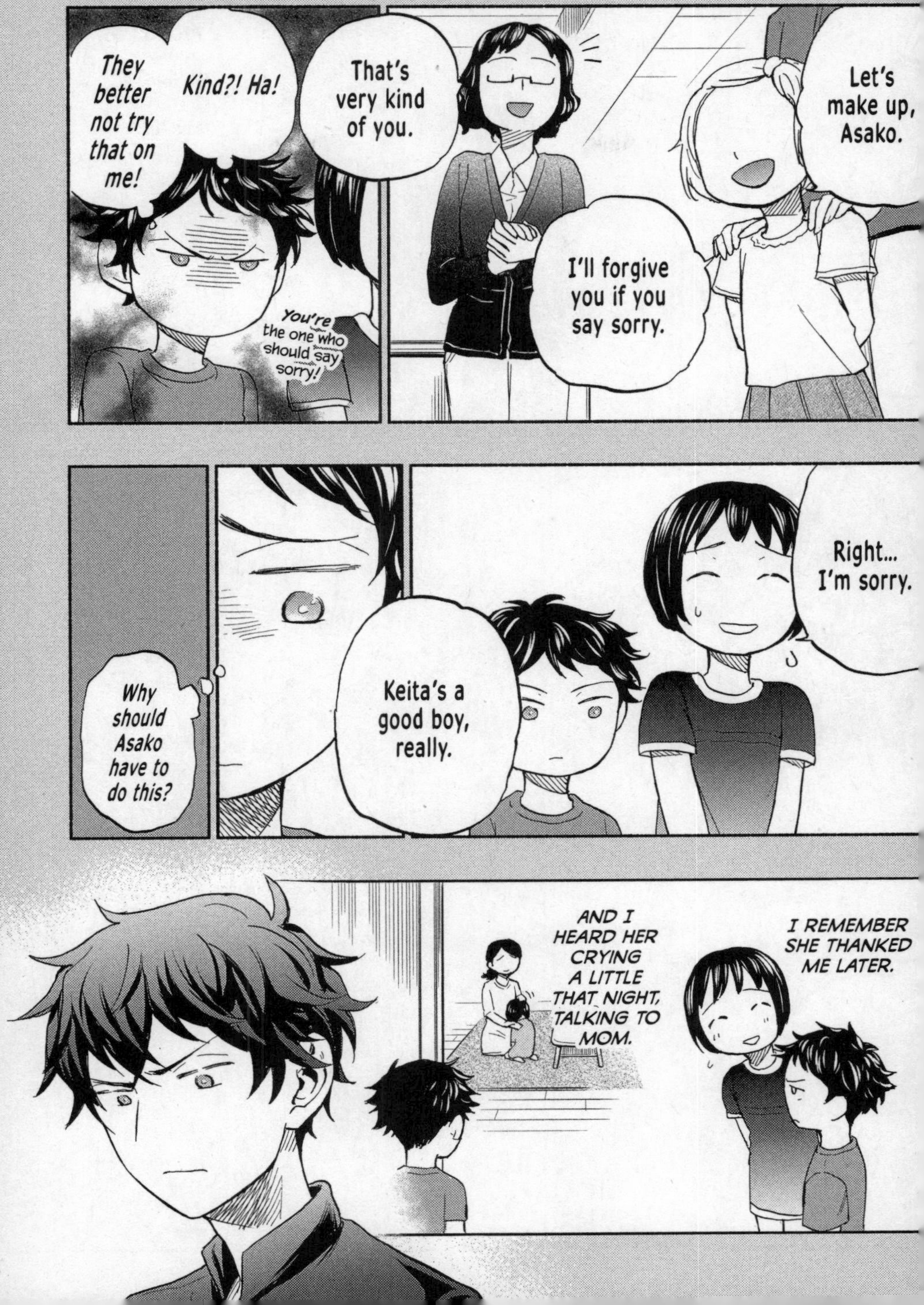
Let's make up, Asako.
I'll forgive you if you say sorry.
That's very kind of you.
Kind?! Ha!
They better not try that on me!
You're the one who should say sorry!
Right... I'm sorry.
Keita's a good boy, really.
Why should Asako have to do this?
I REMEMBER SHE THANKED ME LATER.
AND I HEARD HER CRYING A LITTLE THAT NIGHT, TALKING TO MOM.

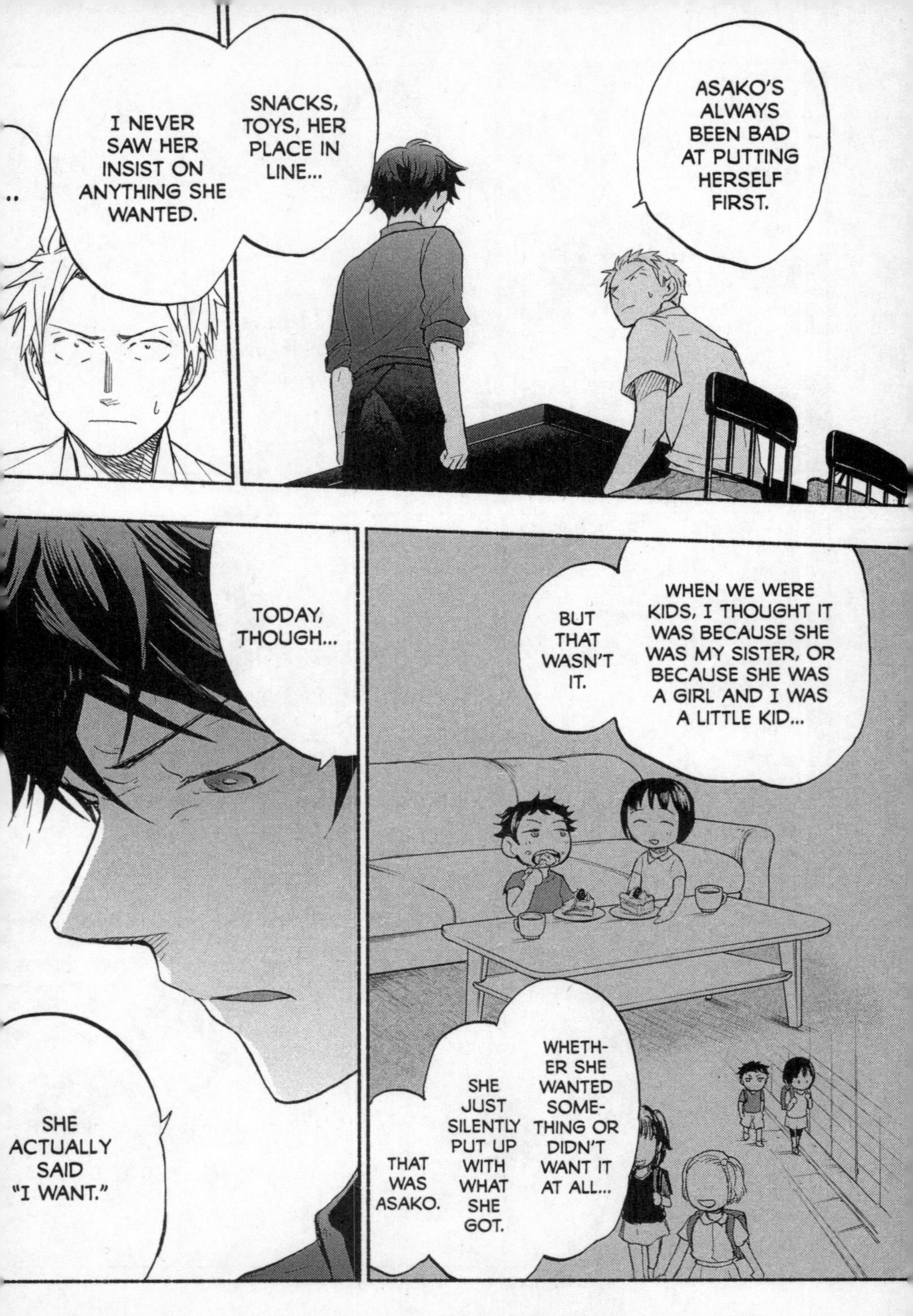
ASAKO'S ALWAYS BEEN BAD AT PUTTING HERSELF FIRST.
SNACKS, TOYS, HER PLACE IN LINE...
I NEVER SAW HER INSIST ON ANYTHING SHE WANTED.
..
WHEN WE WERE KIDS, I THOUGHT IT WAS BECAUSE SHE WAS MY SISTER, OR BECAUSE SHE WAS A GIRL AND I WAS A LITTLE KID...
BUT THAT WASN'T IT.
WHETH-ER SHE WANTED SOME-THING OR DIDN'T WANT IT AT ALL...
SHE JUST SILENTLY PUT UP WITH WHAT SHE GOT.
THAT WAS ASAKO.
TODAY, THOUGH...
SHE ACTUALLY SAID "I WANT."

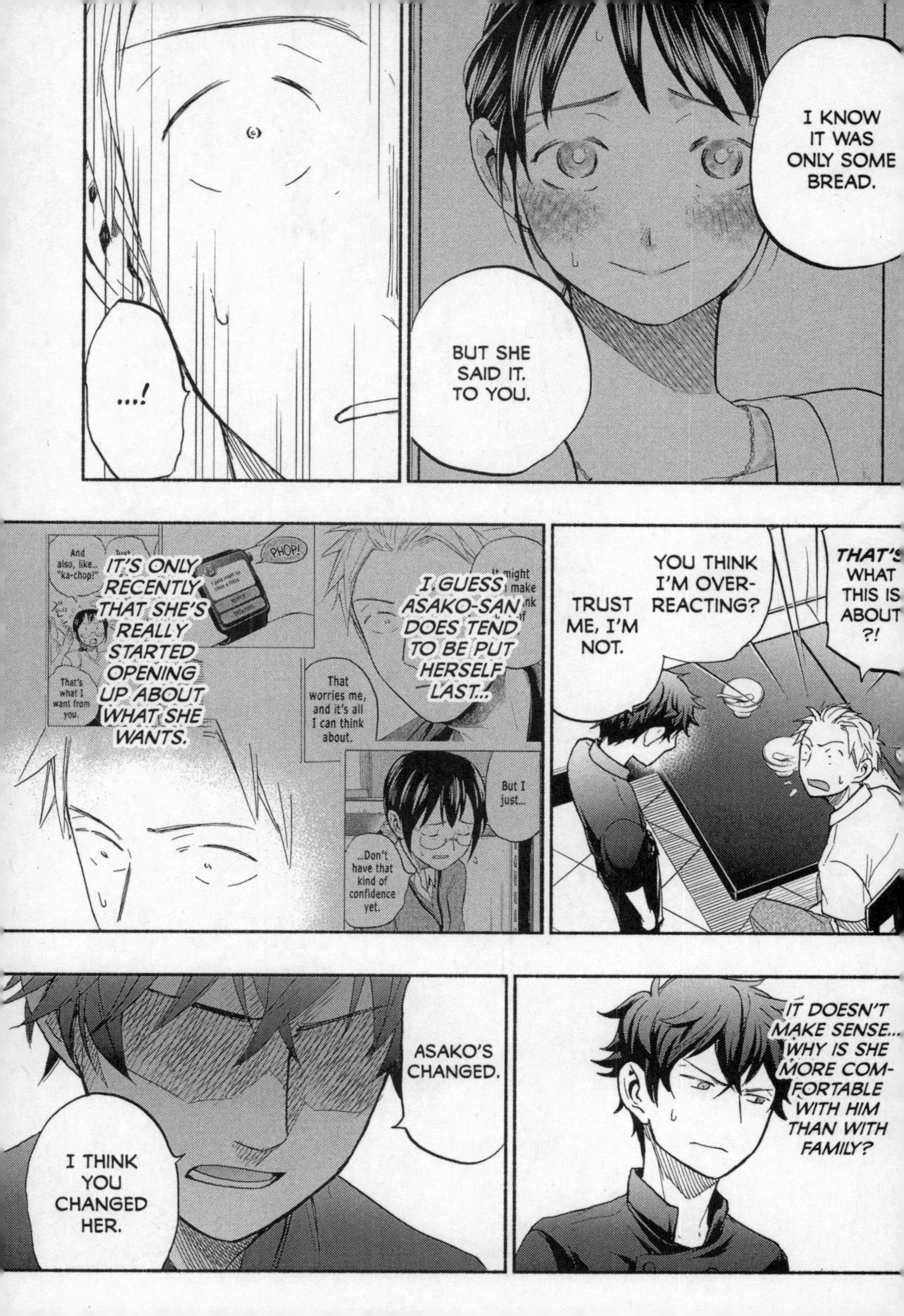
I KNOW IT WAS ONLY SOME BREAD.
BUT SHE SAID IT. TO YOU.
...!
THAT'S WHAT THIS IS ABOUT?!
YOU THINK I'M OVER-REACTING?
TRUST ME, I'M NOT.
I GUESS ASAKO-SAN DOES TEND TO BE PUT HERSELF LAST...
That worries me, and it's all I can think about.
But I just...
...Don't have that kind of confidence yet.
PHOP!
And also, like... "ka-chop!"
That's what I want from you.
IT'S ONLY RECENTLY THAT SHE'S REALLY STARTED OPENING UP ABOUT WHAT SHE WANTS.
IT DOESN'T MAKE SENSE... WHY IS SHE MORE COM-FORTABLE WITH HIM THAN WITH FAMILY?
ASAKO'S CHANGED.
I THINK YOU CHANGED HER.

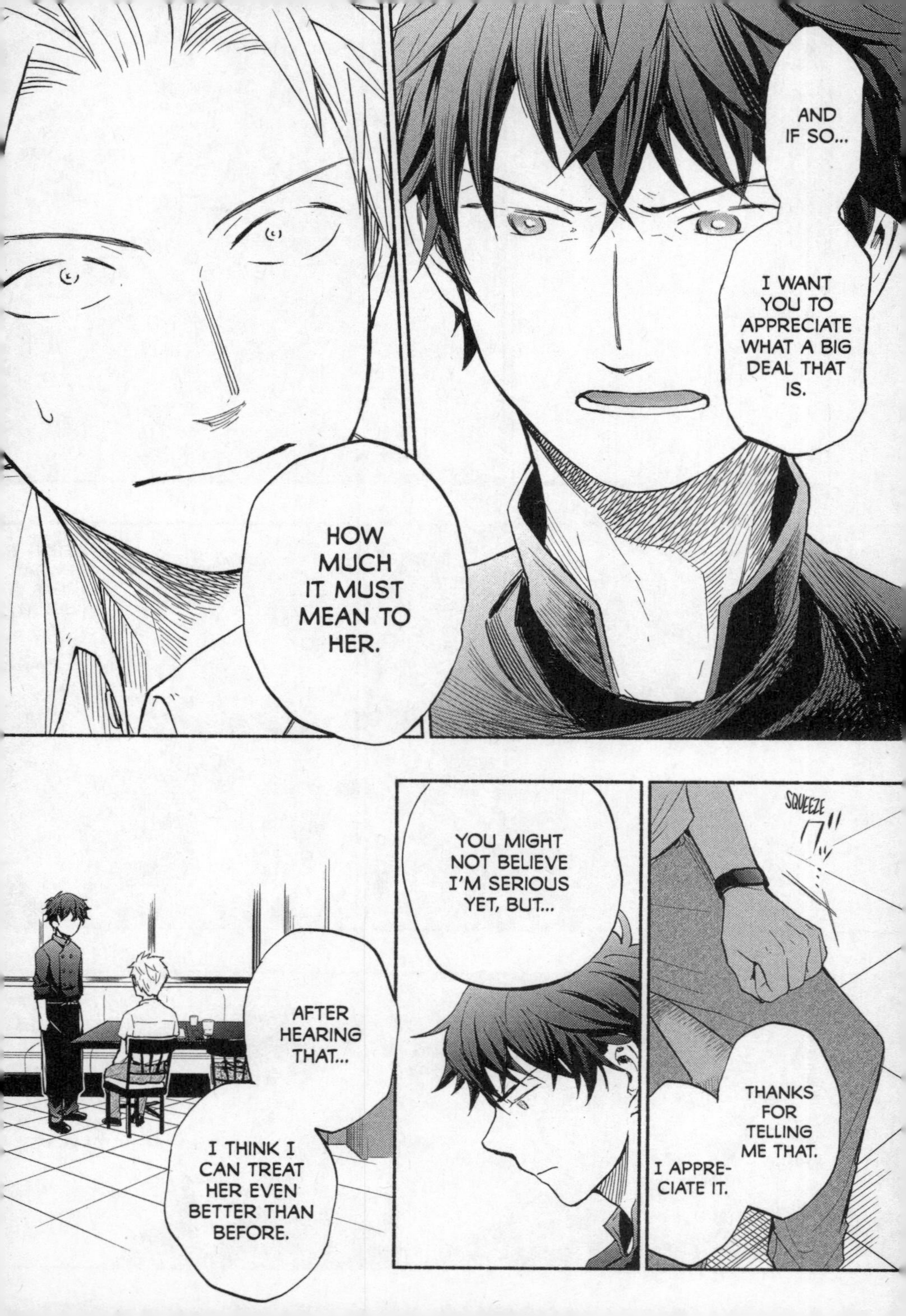

AND IF SO...
I WANT YOU TO APPRECIATE WHAT A BIG DEAL THAT IS.
HOW MUCH IT MUST MEAN TO HER.
SQUEEZE
THANKS FOR TELLING ME THAT.
I APPRECIATE IT.
YOU MIGHT NOT BELIEVE I'M SERIOUS YET, BUT...
AFTER HEARING THAT...
I THINK I CAN TREAT HER EVEN BETTER THAN BEFORE.

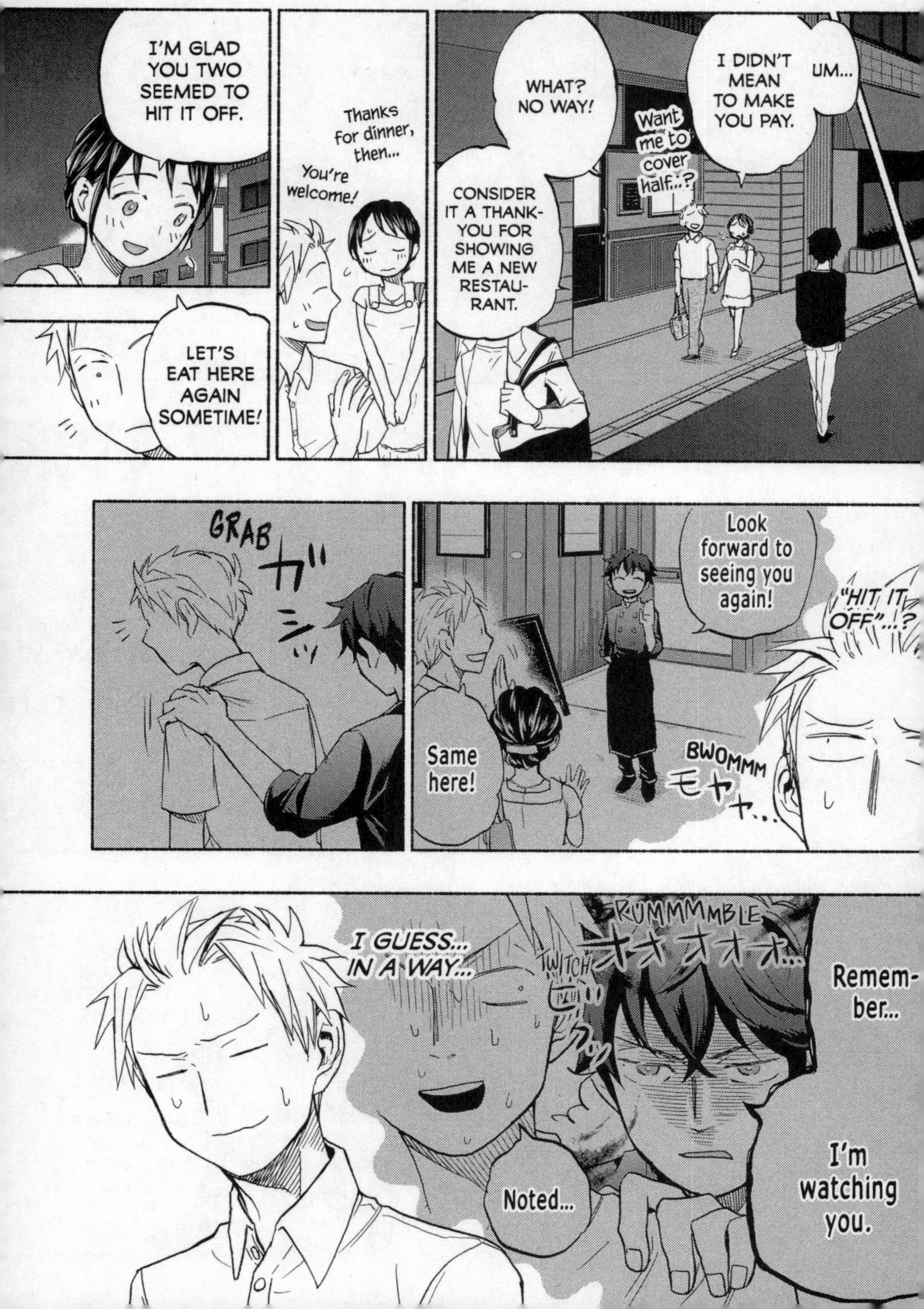
UM...
I DIDN'T MEAN TO MAKE YOU PAY.
Want me to cover half...?
WHAT? NO WAY!
CONSIDER IT A THANK-YOU FOR SHOWING ME A NEW RESTAURANT.
Thanks for dinner, then...
You're welcome!
I'M GLAD YOU TWO SEEMED TO HIT IT OFF.
LET'S EAT HERE AGAIN SOMETIME!
"HIT IT OFF"...?
Look forward to seeing you again!
Same here!
BWOMMM
GRAB
ガッ
Remember...
I'm watching you.
GRUMMMMBLE
オオオオオ...
TWITCH
I GUESS... IN A WAY...
Noted...

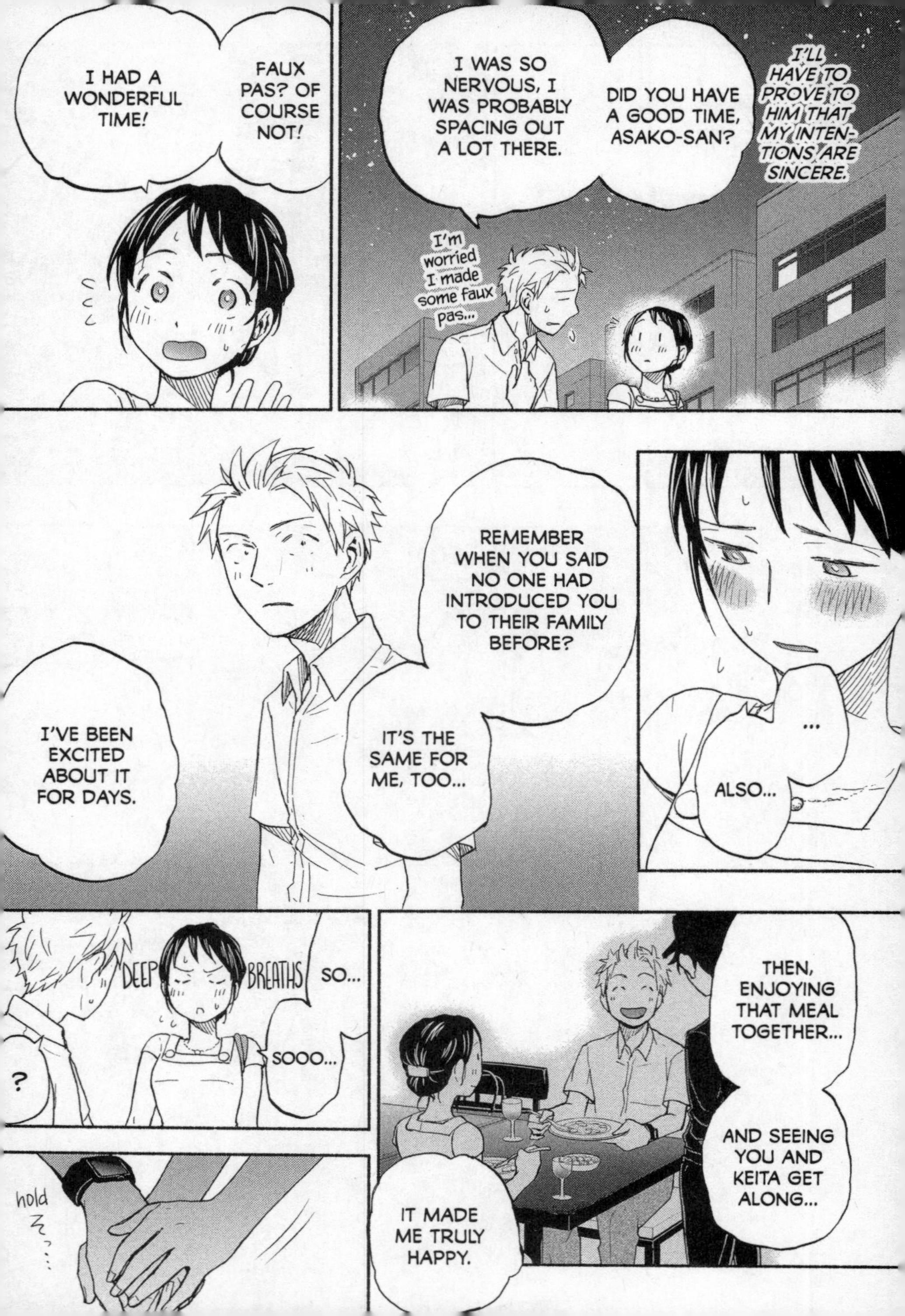
I'LL HAVE TO PROVE TO HIM THAT MY INTENTIONS ARE SINCERE.
DID YOU HAVE A GOOD TIME, ASAKO-SAN?
I WAS SO NERVOUS, I WAS PROBABLY SPACING OUT A LOT THERE.
I'm worried I made some faux pas...
FAUX PAS? OF COURSE NOT!
I HAD A WONDERFUL TIME!
...
ALSO...
REMEMBER WHEN YOU SAID NO ONE HAD INTRODUCED YOU TO THEIR FAMILY BEFORE?
IT'S THE SAME FOR ME, TOO...
I'VE BEEN EXCITED ABOUT IT FOR DAYS.
THEN, ENJOYING THAT MEAL TOGETHER...
AND SEEING YOU AND KEITA GET ALONG...
IT MADE ME TRULY HAPPY.
DEEP BREATHS
SO...
SOOO...
?
hold

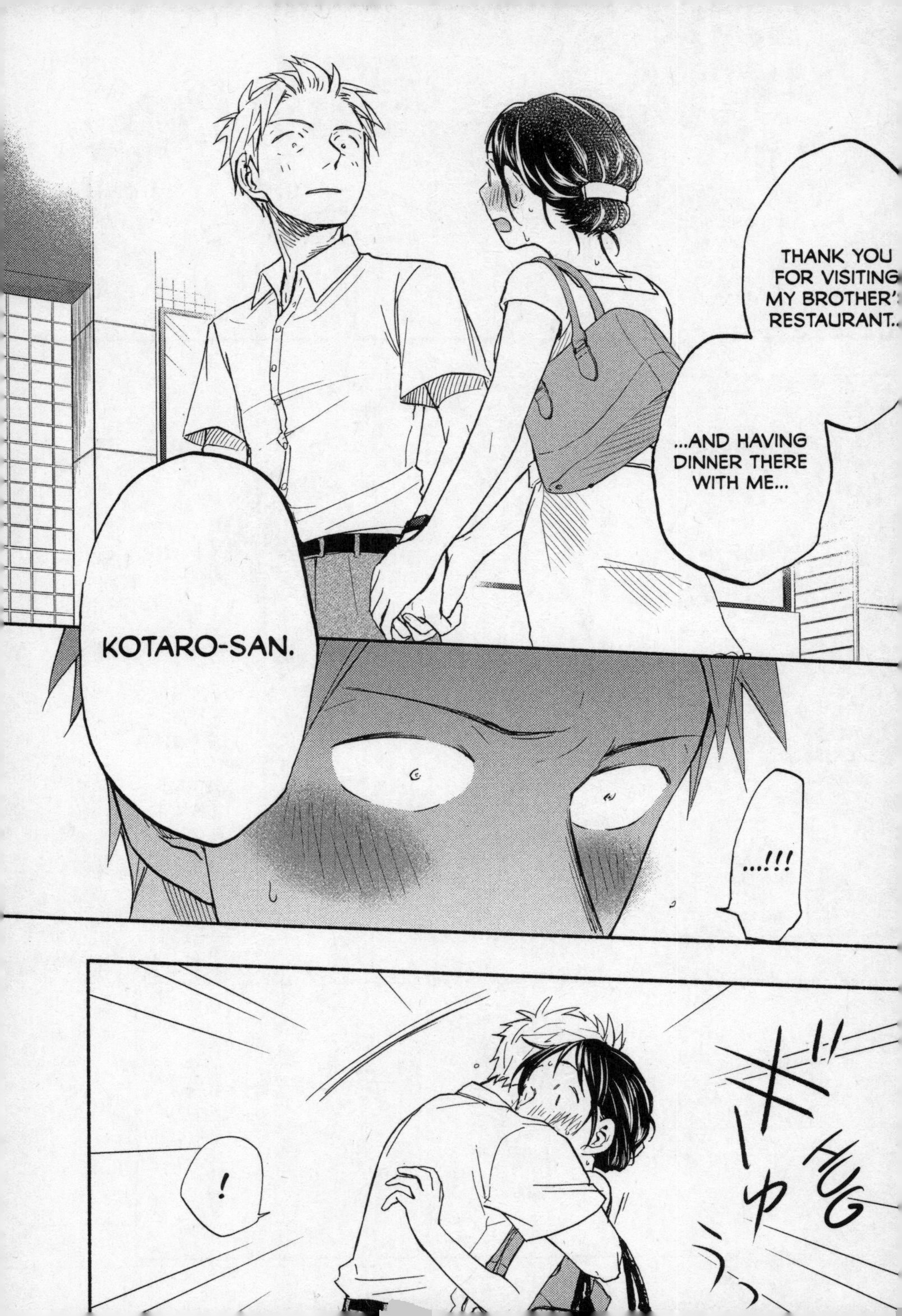
THANK YOU FOR VISITING MY BROTHER' RESTAURANT..
...AND HAVING DINNER THERE WITH ME...
KOTARO-SAN.
...!!!
HUG
!

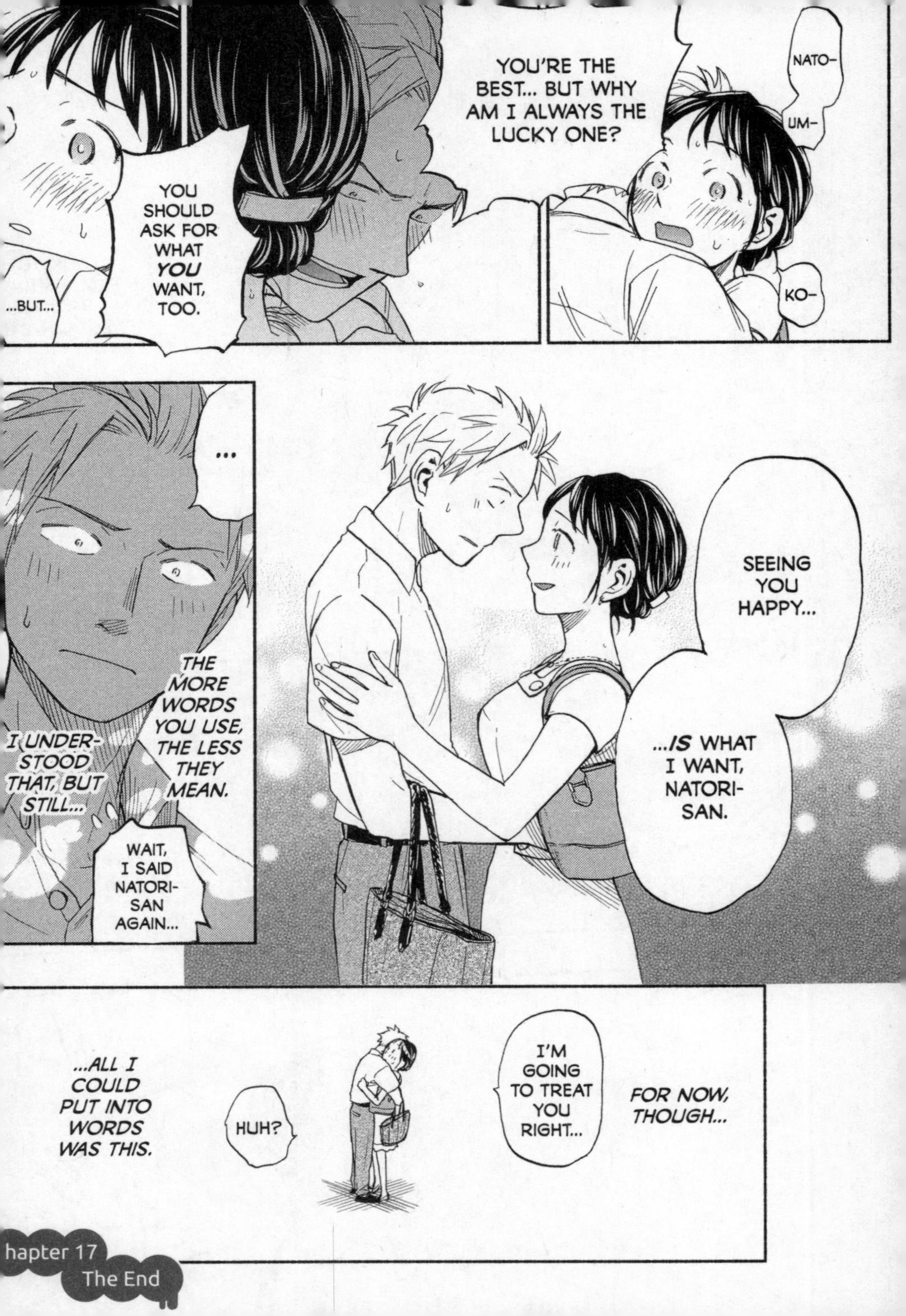
NATO- UM- KO-
YOU'RE THE BEST... BUT WHY AM I ALWAYS THE LUCKY ONE?
YOU SHOULD ASK FOR WHAT *YOU* WANT, TOO.
...BUT...
SEEING YOU HAPPY...
...*IS* WHAT I WANT, NATORI-SAN.
...
THE MORE WORDS YOU USE, THE LESS THEY MEAN.
I UNDERSTOOD THAT, BUT STILL...
WAIT, I SAID NATORI-SAN AGAIN...
FOR NOW, THOUGH...
I'M GOING TO TREAT YOU RIGHT...
HUH?
...ALL I COULD PUT INTO WORDS WAS THIS.
hapter 17
The End

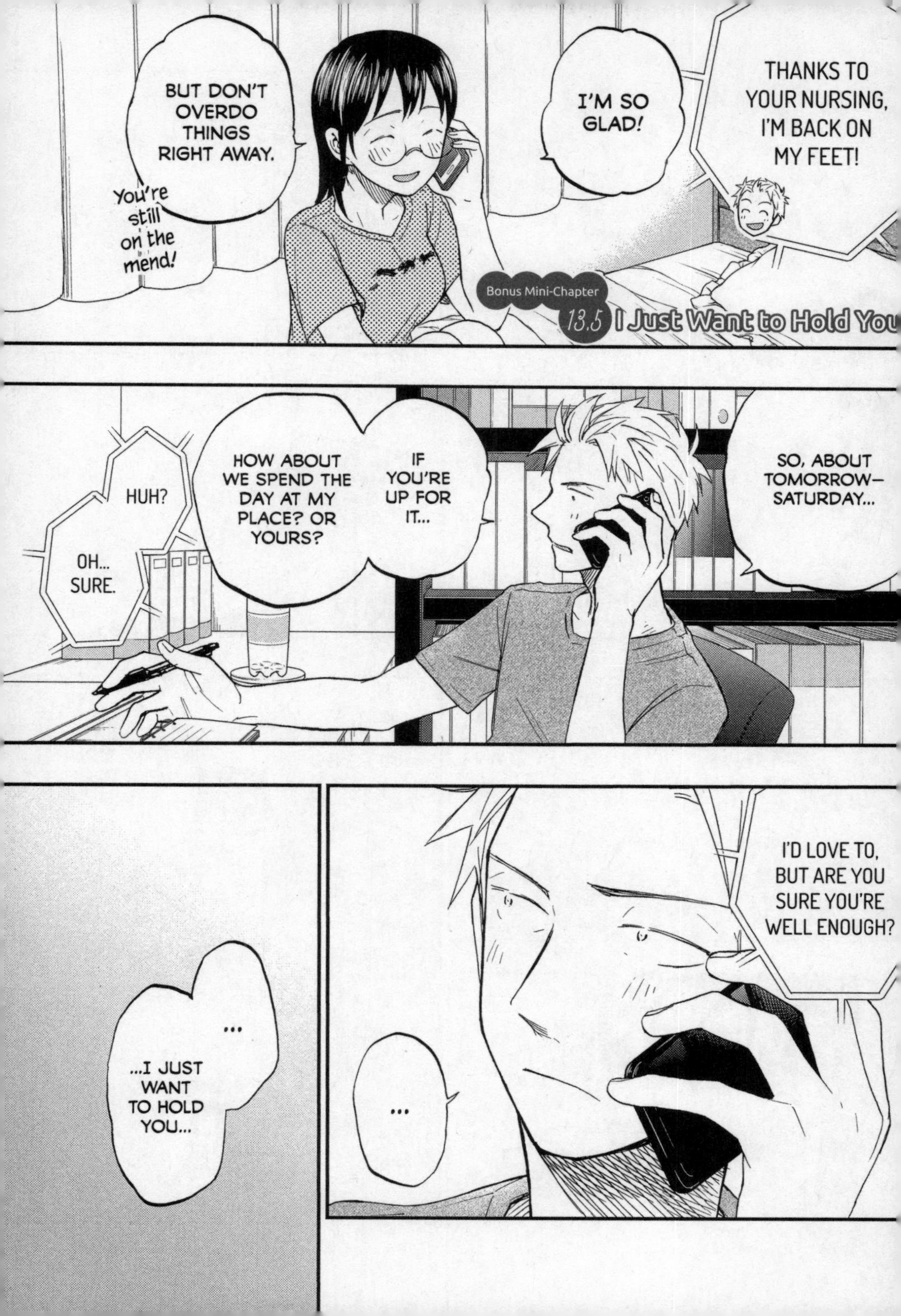
THANKS TO YOUR NURSING, I'M BACK ON MY FEET!
I'M SO GLAD!
BUT DON'T OVERDO THINGS RIGHT AWAY.
You're still on the mend!
Bonus Mini-Chapter
13.5 I Just Want to Hold You
SO, ABOUT TOMORROW—SATURDAY...
IF YOU'RE UP FOR IT...
HOW ABOUT WE SPEND THE DAY AT MY PLACE? OR YOURS?
HUH?
OH... SURE.
I'D LOVE TO, BUT ARE YOU SURE YOU'RE WELL ENOUGH?
...
...
...I JUST WANT TO HOLD YOU...

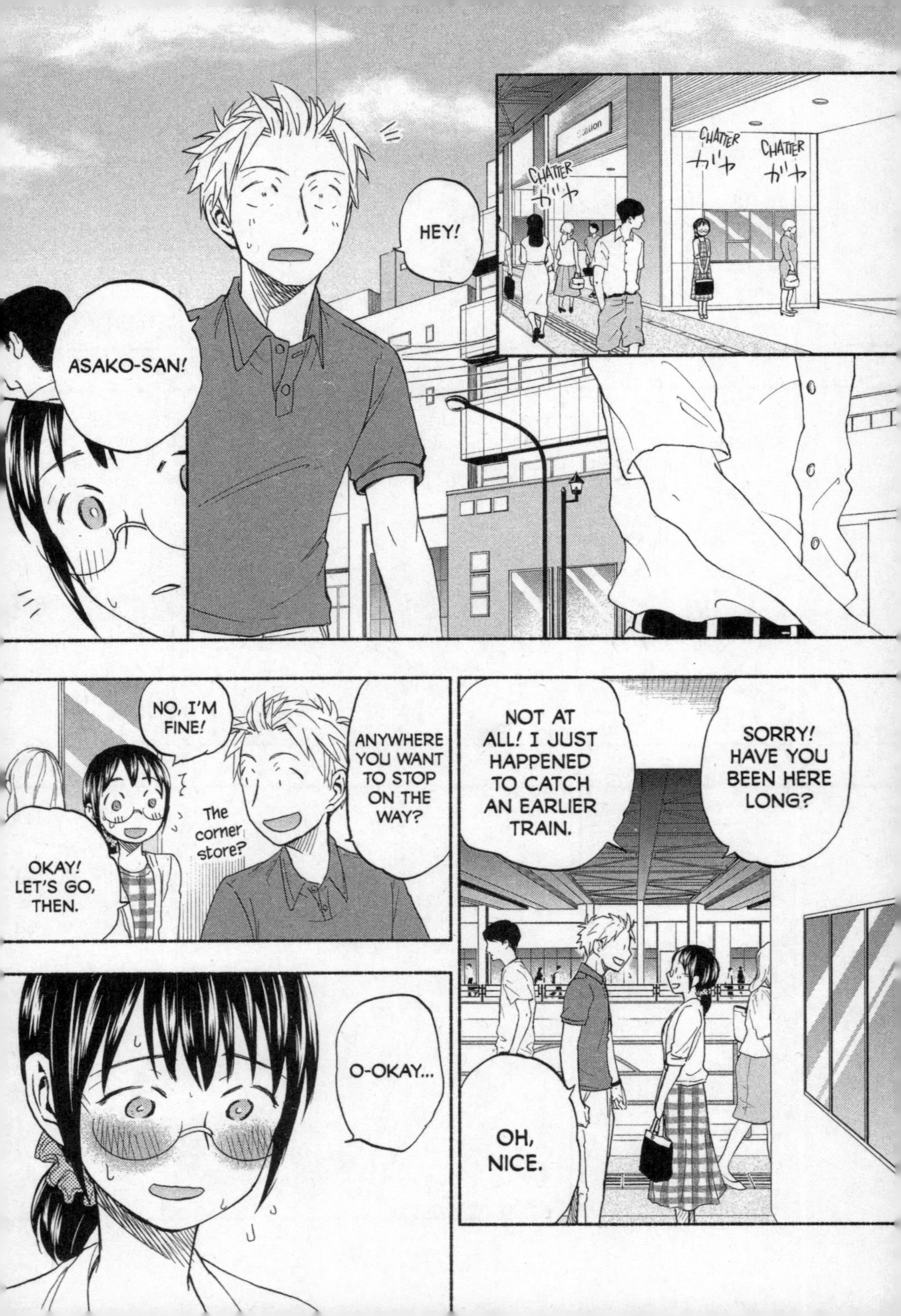
CHATTER
ガヤ
CHATTER
ガヤ
CHATTER
ガヤ
HEY!
ASAKO-SAN!
SORRY! HAVE YOU BEEN HERE LONG?
NOT AT ALL! I JUST HAPPENED TO CATCH AN EARLIER TRAIN.
OH, NICE.
ANYWHERE YOU WANT TO STOP ON THE WAY?
NO, I'M FINE!
The corner store?
OKAY! LET'S GO, THEN.
O-OKAY...

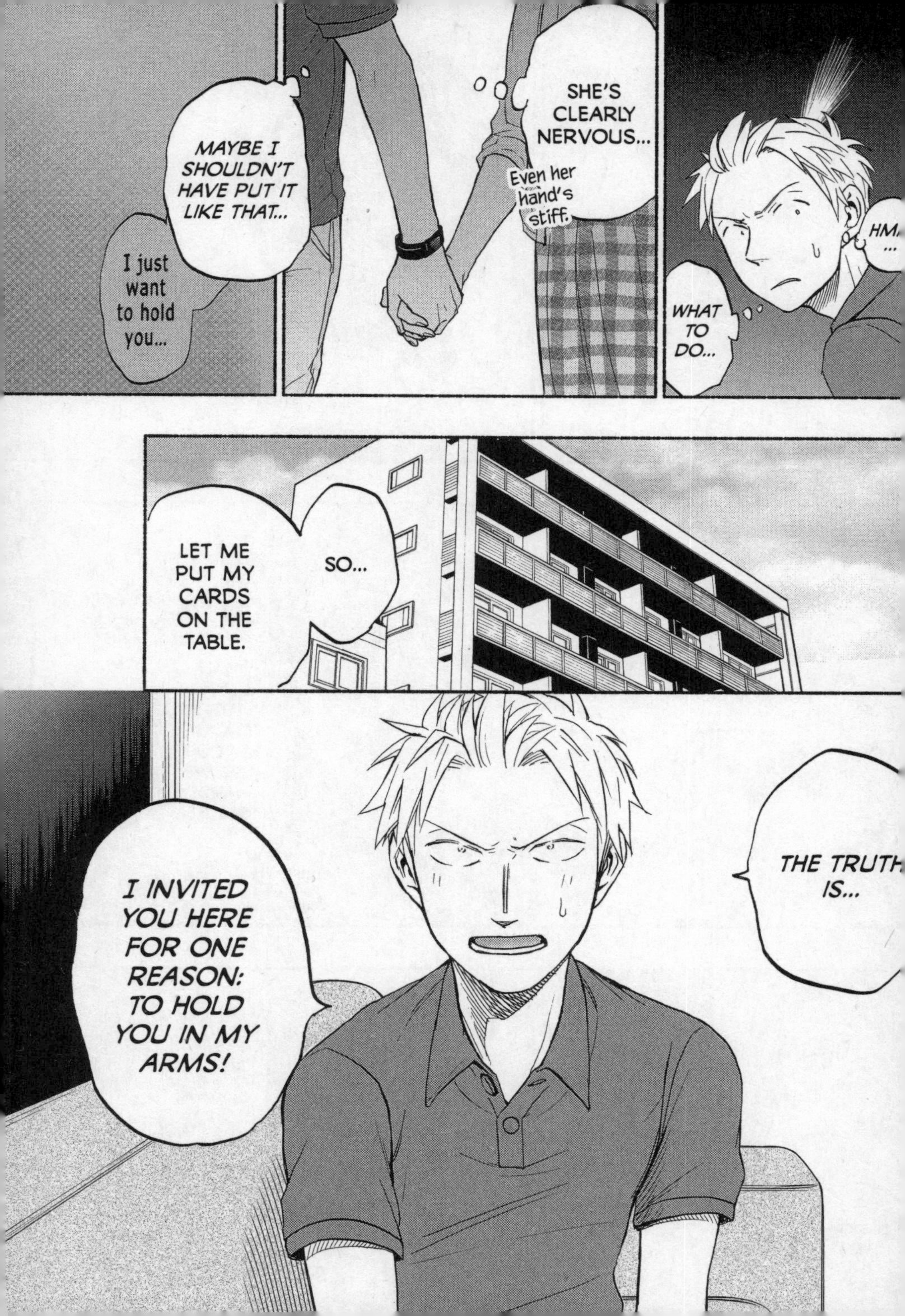
HM...
WHAT TO DO...
SHE'S CLEARLY NERVOUS...
Even her hand's stiff.
MAYBE I SHOULDN'T HAVE PUT IT LIKE THAT...
I just want to hold you...
SO...
LET ME PUT MY CARDS ON THE TABLE.
THE TRUTH IS...
I INVITED YOU HERE FOR ONE REASON: TO HOLD YOU IN MY ARMS!

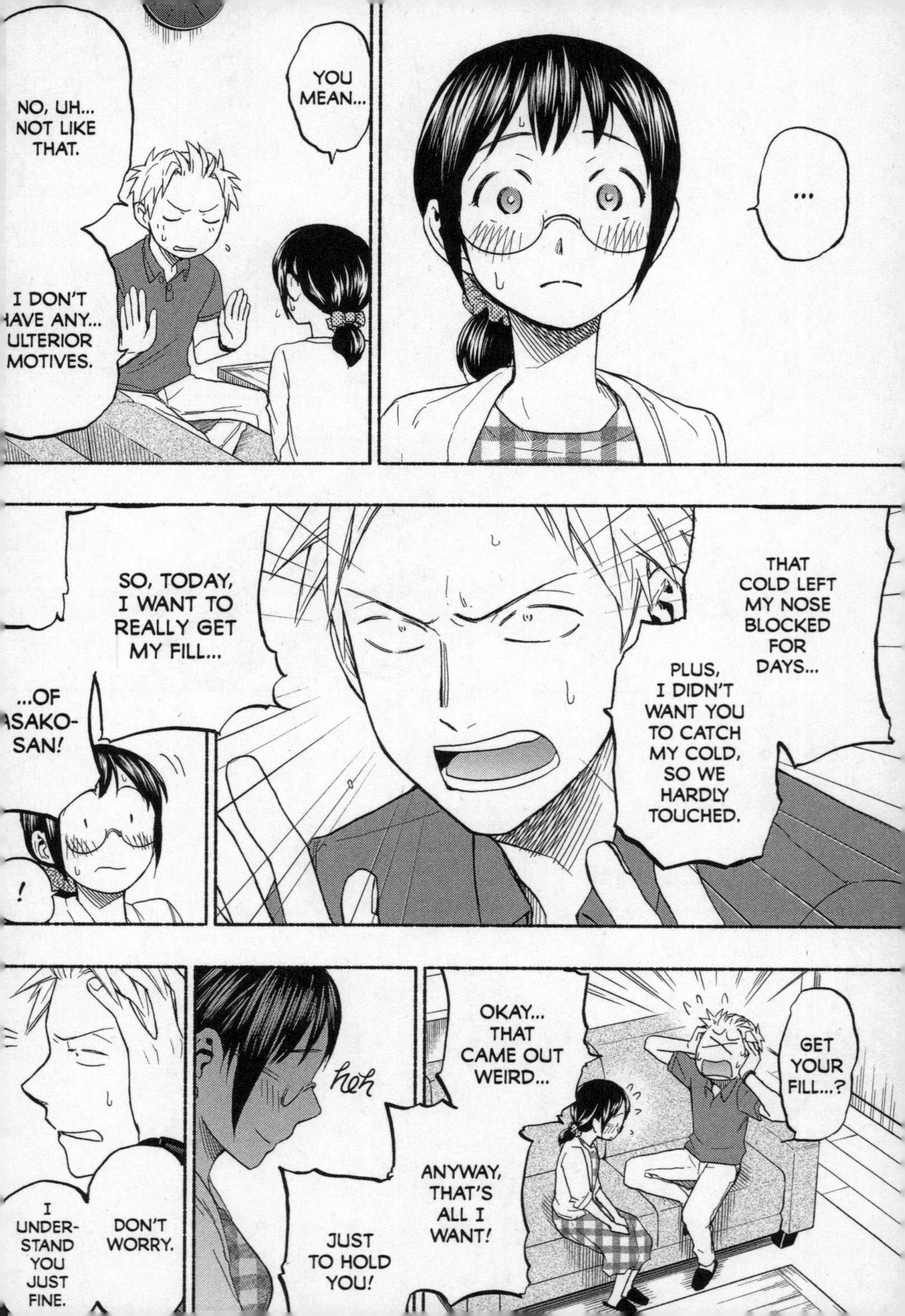
...
YOU MEAN...
NO, UH... NOT LIKE THAT.
I DON'T HAVE ANY... ULTERIOR MOTIVES.
THAT COLD LEFT MY NOSE BLOCKED FOR DAYS...
PLUS, I DIDN'T WANT YOU TO CATCH MY COLD, SO WE HARDLY TOUCHED.
SO, TODAY, I WANT TO REALLY GET MY FILL...
...OF ASAKO-SAN!
!
GET YOUR FILL...?
OKAY... THAT CAME OUT WEIRD...
ANYWAY, THAT'S ALL I WANT!
JUST TO HOLD YOU!
heh
DON'T WORRY.
I UNDER-STAND YOU JUST FINE.

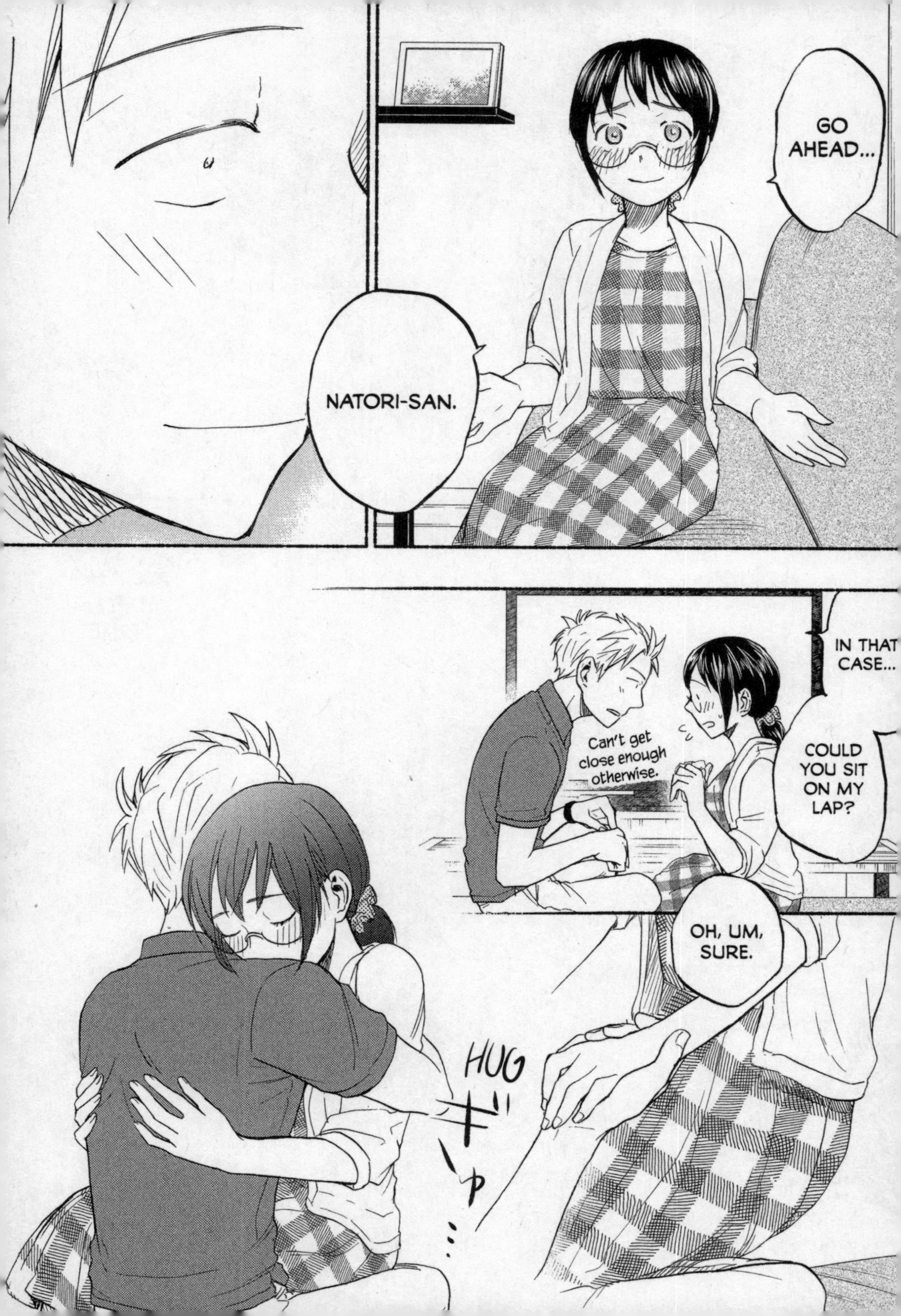
GO AHEAD...
NATORI-SAN.
IN THAT CASE...
COULD YOU SIT ON MY LAP?
Can't get close enough otherwise.
OH, UM, SURE.
HUG
ギゅ…

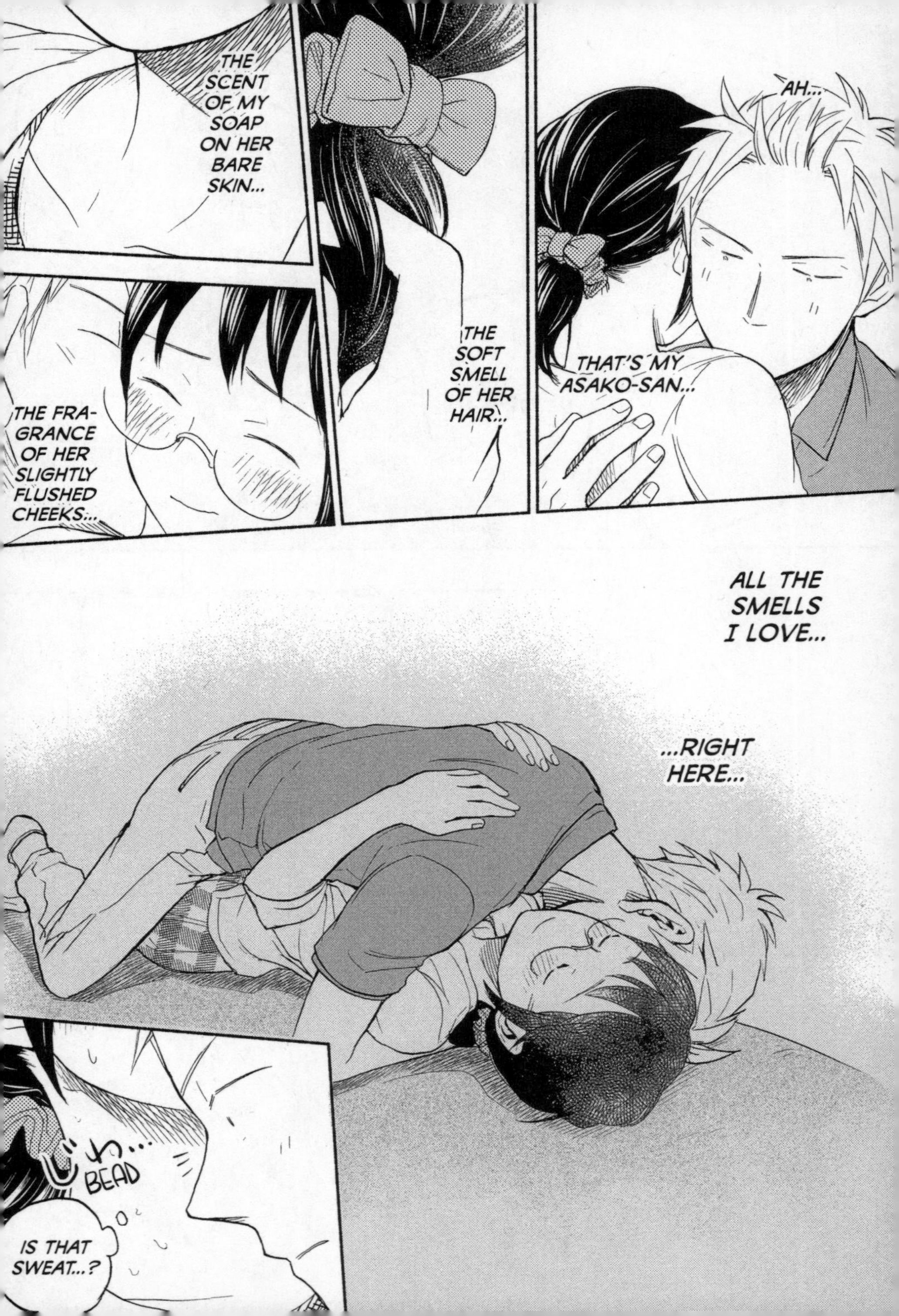
AH...
THAT'S MY ASAKO-SAN...
THE SOFT SMELL OF HER HAIR...
THE SCENT OF MY SOAP ON HER BARE SKIN...
THE FRAGRANCE OF HER SLIGHTLY FLUSHED CHEEKS...
ALL THE SMELLS I LOVE...
...RIGHT HERE...
じわ...
BEAD
IS THAT SWEAT...?

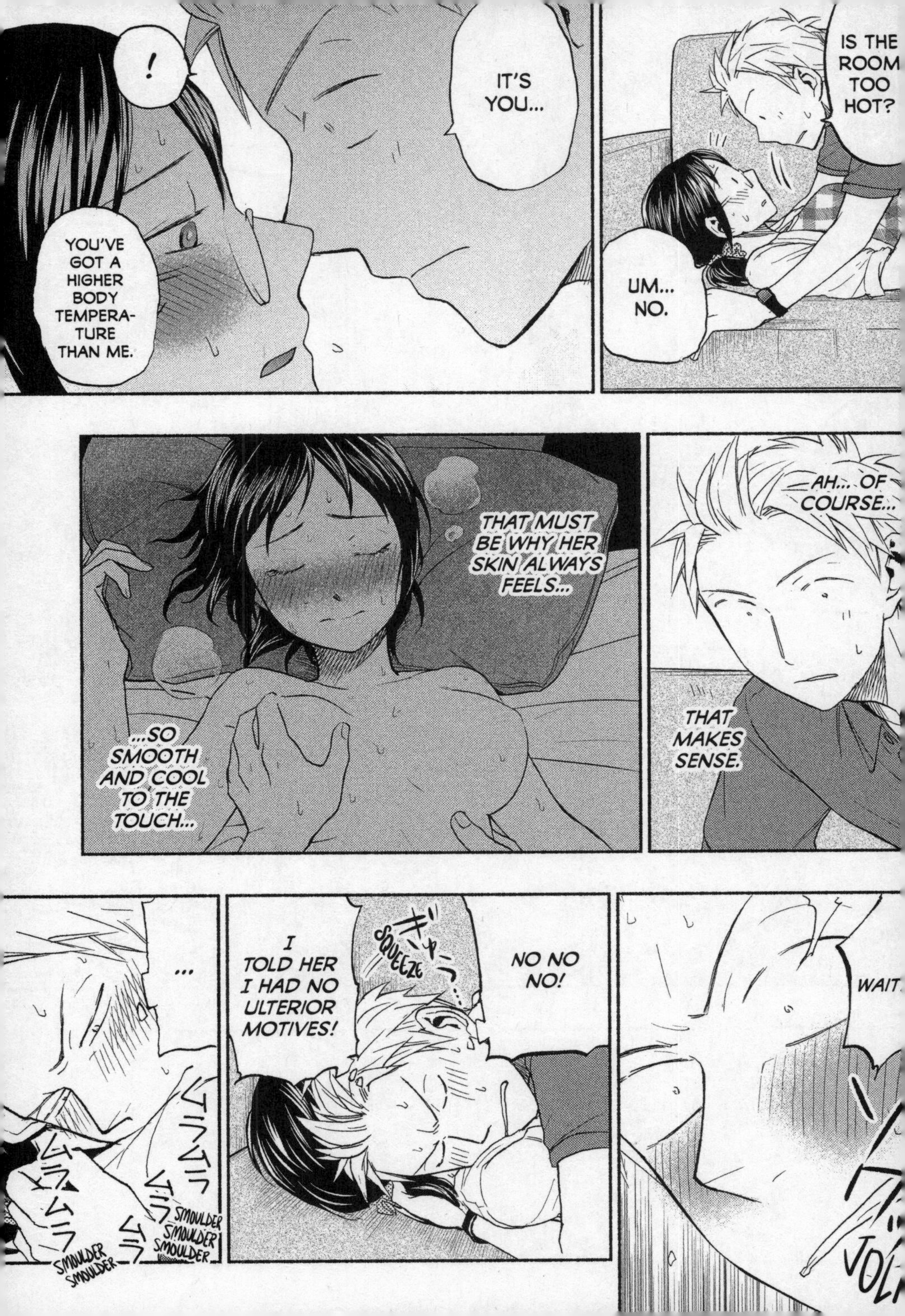
IS THE ROOM TOO HOT?
UM... NO.
IT'S YOU...
!
YOU'VE GOT A HIGHER BODY TEMPERA-TURE THAN ME.
AH... OF COURSE...
THAT MAKES SENSE.
THAT MUST BE WHY HER SKIN ALWAYS FEELS...
...SO SMOOTH AND COOL TO THE TOUCH...
WAIT.
NO NO NO!
SQUEEZE
I TOLD HER I HAD NO ULTERIOR MOTIVES!
...
SMOULDER SMOULDER SMOULDER
SMOULDER SMOULDER

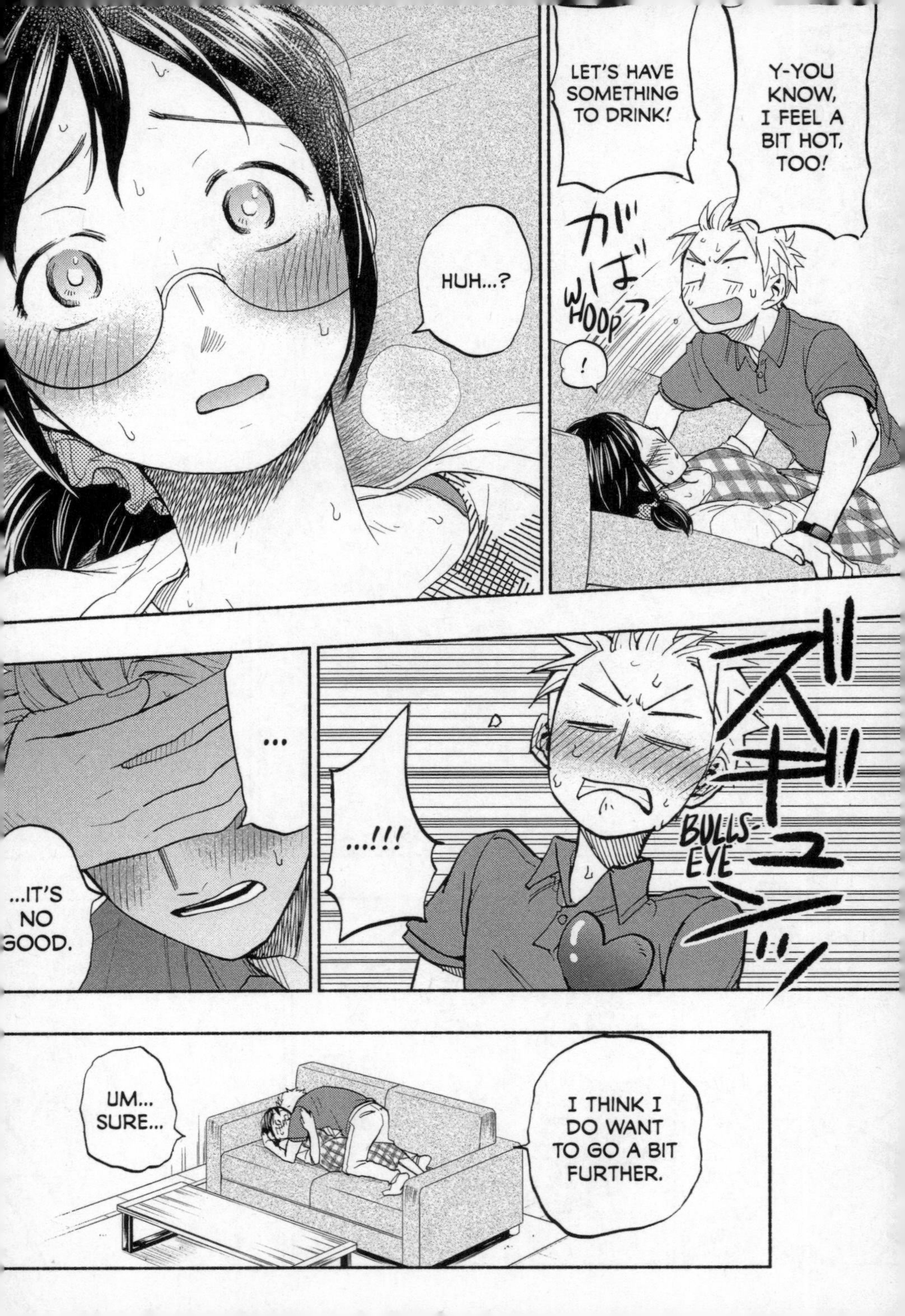
Y-YOU KNOW, I FEEL A BIT HOT, TOO!
LET'S HAVE SOMETHING TO DRINK!
がばっ
WHOOP
!
HUH...?
ズキューンッ
BULLS-EYE
...!!!
...
...IT'S NO GOOD.
I THINK I DO WANT TO GO A BIT FURTHER.
UM... SURE...

Sweat and Soap, Volume 2
The End

SWEAT AND SOAP EXCLUSIVE CHARACTER PROFILES!

BECAUSE SHE HAD SO LITTLE ROMANTIC EXPERIENCE BEFORE NATORI-SAN, ASAKO READS LOTS OF LOVE ADVICE COLUMNS ONLINE NOW. SO, SHE MIGHT BE A LITTLE MORE KNOWLEDGEABLE THAN EXPECTED IN SOME AREAS...

ASAKO YAESHIMA (AGE 26)

HEIGHT: 156 CM (5'4")
BIRTHDAY: MARCH 28
WEIGHT: 51 KG (112 LB)
SIGN: ARIES
BLOOD TYPE: O

FAVORITE FOODS/DRINKS:
JAPANESE FOOD, SOY MILK, HERBAL TEA

NOT A FAN OF:
FATTY PORK

HOBBIES:
SOAP COLLECTING
NEVER BUYS TOO MUCH TO USE BEFORE THE EXPIRY DATE, AND NEVER HAS MORE THAN THREE SOAPS GOING AT ONCE.

SPECIAL TALENTS:
NOTHING IN PARTICULAR YET, BUT WATCH THIS SPACE.
LIKES LOOKING AT CUTE OUTFITS IN FASHION MAGAZINES, EVEN THOUGH SHE CAN'T WEAR THEM HERSELF. ALSO HAS A WEAKNESS FOR CUTE FURNISHINGS AND KNICK-KNACKS.

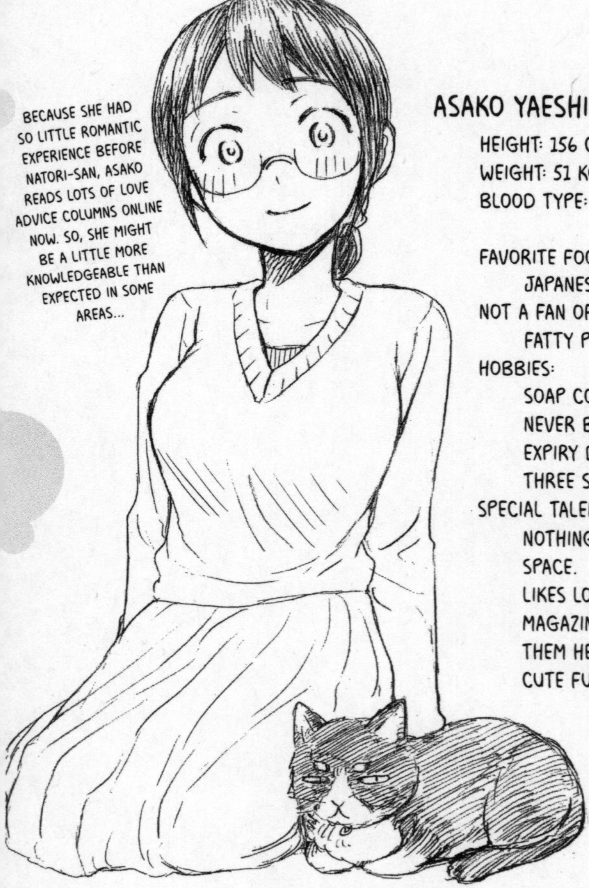

MAROSUKE, THE YAESHIMA FAMILY CAT (MALE, AGE 8)

UGLY CAT ADORED BY THE ENTIRE FAMILY.
ASAKO-SAN LIKES THE SMELT THIEF BECAUSE ITS BRAZENNESS IS EXACTLY LIKE MAROSUKE'S.

KOTARO NATORI (AGE 29)

HEIGHT: 175 CM (5'9")   BIRTHDAY: OCTOBER 1
WEIGHT: 63 KG (139 LB)   SIGN: LIBRA
BLOOD TYPE: B

FAVORITE FOODS/DRINKS:
    SANDWICHES, PASTA, HAMBURG STEAK
NOT A FAN OF:
    CELERY, SPICY THINGS LIKE SICHUAN MAPO
    TOFU, ANYTHING OVERSTIMULATING
HOBBIES:
    RESEARCHING AND CHECKING OUT THINGS
    THAT SMELL GOOD
    LOOKING AT SHOES
SPECIAL TALENTS:
    IDENTIFYING PLEASANT SMELLS,
    GREEN TEA TASTING

NATORI-SAN'S SENSE OF SMELL ISN'T
INBORN (LIKE ABSOLUTE PITCH, ETC.)

HE GOT BETTER THROUGH PRACTICE.
SO HE'S A BIT LESS SENSITIVE WHEN HE'S
DOZING OR TOO TIRED TO CONCENTRATE.
HE LIKES ANIMALS, BUT SOMETIMES
HAS A HARD TIME AT ZOOS.

NATORI-SAN
IS ACTUALLY
REALLY HARD TO
DRAW. HE TAKES
TWICE AS LONG
AS THE OTHER
CHARACTERS...

IF I'M NOT CAREFUL, HE
ENDS UP LOOKING ABOUT
17 YEARS OLD, AND EVEN
WHEN I AM CAREFUL HE
LOOKS MAYBE 23...
IT'S A PROBLEM.

THIS BREED HAS CUTE TAILS

SPECIAL GUEST:
PEMBROKE
WELSH CORGI

I JUST DREW THIS BECAUSE I LIKE THIS BREED.
I ALSO LIKE SHIBA INU.

KEITA DOESN'T HAVE A PET JAGUAR OR ANYTHING. IT'S JUST A SYMBOL OF HIS BATTLE MODE (?).

KEITA IS ACTUALLY THE FIRST MALE CHARACTER I'VE EVER DRAWN WITH REAL IRISES (NOT JUST DOTS). I WAS NERVOUS AT FIRST, BUT THE RESPONSE FROM FEMALE FANS WAS GREAT FROM HIS VERY FIRST APPEARANCE. "HUH," I THOUGHT, "I GUESS IRISES ARE IMPORTANT AFTER ALL."

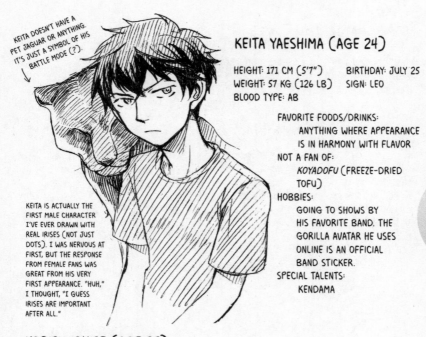

KEITA YAESHIMA (AGE 24)

HEIGHT: 171 CM (5'7") BIRTHDAY: JULY 25
WEIGHT: 57 KG (126 LB) SIGN: LEO
BLOOD TYPE: AB

FAVORITE FOODS/DRINKS:
ANYTHING WHERE APPEARANCE IS IN HARMONY WITH FLAVOR
NOT A FAN OF:
KOYADOFU (FREEZE-DRIED TOFU)
HOBBIES:
GOING TO SHOWS BY HIS FAVORITE BAND. THE GORILLA AVATAR HE USES ONLINE IS AN OFFICIAL BAND STICKER.
SPECIAL TALENTS:
KENDAMA

KORISU ICHISE (AGE 25)

(GIVEN NAME PRONOUNCED "KO-RI-SU")

HEIGHT: 152 CM (5') BIRTHDAY: MAY 10
WEIGHT: 42 KG (93 LB) SIGN: TAURUS
BLOOD TYPE: B
FAVORITE FOODS/DRINKS:
TOMATO RAMEN
NOT A FAN OF:
KAZUNOKO (HERRING ROE)

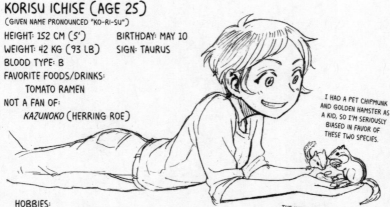

I HAD A PET CHIPMUNK AND GOLDEN HAMSTER AS A KID, SO I'M SERIOUSLY BIASED IN FAVOR OF THESE TWO SPECIES.

HOBBIES:
LOVES PACKAGING AND WRAPPING, SO CAN SPEND HOURS IN PAPER SHOPS
SPECIAL TALENTS:
MAKING POP CARDS, REPEATED SIDEWAYS JUMPING (THE SPORTS TEST CLASSIC)

THE NAME "KORISU" CAME TO MIND AS A GOOD ONE FOR A CHEERFUL GIRL WHO BOUNCES AROUND LIKE A SQUIRREL. (THE WORD *KORISU* CAN ALSO MEAN "LITTLE/BABY SQUIRREL.) I CHOSE THE SURNAME "ICHISE" ("ONE SHORE") AS A KIND OF OPPOSITE TO ASAKO'S "YAESHIMA" ("EIGHTFOLD ISLAND").

SWEAT AND SOAP

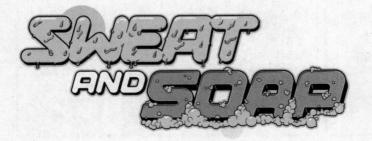

AFTERWORD

BY KINTETSU YAMADA

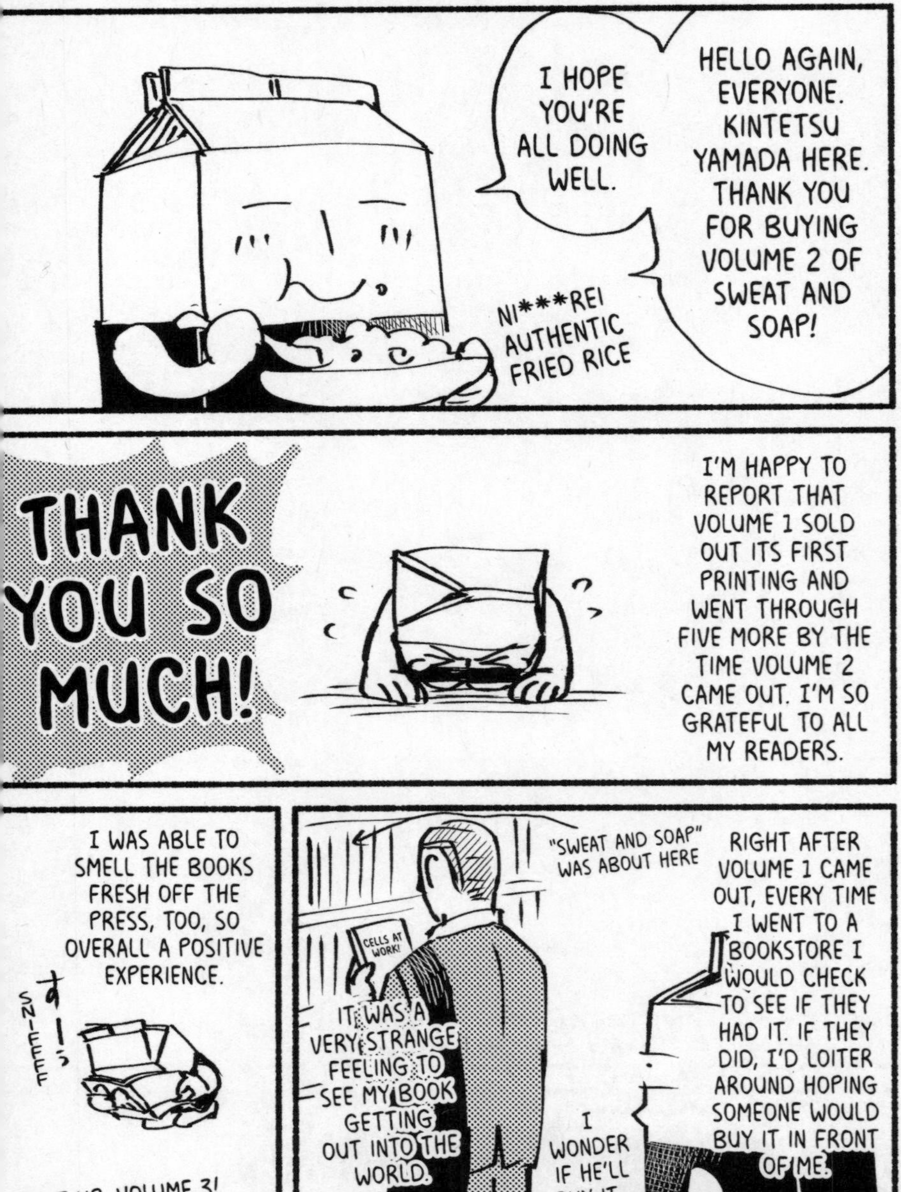
HELLO AGAIN, EVERYONE. KINTETSU YAMADA HERE. THANK YOU FOR BUYING VOLUME 2 OF SWEAT AND SOAP!
I HOPE YOU'RE ALL DOING WELL.
NI***REI AUTHENTIC FRIED RICE
I'M HAPPY TO REPORT THAT VOLUME 1 SOLD OUT ITS FIRST PRINTING AND WENT THROUGH FIVE MORE BY THE TIME VOLUME 2 CAME OUT. I'M SO GRATEFUL TO ALL MY READERS.
THANK YOU SO MUCH!
RIGHT AFTER VOLUME 1 CAME OUT, EVERY TIME I WENT TO A BOOKSTORE I WOULD CHECK TO SEE IF THEY HAD IT. IF THEY DID, I'D LOITER AROUND HOPING SOMEONE WOULD BUY IT IN FRONT OF ME.
"SWEAT AND SOAP" WAS ABOUT HERE
CELLS AT WORK!
IT WAS A VERY STRANGE FEELING TO SEE MY BOOK GETTING OUT INTO THE WORLD.
I WONDER IF HE'LL BUY IT...
I WAS ABLE TO SMELL THE BOOKS FRESH OFF THE PRESS, TOO, SO OVERALL A POSITIVE EXPERIENCE.
すー
SNIEEFF
NEXT UP: VOLUME 3!

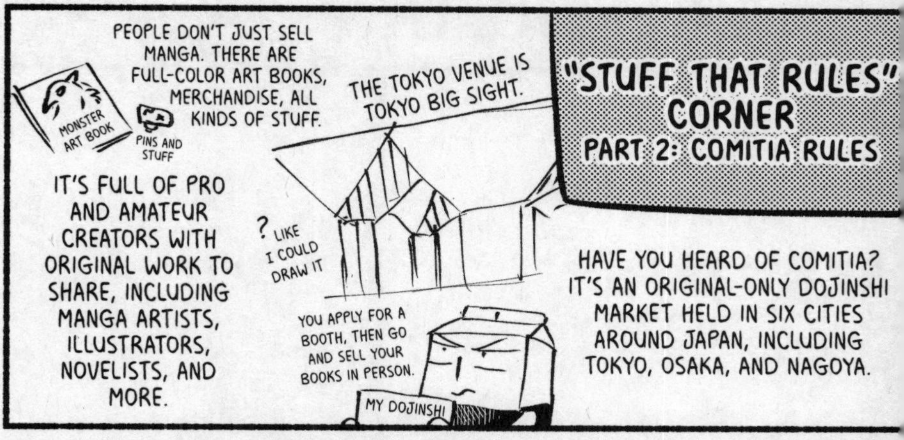
"STUFF THAT RULES" CORNER
PART 2: COMITIA RULES
HAVE YOU HEARD OF COMITIA? IT'S AN ORIGINAL-ONLY DOJINSHI MARKET HELD IN SIX CITIES AROUND JAPAN, INCLUDING TOKYO, OSAKA, AND NAGOYA.
YOU APPLY FOR A BOOTH, THEN GO AND SELL YOUR BOOKS IN PERSON.
MY DOJINSHI
THE TOKYO VENUE IS TOKYO BIG SIGHT.
? LIKE I COULD DRAW IT
PEOPLE DON'T JUST SELL MANGA. THERE ARE FULL-COLOR ART BOOKS, MERCHANDISE, ALL KINDS OF STUFF.
PINS AND STUFF
MONSTER ART BOOK
IT'S FULL OF PRO AND AMATEUR CREATORS WITH ORIGINAL WORK TO SHARE, INCLUDING MANGA ARTISTS, ILLUSTRATORS, NOVELISTS, AND MORE.

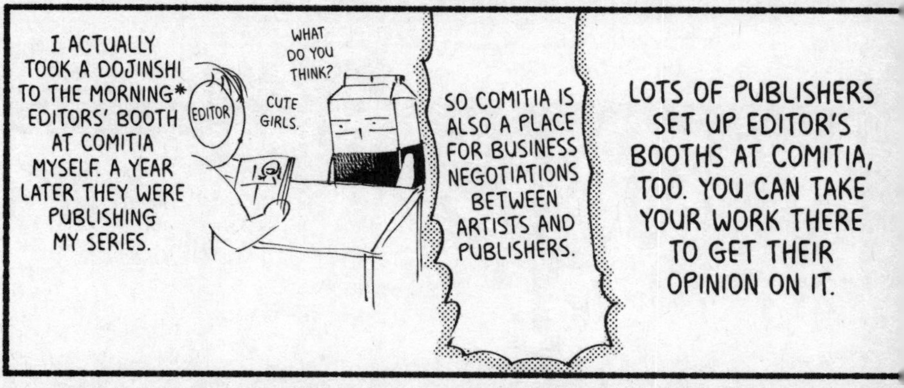
LOTS OF PUBLISHERS SET UP EDITOR'S BOOTHS AT COMITIA, TOO. YOU CAN TAKE YOUR WORK THERE TO GET THEIR OPINION ON IT.
SO COMITIA IS ALSO A PLACE FOR BUSINESS NEGOTIATIONS BETWEEN ARTISTS AND PUBLISHERS.
WHAT DO YOU THINK?
CUTE GIRLS.
EDITOR
I ACTUALLY TOOK A DOJINSHI TO THE MORNING* EDITORS' BOOTH AT COMITIA MYSELF. A YEAR LATER THEY WERE PUBLISHING MY SERIES.

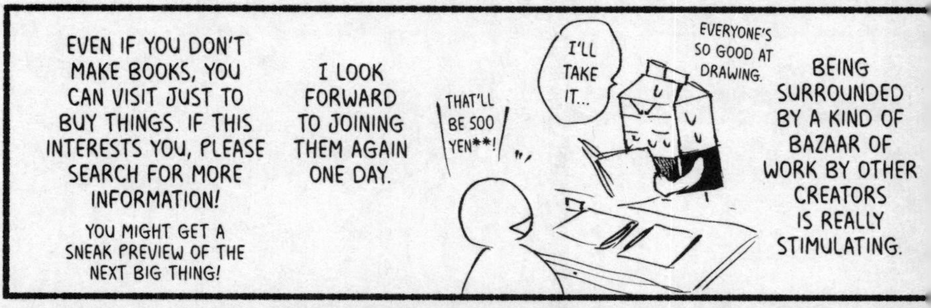
BEING SURROUNDED BY A KIND OF BAZAAR OF WORK BY OTHER CREATORS IS REALLY STIMULATING.
EVERYONE'S SO GOOD AT DRAWING.
I'LL TAKE IT...
THAT'LL BE 500 YEN**!
I LOOK FORWARD TO JOINING THEM AGAIN ONE DAY.
EVEN IF YOU DON'T MAKE BOOKS, YOU CAN VISIT JUST TO BUY THINGS. IF THIS INTERESTS YOU, PLEASE SEARCH FOR MORE INFORMATION!
YOU MIGHT GET A SNEAK PREVIEW OF THE NEXT BIG THING!

SPECIAL THANKS

STAFF
MOE SANADA
SHIJIMA
NONOKO NATSUKI
MAI SETA

EDITOR: SUZUKI

WE HAVE AN OFFICIAL TWITTER NOW:
@ASETOSEKKEN

MINE'S HERE:
@KINTETSUYMD

* *Morning* is the magazine in which *Sweat and Soap* is published in Japan.
** Roughly equals $5.

THE CONVERSATION TAKING PLACE ON THE COVER OF VOLUME 2
(WHILE OUR HEROES ARE ON THE COUCH DURING CHAPTER 15)

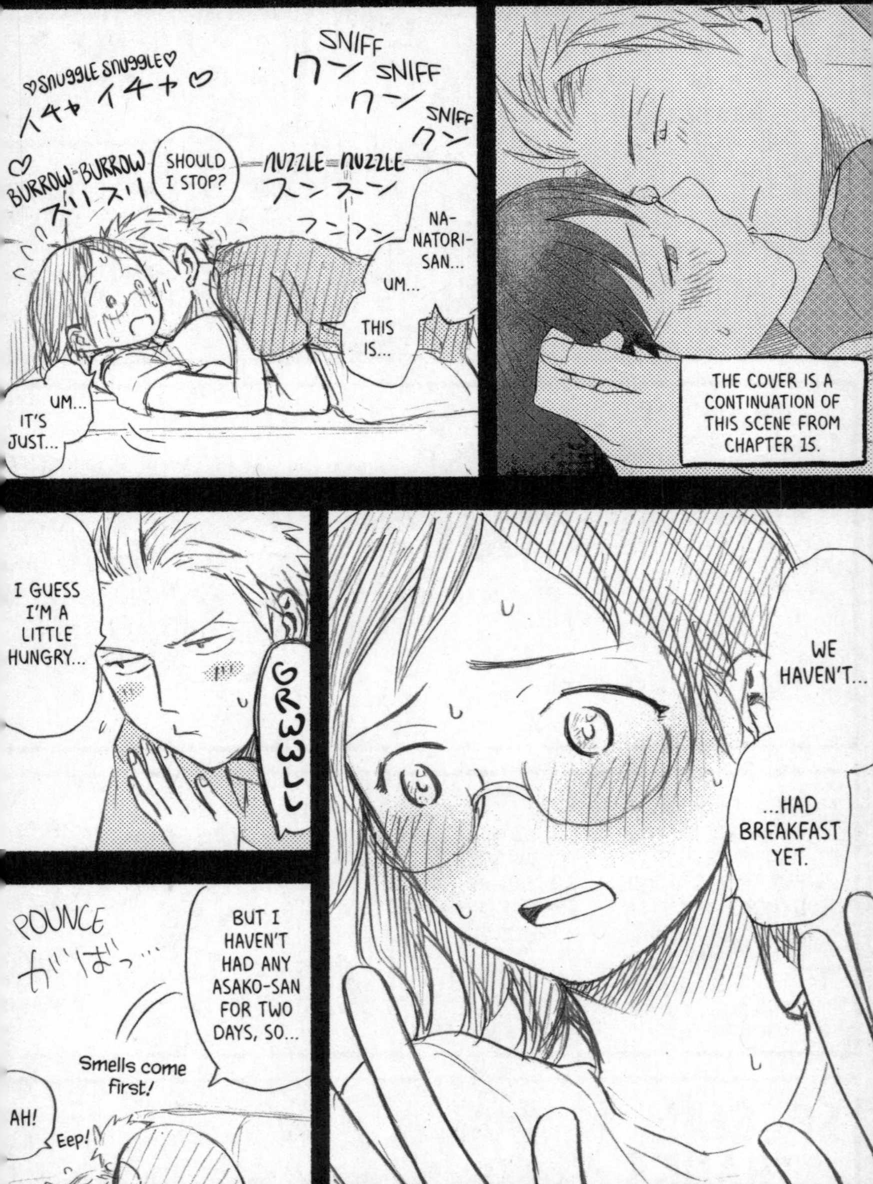
THE COVER IS A CONTINUATION OF THIS SCENE FROM CHAPTER 15.
SNIFF クン
SNIFF クン
SNIFF クン
NUZZLE NUZZLE スンスン
フンフン
NA-NATORI-SAN...
UM...
THIS IS...
♡SNUGGLE SNUGGLE♡ イチャイチャ♡
SHOULD I STOP?
♡BURROW-BURROW ズリズリ
UM... IT'S JUST...
WE HAVEN'T...
...HAD BREAKFAST YET.
I GUESS I'M A LITTLE HUNGRY...
GRRRLL
BUT I HAVEN'T HAD ANY ASAKO-SAN FOR TWO DAYS, SO...
POUNCE がばっ…
Smells come first!
AH!
Eep!

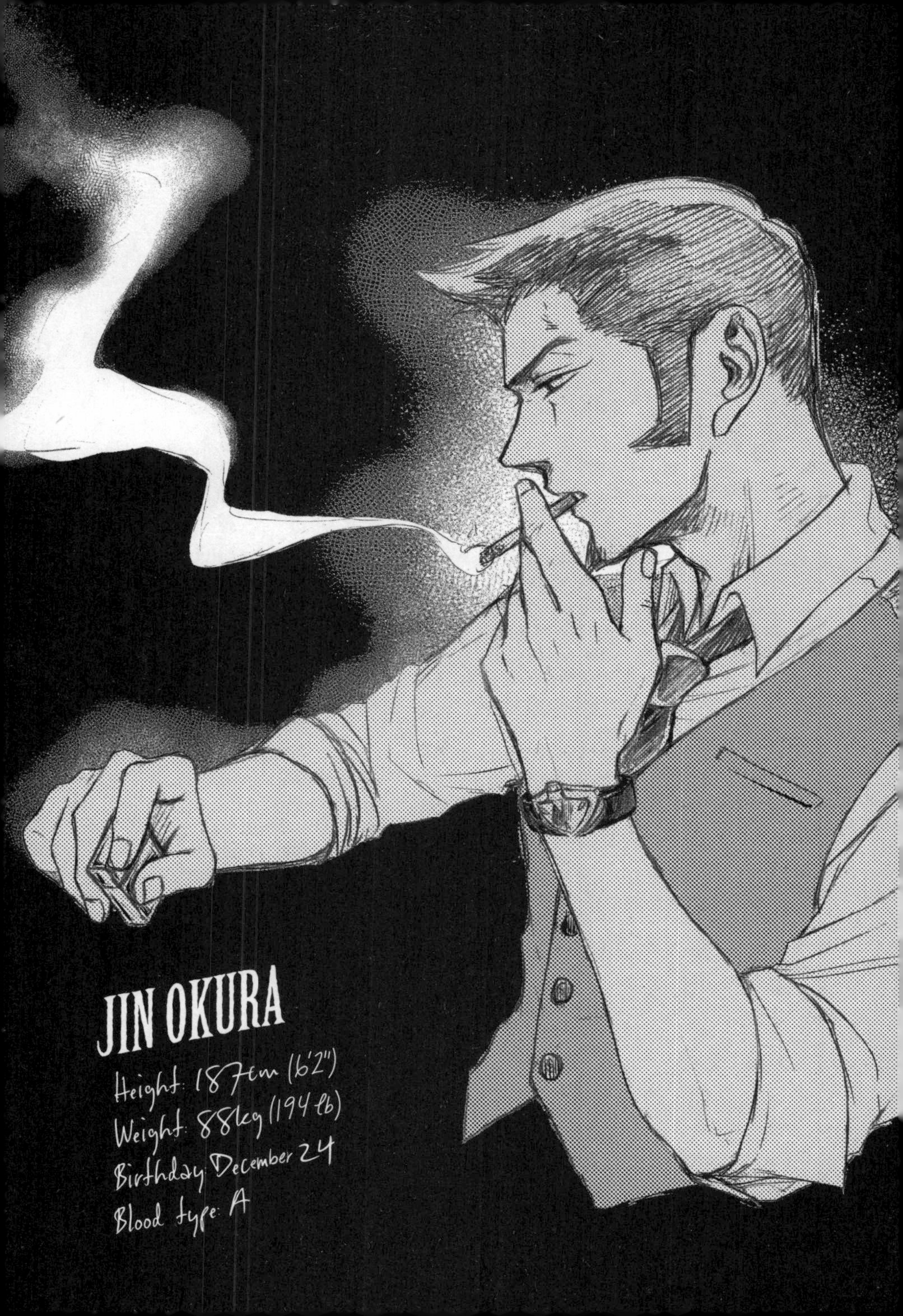
JIN OKURA
Height: 187cm (6'2")
Weight: 88kg (194 lb)
Birthday: December 24
Blood type: A

Translation Notes

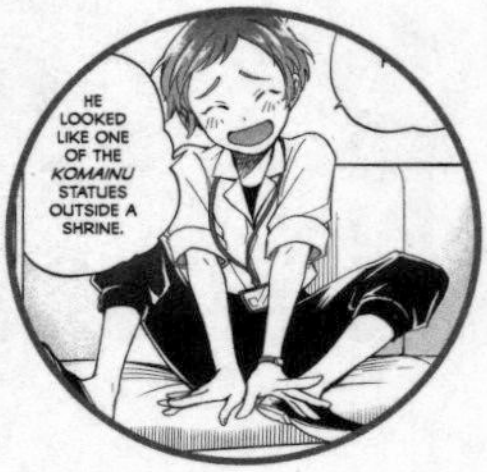
HE LOOKED LIKE ONE OF THE KOMAINU STATUES OUTSIDE A SHRINE.

Komainu, page 9
Stone "lion dog" statues that can often be seen on either side of the *torii* gate at a Shinto shrine. These statues are meant to ward off evil spirits.

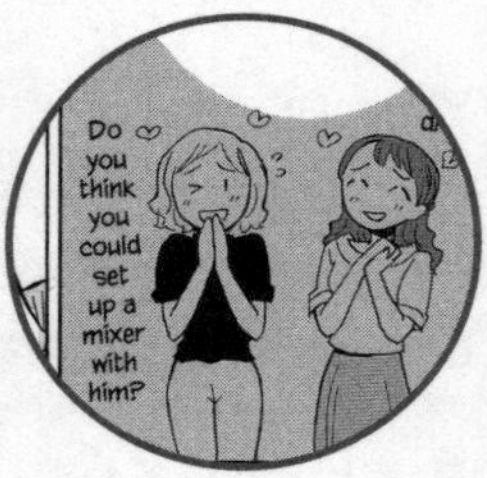
Do you think you could set up a mixer with him?

Mixer, page 13
"Mixer" here is referring to a *gokon*, a kind of group blind date which are usually organized by man and a woman who know each other. Each brings several friends of their same gender, and everyone eats, drinks, and chats together at the same table. Ideally, the outcome is that at least some of the guests will trade numbers by the end of the night.

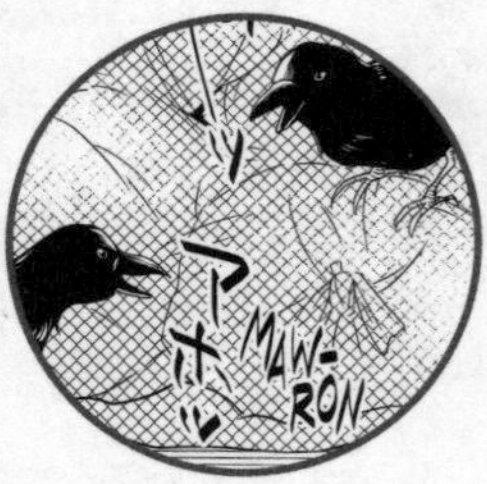
MAW-RON

MAW-RON, page 34
In Japanese, the albatross is known as *ahodori*, and *aho* on its own is a common way of calling someone an idiot. An albatross overhead crying *aho!* is a common gag in manga when someone does something foolish. For some reason, here the crows are saying *aho* instead.

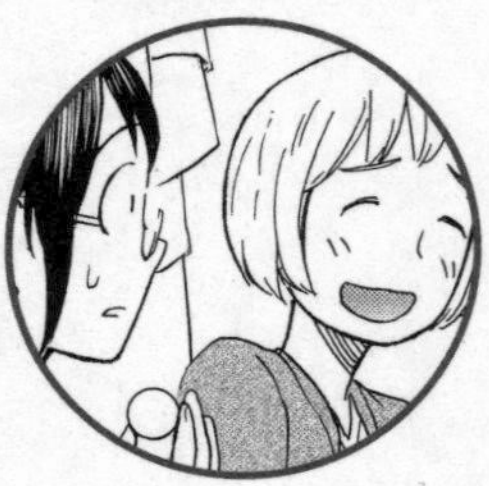

-shi, page 51
A more formal honorific than *san*, here used ironically.

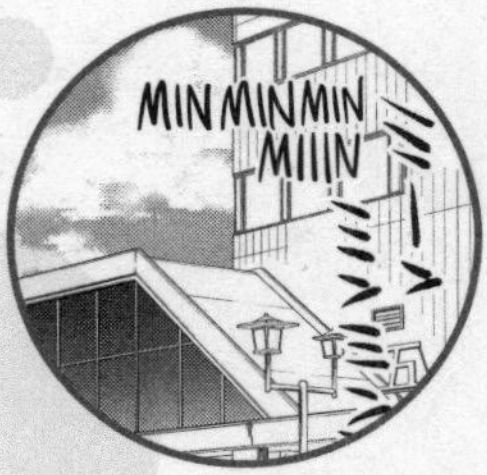
MIN MIN MIN
MIIIN

Cicada cries, page 107
In Japan, cicadas are known by the noises they make, rendered onomatopoeically as *min min min miiii*, *jiii*, *kana kana kana*, *tsukutsuku-boshi*, etc. As cicada cries are an ever-present soundtrack to summer in Japan, their cries often become shorthand for introducing the season.

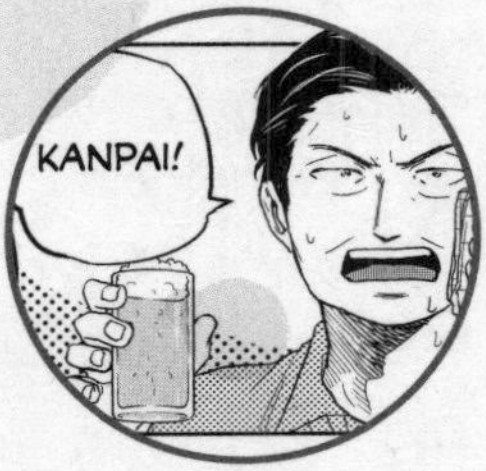
KANPAI!

Kanpai, page 121
Japanese for "Cheers!"

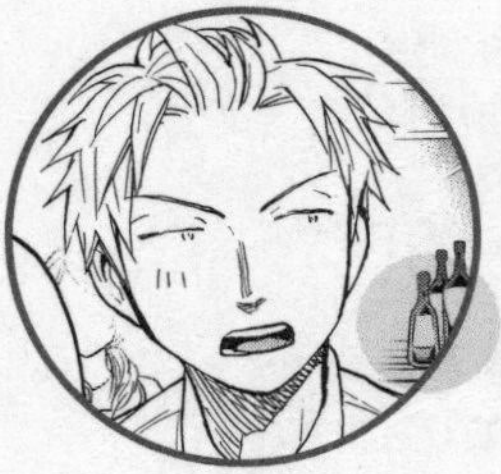

Using someone's first name, page 169
In Japan, the default, polite way to refer to someone is with their surname plus an honorific like *-san*. This applies even to work acquaintances on friendly terms. Switching to given names can be quite a charged event, something like going from *vous* to *tu* in French. Using someone's first name without being close can be considered quite rude.

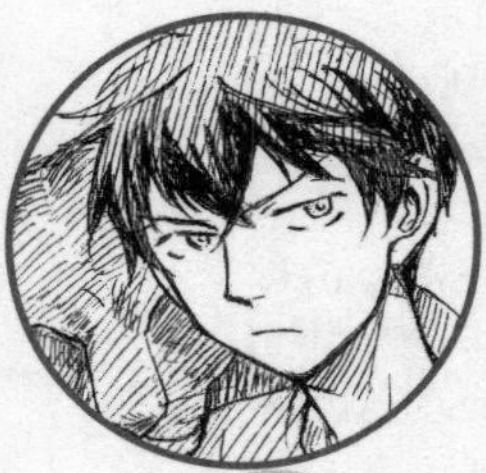

Kendama, page 202
The *kendama* is the Japanese version of the classic cup-and-ball toy. Kendama can be a competitive sport, with the World Cup held in Japan.

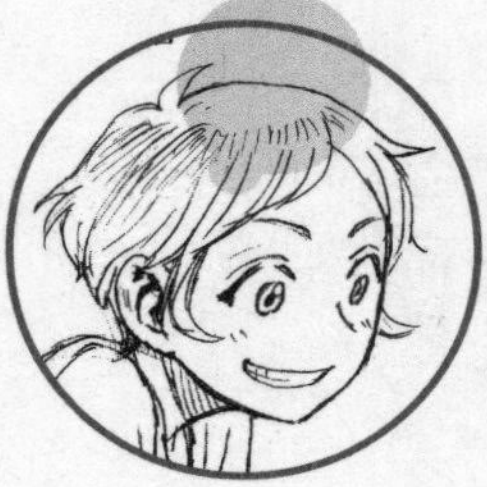

Sideways Jumping, page 202
Literally just jumping sideways (from a standing start). A common element in Japanese fitness tests.

AS SEEN IN SWEAT AND SOAP! CLAM AND KARASUMI PEPERONCINO...IS WHAT I WANT TO MAKE, BUT THAT'S WAY TOO HARD, SO HERE'S A RECIPE FOR

NORMAL SOUP PEPERONCINO

JUST PUT IN A BIT MORE PASTA WATER THAN USUAL!

INGREDIENTS (PER PERSON)

PASTA ... 100 G
GARLIC ... 1 CLOVE
BACON ... TO TASTE
OLIVE OIL ... 2 TBSP
SLICED RED CHILI PEPPER
(*TOGARASHI*) ... TO TASTE
SOY SAUCE ... A DASH

TO MAKE DISH RICHER AND TASTIER

WALNUTS OR PEANUTS (UNSALTED) ... CRUSH THEM UP, POUR THEM IN, AND BE AMAZED AT THE DEPTH AND TEXTURE THEY ADD!

1. FINELY CHOP THE GARLIC AND THINLY SLICE THE BACON.
2. START BOILING THE PASTA. IN A FRYING PAN, WARM THE GARLIC IN THE OLIVE OIL ON LOW HEAT. WHEN THE FRAGRANCE STARTS TO RISE, ADD THE BACON.
3. WHEN THE BACON HAS COOKED A BIT, ADD THE RED CHILI PEPPER. IF YOU'RE ALSO ADDING CRUSHED NUTS, DO THAT NOW TOO.
4. ADD ABOUT 2.5 TO 3 LADLES OF THE PASTA WATER TO THE FRYING PAN AND STIR SLOWLY TO EMULSIFY.
5. MIX IN THE BOILED PASTA, STIR IN SOME SOY SAUCE TO FINISH, AND DINNER IS SERVED!

BE CAREFUL NOT TO ADD TOO MUCH PASTA WATER, OR IT WON'T EMULSIFY PROPERLY AND THE FLAVOR WILL BE WEAK. ALSO SUPER TASTY WITH OTHER INGREDIENTS ADDED.

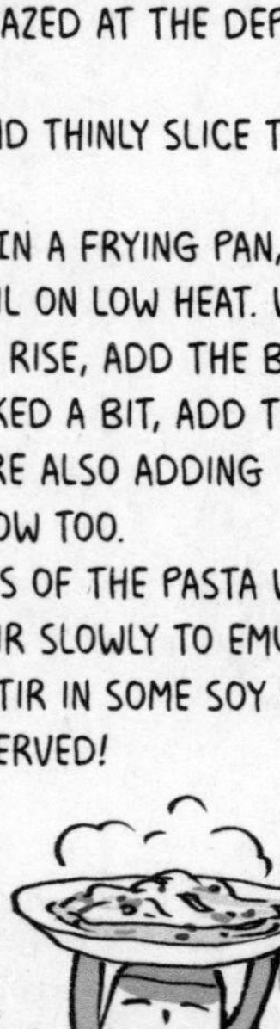
USE A DEEPER DISH THAN USUAL!
THE PASTA ENDS UP HALF-SUBMERGED IN THE SOUP.

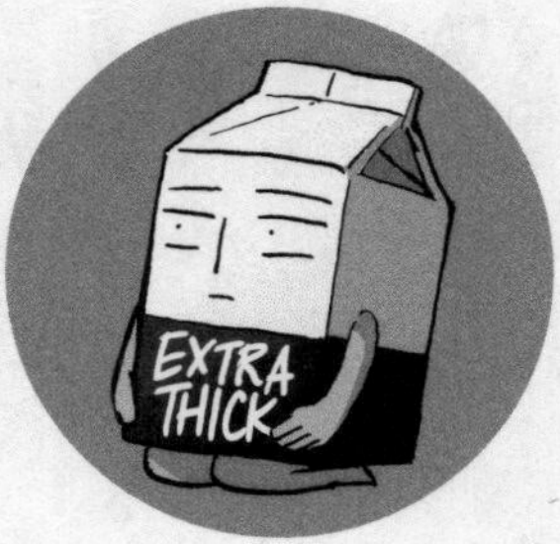
EXTRA
THICK

kintetsu yamada

Drawing the carton of milk for my self-portrait is harder than you'd think. You have to really study how they look when they're opened—the horizontal-vertical ratio and so on—or what you draw won't look like a milk carton at all. So I'm thinking I might have made a mistake here, but I'm a lifelong milk lover so I'll keep drawing my cartons.

Please enjoy volume 2!

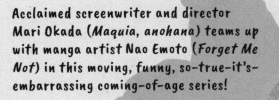

Acclaimed screenwriter and director Mari Okada (*Maquia*, *anohana*) teams up with manga artist Nao Emoto (*Forget Me Not*) in this moving, funny, so-true-it's-embarrassing coming-of-age series!

When Kazusa enters high school, she joins the Literature Club, and leaps from reading innocent fiction to diving into the literary classics. But these novels are a bit more...*adult* than she was prepared for. Between euphemisms like fresh dewy grass and pork stew, crushing on the boy next door, and knowing you want to do that *one thing* before you die—discovering your budding sexuality is no easy feat! As if puberty wasn't awkward enough, the club consists of a brooding writer, the prettiest girl in school, an agreeable comrade, and an outspoken prude. Fumbling over their own discomforts, these five teens get thrown into chaos over three little letters: S...E...X...!

O Maidens in your Savage Season

Anime coming soon!

Mari Okada   Nao Emoto

KC KODANSHA COMICS

ANIME OUT NOW FROM SENTAI FILMWORKS!

A BL romance between a good boy who didn't know he was waiting for a hero, and a bad boy who comes to his rescue!

Masahiro Setagawa doesn't believe in heroes, but wishes he could: He's found himself in a gang of small-time street bullies, and with no prospects for a real future. But when high school teacher (and scourge of the streets) Kousuke Ohshiba comes to his rescue, he finds he may need to start believing after all... in heroes, and in his budding feelings, too.

Hitorijime My Hero

Memeco Arii

KC KODANSHA COMICS

Yuri is My Job! © Miman/Ichijinsha Inc.

Hime is a picture-perfect high school princess, so when she accidentally injures a café manager named Mai, she's willing to cover some shifts to keep her façade intact. To Hime's surprise, the café is themed after a private school where the all-female staff always puts on their best act for their loyal customers. However, under the guidance of the most graceful girl there, Hime can't help but blush and blunder! Beneath all the frills and laughter, Hime feels tension brewing as she finds out more about her new job and her budding feelings...

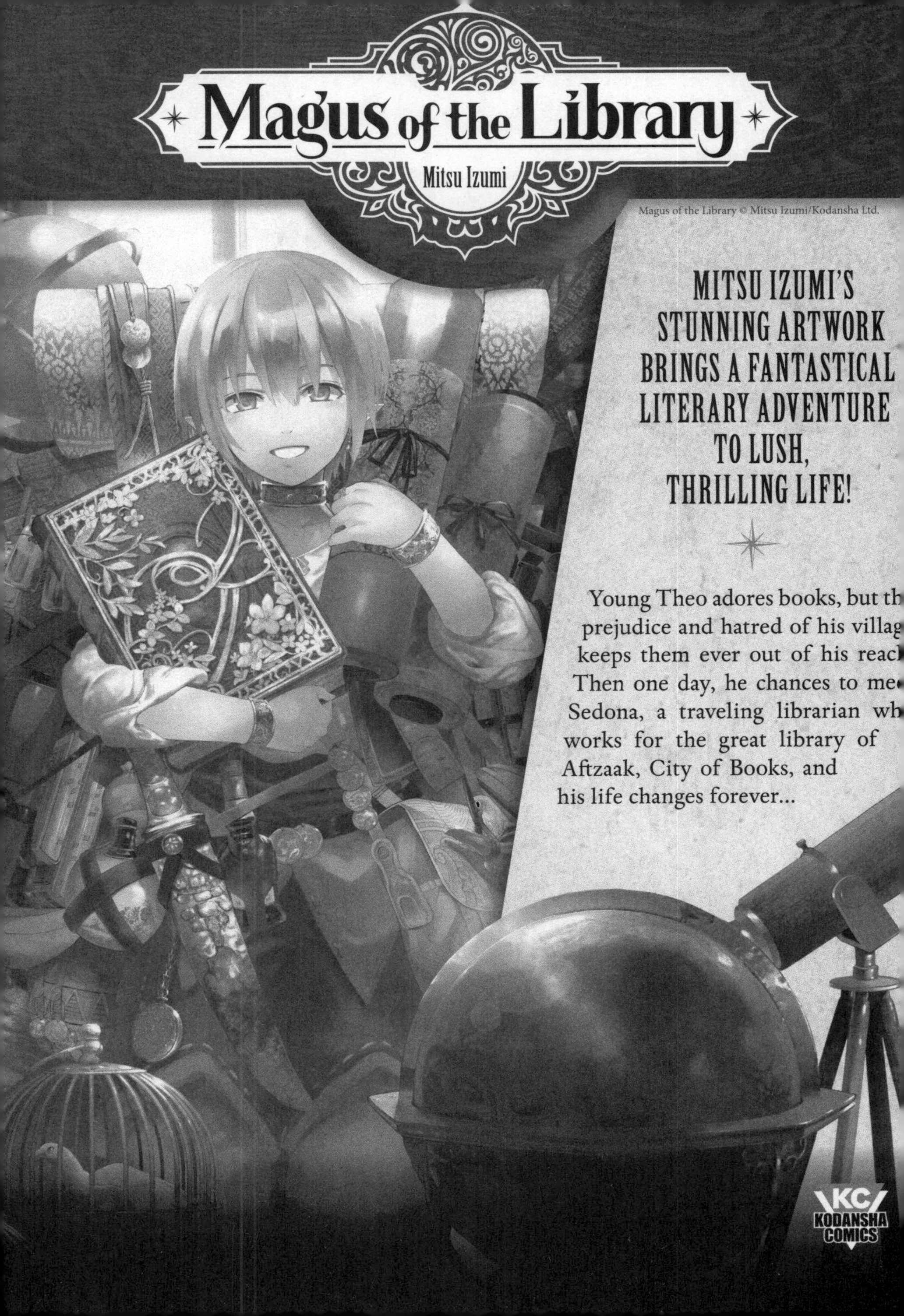
Magus of the Library
Mitsu Izumi
Magus of the Library © Mitsu Izumi/Kodansha Ltd.
MITSU IZUMI'S STUNNING ARTWORK BRINGS A FANTASTICAL LITERARY ADVENTURE TO LUSH, THRILLING LIFE!
Young Theo adores books, but th
prejudice and hatred of his villag
keeps them ever out of his reac
Then one day, he chances to me
Sedona, a traveling librarian wh
works for the great library of
Aftzaak, City of Books, and
his life changes forever...
KC
KODANSHA COMICS

The prestigious Dahlia Academy educates the elite of society from two countries; To the East is the Nation of Touwa; across the sea the other way, the Principality of West. The nations, though, are fierce rivals, and their students are constantly feuding—which means Romio Inuzuka, head of Touwa's first-year students, has a problem. He's fallen for his counterpart from West, Juliet Persia, and when he can't take it any more, he confesses his feelings.

Now Romio has two problems: A girlfriend, and a secret…

Boarding School *Juliet*

By Yousuke Kaneda

"A fine romantic comedy... The chemistry between the two main characters is excellent and the humor is great, backed up by a fun enough supporting cast and a different twist on the genre." –AiPT

A picture-perfect shojo series from Yoko Nogiri, creator of the hit *That Wolf-Boy is Mine!*

Mako's always had a passion for photography. When she loses someone dear to her, she clings onto her art as a relic of the close relationship she once had... Luckily, her childhood best friend Kei encourages her to come to his high school and join their prestigious photo club. With nothing to lose, Mako grabs her camera an moves into the dorm wher Kei and his classmates live. Soon, a fresh take on life, along with a mysterious new muse, begin to come into focus!

LOVE IN FOCUS

Love in Focus © Yoko Nogiri/Kodansha Ltd.

Praise for Yoko Nogiri's *That Wolf-Boy is Mine!*

KC/ KODANSHA COMICS

**THE MAGICAL GIRL CLASSIC THAT BROUGHT A
GENERATION OF READERS TO MANGA, NOW BACK IN A
DEFINITIVE, HARDCOVER COLLECTOR'S EDITION!**

CARDCAPTOR SAKURA
COLLECTOR'S EDITION
C L A M P

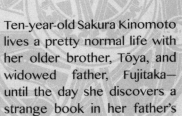

Ten-year-old Sakura Kinomoto
lives a pretty normal life with
her older brother, Tōya, and
widowed father, Fujitaka—
until the day she discovers a
strange book in her father's
library, and her life takes a
magical turn...

- A deluxe large-format
  hardcover edition
  of CLAMP's shojo
  manga classic
- All-new foil-stamped cover
  art on each volume
- Comes with exclusive
  collectible art card

Cardcaptor Sakura Collector's Edition © CLAMP • Shigatsu Tsuitachi Co., Ltd. / Kodansha Ltd.

KC
**KODANSHA
COMICS**

The art-deco cyberpunk classic from the creators of *xxxHOLiC* and *Cardcaptor Sakura*!

"Starred Review. This experimental sci-fi work from CLAMP reads like a romantic version of *AKIRA*."
—Publishers Weekly

CLOVER © CLAMP·ShigatsuTsuitachi CO.,LTD./Kodansha Ltd.

Su was born into a bleak future, where the government keeps tight control over children with magical powers—codenamed "Clovers." With Su being the only "four-leaf" Clover in the world, she has been kept isolated nearly her whole life. Can ex-military agent Kazuhiko deliver her to the happiness she seeks? Experience the complete series in this hardcover edition, which also includes over twenty pages of ravishing color art!

KC KODANSHA COMICS

The beloved characters from *Cardcaptor Sakura* return in a brand new, reimagined fantasy adventure!

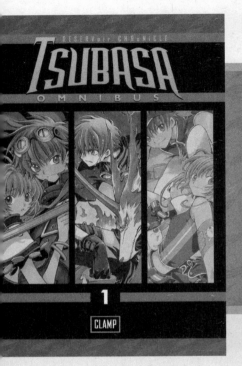

"[*Tsubasa*] takes readers on a fantastic ride that only gets more exhilarating with each successive chapter." —Anime News Network

In the Kingdom of Clow, an archaeological dig unleashes an incredible power, causing Princess Sakura to lose her memories. To save her, her childhood friend Syaoran must follow the orders of the Dimension Witch and travel alongside Kurogane, an unrivaled warrior; Fai, a powerful magician; and Mokona, a curiously strange creature, to retrieve Sakura's dispersed memories!

KC
KODANSHA
COMICS

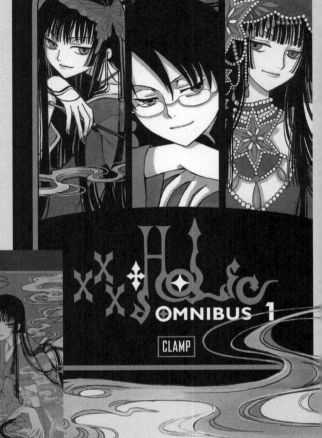

"Clever, sassy, and original....*xxxHOLiC* has the inherent hallmarks of a runaway hit."
—NewType magazine

Beautifully seductive artwork and uniquely Japanese depictions of the supernatural will hypnotize CLAMP fans!

Kimihiro Watanuki is haunted by visions of ghos and spirits. He seeks help from a mysterio woman named Yuko, who claims she can he However, Watanuki must work for Yuko in ord to pay for her aid. Soon Watanuki finds hims employed in Yuko's shop, where he sees things a meets customers that are stranger than anythi he could have ever imagined.

KC
KODANSHA
COMICS

A Kodansha Comics Trade Paperback Original
Sweat and Soap 2 copyright © 2019 Kintetsu Yamada
English translation copyright © 2020 Kintetsu Yamada

Published in the United States by Kodansha Comics, an imprint of Kodansha USA Publishing, LLC, New York.

Publication rights for this English edition arranged through Kodansha Ltd., Tokyo.

First published in Japan in 2019 by Kodansha Ltd., Tokyo as *Ase to Sekken* volume 2.

ISBN 978-1-63236-971-0

Original cover design by Hideyuki Tanaka (Double Trigger)

Printed in the United States of America.

www.kodansha.us

9 8 7 6 5 4 3
Translation: Matt Treyvaud
Lettering: Sara Linsley
Editing: Lauren Scanlan
Kodansha Comics edition cover design by Phil Balsman

Publisher: Kiichiro Sugawara
Vice president of marketing & publicity: Naho Yamada

Director of publishing services: Ben Applegate
Associate director of operations: Stephen Pakula
Publishing services managing editor: Noelle Webster
Assistant production manager: Emi Lotto, Angela Zurlo